alerie &

Best Books ~~~~~~ lren

Valerie & Walter's

Best Books

A Live!

SECOND EDITION

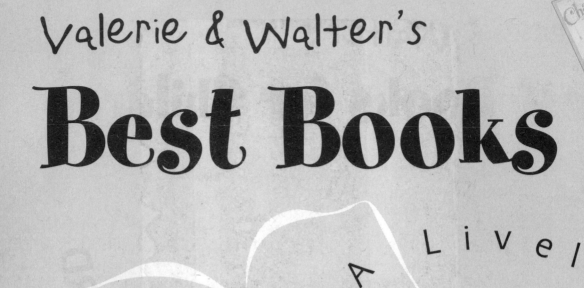

for Children

pinionated Guide

Valerie V. Lewis and Walter M. Mayes

QUILL

A HarperResource Book
An Imprint of HarperCollinsPublishers

HarperCollins books may be purchased for educational, business, or sales promotional use. For information please write: Special Markets Department, HarperCollins Publishers Inc., 10 East 53rd Street, New York, NY 10022.

SECOND EDITION

Designed by Ellen Cipriano
Authors' photo © Renee Fadiman

Library of Congress Cataloging-in-Publication Data

Lewis, Valerie V. (Valerie Valentine)
    Valerie & Walter's best books for children : a lively, opinionated guide / Valerie V. Lewis and Walter M. Mayes.—2nd ed.
        p. cm.
    Includes index.
    ISBN 0-06-052467-7
    1. Children's literature—Bibliography.   2. Children—Books and reading—United States.   I. Title: Best books for children.   II. Title: Valerie and Walter's best books for children.   III. Mayes, Walter M.   IV. Title.

Z1037.L58 2004
011.62—dc22

2003062352

---

04 05 06 07 08   WBC/RRD   10 9 8 7 6 5 4 3 2 1

Acknowledgments

To the vigilant Hicklebee's staff for their book discoveries;
to Ann Seaton who gave us precious time;
to Peggy Rathmann for her spot art of our heads;
to Monica Lewis Holmes for knowing what readers want; and
to Sandra Lewis Nisbet, our personal editor and booster.

Walter's Dedication

To Catherine Mary Regan Van Hest, mother of giants,
source of immeasurable support, and my hero.

Valerie's Dedication

To my grandson Joseph Andrew Vierra
who takes me for walks and makes my heart sing.

The authors wish to thank the following publishers for their permission to use cover art in this book:

Houghton Mifflin Children's Books
Piggie Pie
The Giver
The Silver Pony
Grandfather's Journey
The New Way Things Work
Gossie & Gertie

HarperCollins Children's Books
Charlotte's Web
Goodnight Moon
The Wolves in the Walls
Farfallina and Marcel
Lilly's Purple Plastic Purse
Love That Dog
The Slippery Slope (A Series of Unfortunate
   Events, Book 10)

Penguin Putnam Children's Books
Chato's Kitchen
17 Kings and 42 Elephants
I'll Give You Kisses
So You Want to Be President

The Stinky Cheese Man and Other Fairly
   Stupid Tales
This Land Was Made for You and Me

Candlewick Press
Big Momma Makes the World
Here Comes Mother Goose
Weslandia
So Much
Judy Moody Gets Famous
The Tale of Despereaux

Simon & Schuster Children's Books
Olivia
John Coltrane's Giant Steps
I Love Saturdays y Domingos
Click Clack Moo: Cows That Type
The Spider and the Fly
Nettie's Trip South

Tricycle Press
G is for Googol
George Hogglesberry, Grade School Alien

Bloomsbury USA
The Alphabet Room

Farrar, Straus & Giroux Books for Young Readers
Larky Mavis
Bob
Madlenka's Dog
Holes

Lee & Low Books
The Pot That Juan Built

Handprint Books
The Midnight Ride of Paul Revere

Harcourt Children's Books
How I Became a Pirate
Bubba and Beau
Lives of the Writers

Klutz Press
Face Painting

Scholastic
Bruh Rabbit and the Tar Baby Girl
Talkin' About Bessie
The Thief Lord
Esperanza Rising

Contents

Valerie & Walter's

Best Books for Children

Introduction to the Second Edition

What a joy it is to bring you edition number two of our "highly opinionated" guide to children's books. We've gathered all the latest and greatest. Along with hundreds of new titles (yes, *Harry Potter* is here), many of the old favorites are here, including *Heckedy Peg, Winnie the Pooh,* and *Charlotte's Web.* We've looked them over with care—to make sure they're still in print—and we've kept our heads when it was time to trade in some titles to make room for the new.

This edition features "best books" for children—fiction and nonfiction—up through age twelve. Still, the best-told tales are the ones we're after: adventure, mystery, biography, narrative, and humor. Each one must hold the reader tight and enhance, in some way, his or her perception of and delight in reading.

You'll see a new look in this edition, and we've modified the index, based on notes from our readers. Your positive responses drive us onward!

Six years since the first edition was published, we still love books and love what they do. We still believe in their power, mystery, and magic. And our readers' feedback and enthusiasm show us that they also still believe. It's exciting to trust that this world of books helps open up the real world to young people.

Read this and boost your confidence about choosing books on your own. Start here if you'd like to know more about us and how this book works, or in the back if you know you're looking for a particular kind of book that our extensive thematic appendix can help you find, or go straight to the title listings, more than two thousand of them (fully cross-referenced), and find a wealth of recommendations you can rely on—even if you don't yet know quite what it is you're looking for.

Our Personal Introduction

Introducing: Walter

 I don't remember learning to read. My mother tells me that I was always interested in books and that, as a kindergartner, I had a tendency to read aloud anything I saw. One day I was glancing at the things on my teacher's desk when she heard me read aloud the address on an envelope. I remember a big deal being made out of the fact that I could read. Soon after, I was sent to first grade in the afternoons to practice reading. I stayed in kindergarten for the morning, but left my friends after lunch and went off to the world of readers.

By the time I was in fourth grade, the principal asked me to visit the kindergarten during recess once a week and read stories to the little kids. That was probably a clever effort on his part to channel my aggressively outgoing personality into an acceptable medium. I have always wanted an audience, always wanted accolade and applause, and have always been willing to risk looking foolish to attain them.

My love of books and reading, my compulsive need to perform, along with the belief that we all must do what we can to make the world a better place, have inspired me, after more than twenty years as a bookseller and publisher's sales representative, to create the personality known as Walter the Giant Storyteller. I travel the country making appearances in schools, libraries, bookstores, and at conferences, speaking to children, parents, teachers, and civic groups. Lately, I've also taken on the responsibilities of librarian at a private girls' middle school, where all my opinions and ideas about reading and children are put to use (and tested) daily. I bring a sense of joy to my reading experience and try to instill that joy in others.

Introducing: Valerie

I grew up in a house bulging with books. Reading began first thing in the morning with the newspaper. On Sundays, newsprint was spread across the table and floor as we vied for our favorite sections: my younger sister and I for the "funnies," my brother the sports section, and my two older sisters for the magazine sections and Ann Landers.

But don't think we sat around reading all the time. Five children plus our friends added up to an active household. There were plays to rehearse, cheerleading practice, capture the flag, and street softball. The TV (when we got one) was not often on, except for <u>Ed Sullivan</u> on Sunday nights.

The point is, books were not "special." They were a basic part of our life. We didn't think much about reading. It was always there.

Mom and Dad were steeped in reading, but their approaches to books were very different. Mom's books always had pencil notes in the margins—often eyebrow pencil. If a piece of writing inspired a poem or a thought or a remembered dentist appointment, she'd just jot it down. I suppose, with her five kids, she needed to capture the idea at the moment. Who knew what interruptions would send it off for good?

Mom spent hours in used bookstores finding jewels about dreams or being a woman, or life in Vietnam. Or she'd pick up a book about none of those things just because a face on the cover was intriguing. When Mom died we found valuable insights, verses, and thoughts left behind in the margins.

Dad has first-edition Hemingways on his shelf along with Shakespeare, James Joyce, Dylan Thomas, and Winston Churchill. He would just as soon have his hands removed as to write in a book. He treats them as valued gifts. Mom treated books as a necessity of life—toothbrush, sweater, and a book in case you wait in line or find yourself in a quiet spot. From the two of them, I learned there is more than one way to value a book. Books are a necessity. And they are a valued gift. And I learned that each one of us holds the power to help children love reading—to feel the passion of a good story.

In college I was an art major who was enchanted by books—by the words, the rhythms, and the print on the page. In 1979, with partners, I opened Hicklebee's Children's Bookstore in San Jose, California. It came from my desire to be first in line to see the newest gems published each season—to read aloud pages to strangers, to boast about illustrations as though I had created them myself. My storytelling side—I was always told to "get to the point"—has been satisfied with programs for large groups of adults as well as one-on-one stories with children. After all this time, there is still nothing for me that matches the sight of a child settled on the floor of our store, lost in the magic of a book.

Walter and I have worked together since 1981. When a new book catches my attention, I save a copy to show him. We read passages aloud to anyone who will listen—each of us enjoying our own dramatic telling. Most of the time we agree on shared selections, and when we don't, I figure his judgment is slipping. I don't know anyone with his grasp on which books work best for children. Except, of course, for me.

How This Book Is Organized

Our book is divided into several parts according to a book's listening or interest level. We feel this represents the age of the child to whom the book may be read or who will be interested in the book's subject matter, theme, or style of presentation. We begin our book, for instance, with books of interest to children of all ages. Books of interest follow those listings to babies through preschoolers, followed by books of interest to a mixed listenership of preschoolers and elementary readers, and so on. Within each interest level, their reading levels further categorize books. For instance, in the middle-grade category (don't worry! we're coming to definitions of all these terms), we subdivide listings: those books easily read by a child reading at the elementary level, followed by those that will be read by a child reading at the middle-grade level, etc.

Definitions (or, About Those Levels)

Because a child's readiness for a book is not determined by chronological age, we will use general ranges represented as follows:

All=listeners of all ages
P=from babies to preschoolers
E=Early elementary (grades K–3)
M=Middle elementary (grades 3–6)
M+=Preadolescents (grade 6 and early middle school)

Remember, reading readiness cannot clearly be attached to an age or grade. We recommend a range of listening and reading levels to help you choose books that best fit the needs of your child, student, or family.

In the listening/interest level area, multiple entries indicate that the book will appeal to a group that spans more than one age range.

A dual heading for reading level, such as E/M indicates that a book straddles these two levels; it will challenge an E-level reader but will also satisfy a middle-level reader.

Frankly, these levels have been chosen more from gut reaction and experience than from standard reading-level "recipes." Remember: There is no such thing as a perfect book for all children of a particular age.

Of course, your knowledge of the children for whom you are choosing and their individual interests and abilities should always be the determining factor when you're selecting a book. Our goal is to aim you in the right direction and to help you narrow your path through the forest of choices.

Title Listings

Within each readership category, books are organized alphabetically by title. Here is a sample title listing:

"Slowly, Slowly, Slowly," said the Sloth PICTURE BOOK
AUTHOR/ILLUSTRATOR: Eric Carle
HC: Philomel
THEMES: time; sloths; jungles; animals; Amazon; rain forest

Why are we always in a hurry? Rush. Rush. Rush. We scurry from here to there. We play computer games and then—quick! Click!—we watch TV. We eat fast food . . . Eric Carle's solution? This book. He hopes we can learn a little from the gentle sloth who moves slowly, slowly, slowly. Take the time to read this . . . slowly. You and your youngster will enjoy it.

 This book reminds me of watching Mr. Rogers slowly, slowly, slowly removing each button on his sweater. It wasn't until I had toddlers that I appreciated him and got the importance of taking time, putting on shoes, unbuttoning sweaters. Eric Carle does that here, except he adds his spectacular art.

Each title listing will include some and possibly all of the following:

Title (A star [★] is used to identify standouts/gems/the best of the best in our mutual opinion.)

Author

Illustrator (where applicable)

Hardcover (HC), Paperback (PB), or Board Book (BB) publisher

Format: fiction; picture book; poetry; nonfiction—a basic guide to what kind of book it is.

Themes: Each title includes a list of themes, cross-referenced with the appendix at the back of the book, to offer a multitude of options when matching a child's interests with a book.

Comments: Each entry concludes with our comments, which highlight the distinctive qualities that earned a book its place in our listings. The bulk of the comments come from both of us, written separately, discussed, and revised together until we often cannot tell who wrote what initially.

 I feel certain I would know which reviews I wrote.

Yeah, all the reviews with the word "critter" in them are yours.

From time to time, as above, one of us will have something to say that is in addition to the review we wrote—sometimes responding to the other writer's slightly different take on a book, sometimes recounting an experience linked to a book. You'll also find some reviews identified as either **Valerie's** or **Walter's** alone. This occurs when one of us felt strongly enough about a title and the other one agreed that those feelings pretty much summed it up.

A Note on Finding the Books

We have made every effort to choose books still available from publishers and to list paperback editions, usually less expensive, if available. Find them in your library, or go to your local bookstore to buy the books. Never hesitate to ask a bookseller to special-order a title if you do not see it in the store. As this guide goes into publication, some of our favorites will go "out of print"; that is, they will no longer be available for sale. In those cases, look for them in the library or in used bookstores.

Reading

Why read? Is it just a search for knowledge? If our only goal is for everyone to be able to program the VCR and read a computer manual, then stressing only phonics and word definitions would be all there is to teaching reading. However, if we want to encourage people to think for themselves, then the teaching of reading must have higher priorities. When you nurture the questioning mind, when you allow for the prospect of disagreement or interpretation, and when you develop the power to imagine or even create, then the benefits of reading stretch beyond the obvious and reach past the possible.

Of course reading is good. It's important. You've heard it all your life. The lecture about books and reading ranks right up there with "take your vitamins" and "look both ways before crossing the street." However, one of the reasons children lose interest in books and reading is because of the emphasis put on how "good" it is for them rather than on how exciting it can be. We advocate fewer lectures and more setting an example. Be a reader, both for them and yourself. They'll get the message.

Most meaningful reading is done because the reader wants to, not because he has to. It is the soul that feeds on the adventures of Tom Sawyer and Huck Finn, that grows as a result of Jess's devastating loss in *The Bridge to Terabithia*, that leaps up in gladness at the inspiring words of poets like Nikki Grimes and tellers like Joseph Bruchac.

Reading allows the luxury of retreating from the world into a private place. When you read, you are not limited by where you live, who your relatives are, how much money you have, or if you're the smartest or the fastest. You can travel beyond boundaries and explore the feelings and customs of unfamiliar people, real or imagined. Most of us don't choose to read with such abandon, exploring all those other worlds. We choose what we read with specific tastes and needs in mind. Nevertheless, it's delightful to know that those possibilities are there for us whenever we want them.

As adults, we often read to escape ourselves, or at least our daily lives, but one of the chief reasons children read is to find themselves. Young children frequently measure stories by how closely they echo their own thoughts and feelings. They look for opportunities to identify with characters, their problems, and solutions. They seek approval for themselves and their actions in books and rejoice to find it. As they grow older and their lives become more complex, reading about others with similar concerns and conflicts gives them hope and helps them to feel less alone. Finding oneself in a character or in a story is an incredible feeling. Pride, faith, and confidence in oneself are nurtured by reading as a child reaches for independence.

Create time in your child's life to read for pleasure. In the midst of our hurried lives, when we see our kids settling down with a book, it's hard not to say, "Isn't there something you should be doing?" "Don't you have homework?" Help them find time during the day to experience the excitement of reading a book of their choice. Make this part of every child's daily routine.

Television, Screens, and Reading

Books give children choices. Our concern is that while television dictates a response to a child—when to think something is funny or scary, which characters are good or evil—the child is not learning to develop his own responses. Children need to cultivate their ability to make decisions on their own. One of the great things about reading is how it engages the imagination on so many levels at once yet allows the reader to absorb at her own pace.

Independent readers have the power to control the speed, to reread a page, and to decide if the story works for them regardless of how hard the author worked to shape the tale. The story belongs to them as soon as they read it. They can even choose to put it down and refuse to finish it. That's power!

Family Reading

A Warm Fire, a Comfy Chair, and a Good Book: The classic picture of family life. Our world and our families have changed throughout history, but nothing has taken the place of sharing a good story. It calms, excites, consoles, inspires, motivates, and delights. There is no other family activity that offers more in twenty minutes a day. Once you decide that books will play an important role in the daily life of your family, finding time will be as habitual as eating breakfast and brushing your teeth.

Families who read together get more in the bargain than just well-read kids. It is crucial to the healthy development of the brain that books and stories be read to and made available to even the youngest child. There is plenty of statistical proof that children who have books in their lives have better opportunities and more choices than children who don't. The last four reports from the National Center for Education Statistics have shown a direct correlation between the presence of reading materials in the home and test scores. Kids with books, magazines, newspapers, and other reading materials in their homes, as well as adults who use them, score significantly higher on reading assessment tests than those who do not. Therefore, you are not off the hook once they become readers at age five, six, or seven. Reading together needs to be a constant in your children's lives, a promise that you would not break any sooner than you would break your promise to feed them, love them, or make them wear a coat in winter.

Family reading works best when all members feel involved. When your children begin to read, invite them to read aloud to the family. Some children will be eager to try; others may want to wait and build confidence. Whenever your child is ready, offer books on a variety of subjects and at a reading level that early readers can try.

Reading aloud goes beyond the pages of a book. It is a powerful opportunity to share a common experience and build your quiet connections. Whether your children choose a book or the choice is yours, remember to use this time as an opportunity for joy in your day. You can learn about each other when you share stories and listen to each other. No quizzes are needed; just show that the story interests you. This is not simply a get-it-over-with-and-off-to-bed nightly routine—this is one of the best moments in a family's day.

 Read to them every day you have them. Read to them until they flat-out refuse to stay in the same room with you, and then chase them from room to room with the book in your hand, reading aloud.

A note to grandparents: Take time to read to your grandchild. Begin with him placed cozily on your lap. When he is too big for laps, then cuddle him next to you. Share the fun, excitement, adventure, and magic of a good story. For you it's an opening to talk about your experiences—to impart your wisdom. Most important, you will have made memories and invaluable time with that precious child in your life.

Books on Tape are perfect for family car trips, quiet evenings at home, and calming that noisy carpool. Whether you are traveling eight hours to a vacation destination or spend twenty minutes in a daily commute, a book on tape can be an effective way of sharing the joy of reading with the whole family. There are picture books, folktales, poetry collections, as well as modern and classic novels available in recorded format at your local bookstore or library. Nearly every good novel for children gets recorded, usually in an unabridged format with sensitive, expressive, talented readers.

Children can sit still for unabridged classics. They don't have to hear the entire tape in one sitting. The important thing is that they get the full experience reading aloud provides: rich vocabulary and an opportunity to create a picture in one's mind. It allows the entire family to listen together.

Choosing: Over the years we've seen parents concerned about the grade, reading, developmental, and interest levels of books. Choosing the "right" one can get complicated.

Most people don't know where to start. No wonder they reach for a doll or a truck. It is what it is. After all, you can't judge a book by its cover, but you sure can a toy.

Trust your instincts: When you reach for a children's book, you are most likely attracted by its cover—the title, the illustration. You take it home because it somehow appeals to you. It may be the writing, the subject, or the art. Whatever the reason, it's what makes you different from the next person, and that invites your child to know more about you. So what if you or your child ends up not liking your choice? It's just a book. Each of you bring home a stack of books from the library and take turns reading them. You'll be spending time talking about what appeals to you and getting to know each other's tastes. And

---

Stopping at the peak

There are those times in reading aloud when one moment you've got your children mesmerized, and the next they are bouncing all over the place. Wonder what happens? We are firm believers in stopping at the peak, in direct proportion to age. As children get older they can listen longer. We imagine a graph with an arc going gradually up, getting to a high point, and then plummeting down the other side. It happens when children have had enough. If you can train yourself to stop just before they plummet—not to pick up just one more book while you've got their attention, or read one more chapter—they will be eager for your next read-aloud time. You can extend their listening ability by adding a page or two at each session, but remember to leave them wanting more.

when you are excited about a book yourself, it comes across in body language and feelings as well as words. And remember, there is no such thing as one "right" book. Have fun!

Choosing a Book by More Than Its Cover

Covers are the first things we look at when choosing a book, so if one gets our attention we are more likely to pick up the book. If we do, we are more likely to buy it. However, we've all made wrong choices by letting the cover sell us.

Children—and those who choose books for them—have a better chance than ever to see a wide range in picture-book art. But don't be fooled by stunning illustrations. We've learned in our combined fifty years of pushing books that good illustrations go far in selling the newest titles, but to maintain popularity from year to year, a book depends on the worth of its text. Elsewhere in this book we make light of the "absolute" rules that some people apply to books. We don't mean to imply that there isn't a set of standards that you can use. Here are some of ours:

For babies, try bold colors and contrasts including photographs. Keep it simple. As they get older they love pointing out and naming each character.

Toddlers benefit from busy pictures with lots of things to find on each page. They'll also want to carry around a loved story to read over and over.

As the school years approach, broaden their horizons with a variety of styles. This is a good way to help them become more confident about their own preference.

When choosing a book, assuming you are doing so for reasons other than "I like the art" (which is a good enough reason), *test a page or two* by reading it to yourself. See what connections are made between the words and the pictures. Does the art help you *see* more? Does it tell you things the words do not? Does it add a mood or a feeling to the way words work in your mind *or* does the art distract you from the story? Do the details not match or is there a lack of feeling or personality that makes you feel that the words might be better off by themselves?

 Can you tell that we really don't want to say what is good and bad where pictures are concerned? Everyone's taste is different. Valerie loves some artists' work that I cannot abide and vice versa. When I am forced to come up with a definition I say that a good picture book is one in which the words tell the story without needing pictures and the pictures tell a story without needing words—yet when the two are combined, you cannot imagine them existing apart.

You Can't Judge a Book by Its Low Price

When choosing a book for a child the only wrong choice is not to choose. People ask us what we think about Golden Books and others that can be picked up at grocery counters and drugstores. If a grandmother picks one up at the drugstore and takes it home to read to her grandson, we think it is great. If the new book added to the grocery basket excites a child, we think it is great. It's a step toward reading and a step closer to the library and the opportunity for a child to broaden his reading horizons. Price and format can never be trusted as guarantees of the value a book may have to a child.

What If You Make a Mistake?

There is nothing in the world that can stop a child from wrinkling up his nose at a book for which you've just plopped down eighteen dollars. That's why we suggest learning about what you like as a family at the library, where there is no risk.

When you select a book and bring it to your child to share, you are telling her something about what you value in a book—helping to shape her tastes and making her familiar with yours. But if the only books she sees are ones you like, her tastes will be limited. We advocate buying the books you love and going to the library for a wider selection. Ultimately your child's tastes will become clear.

Remember the Original Version. Publishers are in the business of making money. Though it sets our teeth on edge, we can't really blame them when they try to squeeze every drop of blood out of a successful book in the process of turning it into merchandise. You'll buy them for your children: We bought them for ours. But whether it's a pop-up, poster book, board book, cookbook, bathtub book, or any of the cut-and-paste abridgments, we want to encourage you to seek out the original version. Use your children's love of that character to further their appreciation of its literary source. Besides, if you don't, they may go through life believing they have already read it.

We encourage parents to seek out a book person with the same care they give to choosing their child's doctor or dentist. Know what you're looking for or at least how to ask for help. If your questions are met with an empty stare, or a cursory response, you haven't found the right person. Look for the children's librarian in your local library. Look for the staff member at your locally owned independent bookstore who knows your community and has the knowledge of books to be able to assist you.

"Free, free, free. Libraries are free!" I'm going to keep saying this until you all promise you'll go to the library once a week.

Be honest about your feelings toward a book: If you don't like it, say so. If you just can't stand reading the same book over and over, it is okay to tell the child, but choose another book instead. Don't put down anyone else's choice of reading material; just be up front about your own response to something.

 I know that sprinkles of "doesn't like it" or "thinks it's great" dust float around when you are reading. You are not going to fool anyone by pretending you are enjoying the process if you aren't—and you could send the unintended message that reading itself is no fun.

Let your child choose. It is wonderful when a child has parents who value books enough to buy them and create an at-home library. But we also believe children should have library experience so they can learn to make good choices for themselves. At the library, price is not an issue, money is no object.

 Uh, have I mentioned that libraries are free?

Your child may choose a book because it looks familiar or because the cover is weird, or he may grab it because it's on top. It doesn't matter. If he changes his mind when he gets home, he can return it to the library—no questions asked.

Where Would I Be Without Libraries?

By the time I started the ninth grade I was attending my eleventh school. We moved a lot, and I remember every library at every school I attended. My first school had no library, only a "book room," and by the time I left there (midway through third grade) I had read every book in it that was of interest to me. After two more moves in third and fourth grades, I spent my fifth- and sixth-grade years at a brand-new school, and I was proud to know that my name would be the first one on so many library cards. The libraries at the three junior high schools I went to were lifesavers, and I spent enormous amounts of time there. Then we moved (again!) to California in March of my eighth-grade year. I was devastated and surly and hated my new school. I spent two periods a day in the library, reading the entire works of Madeleine L'Engle, Edward Eager, and others.

My high school years were all spent at the same school, and I knew every nook and cranny of that library. The librarian was the

Library 911

I was asked to observe a library to offer my opinion as to why children were not checking out books. When I walked through the doors, I was confronted with shelves of drab, spine-out volumes set in orderly rows in the stale library air. "Color!" I thought. "This place needs color!" But when I heard the librarian caution a class of second-graders, "Do not touch a book unless you can read it," I recognized the true problem. This librarian didn't understand children. She didn't realize that part of the fun is in the choosing, not just reading. Whether their choices are based on the favorite of a friend, the picture on the front, or the subject matter, children need to go through the process of making a choice. Only when they've had the freedom to do that will they learn to make the right choices for themselves.

mother of a friend of mine, and when I was a senior she allowed me to go through a drawer in her office of books she had acquired but couldn't put out in the stacks for various reasons. Through her I discovered Brautigan, Ferlinghetti, Ginsberg, and Vonnegut.

During the same time, we lived far away from the school, and the nearest branch library was thirty miles away, but we had the Bookmobile! Twice a week I would walk the mile and a half down to where it parked and I would fill up on what they had and badger the librarian for other titles. You could ask them for books and the next week they would *bring them to you!* My only regret was that a lot of the reference books I wanted to get my hands on could not be checked out. So I rode the bus all the way into downtown San Diego (it took about an hour) and went to the big main library. I thought it was heaven! I spent hours in the recordings area, checking out Broadway shows whose soundtracks I didn't own and works by composers I had never heard of, taking them into the private rooms and listening. I was forever asking the reference librarian for some huge atlas or compendium and having her (*always* a her) lug it down off some high shelf and watch me as I merrily plopped myself down in a chair at a table and read the damn thing. I never looked stuff up, wasn't trying to do research. I just wanted to read and absorb. After a few months of this, the staff knew my predilection, and would try to interest me in more obscure tomes of arcane knowledge (weather, mining, invertebrates, folklore, flags, whatever . . .), and they were never surprised when I took the book and read through it. This panned out nicely when, years later, I appeared on *Jeopardy!* and won four games. I always use that anecdote to illustrate to impressionable youth the value of reading. Oh, yeah—don't forget: "Free, free, free. Libraries are free!"

Clip the Strings Attached to Reading

For some reason, we parents feel that our child's reading is our own personal accomplishment. Pregnant women come into Hicklebee's requesting books that will prepare their baby to read. I always recommend something nontoxic. It is practical, and it makes far more sense for an infant to chew on the corners than to try reading the book.

When people offer a child a teddy bear, they do it with love, often holding teddy to themselves before handing it over. No strings . . . just something to love. But with books this invisible thing happens. Those strings are there, and they whisper, "This is the one that will teach him . . ." I wish we could treat a book like a teddy bear. Love it. Hand it over after clutching it fondly to your chest because it is such a prize. That probably would raise reading achievement across the board!

I believe the <u>Nancy Drew</u> and <u>Hardy Boys</u> books continue to be popular because someone who knows the characters by heart often introduces them. The fondness for the series comes across with a sincere, "I've got a book I know you're going to love!" sentiment. Understand, I've been there, showing words to my toddler, thinking this was dif-

A fifth-grader came into my bookstore with his class. His attitude made it clear there wasn't anything of value there for him. He was wearing a T-shirt with "LIFE SUCKS!" printed on the front. I said, "Whoa, that's pretty dreary!" in response to his shirt and then asked if there was anything he would like me to show him. He snickered, looking around me at his friends, and said, "You don't have a book about bikes do you?" I led him to a shelf that offered several titles. He mentioned that he had just modified an old Schwinn so that it was "way cool." I pulled out a book showing photos and illustrations of modified bikes. His face lit up as he settled down, book in hand, friends surrounding him, and he began pointing to pictures describing parts and paint. When it was time to go, he found me and offered a casual "thanks." As he filed past with his class, I noticed his T-shirt had been turned inside out.

ferent; after all, wasn't she a bit brighter than most kids? We're only human but we should not take this early-reader business too seriously. If you love reading, and you let your children know it through your example and enthusiasm—for your books, for theirs, for the library and the bookstore—you'll grow a reader almost effortlessly.

Picture books are for all ages. Regardless of your child's reading skill, no child is too old to enjoy illustrations. Some of the best readers request picture books.

My stepsister Paula announced, upon graduating from high school, that she was so glad, because "I never have to read another book again, as long as I live!" My grandmother nearly had a heart attack. What she heard was an emphasis on the word *never*. Paula's emphasis was on *have to*. The process of reading had been made so odious to her, with no adult around to shepherd her through the tough times (we who turn to literature early and often are true anomalies and frequently do so in a solitary fashion) that she associated all reading with everything she loathed about school. She is now a preschool teacher and the mother of four and, like most of my siblings, she came to reading for pleasure in her own good time. I get reports from my stepsister Letha's house that my sisters and nieces sit around the pool on summer afternoons reading books and discussing them. I am so proud!

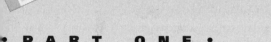

PART ONE

Books for All Ages

Books are way better than television.
For one thing, books don't have commercials.
For another thing, you can't use a television to squash a bug.
(Well, you can, but it has to be a very slow bug.)

—DAVE BARRY, HUMORIST

Listening/Interest Level: All/ Reading Level: Early Elementary (E)

Here is a collection of books for sharing that will not only interest the widest possible range of listeners, but are easy enough so that early readers can join in the fun.

★ 17 Kings and 42 Elephants
PICTURE BOOK

AUTHOR: Margaret Mahy • ILLUSTRATOR: Patricia MacCarthy
HC: Dial
THEMES: elephants; journeys; kings; jungles; math; rhythm

A magical collaboration, one that is an example of the best kind of picture-book storytelling. Mahy's evocative poetry, telling of a journey full of mystery, is complemented by MacCarthy's beautiful batik paintings; together they make a masterpiece. This story raises more questions than it answers. Where are the kings going? Where are they from? What do seventeen kings need with forty-two elephants, anyway? There is plenty of opportunity for discussion long after the reading ends.

All the Way to Lhasa: A Tale From Tibet
PICTURE BOOK

AUTHOR/ILLUSTRATOR: Barbara Helen Berger
HC: Philomel
THEMES: Tibet; parables; goals; perseverance; triumph; journeys; folklore

"One foot in front of the other . . ." a small boy and his yak persevere along the difficult way to the holy city of Lhasa, succeeding where others failed.

Berger's soft pictures and lyrical prose make this "tortoise and hare"-style story one the entire family will enjoy.

Annie Bananie

PICTURE BOOK

AUTHOR: Leah Komaiko • ILLUSTRATOR: Laura Cornell
HC/PB: HarperCollins
THEMES: friendship; moving; loss

Anyone who has had a best friend move away will understand Annie Bananie. Komaiko, who has a talent for rhythm and for understanding true friendship, has captured the feelings in her words. Cornell has echoed the feelings in her art.

Anno's Journey

PICTURE BOOK

AUTHOR/ILLUSTRATOR: Mitsumasa Anno
PB: Paperstar
THEMES: wordless; Europe; geography; social studies; journeys

Float invisibly from one perspective to another in this wordless journey through northern Europe. Anno's stunning watercolors offer details as an antidote to geography-shy readers.

Art Dog

PICTURE BOOK

AUTHOR/ILLUSTRATOR: Thacher Hurd
HC/PB: HarperCollins
THEMES: art; dogs; heroes; creativity; humor; puns; jobs; taking action;
    artists; theft; museums

Using the complete range of colors in his palette, Hurd tells the story of the mysterious hero, Art Dog, and his rescue of priceless masterpieces stolen from the Dogopolis Museum of Art. Funny, loaded with puns and inspiring to future artists; a fun book to read before visiting an art museum for the first time.

Ben's Trumpet

PICTURE BOOK

AUTHOR/ILLUSTRATOR: Rachel Isadora
HB: Greenwillow
THEMES: music; cities; musical instruments; community; jazz; musicians;
    yearning

Ben yearns to play a real trumpet, not just the pretend one that nobody else can see. It's the early 1920s and his dream comes true with the help of a trumpeter from the neighborhood jazz club. Black-and-white Caldecott Honor illustrations are breathtaking.

Others in this series, where each page reveals the magic of nature are *Plants That Never Ever Bloom* and *The Reason for a Flower.*

Robert Sabuda, Master of the Pop-Up

Widely acknowledged as a master of paper engineering, Robert Sabuda has brought new life and energy to a tired format with his fascinating, astounding works of art. Many of his creations become collector's items. For the holidays he has illustrated The *Night Before Christmas*, *The 12 Days of Christmas*, *A Kwanzaa Celebration Pop-up Book* by Nancy Williams, and his celebrated *The Christmas Alphabet.* Sabuda's art is not only about holidays. Here is a sampling of his other books, suitable for all ages:

ABC Disney: An Alphabet Pop-Up (out of print, but worth tracking down)
The Movable Mother Goose
Young Naturalist Pop-up Handbook; Butterflies (with Matthew Reinhart)
The Wonderful Wizard of Oz: A Commemorative Pop-up by L. Frank Baum

Chickens Aren't the Only Ones   PICTURE BOOK NONFICTION

AUTHOR/ILLUSTRATOR: Ruth Heller
HC: Price Stern & Soan • PB: Paperstar
THEMES: science; chickens; eggs; birds; snakes; dinosaurs; frogs; fish; spiders; nature

"Chickens aren't the only ones, most snakes lay eggs and lizards, too, and crocodiles and turtles do, and dinosaurs who are extinct, but they were reptiles, too." Heller's brilliant illustrations and simple text pique the interest of young scientists as well as any child interested in how things come to be.

The Christmas Alphabet   POP-UP

AUTHOR/ILLUSTRATOR: Robert Sabuda
HC: Orchard
THEMES: Christmas; guessing

Each letter of the alphabet is placed on its own door, concealing a pop-up prize. Guess what is behind each door, and marvel at all twenty-six dazzling paper creations.

Clown   PICTURE BOOK

AUTHOR/ILLUSTRATOR: Quentin Blake
HC/PB: Henry Holt
THEMES: adventure; wordless; homelessness; toys; poverty; friendship; home; clowns; problem solving

A clown begins this tale in a garbage can, and ends it with a happy-ever-after family. In between, adventures keep the pages turning—and all without a word. Hooray for Blake! His action-filled plot with its heart-tugging moments makes this book a worthwhile addition to anyone's library.

Dealing with Death

What do you offer a child who has experienced the death of a family member, neighbor, school chum—or even a cherished pet? There are excellent books available, but we suggest you read them aloud before they are needed. Even with the best intentions, family members who want to ease the sorrow and answer difficult questions are often upset themselves. While even the best book can only begin to help ease the grief, if a story and its ideas are already familiar, it will be more of a comfort. And even a child fortunate enough to never have to go through one of these experiences may need help understanding a friend's situation.

We strongly recommend *Badger's Parting Gifts [PAGE 164]* and *Lifetimes [PAGE 48]*. Each has a different approach and works as a starting point for discussion. *Badger* is told in story format and deals primarily with feelings about loss. *Lifetimes* is nonfiction, a straightforward account of living and dying.

Other titles you may wish to consider: for younger children: *You Hold Me and I'll Hold You, Goodbye Mousie, The Tenth Good Thing About Barney, Waiting for the Whales, I'll See You in My Dreams, Grandad Bill's Song, Dog Heaven, Cat Heaven, The Dead Bird, Everett Anderson's Goodbye, I'll Always Love You, Annie and the Old One, Nana Upstairs, Nana Downstairs*. For older children: *Mick Harte Was Here, The Bridge to Terabithia, The Heavenly Village, Missing May,* and *On My Honor*.

The Dead Bird   PICTURE BOOK

AUTHOR: Margaret Wise Brown • ILLUSTRATOR: Remy Charlip
PB: HarperCollins
THEMES: death; rituals; birds; problem solving

A straightforward look at a child's first encounter with death. Children find a dead bird, examine it, bury it, sing a song for it, honor it, and finally forget about it. Simple text on white pages alternates with Charlip's unaffected art, making this a profoundly moving book and one that will serve as a snapshot of a nearly universal moment of childhood.

Doctor De Soto

PICTURE BOOK

AUTHOR/ILLUSTRATOR: William Steig
HC: Farrar, Straus & Giroux • PB: Sunburst
THEMES: dentists; mice; foxes; humor; teeth

Doctor De Soto is a mouse dentist who makes his practice available to just about anyone who isn't a danger to mice. But then one day Fox comes crying in agony with a terrible toothache. What's a good dentist to do? If it's like pulling teeth to get your child to sit down for a story, try this witty one. For more adventures, see *Doctor DeSoto Goes to Africa*.

The Empty Pot

PICTURE BOOK

AUTHOR/ILLUSTRATOR: Demi
HC/PB: Henry Holt
THEMES: truth; gardening; folklore; China; flowers

Demi has created many other books with detailed illustrations and well-told stories—fiction and non. Some are *King Midas: The Golden Touch*; *Kites: Magic Wishes That Fly Up to the Sky*; and the out-of-print but worth searching for *Demi's Dragons and Fantastic Creatures*.

An elderly emperor proclaims to the children in his land that his successor will be "whoever can show me their best in a year's time." He then gives special flower seeds to each. Young Ping is especially happy: after all, he has always been a successful gardener. But as hard as he tries, nothing grows. At the end of the year, he is the only child with an empty pot. We don't want to ruin this story for you, but we can tell you that the ending is a happy one that comes with a lesson in honesty. Demi's beautiful art is in a style unique to her.

Everett Anderson's Goodbye

PICTURE BOOK

AUTHOR: Lucille Clifton • ILLUSTRATOR: Ann Grifalconi
PB: Henry Holt
THEMES: death; loss; fathers; anger; denial; African American

Everett Anderson's father has died. This quiet, sensitive story shows the stages of grief he experiences before being able to say, "I knew my daddy loved me through and through, and whatever happens when people die, love doesn't stop, and neither will I." Although Everett is a very young boy, any age child will understand the emotions experienced in this treasure. Other stories about Everett Anderson, dealing with less traumatic topics, include *Everett Anderson's 1 2 3*, *Everett Anderson's Friend*; *Some of the Days of Everett Anderson*, and *One of the Problems of Everett Anderson*.

★ Fables

AUTHOR/ILLUSTRATOR: Arnold Lobel
HC/PB: HarperCollins
THEMES: animals; fables; folklore; lessons

Published in 1980, *Fables* has become a classic. Lobel's twenty original stories each fit on a single page with a facing award-winning full-color illustration. The tales are a delight to read aloud, and the morals at the end of each add value on their own. This is the book to take to children's appointments. Open to any page for a complete story, a chuckle, and a perfect way to pass waiting-room time.

Farm Morning

PICTURE BOOK

AUTHOR/ILLUSTRATOR: David McPhail
PB: Harcourt Brace
THEMES: farms; farm animals; morning; fathers and daughters; rituals

A perfect father/daughter book, as well as a glimpse of farm life, *Farm Morning* details the daily rituals of tending farm animals with lovely, gentle words and watercolors.

Fortunately

PICTURE BOOK

AUTHOR/ILLUSTRATOR: Remy Charlip
PB: Aladdin
THEMES: self-respect; repetition; luck; travel; mail; comparisons

"Fortunately one day, Ned got a letter that said, 'Please Come to a Surprise Party': But unfortunately the party was in Florida and he was in New York." First published in 1964, *Fortunately* continues to delight youngsters, who repeat an enthusiastic "fortunately" followed by an exasperated "unfortunately" for weeks following this story. And why not? They have experienced Charlip, who, fortunately, is an artist whose wit, talent, and understanding of children has created books that continue to delight over the span of ages, no unfortunately about it.

Free Fall

PICTURE BOOK

AUTHOR/ILLUSTRATOR: David Wiesner
HC: Lothrop • PB: Mulberry
THEMES: wordless; dreams; adventure; connections

No words are necessary. Wiesner's adventure comes to life as the pages of a sleeping boy's book break loose and sweep away into new forms connecting and changing from page to page. Let your child enjoy this one at his own pace.

★ The Gardener
PICTURE BOOK

AUTHOR: Sarah Stewart • ILLUSTRATOR: David Small
HC: Farrar, Straus & Giroux • PB: Sunburst
THEMES: gardening; mail; family; separation; generosity; U.S. history, the Depression; uncles; nieces; baking; bakers; optimism; resourcefulness; emotions; compassion; neighbors; gardens; country life; diversity; city life; gardeners

Lydia Grace's uncle doesn't smile. That's what she discovers when she is sent to live with him during her family's difficult times. But his crabby expression is no match for Lydia's cheery disposition. In no time, with her green thumb at work, she brightens up the world around her uncle's bakery and learns that people show love in various ways. Small's full-page art transforms bigs to enormous, littles to minuscule, and flowers to joy. This sweet story, told through art and letters home, will touch your heart.

George and Martha
PICTURE BOOK

AUTHOR/ILLUSTRATOR: James Marshall
HC/PB: Houghton Mifflin
THEMES: friendship; humor; relationships

The perfect expression of friendship in picture-book form. Two hippos, lovingly but hilariously rendered in Marshall's droll, minimalist style (both pictures and words), star in a series of adventures that will have everyone laughing. The limits of being a friend are tested time and again in these books, but nothing can keep George and Martha apart for long. Underneath all the fun, there are some valuable lessons about trust, loyalty, and maintaining a sense of humor. There are seven George and Martha titles in all, including a one-volume omnibus edition.

 Though Marshall never comes right out and says it, it seems clear to the adult eye that G & M are more than just friends. I have always felt that these books should be given as a set to any couple about to embark upon a long-term relationship. George and Martha are role models for us all!

Good Dog, Carl

PICTURE BOOK

AUTHOR/ILLUSTRATOR: Alexandra Day
HC/BB: Simon & Schuster • PB: Aladdin
THEMES: wordless; dogs; babysitters; babies

When Carl the dog is told "Look after the baby, Carl, I'll be back shortly," the text ends and the action begins. Carl works like a dog—keeping the baby safe as it ventures from one room to the other. This is the first and our favorite of several Carl books.

The Grey Lady and the Strawberry Snatcher

PICTURE BOOK

AUTHOR/ILLUSTRATOR: Molly Bang
HC: Simon & Schuster • PB: Aladdin
THEMES: wordless; strawberries; adventure; theft; chases; blackberries; monsters

The strawberry snatcher is in hot pursuit of the Grey Lady's strawberries, until he discovers blackberries. A full-color, action-packed wordless treasure.

Hippos Go Berserk

PICTURE BOOK

AUTHOR/ILLUSTRATOR: Sandra Boynton
HC/BB: Simon & Schuster • PB: Aladdin
THEMES: counting; humor

A counting book featuring forty-five hippos and an unidentified creature romping out of control. Funny, and the kind of book that begs to be read again and again.

If...

PICTURE BOOK

AUTHOR/ILLUSTRATOR: Sarah Perry
HC: Getty Trust Publications
THEMES: imagination; fantasy

"If toes were teeth . . . If caterpillars were toothpaste . . ." Striking illustrations demand attention as you venture from one page to the next in this visual stretch of the imagination.

Another book that conjures up possibilities through imagination is *Imagine A Night* by Canadian artist Rob Gonsalves, who paints the images formed between sleep and wakefulness when one's mind frees itself to soar beyond the boundaries of everyday experiences.

I'll Give You Kisses

PICTURE BOOK

AUTHOR/ILLUSTRATOR: Diane Paterson
PB: Dial
THEMES: humor; aunts; babies

Formerly titled *Smile for Auntie,* this uproarious tale of an aunt doing every-thing she can to get a baby to smile is back in print with its close-up, exag-gerated illustrations intact. We all remember a family member or friend trying to elicit a response from us as children. Then we become adults and find ourselves doing the same thing to the children of our loved ones. Read this book and chuckle with familiarity as the child responds warily to Auntie, only to smile as she leaves.

 My daughter, Laura, was thrilled to hear this book was back in print. Then I told Laura the title had been changed. "No!" she said. "The new title turns the plea into a bribe. I hate it!" Ah, it isn't a good idea to fool with a beloved book. I agree with Laura.

Jeremy's Decision

PICTURE BOOK

AUTHOR: Ardyth Brott • ILLUSTRATOR: Michael Martchenko
PB: Kane/Miller
THEMES: music; jobs; orchestras; siblings; fathers and sons; individuality;
  dinosaurs; choices

Jeremy has gotten tired of everyone's asking if he's going to be like his father, a famous symphony conductor, when he grows up. He has his own interests—dinosaurs—but has endured the well-meaning questions out of politeness. With a satisfying and surprising conclusion, here is a book for every child who fears living up to adult expectations.

Lunch

PICTURE BOOK

AUTHOR/ILLUSTRATOR: Denise Fleming
HC/PB/BB: Henry Holt
THEMES: concepts; vegetables; fantasy; color; food; mice; fruit; vocabulary

A spunky mouse eats his way through a feast of oversized, brightly colored fruits and vegetables. This is a great color concept book, but it's one we'd use with older readers to stretch the vocabulary. Fleming uses two words to describe each vegetable or fruit: crisp white turnip; tasty orange carrots. Have third- or fourth-graders (or older) rewrite her story, replacing the adjectives with others that fit.

Mike Mulligan and His Steam Shovel

PICTURE BOOK

AUTHOR/ILLUSTRATOR: Virginia Lee Burton

HC/PB: Houghton Mifflin

THEMES: machines; buildings; digging; jobs; change; towns; problem solving; resourcefulness; performing

Sweetly old-fashioned, it's the story of a man and his beloved steam shovel, Mary Ann. They dig themselves into a hole, and it takes the ingenuity of a small boy to come up with the perfect solution.

Mole Music

PICTURE BOOK

AUTHOR/ILLUSTRATOR: David McPhail

HC/PB: Henry Holt

THEMES: music; peace; conflict and resolution; musicians

> Another wonderful story is McPhail's *Teddy Bear*, about a lost-then-found-then-lost-again bear and the heart-warming resolution between his two owners.

A simple tale of a mole who longs to make music and who, having studied the violin, gives the world an unsuspected gift. McPhail's gift for gentle poignancy never veers into the mawkish, making him one of our favorite writers who can deliver that "Awwww!" feeling.

My Map Book

PICTURE BOOK

AUTHOR/ILLUSTRATOR: Sara Fanelli

HC: HarperCollins

THEMES: maps; point of view; drawing; self-respect; human body; community

Maps of "my room" and "my neighborhood" we've seen before, but a map of "my stomach" and "my heart"? The concept is clever, but the art seemed weird to us at first. Now we're convinced that it's just what young children need to encourage them to use maps to help them explore their own worlds.

Noah's Ark

PICTURE BOOK

AUTHOR/ILLUSTRATOR: Peter Spier

HC: Doubleday • PB: Dell

THEMES: Bible stories; floods; animals; faith; courage; wordless

Winner of the Caldecott Medal, this wordless retelling of the story of Noah will captivate children, allowing them to tell the story in their own fashion. For another look at Noah's story, read *On Noah's Ark* by Jan Brett.

Next Please
PICTURE BOOK

AUTHOR/ILLUSTRATOR: Ernst Jandl and Norman Junge
HC: Putnam
THEMES: doctors; illness; toys; patience; fear

Five toys, each with the waiting-room willies, go through the gamut of emotions as they wait their turn. Soon there is only one left. With few words, and extraordinary pictures, this gem should be required for the shelves of every waiting room.

 I must have turned the pages back and forth twenty times, checking the subtle changes in the toys' expressions. Those so inclined might want to use this book as an opportunity to talk about how each character may be feeling.

★ Officer Buckle and Gloria
PICTURE BOOK

AUTHOR/ILLUSTRATOR: Peggy Rathmann
HC: Putnam
THEMES: safety; friendship; police; dogs; school; humor; mishaps; teamwork

Here's a story that is kid-friendly. Officer Buckle's boring safety assemblies get livened up by the addition of Gloria, a dog of more than a few tricks. There's a message everyone can agree on—safety is important, but friendship is the most important thing—and a humorous illustration style that is so tightly woven into the narrative, you cannot imagine the book existing any other way. We have read this book countless times and are still noticing the cleverness of Rathmann's eye for detail—check out Officer Buckle's pajamas. This is one funny book!

Old Turtle
PICTURE BOOK

AUTHOR: Douglas Wood • ILLUSTRATOR: Cheng-Khee Chee
HC: Scholastic
THEMES: fables; God; the earth; nature; environment; peace; turtles; hope

When all the beings of the world began to understand one another, they argued about what God was. "God is a swimmer, in the dark blue depths of the sea. 'She is a hunter,' roared the lion. 'God is gentle,' chirped the robin." And then Old Turtle spoke. He spoke of what God is and of what was to come. A family gift that celebrates life, nature, peace, and beauty. A sequel, *Old Turtle and the Broken Truth*, with illustrations by Jon J. Muth, is also available.

The Paperboy

AUTHOR/ILLUSTRATOR: Dav Pilkey
HC/PB: Orchard
THEMES: morning; jobs; pets

PICTURE BOOK

A quiet ode to a paperboy's early morning routine. The quality of writing is matched by the shadowy paintings, making this a lovely book to share in quiet moments. Hush, or you'll break the magic of its spell.

The Rolling Store

AUTHOR: Angela Johnson • ILLUSTRATOR: Peter Catalanotto
HC: Orchard
THEMES: African American; stores; grandfathers; friendship

PICTURE BOOK

A young girl recounts the tale of her grandfather's childhood, when a big truck would come out to the country, a store on wheels with something for everyone. Past and present converge and the rolling store rolls once more.

Shoes, Shoes, Shoes

AUTHOR: Ann Morris • ILLUSTRATOR: Ken Heyman
    (photographs)
PB: MULBERRY
THEMES: cultural diversity; shoes

PICTURE BOOK

Other Morris and Heyman titles include *Bread, Bread, Bread; Hats, Hats, Hats; Houses and Homes; Loving; On the Go; Work;* and *Tools.*

This sparkling photo-essay, which uses footwear around the world to point out our differences and similarities, is typical of Ann Morris's outstanding work. With photographer Ken Heyman, Morris has given us a treasure trove of books on a variety of topics, all suitable for use with children from the very young up to middle school. These make us look at things we take for granted and really see them, and the conversations with children that result from viewing her books are full of insight. Highly recommended.

Sisters

AUTHOR/ILLUSTRATOR: David McPhail
HC/PB: Harcourt Brace
THEMES: sisters; comparisons; family; siblings; individuality

PICTURE BOOK

They aren't very much alike. They don't agree about baseball, or what to wear, or when to wake up. But there is something they have in common: Each one loves her sister.

★ So Much

PICTURE BOOK

AUTHOR: Trish Cooke • ILLUSTRATOR: Helen Oxenbury
PB: Candlewick
THEMES: family; relatives; babies; love; birthdays; fathers; mothers; aunts; uncles; cousins; grandmothers; birthday parties; surprises

Sitting at home, doing "nothing really," Mom and the baby are joined by Auntie Bibba, Uncle Didi, Nannie and Gran-Gran, Cousin Kay-Kay, and Big Cousin Ross. Each family member makes a big deal over the baby, showing affection for him in a variety of ways, always ending in "so much!" Cooke's repetitive, demands-to-be-read-aloud text is full of Anglo-Caribbean rhythms, and Helen Oxenbury's art adds the right touches to this testament to love, making it a must for all families to share.

 Raucously and with a Caribbean dialect!

 Quietly and in your own voice works just as well.

Some Smug Slug

PICTURE BOOK

AUTHOR: Pamela Duncan Edwards • ILLUSTRATOR: Henry Cole
HC/PB: HarperCollins
THEMES: slugs; confidence; vocabulary; animals; alliteration

"Slowly the slug started up the steep surface, stringing behind it scribble sparkling like silk." Read-out-loud language that leaves images may be the best part of this incredible book, although some might argue it's the full-page illustrations that offer a bug's-eye view. Whatever it is, the ending will surprise the reader as much as it does one overconfident slug. If there is a moral here, it's "take your mind off of yourself long enough to open your eyes and your ears."

Time Flies

PICTURE BOOK

AUTHOR/ILLUSTRATOR: Eric Rohmann
HC: Crown
THEMES: wordless; dinosaurs; birds; museums

For a look at Rohmann illustrating in a very different style, check out his Caldecott winner, *My Friend Rabbit.*

Inspired by the theory that birds are the modern relatives of dinosaurs, Rohmann's oversize oil paintings lead the reader from page to page on a wordless journey into a museum, through the dinosaur exhibit and through time.

Other terrific nature titles by Jenkins include: *Big and Little*; *Hottest, Coldest, Highest, Deepest*; *Looking Down*; *Biggest, Strongest, Fastest*; *Top of the World: Climbing Mount Everest*; and *Life on Earth: The Story of Evolution*.

Tuesday
PICTURE BOOK

AUTHOR/ILLUSTRATOR: David Wiesner
HC/PB: Clarion
THEMES: wordless; frogs; imagination; fantasy; adventure

Except for the day and time, this book has no words. It is a flying-frog fantasy adventure that will keep you turning the pages. The art is stunning. The story is mysterious. Truly original.

★ Voyage to the Bunny Planet: First Tomato, Moss Pillows, The Island Light
PICTURE BOOK BOXED SET

AUTHOR/ILLUSTRATOR: Rosemary Wells
HC: Viking
THEMES: self-respect; dreams; imagination; comfort; bad days

We treasure this set and have probably given it to as many adults as children. Each of the stories in Wells's three-book box tells of the beginning of a difficult day. And then (ta dah!): "Far beyond the moon and stars, Twenty light-years south of Mars, Spins the gentle Bunny Planet, And the Bunny Queen is Janet." And Janet's role? To give the child "the day that should have been." Here's the perfect way to show your child that you do understand.

What Do You Do When Something Wants to Eat You?
PICTURE BOOK NONFICTION

AUTHOR/ILLUSTRATOR: Steve Jenkins
HC: Houghton Mifflin
THEMES: animals; predators; animal defenses; food chain

Jenkins's fascinating nature books have delighted us with their mix of ingenious juxtapositions of facts and terrific cut-and-torn-paper art. This book is no exception. Looking at the relationship between the hunter and the hunted introduces the ways animals have developed defenses and strategies to protect themselves from being devoured.

★ Where the Wild Things Are

AUTHOR/ILLUSTRATOR: Maurice Sendak
HC/PB: HarperCollins
THEMES: mischief; fantasy; monsters; adventure; journeys;
    belonging; confidence; courage

Max causes so much trouble at home that he is sent to bed without supper. When his room becomes a forest from which he magically sails away, he finds himself in a land dominated by huge, grotesque beasts—wild things! Quite a bit wild himself, Max is more than a match for these creatures, and he tames them. When the fun is over, he longs for a place "where someone loved him best of all," so he returns home to find the loving gift of his supper waiting for him . . . "and it was still hot." In this simple yet never simplistic story, a child's fantasy life moves to center stage, allowing him to achieve mastery over feelings and fears through Sendak's stunning, award-winning illustrations. A classic that begs to be read again and again.

> "The best time to start reading aloud to a baby is the day it is born. The lilting rhythm of a simple bedtime book on that first thrilling, exhausting day is soothing for the tremulous parents and the new child and adds to the bonding between them."
> —*Mem Fox, from* Reading Magic: Why Reading Aloud to Our Children Will Change Their Lives Forever

★ Wilfrid Gordon McDonald Partridge

PICTURE BOOK

AUTHOR: Mem Fox • ILLUSTRATOR: Julie Vivas
HC/PB: Kane/Miller
THEMES: elderly and children; aging; memory;
    wisdom; friendship; gifts; diversity; memories

A small boy "who isn't very old either" shows wisdom beyond his years in this perfectly paced tale. Lovingly presented, this book has such reverence for age and the common bonds between the very young and very old that it is difficult to read it without a lump in the throat. How Wilfrid assists Miss Nancy in reclaiming her lost memories is a story you won't soon forget.

Willy the Wimp

PICTURE BOOK

AUTHOR/ILLUSTRATOR: Anthony Browne
PB: Candlewick
THEMES: apes; bullies; gentle boys; clumsiness; shyness

Willy is a chimp who could use a big dose of self-esteem. Slight, bespectacled, and shy, he is the very picture of a spineless wimp. Browne's paintings and story bring Willy vividly to life, endearing him to readers who may be a little unsure of themselves as well. Willy's adventures continue in *Willy and Hugh, Willy the Champ, Willy the Wizard,* and *Willy's Pictures.*

Yellow Umbrella
PICTURE BOOK

AUTHOR/ILLUSTRATOR: Jae Soo Liu • MUSIC: Dong Il Sheen
HC: Kane/Miller
THEMES: rain; wordless; journeys; colors

Follow a child to school on a rainy day, as seen from above with only a bright yellow umbrella to identify him or her. All we see in this whimsical look at children's rainy day play is a rainbow of umbrellas and the occasional boot or two. A delightful CD of "raindrop" musical accompaniment is provided, but the book can be enjoyed with or without music.

Zoom
PICTURE BOOK

AUTHOR/ILLUSTRATOR: Istvan Banyai
PB: Puffin
THEMES: wordless; art; infinity; perspective; point of view

Zoom takes the reader into the infinite. Each page moves you back farther and farther from the previous image. Just when you think you know where you are, back you go. There isn't a single word, but you won't put it down until you see how it ends. A sequel, *Re-Zoom*, examines the process in reverse.

Listening/Interest Level: All/ Reading Level: Early and Middle Elementary (E/M)

Perfect for family read-alouds, this fascinating mix—fiction and nonfiction—allows a wide age span of children to listen at once. Although these books may challenge early readers, older siblings can participate.

A Is for . . . ?: A Photographer's Alphabet of Animals

PICTURE BOOK
NONFICTION

AUTHOR/ILLUSTRATOR: Henry Horenstein
HC: Harcourt
THEMES: alphabet; guessing; animals

Sepia-toned photographs provide clues to the identity of the animal for each letter. Fascinating, and not as easy to guess as you might think.

Alison's Zinnia

PICTURE BOOK

AUTHOR/ILLUSTRATOR: Anita Lobel
HC: Greenwillow • PB: Mulberry
THEMES: gardening; alphabet; alliteration; connections; names

ABC alliterations, full-page flower paintings, and a clever girl-verb-flower link from one page to the next keep the interest blooming for the whole family. "Alison acquired an amaryllis for Beryl. Beryl bought a begonia for Crystal. Crystal cut a chrysanthemum for Dawn." A vocabulary stretcher, guessing game, and flower primer all in one.

Alphabet City

PICTURE BOOK

AUTHOR/ILLUSTRATOR: Stephen T. Johnson
HC: Viking • PB: Puffin
THEMES: alphabet; city scenes; architecture; wordless

Find the alphabet—all capital letters—in realistic paintings of objects. (We had to look twice to be sure they weren't photos.) Some of the letters in these city scenes stand out; others are subtle and require a closer look. There is pleasure enough discovering letters at each turn of the page, but an added bonus invites readers of all ages to venture beyond the pages to the outside world and discover alphabetical images of their own.

Amazing Grace

PICTURE BOOK

AUTHOR: Mary Hoffman • ILLUSTRATOR: Caroline Binch
HC: Dial
THEMES: strong girl; family; grandmothers; storytelling; imagination; prejudice; self-respect; determination; African American; plays; gender roles; pretending

In this beautifully illustrated picture book, we are introduced to story-loving Grace, an only child with a rich imagination and the ability to put it to good use. Stories are so integral a part of her life that acting them out is a daily ritual. When the play of *Peter Pan* is being put on at school, her classmates tell her that she cannot be Peter because she is a) a girl, and b) black. With the help of her wise grandmother, she reaffirms what she already knows: She can be anything she wants, if she puts her mind to it. A life-affirming book made special by Hoffman's stirring message and Binch's extraordinary paintings.

Hoffman brings us a new tale of a slightly older Grace every few years, with a picture-book sequel, *Boundless Grace;* an early reader, *Starring Grace;* and a chapter book, *Encore Grace!* continuing her story.

Annie and the Wild Animals

PICTURE BOOK

AUTHOR/ILLUSTRATOR: Jan Brett
HC/PB: Houghton Mifflin
THEMES: animals; winter; hunger; friendship

A sweet encounter between a young girl and the hungry animals of the wintry forest. Annie's corn cakes are delicious, and every day there are more animals outside that are hungry, until things get out of hand. Brett's precious illustrations lend a charming air, and her skill at visual narrative is evident when the observant reader notices the story going on in the margins of every page.

Arlene Sardine   PICTURE BOOK
AUTHOR/ILLUSTRATOR: Chris Raschka
HC: Orchard
THEMES: fish; death; life cycle; food

Arlene is a little fish who wants to be a sardine. In order to become one, however, she must be caught, smoked, and put into a can. This archly told tale of the life and death of the title character gives some adults pause, but children find it interesting. Multifaceted enough to be interpreted as a fable about being careful what you wish for, a story of dreams fulfilled, or a subtle entreaty to vegetarianism, this is yet another inventive, mischievous tale from one of our favorite creators of children's books.

As shocking as it is, I couldn't stop laughing.

Away from Home   PICTURE BOOK
AUTHOR/ILLUSTRATOR: Anita Lobel
HC: Greenwillow
THEMES: alliteration; guessing; cultural diversity; travel; theater; costumes;
    alphabet; geography

An alliteration of friends from A to Z travel the world in twenty-five scenes. "Isaac idled in Innsbruck. John juggled in Jerusalem." Readers have fun with words while they play a geographical guessing game. Match the cities to the countries. Notice the costumes in each scene. Lobel has paid attention to detail, from A to Z. The last page describes specific locations pictured in this journey.

Be Good to Eddie Lee   PICTURE BOOK
AUTHOR: Virginia Fleming • ILLUSTRATOR: Floyd Cooper
HC: Putnam • PB: Paperstar
THEMES: handicaps; friendship; Down's syndrome

Eddie Lee's friends discover he has something of value to offer. This beautifully illustrated story about a boy with Down's syndrome never becomes condescending.

Blueberries for Sal

PICTURE BOOK

AUTHOR/ILLUSTRATOR: Robert McCloskey
HC: Viking • PB: Puffin
THEMES: fruit; bears; mothers and daughters; eating; comparisons; repetition

Two mothers go picking blueberries with their respective offspring. Each child wanders off in search of berries of her own to eat, and they inadvertently switch places. That one of the mothers is a bear makes the mix-up more interesting, but McCloskey's gentle, repetitive prose and lovely blue-and-white illustrations never let the story become threatening.

★ Bob

PICTURE BOOK

AUTHOR/ILLUSTRATOR: Tracey Campbell Pearson
HC: Putnam
THEMES: roosters; farm animals; animal sounds; triumph; problem solving

A dry-humored read-aloud about a rooster in search of his crow. Along the way he picks up other animal sounds, all of which help save the day. We howled.

 If you read to groups of children, or if you speak to groups of adults, you'll want to add this to your collection. Bob learns new animal noises with the turn of each page. Before I begin to read aloud, I divide the group into "meow-meow," "woof-wag," "ribbet-ribbet-hop-hop," and Bob's other noises. When that sound comes up in the story, I point, rather than read, and the folks representing that animal erupt with their appropriate sounds until the finale, when the room is filled with animal music. Delightful. Everyone howls.

Book

PICTURE BOOK

AUTHOR: George Ella Lyon • ILLUSTRATOR: Peter Catalanotto
HC: DK Ink
THEMES: books; reading; writing

From one of our favorite teams comes a rapturous ode, in words and watercolors, to the almost indescribable joy of reading. This would be great to use for teaching writing to young people.

The Butterfly Jar

POETRY COLLECTION

AUTHOR: Jeff Moss • ILLUSTRATOR: Chris Demarest
HC: Bantam
THEMES: humor; self-respect; friendship; wordplay; loss; rhyme

The late Jeff Moss used to write songs for *Sesame Street*, including such childhood standards as *"Rubber Ducky"* and *"I Love Trash."* In this, his first and best collection of poetry for children, he covers the gamut from the ridiculously silly to the serious. A terrific collection that can stand beside the best light children's verse.

Canyon
PICTURE BOOK NONFICTION

AUTHOR: Eileen Cameron • ILLUSTRATOR: Michael Collier (photographs)
HC: Mikaya Press
THEMES: geology; water; rivers; photographs; nature

"Water falls softly in cold snow crystals onto the mountaintop," beginning its journey down the mountain, through crannies, over rocks, digging the river bed until a canyon is born. Spare text and stunning photographs offer the young reader a breathtaking introduction to geology.

Chicken Sunday
PICTURE BOOK

AUTHOR/ILLUSTRATOR: Patricia Polacco
HC: Philomel • PB: Paperstar
THEMES: neighbors; friendship; African American; Russian American; hats; rituals; family; gifts; religion; eggs; grandmothers; cultural diversity

This tender story of a Russian American girl who, in a solemn backyard ceremony, pledges to be friends for life with her African American neighbor, comes from Polacco's own childhood. Young readers will see the wealth in a community where neighbors who are not the same race or religion can join in each other's traditions and in the joy of friendship.

★ Come a Tide
PICTURE BOOK

AUTHOR: George Ella Lyon • ILLUSTRATOR: Stephen Gammell
HC/PB: Orchard
THEMES: floods; family; courage; disaster; U.S.A., Appalachia

This warmly told tale, full of quirky characterizations and humorous details about a rural family experiencing a flood, enchanted us both from the start. But it wasn't until we had the opportunity to read it in communities where disaster had recently occurred that we began to realize its greater value. Gammell's artwork is a plus for any book, but his depiction of the water coming down, rising, and receding is simply superb.

Disaster

No matter what the natural disaster, at some point in the picking-up-and-putting-it-all-back-together stage, children will likely want to know why they have to live in a place where such things happen—"Why don't we move to where disaster can't harm us?" Books like *Come a Tide* can be very helpful in explaining that the love of home and family are strong in many of us—so strong that we often choose to stay and rebuild. Another book that deals powerfully with a disastrous flood, but for an older audience, is Jane Kurtz's *River Friendly, River Wild*. Kurtz's personal experience with the 1997 Red River flood informs her look at what it's like to survive a flood, and how one deals with the sludge, the smell, and the deep sense of loss when it's over. From the perspective of a young girl, this story about putting pieces back together is told in eighteen affecting poems.

Look for these books dealing with other natural disasters:

TORNADOES

The Bravest of Us All by Marsha Diane Arnold, illustrated by Brad Sneed
The Storm by Marc Harshman, illustrated by Mark Mohr
One Lucky Girl by George Ella Lyon, illustrated by Irene Trivas

HURRICANES

Hurricane! by Patricia Lakin, illustrated by Vanessa Lubach
Hurricane by Jonathan London, illustrated by Henri Sorensen

STORMS

Williwaw! by Tom Bodett
The Gullywasher by Joyce Rossi

EARTHQUAKES

Earthquake Terror by Peg Kehret
Earthquake by Milly Lee, illustrated by Yangsook Choi
Quake!: A Novel by Joe Cottonwood
I Am Lavina Cumming by Susan Lowell

VOLCANOES

The Shark Callers by Eric Campbell (also about tidal waves)
Sasquatch by Roland Smith

★ Dem Bones

AUTHOR/ILLUSTRATOR: Bob Barner
HC: Chronicle
THEMES: science; songs; music; bones; human body

"Toe bone connected to da foot bone . . . Foot bone connected to da ankle bone. . . ." Children have been singing this popular tune for ages. Barner's lively, colorful illustrations of skeletons dance, horns blaring, through the pages of this anatomy book for youngsters. "The foot bones are the basement of your skeleton. The twenty-two bones in your foot support the entire weight of your body." As the song bounces through the pages Barner also relates facts about different bones in the human body.

Have fun with <u>Dem Bones</u>*. It's a sing-along book. It's a science book. I like to go from page to page, singing and pointing out the clever scientific facts as though they were coming from my brain. Why not? You won't get caught unless you share this with a reader.*

Bob Barner's visual storytelling skill makes subjects come to life. For more fun with bones, this time of the prehistoric variety, look for Barner's <u>Dinosaur Bones</u>*.*

Sing Along

Here in picture-book form are our favorite versions of the classic childhood songs and lullabies children and grown-ups have been singing for years:

Dem Bones by Bob Barner
Down by the Station by Will Hillenbrand
The Eensy-Weensy Spider by Mary Ann Hoberman
Fiddle-I-Fee by Will Hillenbrand
Frog Went A-Courtin' by John Langstaff
Getting to Know You!: Rodgers and Hammerstein Favorites illustrated by Rosemary Wells
Hush Little Baby by Sylvia Long
Knick Knack Paddy Whack: A Moving Parts Book by Paul Zelinsky
Old MacDonald Had a Farm by Glen Rounds
She'll Be Comin' Round the Mountain by Tom Birdseye
The Teddy Bears' Picnic by Jerry Garcia, Bruce Whatley, and David Grisman
The Tree in the Wood: An Old Nursery Song by Christopher Manson (Illustrator)
The Wheels on the Bus: The Traditional Song by Paul Zelinsky

Edward and the Pirates

PICTURE BOOK

AUTHOR/ILLUSTRATOR: David McPhail
HC: Little Brown
THEMES: reading; imagination; courage; fathers and sons; mothers and sons;
   parents; adventure

A wonderful ode to reading and the power of the imagination. Edward's story-induced adventures are epic in scope and full of bravery and cleverness, but the fact that his parents are a large part of the story makes this a must for family reading time. More adventures can be found in *Santa's Book of Names* and *Edward in the Jungle*.

Eulalie and the Hopping Head

PICTURE BOOK

AUTHOR/ILLUSTRATOR: David Small
PB: Farrar, Straus & Giroux
THEMES: frogs; dolls; mistaken identity; adoption; mothers and daughters

When a child is left alone in the forest, it is up to Mother Lumps and her daughter, Eulalie, to take her in and try to provide for her. The young reader knows right away that the child is merely a doll, but Eulalie and Mother Lumps, being frogs, are slower to catch on. It is only when Eulalie crawls inside the doll's head (don't ask!) and much excitement ensues that things are finally put right. Slyly hilarious, with lines like "On the way home, the child's head fell off six more times" that are sure to please adults and children alike.

Five Little Fiends

PICTURE BOOK

AUTHOR/ILLUSTRATOR: Sarah Dyer
HC: Bloomsbury
THEMES: moon; sun; sky; sharing; earth; beauty; monsters; connections

Five little fiends, each bright red, marvel at their favorite parts of the world. One day each decides to take the one thing they like best. Soon they discover that when the sun, land, sky, sea, and moon are no longer connected, they lose their beauty. Here's a first lesson in sharing and a delightful introduction to environmental links.

Free to Be You and Me

ANTHOLOGY

AUTHOR: Marlo Thomas, et al.
PB: Running Press
THEMES: poems; songs; diversity; community

Marlo Thomas brought together an amazing crew of contributors to this classic, first published in 1974. These authors, illustrators, actors, and various celebrities include Shel Silverstein, John Steptoe, Judy Blume, Harry Belafonte, Mel Brooks, and lots more. His or her poems, songs, stories, and art celebrate the uniqueness of each person.

 I still laugh when I remember my daughters and I singing, "It's all right to cry" at the top of our lungs along with Rosey Grier.

Freedom Summer

PICTURE BOOK

AUTHOR: Deborah Wiles • ILLUSTRATOR: Jerome Lagarrigue
HC: Simon & Schuster
THEMES: friendship; civil rights; prejudice; swimming; US History, the '60s

Wiles provides a thought-provoking look at the effects of racism on two southern boys, one white, one black. Rather than allow a public swimming pool to be desegregated, the town decides to get rid of it, leading to disappointment for both boys and the kindling of understanding in the white boy of the injustice his friend must face on a daily basis.

Gathering the Sun: An Alphabet in Spanish and English

PICTURE BOOK NONFICTION

AUTHOR: Alma Flor Ada • ILLUSTRATOR: Simon Silva
HC: Lothrop • PB: HarperTrophy
THEMES: Spanish language; bilingual; Mexican American; migrant
     farmworkers; alphabet

Poems and paintings come together to create an alphabetical treasure, celebrating the lives, experiences, and culture of the Spanish-speaking people who work the farmland of the American West. Silva's paintings reflect the bold, colorful art found in Mexico, where he was born.

Gila Monsters Meet You at the Airport

PICTURE BOOK

AUTHOR: Marjorie Weinman Sharmat • ILLUSTRATOR: Byron Barton
PB: Puffin
THEMES: New York; comparisons; moving; U.S.A., the West; change; fear of
     new things; airports

A boy moving west from New York City is full of apprehension—he's heard it's really strange out west! He meets a boy at the airport who is moving to

New York with similar fears. A fun look at the misinformation we sometimes let rule our choices.

God Bless the Gargoyles

AUTHOR/ILLUSTRATOR: Dav Pilkey
HC/PB: Harcourt Brace
THEMES: gargoyles; angels; loneliness; misunderstanding

A gentle, loving ode to the misunderstood, with gargoyles standing in for humanity's downtrodden and mistreated. Moving and peaceful, like a prayer at bedtime, which it resembles.

Gopher Up Your Sleeve

POETRY

AUTHOR: Tony Johnston • ILLUSTRATOR: Trip Park
HC: Rising Moon
THEMES: poetry; humor; animals

"A parrot's like a green leaf walking. The difference is the parrot's squawking." Short whimsical rhymes and comical pictures describe animals as ordinary as a frog and as unusual as a vinegarroon.

Happy to Be Nappy

PICTURE BOOK

AUTHOR: bell hooks • ILLUSTRATOR: Chris Raschka
HC/BB: Hyperion
THEMES: self-respect; hair; African American; girls, strong; getting along; joy

Renowned feminist and social critic bell hooks (yes, she spells her name without capital letters) looks at young African American girls and their hair in this uplifting and whimsical picture book. Raschka's illustrations complement the tone of the text so well, it is hard to imagine a book more encouraging of all girls to love and accept themselves (and others) just the way they are. A similar generous, loving gift of a book is given to boys in the same team's *Be Boy Buzz*.

Head, Body, Legs: A Story from Liberia

PICTURE BOOK

AUTHORS: Won-Ldy Paye and Margaret H. Lippert • ILLUSTRATOR: Julie Paschkis
HC: Henry Holt
THEMES: folklore; Africa; human body; cooperation

"Long ago, Head was all by himself. He had no legs, no arms, no body. He rolled everywhere." It was inconvenient, to say the least. This creation tale from Liberia shows how head, body, legs, and arms worked together to make up the human body.

This is the kind of tale I choose to read to a small group. You can tell that young children get it as they roll their eyes and laugh out loud.

★ Heckedy Peg   PICTURE BOOK
AUTHOR: Audrey Wood • ILLUSTRATOR: Don Wood
HC: Harcourt Brace • BP: Voyager
THEMES: mothers; witches; magic; food; strangers; disobeying; courage;
    rescue

If this tale doesn't convince children to listen to their mothers, we don't know what will. Seven children, each named for a day of the week, are warned about strangers. But when Heckedy Peg hobbles to their window—"I'm Heckedy Peg. I've lost my leg. Let me in!"—they let her in. The witch is so witchy it's hard to read this aloud without a croak in your voice. She casts a spell that only a mother can break. The Woods too have cast a spell. The result: a book rich in art and story that proves it's not smart to mess with someone's mother! Who modeled for the witch? It wasn't Audrey. And it wasn't the Woods' son, Bruce. . . .

 I love to perform this book, and I carry it with me wherever I go, as it works when no other tale will. When I watch the faces of the audience, it is usually the mothers who show fear, not the children. I often see moms lift their little ones onto their laps during the scary parts, but the children handle their fears much better than their parents do.

 I'm one of those moms. Although some very young ones love it, I saved it for my five-year-olds.

The House on East 88th Street   PICTURE BOOK
AUTHOR/ILLUSTRATOR: Bernard Waber
HC/PB: Houghton Mifflin
THEMES: family; New York; crocodiles; friendship; fitting in; city life

Welcome to the world of lovable Lyle, the urban crocodile. These charming tales (including *Lyle, Lyle Crocodile,* and *Lyle at the Office)* won't tell you much about how real crocodiles behave, but watching Lyle interact with people in the city will give you plenty of chuckles.

★ I Like the Music
PICTURE BOOK

AUTHOR: Leah Komaiko • ILLUSTRATOR: Barbara Westman
PB: HarperCollins
THEMES: music; orchestras; cities; grandmothers and granddaughters; rhythm

 ". . . and I rapa-tapa-tapa on the hot concrete." The rhythm takes over and bounces within me for hours. I want to chant it and celebrate it. It is so clever, you should try it. "I like the beat Of my feet When my shoes hit the street And I rapa-tapa-tapa On the hot concrete." Komaiko's chant moves from the beat of the street to the rhythm of the orchestra and back again. Read it through a couple of times to fully appreciate this masterpiece.

I Saw Esau
POETRY COLLECTION

AUTHORS: Iona and Peter Opie • ILLUSTRATOR: Maurice Sendak
HC/PB: Candlewick
THEMES: rhyme; childhood; chants; playing

Why is it that adults often try to make us believe that childhood is nice? It certainly isn't a lot of the time, and the Opies know it. This classic collection of chants and rhymes will take you back to your school days. The Opies made a life's work of chronicling the language, poetry, and song of childhood, and the taunts and teases are in here along with the riddles, counting songs, and those playground hits from long ago. Sendak's illustrations are as irreverent as the rhymes and add the perfect touch to the collection.

I Spy Mystery: A Book of Picture Riddles
PICTURE BOOK

AUTHOR: Jean Marzollo • ILLUSTRATOR: Walter Wick (photographs)
HC: Scholastic
THEMES: rhyme; riddles; photographs; searching game; puzzles

I spy a hammer, a rabbit, a pail,
A whistle, a button, a horse on its tail

Each colorful page is jam-packed with interesting items to find: Photographed sets of hundreds of fascinating antique and contemporary toys, jewelry, plants, and other props that appeal to all ages. When you've finally gotten through your search, Extra Credit Riddles and More Mysteries send you back again. New titles appear regularly.

In addition to Marzollo's marvelous I Spy mysteries, take a look at the *Can You See What I See?* books by Walter Wick, also full of objects to discover.

I'll Always Love You

PICTURE BOOK

AUTHOR/ILLUSTRATOR: Hans Wilhelm
HC/PB: Crown
THEMES: dogs; death; loss; love; grief

A poignant reminder of how our loved ones live on with us after we die. This is a good book to use in the event of a pet's death, as its comforting message and warm illustrations will help to soothe as well as give strength.

Imogene's Antlers

PICTURE BOOK

AUTHOR/ILLUSTRATOR: David Small
HC: Crown • PB: Dragonfly
THEMES: change; strong girls; humor; fantasy

Taking an absurd notion and treating it as if it were possible is one of the trademarks of David Small's picture books. Here, Imogene wakes up one morning with quite an impressive rack, and though she takes it in stride, the rest of the world has trouble coping. Hilarious!

Incredible Ned

PICTURE BOOK

AUTHOR: Bill Maynard • ILLUSTRATOR: Frank Remkiewicz
HC: Putnam • PB: Paperstar
THEMES: imagination; art; creativity; problem solving

An ode to creativity! Ned's ability to make real whatever he imagines proves to be a burdensome gift, until his art teacher realizes that the solution is to encourage him to draw what he sees. Individuals like Ned need to be encouraged, not stifled. This is sure to captivate as a read-aloud and give a boost of confidence at the same time.

Storytelling Advice from the Mouth of the Giant

I am asked all the time if there are any rules to storytelling, any simple principles to remember. For me, there are three:

- You must make the story personal. Find the connection between yourself and the tale you tell, or find a different story. Allow yourself to express the emotions the story creates in you. If a story doesn't make us feel something, what good is it?
- You must make the story interesting. The teller has a responsibility to his listeners to consider what will hold and enthrall them. There is nothing worse than being on the receiving end of a boring story.
- Lastly, you must *hold nothing back* as you tell, especially to children. They spend so much of their lives being told their actions are inappropriate ("Sit still! Put that down! Remember your manners! Don't pick at that!"). When they encounter an adult with the chutzpah to throw caution to the wind while telling a story, not caring how foolish it may look, they sit up and pay attention. Now, I am not expecting people to tell stories the same way I do, but I do want them to be as uninhibited as they can be, within the bounds of their personalities. A little less reserve and a little more foolishness can go a long way toward getting a listener involved in a story.

My grandmother Mayes was one of the greatest natural storytellers I ever knew and a major influence on my life. She was refined, gracious, extremely well read, and the only person I have ever known who could do several things at once and do them all well. (Today we call it multitasking, but Gramma just liked to keep busy.) She did not, however, suffer fools gladly. When I would launch into one of my long, seven-year-old's recitation about my day, the playground, and what injustices my brother had visited upon me, she would let me go on only so long, digressing within digressions, before she would stop me by saying, "Dear, just because it happened to you does not necessarily make it interesting." And she was right. "A tale should not get lost in the telling," she used to say. I try to live by those words today.

A Response to the Giant's Advice

I love it when a storyteller looks into my eyes for just a moment, leans forward in his place, and lures me into his spell as though I am one of the chosen few to be let in on the tale. "Not holding back" isn't about noise but about the sincerity of the teller, regardless of style.

★ John Coltrane's Giant Steps

PICTURE BOOK

AUTHOR/ILLUSTRATOR: Chris Raschka

HC: Atheneum

THEMES: music; performing; snow; raindrops; kittens; imagination

"Good evening. And thank you for coming to our book. We have something very special for you tonight . . . Why not stay and see it?" Chris Raschka presents John Coltrane's "marvelous and tricky composition," *Giant Steps*, playfully performed by a box, a snowflake, some raindrops, and a kitten. As with his earlier jazz work, *Mysterious Thelonious*, Raschka offers a very different kind of picture book, a celebration of music and rhythm blended with strokes of a paintbrush that present readers (and listeners) of all ages a unique experience.

 This is one of my favorites to read aloud. Start slowly; the words build tempo on their own. You'll want to raise your hands at the end with a "Bravo! Bravo Chris Raschka! Bravo everyone!"

★ The Keeping Quilt

PICTURE BOOK

AUTHOR/ILLUSTRATOR: Patricia Polacco

HC: Simon & Schuster

THEMES: Russia; quilts; family; weddings; celebrations; Jews; immigration; symbols

For four generations, a quilt made from Anna's babushka, Uncle Vladimir's shirt, Aunt Havelah's nightdress, and scraps from a basket of other old clothes is passed from mother to daughter, from celebration to celebration. Moving and rich in family tradition, Polacco's story of her own Russian family gives young readers an understanding of the value of tradition.

 Children may not recognize their own family traditions. Here's a perfect chance to point them out. Mine included Hawaiian leis and hot bread pudding at Christmastime.

★ King and King

PICTURE BOOK

AUTHORS/ILLUSTRATOR: Linda De Haan and Stern Nijland

HC: Tricycle Press

THEMES: marriage; love; kings; gay

 It took long enough, and it had to be imported from the Netherlands, but there is finally a picture book that deals with same-sex relationships in a matter-of-fact way, is child-friendly as opposed to didactic, and is fun to read. The story of a young prince who finds his mate in another prince and lives happily ever after with him is not just for families with gay parents but for everyone.

★ Larky Mavis   PICTURE BOOK

AUTHOR/ILLUSTRATOR: Brock Cole
HC: Farrar, Straus & Giroux
THEMES: family; adoption; fitting in; community; angels; kindness; outcasts

Whimsical, endearing, thought-provoking, and a little bit odd, this compassionate story is one of the best we have found about outcasts and community. You need to look closely at the pictures, perhaps requiring multiple readings, to appreciate the depth of Cole's storytelling mastery, and there are more questions raised than answered, which we think makes the story all the richer.

 Besides, the writing is so fine it forces you to read it aloud, even if you are alone.

 This book reminds me of Maurice Sendak's great, misunderstood book about caring for all our children, *We Are All in the Dumps with Jack and Guy*, another deeply rich and profound book.

The Library Dragon   PICTURE BOOK

AUTHOR: Carmen Agra Deedy • ILLUSTRATOR: Michael P. White
HC: Peachtree
THEMES: dragons; librarians; libraries; school; books; reading; change

A fun read-aloud about a library with an actual dragon for a librarian! Miss Lotta Scales is more concerned with keeping her library in order—DO NOT TOUCH THE BOOKS, the sign reads—than with the children who come there, and her fiery personality has scared everyone away. When a nearsighted child dares to read aloud in the library, a remarkable transformation occurs. Every librarian in America needs a copy of this for story hour.

Lifetimes: The Beautiful Way to
Explain Death to Children   PICTURE BOOK NONFICTION

AUTHOR: Bryan Mellonie • ILLUSTRATOR: Robert Ingpen (PHOTOGRAPHS)
PB: Bantam
THEMES: death; loss; life cycle; love; change; healing

Eloquent and simple, this is a book for healing the pain of loss. Using photographs of the cycle of nature, it illustrates that all things have a birth, a life, and a death. It is never sappy, never preachy, but is a gentle way to help children understand. We recommend it be read to children as a matter of course and not just in the event of a loss.

Little Red Riding Hood

PICTURE BOOK

AUTHOR/ILLUSTRATOR: Trina Schart Hyman
HC/PB: Holiday House
THEMES: folklore; strong girls; grandmothers; wolves; forests; consequences;
    disobeying

Trina Schart Hyman can illustrate anything she wants, and we will probably find it compelling. In fact, we love her art so much that we forget she is often a skilled reteller of the tales she chooses to illustrate. This version of the Grimm Brothers' tale has not been cleaned up—the wolf eats Red Riding Hood and the huntsman has to cut him open to save her. It is once again a reminder of the price to pay for straying from the path. We think it is good to see folktales with a clear eye and encourage discussion of the ways that stories are used to influence and manipulate.

Lon Po Po: A Red-Riding Hood Story from China

PICTURE BOOK

AUTHOR/ILLUSTRATOR: Ed Young
HC: Philomel • PB: Paperstar
THEMES: China; fairy tales; sisters; wolves; strong girls; folklore

Young's dramatic use of watercolors and pastels will get your attention in this powerful book. Look for a moment at his first haunting image of a wolf. Then go on to enjoy every word of this ancient Red Riding Hood tale from China.

Look Alikes

PICTURE BOOK

AUTHOR/ILLUSTRATOR: Joan Steiner (photographs)
HC: Little Brown
THEMES: transformation; guessing; searching game; puzzles;
    photographs

For everyone who loves *I Spy* (or who hates them, for that matter), this complex book of photos will occupy anyone from five to ninety for hours. Each scene is completely constructed out of objects that you have to look twice at to tell what they are. The longer you look, the more you see, and the more you are amazed at the ingenuity of Steiner's work. *Look Alikes, Jr.* offers a simpler set of pictures for a younger audience.

The Magic School Bus in the Time of the Dinosaurs

PICTURE BOOK NONFICTION

AUTHOR: Joanna Cole • ILLUSTRATOR: Bruce Degen
HC/PB: Scholastic
THEMES: dinosaurs; science; adventure; nature; animals, prehistoric

Fasten your seat belts and get ready for a tour of the Triasic, Jurassic, and Cretaceous periods with one of the country's favorite teachers—Ms. Frizzle! This time her Magic School Bus goes to *The Time of the Dinosaurs*. Author Cole and illustrator Degen have fun with this one—from the fact-filled pages to their author photos where they emerge as Joannasaurus Rex and Bruceratops! In addition to dinosaurs, this remarkable series takes on most science topics of interest to kids and delivers them with a touch of comic-book style that draws readers into the words. A ton of information gets conveyed in these books, and there are gobs of outstanding titles to check out, including *Magic School Bus* adventures . . . *Lost in the Solar System,* . . . *Inside a Beehive,* . . . *Inside the Body,* and . . . *At the Waterworks.*

Make Way for Ducklings

PICTURE BOOK

AUTHOR/ILLUSTRATOR: Robert McCloskey
HC: Viking • PB: Puffin
THEMES: Boston; mothers; ducks; safety; home

A book so beloved that there are nine statues of the ducks in Boston's Public Garden. The story of a mother duck who stops traffic to move her ducklings is a true delight, and McCloskey's drawings are splendid. Want to know the secret to remembering the names of all the ducklings? They all end in "ack" and start with the letters *J–O,* going in order: Jack, Kack, Lack, Mack, Nack, Oack, Pack, and Quack!

AUTHOR SPOTLIGHT ON
JOANNA COLE

If Joanna Cole had contributed nothing to the world of children's books other than her *Magic School Bus* books, her popularity would still be assured. That phenomenon has brought science into the homes of countless children and made many a schoolteacher wish that she were as gifted as the fictional Ms. Frizzle. But there is so much more that Joanna Cole has to offer children.

Ms. Frizzle has set out on her own lately, aiming to do for social studies what she has so successfully done for science in *Ms. Frizzle's Adventures: Ancient Egypt*, albeit without the aid of a magic bus.

Science is clearly a love of hers, and her series of younger books that look at the bodies of animals (*A Bird's Body, A Cat's Body, A Dog's Body*) belong in every library in the country. Featuring clear and precise text accompanied by black-and-white photos, these are perfect nature books for the young and curious.

Her concern for the trials and tribulations of childhood is evident in her books about children's rites of passage: *Asking About Sex and Growing Up, How I Was Adopted, Your New Potty*, and *The New Baby at Your House*.

As a collaborator with gifted artists like illustrator Bruce Degen and photographer Jerome Wexler, she is expert at blending the visual and the word. As a cowriter with Stephanie Calmenson, Cole has created a series of books that archive the folklore of childhood: *Anna Banana: 101 Jump-Rope Rhymes; Give a Dog a Bone: Stories, Poems, Jokes, and Riddles About Dogs; Pin the Tail on the Donkey and Other Party Games;* and *Pat-A-Cake and Other Play Rhymes.*

As if all this weren't enough, she has compiled some of the best anthologies for family reading in her books *Ready . . . Set . . . Read!: The Beginning Reader's Treasury; Ready . . . Set . . . Read—And Laugh: A Funny Treasury for Beginning Readers;* and *The Read-Aloud Treasury.* Each volume presents delightful excerpts and complete renditions of books that are (or ought to be) childhood favorites. Through these reasonably priced anthologies, families are offered a look at a wide range of stories and appealing illustrations, and through her exemplary work, Joanna Cole has helped to introduce thousands of families to the joys of reading and the windows reading opens to many of life's other joys.

Mama Provi and the Pot of Rice

PICTURE BOOK

AUTHOR: Sylvia Rosa-Casanova • ILLUSTRATOR: Robert Roth
HC: Atheneum • PB: Aladdin
THEMES: food; grandmothers; cultural diversity; sharing

Mama Provi's rice is the perfect comfort food for an ailing grandchild. She lives on the ground floor of her urban apartment building, with six floors separating her from her granddaughter. As she walks up the stairs to deliver her rice, a different smell awaits her on every landing. Each resident she meets offers some of her particular ethnic treat in exchange for some of the delicious rice, so that by the time she reaches her granddaughter's apartment she has a multicultural feast to share.

Manneken Pis: A Simple Story of a Boy Who Peed on a War   PICTURE BOOK

AUTHOR/ILLUSTRATOR: Vladimir Radunsky
HC: Atheneum
THEMES: war; peace; gentle boys; families; Belgium; fighting

This is the story of the legendary Belgian boy who stopped a war by peeing (quite by accident) on the fighting soldiers. The responses to this indignity—from the soldiers to the people of the town—is hysterical laughter. One can hardly fight a war while one is laughing. Children will think this is funny. Parents may not. We're on the kid's side here. After all, what is more revolting than the war itself? Most of us have seen the statue of a boy peeing in the water. The original is in Brussels, Belgium.

★ Monster Mama   PICTURE BOOK

AUTHOR: Liz Rosenberg • ILLUSTRATOR: Stephen Gammell
HC: Putnam • PB: Paperstar
THEMES: mothers and sons; family; monsters; courage; single parent; point of view; bullies

A book that can be read two ways: one as a fantasy tale of a boy with a bonafide monster for a mother, and the other as a healing story about living with a dysfunctional but loving parent. Monster Mama is right up there with the mom from Heckedy Peg as one of the all-time great mothers in children's books. A brilliant, funny, powerful book useful for those times in all parents' lives when we see ourselves reflected back as a monster in our children's eyes.

My Father's Dragon   FICTION

AUTHOR/ILLUSTRATOR: Ruth Stiles Gannett
PB: Knopf
THEMES: fantasy; dragons; family

A fantasy that will hold the interest of a child just becoming comfortable with chapter books. It has all the elements of fantasy writing and can be read aloud in one long sitting by an adult. The sequels, written in the same charming style, are *The Dragons of Blueland* and *Elmer and the Dragons*.

My Painted House, My Friendly Chicken, & Me

PICTURE BOOK NONFICTION

AUTHOR: Maya Angelou • ILLUSTRATOR: Margaret Courtney Clarke
        (photographs)
PB: Knopf
THEMES: South Africa; creativity; community; chickens; art

Maya Angelou joins photographer Margaret Courtney Clarke in introducing Thandi, a girl who lives in a painted village in South Africa. Her people do not call anything beautiful. They say that the best thing is good. This is a beautiful—we mean good—way to introduce young readers to a new culture.

★ Oh, the Places You'll Go!

PICTURE BOOK

AUTHOR/ILLUSTRATOR: Dr. Seuss
HC: Random House
THEMES: self-respect; rhyme; journeys; future;
        individuality; change

You have brains in your head.
You have feet in your shoes.
You can steer yourself any direction you choose.

This ode to the future packs the kind of forward surge found in the best marching bands. It's a cheer for individuality, a push up and over the mountain of success. For a newborn, nursery school grad, or CEO, read it aloud with the promise that she too will succeed "98 and ¾ percent guaranteed."

On the Day You Were Born

PICTURE BOOK

AUTHOR/ILLUSTRATOR: Debra Frasier
HC: Harcourt Brace

When my children were growing up, reading aloud to them was a very special part of our time together. Little did I suspect that as adults my son and daughter would recall these reading sessions to teach their mother a valuable lesson.

One day I was feeling discouraged and daunted in the face of an obstacle. My kids sat me down and handed me the Dr. Seuss book *Oh, the Places You'll Go!*, the same children's book I had read to them years ago. My son told me to read it aloud and listen to the story's message.

The book describes the wonders of life and the ups and downs that are possible. It tells of the "high Heights" as well as the disappointments that happen to even the best of us. Through this wise little book, my children reminded me that as long as you try your best you are always a winner.

—*Barbara Boxer,
California senator*

THEMES: birth; nature; planets; the earth; music; birthdays; the
environment

"On the eve of your birth, word of your coming passed from animal to animal . . . and the marvelous news migrated worldwide." This is a book to celebrate a new birth, becoming a parent or grandparent, birthdays, graduation, and most events that honor life's changes and celebrate our arrival on earth. Frasier blends natural facts, rhythms, and vivid collage cutouts to show how the natural world welcomes each new human member.

The Paper Bag Princess
PICTURE BOOK

AUTHOR: Robert Munsch • ILLUSTRATOR: Michael Martchenko
PB: Annick Press
THEMES: princesses; strong girls; dragons; gender roles

"Well, a princess! I love to eat princesses, but I have already eaten a whole castle today. I am a very busy dragon. Come back tomorrow." Princesses who have had their castle burnt up, left with only a paper bag to wear, who have trudged along the whole day trying to save the poor prince—well, they just don't take no for an answer. Our princess Elizabeth tricks the dragon, saves the prince, and will more than likely live very happily ever after. And when you reach the ending of this turn-the-tables tale, you'll feel quite happy yourself!

★ Piggie Pie
PICTURE BOOK

AUTHOR: Margie Palatini • ILLUSTRATOR: Howard Fine
HC/PB: Clarion
THEMES: wordplay; humor; folktale variation; witches; disguises; farms;
hunger; farm animals; cooking; triumph

Hilarious! One of the funniest books we know. Very strong visuals make this a small-group book, but you will love reading it to your own child. Gritch the witch is on a search for piggies to put into her pie, but the pigs outsmart her at every turn. When she meets up with a wolf, also the victim of the pigs' cleverness, the two very hungry nasties go off arm in arm to an imagined conclusion that is fitting and funny.

A Pinky Is a Baby Mouse and Other Baby Animal Names
PICTURE BOOK NONFICTION

AUTHOR: Pam Muñoz Ryan • ILLUSTRATOR: Diane deGroat
PB: Hyperion
THEMES: nature; animal babies

I am a sucker for books that have cute baby animals and interesting facts. This book is a terrific collaboration and one of my favorites. See if you know all the names of the babies; I sure didn't.

★ The Polar Express

PICTURE BOOK

AUTHOR/ILLUSTRATOR: Chris Van Allsburg
HC: Houghton Mifflin
THEMES: trains; journeys; Christmas; Santa Claus; faith; childhood; gifts

A modern classic. This tale of a young boy's magical journey to the North Pole offers an antidote to the saccharine, overmerchandised holiday tales that flood the airwaves and marketplace every year. As with most Van Allsburg stories, there is a bittersweet truth at the heart of this fantasy. You will hear Christmas bells differently once you've read this.

Christmas

There is no shortage of books dealing with the Christmas season. Every year we are inundated with new books from publishers designed to cash in on this, the most active book-buying season of the year. Each family will come up with a list of its own favorites according to the ages and interests of their children. Here are our favorites broken down into categories.

CLASSICS

The Night Before Christmas (also known by its original title, *A Visit from Saint Nicholas*)
   First published in a newspaper in 1823, Clement Clarke Moore's well-known poem has been adapted so many times to song and story that there must be a version of this book for everyone's taste. Though the interpretations run the gamut of those by artists such as Grandma Moses and Jesse Wilcox Smith, to sticker books, pop-up books, and versions for Cajuns to Oregonians that bend and abridge the text shamelessly, we are most fond of the full-length poem in its original illustrated format.

The Twelve Days of Christmas
   Again, there are many to choose from. Our favorites are by Hilary Knight and Jan Brett, as well as Robert Sabuda's pop-up version.

The Nutcracker by E.T.A. Hoffman
   Grandmothers across the country visit bookstores and libraries in December in search of a book version to accompany what is often their grandchild's first trip to the ballet. Here is a

situation in which grandma may want to retell the story in her own words, perhaps accompanied by a recording of the music, rather than subject her child to the original complex and dark tale that could create dread about going to the ballet. Though we generally do not recommend abridged work, we also do not wish to argue with grandma—if she wants a simplified version, we will get her one! We recommend Deborah Hautzig's *The Nutcracker Ballet* (part of the Step Into Reading Series) or David and Noelle Carter's pop-up version in such occasions. Another option would be to introduce the child to the ballet via books that deal with going to or dancing in the Nutcracker such as *Noelle of the Nutcracker* by Pamela Jane, illustrated by Jan Brett, or Rachel Isadora's *Lili On Stage*. When it is time for Hoffman's full-length story, we favor the gorgeously illustrated gift editions by Maurice Sendak or Roberto Innocenti.

How the Grinch Stole Christmas by Dr. Seuss
    There is no replacing the original story. Read this instead of renting the overproduced movie.

MODERN FAVORITES

Many new Christmas books come out each year but most are forgotten by January. Some books do rise above the pack and become perennial favorites. Try introducing your family to these:

Too Many Tamales by Gary Soto
Olive, the Other Reindeer by J. Otto Seibold and Vivian Walsh
Truffle's Christmas by Anna Currey
How Murray Saved Christmas by Mike Reiss
Harvey Slumfenberger's Christmas Present by John Burningham
Mr. Willoughby's Christmas Tree by Robert Barry
On Christmas Eve by Liz Rosenberg
The Animals' Christmas Carol by Helen Ward
Santa's Favorite Story by Aoki Hisako and Ivan Gantschev
Tree of Cranes by Allen Say
Wombat Divine by Mem Fox
One Wintry Night by Ruth Bell Graham

CHRISTMAS READ-ALOUDS

Every Christmas needs one good read-aloud story to pull at the heart strings. Yes, you could watch *It's a Wonderful Life* (we do), but we're talking about having a house full of family and friends that serves as the perfect captive audience for reading aloud. In addition to *The Polar Express* (Chris Van Allsburg), try these:

A Christmas Memory by Truman Capote
Star Mother's Youngest Child by Louise Moeri
A Child's Christmas in Wales by Dylan Thomas
A Christmas Carol by Charles Dickens
The Christmas Miracle of Jonathan Toomey by Susan Wojciechowski
Santa Calls by William Joyce

The Gift of the Magi by O. Henry
The Velveteen Rabbit by Margery Williams
The Miracle on 34th Street by Valentine Davies

CHRISTMAS TREASURIES

There are many handsome volumes of songs, stories, poems, and even recipes collected for the holiday season, often with wonderful art. These are our favorites:

Jan Brett's Christmas Treasury
A Christmas Treasury: Very Merry Stories and Poems (Kevin Hawkes)
Michael Foreman's Christmas Treasury
The Oxford Treasury of Christmas Poems (Michael Harrison, ed.)
The Golden Books Treasury of Christmas Joy: Favorite Stories, Poems, Carols, and More (Skip Skwarek, ed.)
Joy to the World: A Family Christmas Treasury (Ann Keay Beneduce, ed.)
Michael Hague's Family Christmas Treasury
Tomie dePaola's Book of Christmas Carols

Puffins Climb, Penguins Rhyme

PICTURE BOOK NONFICTION

AUTHOR/ILLUSTRATOR: Bruce McMillan (photographs)
HC/PB: Gulliver
THEMES: puffins; penguins; Iceland; Antarctica; wordplay; vocabulary; parts of speech; comparisons

While puffins live at the top of the world in Iceland and penguins at the bottom in Antarctica, readers can observe them through photographs. Each two-page spread is made up of simple, four-word rhymes. "Puffins land. Puffins stand." "Penguins glare. Penguins share." Cover up the last word on each second page and ask your child to guess which word is hidden. Some will come up with the same word and others will find new words that work just as well. It's a fun way to boost verb vocabulary.

Ramadan

PICTURE BOOK

AUTHOR: Suhaib Hamid Ghazi • ILLUSTRATOR: Omar Rayyan
HC/PB: Holiday House
THEMES: Ramadan; Islam; fasting; family

In the guise of a story about a young boy named Hakeem, the reader is introduced to the facts about the month-long observance of the Muslim faith. Beautiful art and an attention to detail in the words and pictures make this an excellent book to introduce Western children to Islam.

Seven Candles for Kwanzaa

PICTURE BOOK NONFICTION
AUTHOR: Andrea Davis Pinkney • ILLUSTRATOR: Brain Pinkney
HC: Dial
THEMES: Kwanzaa; African American; celebrations; traditions

Kwanzaa, which is Swahili for "first fruits of the harvest," is an African American holiday celebrated by millions every year between December 27 and January 1. The Pinkney team's book about Kwanzaa is both beautiful and informative.

Sing Sophie!

PICTURE BOOK
AUTHOR: Dayle Ann Dodds • ILLUSTRATOR: Roseanne Utzinger
HC/PB: Candlewick
THEMES: thunder; creativity; strong girl; songs; music; imagination; singing; rhyme

Make up your own tune to this cowgirl song fest. Sophie Adams will give you the words. "My dog ran off, my cat has fleas, my fish won't swim, and I hate peas. But I'm a cowgirl through and through yipee-ky-yee! yippee-ky-yuu!" We like her words, but her family would just as soon she go off somewhere else to sing. They change their tune when one of her songs saves the day. Be prepared for a rousing singing response to this rollicking read-aloud.

Star Mother's Youngest Child

PICTURE BOOK
AUTHOR: Louise Moeri • ILLUSTRATOR: Trina Schart Hyman
HC: Houghton Mifflin
THEMES: Christmas; loneliness; celebrations; elderly and children; gifts; pets; dogs

In a hut at the edge of a forest a grumpy, lonely old woman shouted, "Just once! I'd like to celebrate a Christmas! Is that too much to ask?" While up in the sky the Star Mother's Youngest Child complained, ". . . just once I want to celebrate Christmas like they do down there!" And so on Christmas day a grumbling, cranky old woman and an ugly, raggedy child find themselves together, making memories. Read this out loud on Christmas Eve and make some memories of your own.

Tar Beach
PICTURE BOOK

AUTHOR/ILLUSTRATOR: Faith Ringgold
HC: Crown • PB: Dragonfly
THEMES: African American; family; fantasy; flying; picnics; bridges; skyscrapers; New York; imagination

Ringgold's story quilts are adapted into book form in this loving reminiscence of hot summer nights, family dinners on the roof, and the longing to fly.

Ten Sly Piranhas: A Counting Story in Reverse (A Tale of Wickedness–and Worse!)
PICTURE BOOK

AUTHOR: William Wise • ILLUSTRATOR: Victoria Chess
HC: Dial
THEMES: rhythm; humor; math; counting; fish

A school of ten sly piranhas gradually dwindles as they waylay and eat each other. There's read-aloud rhythm in numbers from ten to one, and Chess's chunky pictures are bound to make you laugh.

This Land Is My Land
PICTURE BOOK NONFICTION

AUTHOR/ILLUSTRATOR: George Littlechild
HC/PB: Children's Book Press
THEMES: Native American; family history

A perfect family book to celebrate, understand, and learn from the lives of the first Americans. Littlechild's family represents all American families.

The Three Little Wolves and the Big Bad Pig
PICTURE BOOK

AUTHOR: Eugene Trivizas • ILLUSTRATOR: Helen Oxenbury
HC: Macmillan • PB: Aladdin
THEMES: folktale variations; wolves; pigs; triumph; violence; conflict and resolution

Who would have thought that there was another twist in this tale? Well, this is more than clever and is a welcome and funny addition to the canon of retold tales. Helen Oxenbury's illustrations add the perfect touch of hilarity.

But there is another aspect to the book that makes it doubly valuable; as the wolves build stronger houses (bricks, concrete, and then armor plates and iron bars), the pig destroys them with more violence—from a sledgehammer to a pneumatic drill and then dynamite! When the last house gets built from flowers and the pig has a completely unexpected and silly response, the cycle of violence is undercut and the children get a fun example that never preaches.

The Toll-Bridge Troll   PICTURE BOOK

AUTHOR: Patricia Rae Wolff • ILLUSTRATOR: Kimberly Bulcken Root
PB: Harcourt
THEMES: trolls; school; riddles; cleverness; playing tricks; lessons

Every day on his way to school, Trigg comes upon a young troll who demands a penny to cross his bridge. Trigg knows that over time a penny a day could become expensive, so each day he comes up with a riddle to out-smart the troll. The ultimate lesson here is that to become smart, it's a good idea to go to school.

Tom Thumb   PICTURE BOOK

AUTHOR/ILLUSTRATOR: Richard Jesse Watson
PB: Harcourt Brace
THEMES: folklore; courage; knights; little folk

A gloriously illustrated version of the tale of a boy no bigger than a thumb. Tom's exploits are the stuff that dreams are made of, and Watson's retelling is full of adventure and daring. Read this aloud to your five-year-old and watch his eyes light up.

Toot & Puddle: Top of the World   PICTURE BOOK

AUTHOR/ILLUSTRATOR: Holly Hobbie
HC: Little Brown
THEMES: travel; friendship; Nepal

Two pigs, Puddle the worrier and Toot the adventuresome, are pals. Toot travels far and wide, always remembering to send a postcard. Puddle stays home and tends to fret a bit. Like George and Martha, Frog and Toad, and Henry Huggins and his dog, Ribsy, Toot and Puddle are best friends children will adore. Holly Hobbie's watercolors add a further element of charm to each story. Look for other books about Toot and Puddle, including *I'll Be Home for Christmas, A Present for Toot*, and *Toot & Puddle: Charming Opal*.

The Twelve Days of Christmas

AUTHOR/ILLUSTRATOR: Jan Brett
HC: Dodd, Mead & Co. • PB: Paperstar
THEMES: Christmas; repetition; songs; Christmas carols; music; numbers; counting

As with many of Jan Brett's colorfully illustrated books, you don't want to miss the details in the margins. You'll find "Merry Christmas" in eleven languages, a love story, a family preparing for Christmas, and a forest filled with animals. And for those of you who would like to play and sing along to this classic carol, Brett has included the music.

Visiting Day

AUTHOR: Jacqueline Woodson • ILLUSTRATOR: James E. Ransome
HC: Scholastic
THEMES: prison; family; fathers and daughters; grandmothers and granddaughters; loss; patience; separation; yearning

A young girl's love for her father is not diminished by the fact that he is in prison. Her family is held together by her loving grandmother, who understands the importance of the monthly ritual of the long bus ride to prison on visiting day. A gentle look at a difficult experience.

The Whales' Song

AUTHOR: Dyan Sheldon • ILLUSTRATOR: Gary Blythe
PB: Puffin
THEMES: whales; storytelling; gifts; grandmothers

Young Lily listens to her grandmother's stories of the gifts she gave to the whales long ago. Despite her uncle's warnings against listening to such rubbish, Lily gives a gift to the whales and gets a marvelous surprise. The art is exquisite and adds much richness to this story.

When Africa Was Home

AUTHOR: Karen Lynn Williams • ILLUSTRATOR: Floyd Cooper
PB: Orchard
THEMES: friendship; Africa; homesickness; cultural diversity; change; family; community

There are many books about missing home. This is one of the finest, not just for the unusual perspective of a white boy missing his African homeland, but for the brilliant paintings of Floyd Cooper and the text of Karen Lynn Williams, who knows how to take a story about a specific longing and make it universal.

The Wing Shop
PICTURE BOOK

AUTHOR: Elvira Woodruff • ILLUSTRATOR: Stephen Gammell
HC/PB: Holiday House
THEMES: homesickness; home; wings; flying; fantasy

Matthew hates his new neighborhood and wants to go back to his old house. On his journey, he stumbles upon Featherman's Wing Shop, where the wings are "guaranteed to get you somewhere or your money back." The adventures he has when he tries on several pairs of wings convince him to give his new home a try.

Wings: A Tale of Two Chickens
PICTURE BOOK

AUTHOR/ILLUSTRATOR: James Marshall
HC/PB: Houghton Mifflin
THEMES: chickens; foxes; reading; disguises; adventure

In *Wings,* James Marshall creates a character that makes his beloved *Stupids* look smart by comparison. Winnie the chicken is so clueless, she gives new meaning to the term *dumb cluck.* It is only through the efforts of her smarter sister Harriet—smart because she reads!—that Winnie is saved from the clutches of a dastardly fox. Told in a melodramatic style that reads aloud wonderfully.

You Hold Me and I'll Hold You
PICTURE BOOK

AUTHOR: Jo Carson • ILLUSTRATOR: Annie Cannon
HC/PB: Orchard
THEMES: comfort; death; family; funerals; loss; grief

A useful book about grief. A young girl whose aunt has just died observes the preparations for the funeral. With commentary on the way adults handle loss that is honest and simple, the book is never maudlin. The comforting solution is found in the story's title.

Zeke Pippin
PICTURE BOOK

AUTHOR/ILLUSTRATOR: William Steig
PB: HarperCollins
THEMES: music; magic; family; problem solving; running away; bullies; adventure

While moseying down his street one morning, Zeke Pippin picks up a harmonica that fell out of a garbage wagon. Zeke proves to be quite a good musician, but the magic in that piece of fallen garbage works like a sleeping pill—which children soon discover has its bad points and its good. Steig is an expert at painting pictures with words and at illustrating his words with pictures.

Listening/Interest Level: All/ Reading Level: Middle Elementary (M)

These books, often longer and with more involved language than in those written for early readers, are chosen as examples of books to read to your older children while still engaging your younger ones— a trick that we feel is important to maintain family reading time into the teenage years.

10 (Ten)

PICTURE BOOK

AUTHOR/ILLUSTRATOR: Vladimir Radunsky
HC: Putnam
THEMES: armadillos; pregnancy; babies; family; love; counting; zany

Two armadillos meet, fall in love, have ten babies, and live happily ever after in this wacky but heartfelt ode to family. We encourage you not to be put off by how weird this book may seem at first glance. There are rewards of warmth and hilarity for readers of all ages. For another laugh-out-loud experience, try Radunsky's *1(One)* where the sixth child in the armadillo family decides he's #1.

Alice Nizzy Nazzy: The Witch of Santa Fe

PICTURE BOOK

AUTHOR: Tony Johnston • ILLUSTRATOR: Tomie dePaola
HC: Putnam • PB: Paperstar
THEMES: Spanish words; witches; triumph; folklore, U.S.A., the Southwest; folktale variations

Writer Tony Johnston says, "There's nothing like a good witch to stir the imagination. But the witch I love best, Russia's Baba Yaga, has a story told countless times." So she moves Baba to Santa Fe, gives her a horned lizard for a pet, an old adobe hut with road-runner legs, and calls her Alice Nizzy Nazzy. A fun read-aloud with three voices: a Spanish-speaking lizard, a young girl who can't find her sheep, and Alice Nizzy Nazzy. Blend repetition, good-over-evil, and the charm of the Southwest, then add Tomie dePaola's wild illustrations, and you have a character that will cause children to cackle!

Alphabet Books: Animals and Insects

If you like books like *Animalia*, you will want to look in your library for other animal ABC books. Here's a sampling: *A is for . . . ?*; *A Photographer's Alphabet of Animals*; *ABCD: An Alphabet Book of Cats and Dogs*; *Animal Alphabet*; *Antler Bear Canoe*; *Appaloosa Zebra: A Horse Lover's Alphabet*; *Butterfly Alphabet*; *Flora McDonnell's ABC*; *Into the A, B, SEA*; *Jungle ABC*; *Nutshell Library: Alligators All Around*; *Old Black Fly*; *Trunks All Aboard: An Elephant ABC*; and *Zoo Flakes ABC*.

Animalia   PICTURE BOOK
AUTHOR/ILLUSTRATOR: Graeme Base
HC: Abrams • PB: Puffin
THEMES: animals; alphabet; fantasy; searching game; alliteration; wordplay; vocabulary

"An Armored Armadillo Avoiding An Angry Alligator." Base has created not a typical ABC book, nor simply a play with alliterations, but a family volume to read together with enthusiastic shouts, or to be taken off alone for hours of perusal. Each stunning page is filled top to bottom with animals exotic and familiar, and hidden on each page is the artist himself. Identify each figure beginning with the appropriate letter, but don't try to complete this task in one sitting—even with the help of the whole family.

Ashanti to Zulu: African Traditions   PICTURE BOOK
AUTHOR: Margaret Musgrove • ILLUSTRATOR: Leo and Diane Dillon
HC: DIAL • PB: Puffin
THEMES: alphabet; Africa; traditions

Award-winning art and informative text have kept this stunning ABC primer of African culture in print for over twenty years.

Badger's Bring Something Party   PICTURE BOOK
AUTHOR: Hiawyn Oram • ILLUSTRATOR: Susan Varley
HC: Lothrop
THEMES: fitting in; friendship; self-respect; parties; gifts; emotions; embarrassment

Everyone brought something to *Badger's Bring Something Party*. Everybody but mole, that is. He goes to the party ". . . without anything, just himself. His muddy, unwashed, unslicked-down self, not at all neat or dressed up." He feels self-conscious and embarrassed until he is reminded about his "interesting" self who has been forgotten. Children sometimes find themselves feeling like mole, and will certainly have something to say about how different characters behave in this tale.

Bein' With You This Way

PICTURE BOOK

AUTHOR: W. Nikola-Lisa • ILLUSTRATOR: Michael Bryant
HC/PB: Lee & Low
THEMES: neighbors; rhythm; cultural diversity; friendship; community

This neighborhood rap has a finger-snapping rhythm so catchy that young readers will memorize it. Author Nikola-Lisa and illustrator Bryant have created a canvas that points out our differences and chants our similarities.

Big Momma Makes the World

PICTURE BOOK

AUTHOR: Phyllis Root • ILLUSTRATOR: Helen Oxenbury
HC: Candlewick
THEMES: creation; myths; mothers; strong women; babies

With a baby on her hip and laundry piling up, Big Momma creates the world and everything in it. She does what she sees needs to be done, but by the sixth day Momma is ready for a rest. She lines up the folks she has made and says, "This is a real nice world we got here, and you all better take some good care of it." Fun, down-home language and enchanting paintings make up a creation myth that will leave readers thinking, "That's good. That's real good."

 This is moving into first place on my what-to-give-new-mothers list. You've got to love this bigger-than-life mom.

 I love this book too, but as a storyteller, I have questions about its appropriate use. This is clearly a retelling of Genesis, and though it is not a sacred text of mine, I wonder why it is okay to use that creation story in a way many would never dream of using a non-Christian one. Just asking . . .

 Walter, creation stories have been embellished since the beginning of time. But maybe you'd feel more comfortable with Gerald McDermott's spectacular, <u>Creation</u>. With Genesis as the foundation, he shows the beauty of light, water, earth, and the creatures of the world, and tells how man and woman were created to be the keepers of this beauty.

The Blue Fairy Book (and others)
FOLKLORE COLLECTION

AUTHOR: Andrew Lang • ILLUSTRATOR: H. J. Ford
PB: Dover
THEMES: folklore; fairy tales

There was a time when the sun never set on the British Empire. Keep that in mind as you read Andrew Lang's introductions to his collections of tales from around the world. His imperialistic tone is shockingly out of place in today's society, and so it is worthwhile to remember him as a man of his time when reading his books. These low-priced paperbacks are a must for any serious collector of folklore and will serve as an interesting take on different versions of the stories and tales. There are twelve in all.

> "As a child I was most often found curled up with a book . . . and to this day it is still one of life's greatest pleasures. Reading counts. Words matter."
> —*Julie Andrews, author of* Little Bo in France: The Further Adventures of Bonnie Boadicea

★ Chato's Kitchen
PICTURE BOOK

AUTHOR: Gary Soto • ILLUSTRATOR: Susan Guevara
HC: Putnam • PB: Paperstar
THEMES: Spanish words; survival; Hispanic; cats; mice; Los Angeles; triumph, cleverness; humor; meals

Soto's words and Guevara's hilarious paintings turn this read-aloud into a "tell it again" repeater. Chato is the coolest low-riding cat in East L.A. and he has just discovered that his new next-door neighbors are the plumpest, juiciest, tastiest-looking family of mice to move into the barrio in a long time. There is great language here, in English and Spanish. A glossary of Spanish words is included.

★ Children Just Like Me: A Unique Celebration of Children Around the World
NONFICTION

AUTHOR: Barnabas Kindersley • ILLUSTRATOR: Anabel Kindersley (photographs)
HC: DK Publishing
THEMES: cultural diversity; nations; home; family; school; United Nations; comparisons

In celebration of UNICEF's fiftieth anniversary, this photo essay spans the globe in search of what makes us different and the same. The richness and diversity of children's daily lives—where they live, what they do, and where they go to school—is celebrated.

For a similar look at celebrations, holidays, and festivals around the world, find *Children Just Like Me—Celebrations!*

The Creation

PICTURE BOOK

AUTHOR: James Weldon Johnson • ILLUSTRATOR: James Ransome
HC/PB: Holiday House
THEMES: religion; God; creation; African American; Bible stories; speeches

Read-aloud rhythm and a touch of Southern imagery make this telling of the creation story accessible to all ages. In his Illustrator's Note, Ransome explains he has "tried to remain faithful to the spirit of Mr. Johnson's text by interspersing creation scenes with images of a southern country storyteller." He does it beautifully.

D Is for Doufu: An Alphabet Book of Chinese Culture

PICTURE BOOK NONFICTION

AUTHOR: Maywan Shen Krach • ILLUSTRATOR: Hongbin Zhang
HC/PB: Shen's Books
THEMES: China; language; alphabet

An invaluable introduction to Chinese language and culture. Beautifully produced, with notes of interest to any age child, this handsome book is illustrated with folk art and carefully rendered Chinese characters.

De Colores and Other Latin-American Folksongs for Children

SONGBOOK

TRANSLATOR: Jose-Luis Orozco • ILLUSTRATOR: Elisa Kleven
HC: Dutton
THEMES: music; bilingual; Mexico; Spanish; folksongs

Beaming with color and music, this bilingual book includes twenty-seven songs, chants, and rhymes. Orozco has added games and special performance suggestions along with musical arrangements for piano, voice, and guitar. Two sequels, *Diez Deditos* and *Fiestas* are also available.

★ Don't Fidget a Feather

PICTURE BOOK

AUTHOR: Erica Silverman • ILLUSTRATOR: S. D. Schindler
PB: Aladdin
THEMES; competition; friendship; geese; ducks; foxes

This one captured us immediately! Duck and Gander have a freeze-in-place contest to decide who is the champion of champions. Bees, bunnies, crows, not even the wind can get them to move . . . not even Fox, who stuffs them into a bag and takes them home for dinner. We've tested this tale on various elementary ages. Stop reading just after Fox lifts Gander high over the soup pot and says, "In we go." Children's pleas of "go on!" and "don't stop now!" add to the fun.

 This one has never failed me.

Drawing for the Artistically Undiscovered
NOVELTY

AUTHOR/ILLUSTRATOR: Quentin Blake
HC: Klutz Press
THEMES: creativity; art; artists; drawing

Nearly every page is filled with large white spaces, and lurking in the margins are huge piles of inspirational artwork, helpful technique tips, and plenty of "what to draw" ideas. A sketch pen and two watercolor pencils are included in this two-color, spiral-bound treasure.

 I advise you to put your mark on the first page so you won't be afraid to "mess it up." This is one of the best how-to-draw books I've encountered, for any age.

 It even got me to draw!

Earth from Above for Young Readers
PICTURE BOOK

AUTHOR: Robert Burleigh • ILLUSTRATOR: Yann Arthus-Bertrand (photographs)
HC: Abrams
THEMES: photography; geography; diversity

Remarkable pictures of villages, terraced rice fields, vats of dye, floating wood down the Amazon—all photographed from above. This incredible look at the world from a bird's-eye view is enriched with Burleigh's commentary.

At first you'll want to flip through the pages to look at the photographs. But I recommend that you then take time with your child to read aloud the text. In some cases it becomes a search-and-find book. Burleigh asks questions of the reader such as, "Can you find the two streets running from the top to the bottom of the picture?" Sometimes his comments encourage a search: "If you look carefully, you'll see bunches of crops lying on roofs here and there." This is a perfect invitation to careful scrutiny and adds another dimension to the book.

Plan some of your family activities around book themes or vice versa. It can be as simple as playing "freeze in place" after reading *Don't Fidget a Feather* by Erica Silverman, or writing a letter to the Amazonia Foundation following *Amazon Diary: The Jungle Adventures of Alex Winters* by Hudson Talbott. Your children will notice a direct connection between reading and how it positively affects their lives and you'll all have fun in the process!

Finster Frets

PICTURE BOOK

AUTHOR: Kent Baker • ILLUSTRATOR: H. Werner Zimmermann
PB: Stoddart
THEMES: humor; hats; birds; problem solving; worry

Old Finster awakens one morning with a bird's nest in his hair. "What's this?" he says. "Has someone strawed my topside? Has someone broomed my brain?" He then goes to his wife for help. "Holly Berry, my faithful, my fortress, my white-haired puppy love, look what I have on my head!" Their attempts to get rid of the hatlike intruders not only makes a funny read-aloud, but also leaves a place at the end for guessing.

★ From Sea to Shining Sea

ANTHOLOGY

EDITOR: Amy Cohn • ILLUSTRATOR: Various
HC: Scholastic
THEMES: songs; music; poetry; folklore; U.S. history; artists; cultural diversity

More than 140 folk songs, tales, poems, and stories tell the history of America and reflect its multicultural society. Fifteen Caldecott Award and Honor winners add their art for illustrations.

The Great Ball Game: A Muskogee Story

PICTURE BOOK

AUTHOR: Joseph Bruchac • ILLUSTRATOR: Susan L. Roth
HC: Dial
THEMES: Native American; competition; diversity; cooperation; bats; solitude; comparisons; games; folklore

Bruchac's retelling of a Muskogee Indian story shows how the bat came to be accepted as an animal instead of a bird, and why it is that birds fly south each winter. This legend will pique curiosity about bats.

Harvey Potter's Balloon Farm

PICTURE BOOK

AUTHOR: Jerdine Nolen • ILLUSTRATOR: Mark Buehner
HC: Lothrop • PB: Mulberry
THEMES: balloons; farms; farmers; individuality; magic; fantasy

"Harvey Potter was a very strange fellow indeed. He was a farmer, but he didn't farm like my daddy did. He farmed a

---

Bats . . .

are not blind. In fact, they can see very well. There are close to a thousand different kinds of bats in the world. Baby bats are called pups, and mother bats carry them when they search for food. *Bats: Night-fliers* by Betsy Maestro reveals fascinating facts about these highly unusual, intelligent animals. *Stellaluna* by Jannell Cannon will also lead readers into seeking more information about bats. Other bat titles include *Zipping Zapping Zooming Bats; Shadows of the Night;* and *Outside Inside Bats.*

genuine, U.S. Government Inspected Balloon farm. No one knew exactly how he did it. Some folks say that it wasn't real, that it was magic. But I know what I saw, and those were real, actual balloons growing out of the plain ole ground!" Buehner's vivid, colorful paintings bring the reader right into the pages. A fantastic read-aloud.

I Have a Dream
PICTURE BOOK NONFICTION

AUTHOR: Dr. Martin Luther King Jr. • ILLUSTRATOR: Various
HC: Scholastic
THEMES: civil rights; African American; U.S. history, the 1960s; prejudice; artists; speeches

Thirteen artists, all winners of the Coretta Scott King Award or Honor for African American illustrators, offer their own beautiful interpretations of one of the greatest speeches in our nation's history.

I Hear America Singing: Folksongs for American Families
SONGBOOK WITH CD

EDITOR: Kathleen Krull • ILLUSTRATOR: Allen Garns
HC: Knopf
THEMES: music; songs; folksongs; USA

Every library needs one solid compilation of American folksongs. For our money, this is one of the best. This collection gives the background to the songs, letting the reader learn the history as well as the words and the tune. A twenty-three song CD is an added bonus.

I Want to Be
PICTURE BOOK

AUTHOR: Thylias Moss • ILLUSTRATOR: Jerry Pinkney
PB: Puffin
THEMES: milestones; imagination; self-respect

Poet Thylias Moss answers the question "What do you want to be?" in metaphors that touch the senses. "I want to be still but not so still that I turn into a mannequin or get mistaken for a tree." This lovely book, illustrated by Caldecott Honor artist Jerry Pinkney, encourages children to stretch their imaginations. Don't limit this to the very young. It's a perfect gift for milestones: birthdays, graduations, new jobs.

In Daddy's Arms I Am Tall: African Americans Celebrating Their Fathers

POETRY ANTHOLOGY

AUTHOR: Various • ILLUSTRATOR: Javaka Steptoe
HC/PB: Lee & Low
THEMES: African American; fathers; family; jobs

Twelve African American poets write about fathers and sons in this affecting and beautiful collaboration. Steptoe's rich and varied art holds this book together, using a wide range of styles to bring the right touch to each poem. Read this aloud. Give it to fathers to cherish for generations.

★ It's Perfectly Normal

NONFICTION

AUTHOR: Robie H. Harris • ILLUSTRATOR: Michael Emberley
HC/PB: Candlewick
THEMES: sex; human body; health; change; growing; love; sexuality; diversity

One of the best books we have seen for introducing children to the topic of their bodies and their sexuality. A brilliant balance is struck between the "eww, gross!" parts and the stuff that holds us all in total fascination. This is the book you need to buy when your kids are five, and keep on hand where they can find it throughout their childhood and adolescence, and refer to when the topics of sex and bodies come up. Our friend Nicky Salan says that if you put this book in the bathroom and leave it there it will get read (you can count on it), and they'll get correct information without having to embarrass themselves or you.

The Macmillan Dictionary for Children

REFERENCE

AUTHOR: Robert B. Costello, Editor in Chief • ILLUSTRATOR: Photographs
HC: Simon & Schuster
THEMES: words; language; spelling; vocabulary

 The concept of a dictionary for children was completely lost on me as a child. We had an old Webster's Unabridged and as soon as I started asking "What's that mean?" I was told to go look it up. That dictionary was, and still is, a friend to me. When, for my seventh birthday, I received a copy of a *children's* dictionary from a well-meaning adult, I was highly insulted and my response was not kind, resulting in a lecture from my mother about gracious behavior. As an adult, I realize that there are many fine uses for a children's dictionary and that many children may be daunted by the task of finding the right word in the big adult book, so I have happily recommended the Macmillan version for as long as I can remember. It has everything that I ask for of a dictionary, just a little bit less. . . .

So, Walter, let's get to what it is about this dictionary we like: 1) Each word is followed by a simple, straightforward definition; other uses follow, with examples of its proper use in a sentence. 2) Word history and origin notations, and science terms and language use are offered as points of interest. 3) Larger type and carefully chosen words (over 35,000) make this a volume at once accessible and useful to children.

For another look at dramatic lighting and vivid panoramas in an entirely different style, see Ted Rand's version, *Paul Revere's Ride*. If you are intrigued by attention to detail—costumes, location, architecture—seek out *Paul Revere's Ride, The Landlord's Tale*, illustrated by Charles Santore.

The Midnight Ride of Paul Revere
PICTURE BOOK NONFICTION

AUTHOR: Henry Wadsworth Longfellow • ILLUSTRATOR: Christopher Bing

HC: Handprint Books

THEMES: poem; classics; war; U.S. history, Colonial America; maps

"Listen, my children, and you shall hear/ of the midnight ride of Paul Revere." Bing's illustrations will get your attention: scratchboard tinted with watercolors in various shades; wondrous use of light and shadow; pictures of found objects including antique glasses, coins, a quill pen; and documents, including the general's orders as well as Revere's own account of the events described in Longfellow's epic poem. Read it twice: once for the cadence of the poem and then again for the details in the art.

The Mouse and the Motorcycle
FICTION

AUTHOR: Beverly Cleary • ILLUSTRATOR: Louis Darling

HC: Morrow • PB: Avon

THEMES: mice; adventure; motorcycles; friendship; secrets; humor

The first of three novels that tell the tale of a motorcycle-mad mouse named Ralph, befriended by a boy named Keith, who keeps the secret of their adventures despite Ralph's impetuous nature. Ralph is the hero of this fun and involving read that will delight young readers embarking on long chapter books for the first time. Subsequent books are: *Runaway Ralph* and *Ralph S. Mouse*.

Mufaro's Beautiful Daughters
PICTURE BOOK

AUTHOR/ILLUSTRATOR: John Steptoe

HC: Lothrop

THEMES: African culture; folklore; fairy tales; kings; family; journeys; marriage; cruelty; folktale variations; greed; choices; judging; Africa

The King is searching for "the most worthy and beautiful daughter in the land" to be his wife. Mufaro has two. Nyasha is beautiful and kind. Her sister, Manyara, while physically attractive, is mean-spirited. With breathtaking paintings, rich in texture and light, Steptoe weaves a magical tale to be read aloud, but not to a crowd, unless each listener can clearly see the art.

★ The New Way Things Work NONFICTION

AUTHOR/ILLUSTRATOR: David Macaulay
HC: Houghton Mifflin
THEMES: way things work; inventions; science; mammoths

From a simple zipper to computer microchips, if it works, this book tells how. Interesting information such as "The high-speed drill that a dentist uses to cut into your teeth is a miniature descendant of the first windmill . . ." keeps the pages turning. We guarantee that even the least mechanically minded reader will want to follow the entertaining adventures of the woolly mammoth as he demonstrates principles found throughout the book. A section at the end on technical terms is fascinating as well as helpful.

One Wintry Night PICTURE BOOK

AUTHOR: Ruth Bell Graham • ILLUSTRATOR: Richard Jesse Watson
HC: Baker Books
THEMES: Christianity; Christmas; Bible stories; winter; God

This retelling of several key stories from the Christian tradition, leading up to the life of Christ, is complemented by the breathtaking illustrations. A good look at the basics of Christianity, beautifully written and illustrated.

People PICTURE BOOK

AUTHOR/ILLUSTRATOR: Peter Spier
HC/PB: Doubleday
THEMES: cultural diversity; diversity; characteristics; comparisons

The best book we have found that compares in detail the similarities and differences between people. Spier's hilarious pictures feature everything from noses (fifty-four drawings) to people's likes and dislikes (". . . not everybody's idea of a good time is alike"). Each page deserves hours of investigation, so leave it out where your child can peruse it on his own.

The People Who Hugged Trees: An Environmental Folk Tale
PICTURE BOOK

AUTHOR: Deborah Lee Rose • ILLUSTRATOR: Birgitta Saflund
HC/PB: Roberts Rinehart
THEMES: trees; forests; environment; strong girls; India; conflict and
resolution; courage; taking action; folklore

This book has a strong message that never preaches or sacrifices the story to
get the moral across. Amrita Devi refuses to allow the forest near her village
to be cut down, and with her determination helps to convince others to
become Chipko, the people who hug the trees. This classic Indian folktale is
a great way to let kids know how one person can make a difference.

★ The Pot That Juan Built
PICTURE BOOK

AUTHOR: Nancy Andrews-Goebel • ILLUSTRATOR: David Diaz
HC: Lee & Low
THEMES: cumulative; artists; Mexicans; art; work; Mexican culture

A stunning blend of rhyming storytelling and biography that makes for two
wonderful reading experiences in one and a book that will grow with your
child. Written in the repetitive style of "The House That Jack Built" on each
left-hand page, with the right-hand page offering a prose account of the life
and work of Mexican potter Juan Quezada. You can read the poetry only,
peppering your account with facts from the other pages as you go, or your
child can read the biography of a man who brought back a lost art to great
acclaim. Diaz's luminous illustrations in combination with the photographs
in the *Afterword* of Quezada's village are bound to create a desire in some
readers to visit Mexico, as well as the nearest pottery wheel to try their hand
at Quezada's technique.

The Queen's Progress: An Elizabethan Alphabet
PICTURE BOOK NONFICTION

AUTHOR: Celeste Davidson Mannis • ILLUSTRATOR: Bagram Ibatoulline
HC: Viking
THEMES: ABCs; queens; England; history, the Renaissance

Each year Queen Elizabeth I traveled across the English countryside in what
became known as the Queen's Progress. Rhyming verse for each letter of the
alphabet, beautifully detailed art, and interesting notes about each alphabetical
topic—*J* is for jester, *T* is for traitor—makes this journey through Elizabethan
England one the reader will want to repeat, especially to catch the details.

The Rainbow Fairy Book
FOLKLORE COLLECTION

AUTHOR: Andrew Lang • ILLUSTRATOR: Michael Hague
HC: Morrow
THEMES: folklore; fairy tales

A one-volume compilation of Hague's favorite stories from all twelve volumes of the Lang fairy-tale collections. See also *The Blue Fairy Book* (page 67).

A Regular Flood of Mishap
PICTURE BOOK

AUTHOR: Tom Birdseye • ILLUSTRATOR: Megan Lloyd
HC/PB: Holiday House
THEMES: mishaps; mistakes; family; country life

Those who enjoyed *Airmail to the Moon* with its spunky heroine and rustic dialogue will find Ima Bean from Mossyrock Creek an unforgettable character. She means well, but every time she tries to help out, she goofs, resulting in a chain of events that spin wildly and hilariously out of control. Fun to read aloud.

Rootabaga Stories, Part One
STORY COLLECTION

AUTHOR: Carl Sandburg • ILLUSTRATOR: Michael Hague
HC/PB: Harcourt Brace
THEMES: fantasy; humor; imagination

Who marched in the procession when the Rag Doll married the Broom Handle? "Well, first came the Spoon Lickers. Every one of them had a tea spoon, or a soup spoon, though most of them had a big table spoon. On the spoons, what did they have? Oh, some had butter scotch, some had gravy, some had marshmallow fudge . . ." Carl Sandburg's collection of stories will animate a child's daily routine and send imaginations soaring. While the current editions include art by Michael Hague and Paul Zelinsky (*More Rootabagas*), we also recommend looking for the older editions with the original art by Maud and Miska Petersham for a nostalgic treat.

Sacred Places
POETRY COLLECTION

AUTHOR: Jane Yolen • ILLUSTRATOR: David Shannon
HC: Harcourt Brace
THEMES: religion; geography; cultural diversity; rituals; traditions

"Hush, this is a holy place, a sacred place, where the visions dwell, where the dreaming of a race began . . ." And this incredible collection of twelve poems, describing twelve holy places, illustrated with twelve beautiful paintings, will enrich anyone's library whatever their faith.

AUTHOR SPOTLIGHT ON
JANE YOLEN

We are often stunned by the work of Jane Yolen. Not for her sheer output, though she can rival any writer today with the number of books she has written and edited (more than two hundred and counting), but by the wide range of her writing style and her ability to achieve excellence in every field she chooses. Author of picture books, folktales (both original and retellings), poetry, as well as short stories and novels for readers from beginners to adults, she skillfully employs her superb command of language to create fantasy as well as realism in her work. As an editor, anthologizer, and compiler of collections of poetry, short stories, and songs, her ability to bring to light the talents of authors has given numerous writers entry into the world of children's books.

Whether crafting stories of dragons, Arthurian legends, or wizards, Yolen has no peer in fantasy writing, winning numerous awards for her adult work. J.K. Rowling didn't invent the wizard boarding school, you know. For that matter, neither did Jane Yolen, but her *Wizard's Hall* predates Harry by several years and is a great book to give to those older post-Harry readers. Familiar, but less broadly stylized than Rowling's books, this is also a much more compact read, with a humorous style and a love of wordplay that will delight fantasy readers of all ages.

Here are some of our favorite Jane Yolen books, arranged by category, though many titles could easily reside in several:

PICTURE BOOKS

All Those Secrets of the World
Ballad of the Pirate Queens
Dove Isabeau
Encounter
Good Griselle
How Do Dinosaurs Say Goodnight?
How Do Dinosaurs Get Well Soon?
Letting Swift River Go
Miz Berlin Walks
Off We Go!
Owl Moon
Piggins
Unsolved Mysteries from History series: The Wolf Girl; The Mary Celeste; Roanoke: The Lost Colony

POETRY

How Beastly! A Menagerie of Nonsense Poems
Sacred Places
Sleep Rhymes Around the World

NOVELS

Commander Toad series
The Devil's Arithmetic
The Gift of Sarah Barker
The Queen's Own Fool (with Robert J. Harris)
Sword of the Rightful King: A Novel of King Arthur

COLLECTIONS AND ANTHOLOGIES

Baby Bear's Bedtime Book
The Haunted House: A Collection of Original Stories (ed. with Martin Greenberg)
Jane Yolen's Old MacDonald Songbook
The Three Bears Holiday Rhyme Book

FOLKLORE AND FAIRY TALES

The Emperor and the Kite
The Girl Who Cried Flowers and Other Tales
Mightier Than the Sword: World Folktales for Strong Boys
Not One Damsel in Distress: World Folktales for Strong Girls
Sleeping Ugly

FANTASY

Boots and the Seven Leaguers: A Rock-and-Troll Novel
The Pit Dragon Trilogy (Dragon's Blood, Heart's Blood, and A Sending of Dragons)
Wizard's Hall
The Young Merlin Trilogy (Passager, Hobby, and Merlin)

. . . and there are many more.

It is not an overstatement to say that no matter what the stage of a reader's life, Jane Yolen has provided a book just right for it. From the perfect toddler-go-to-bed picture book *How Do Dinosaurs Say Goodnight?* to her magnificent reimagination of King Arthur, *Sword of the Rightful King*, and beyond to adult science fiction, fantasy, and poetry, the bounty of her talent enriches us all.

Say Hola to Spanish

PICTURE BOOK

AUTHOR: Susan Middleton Elya • ILLUSTRATOR: Loretta Lopez
HC/PB: Lee & Low
THEMES: communication; rhyme; Spanish words; vocabulary

"Your hair is your pelo, your nose is nariz. Your grandmother's pelo is probably gris." These ridiculous rhymes using everyday words will tickle and teach at the same time. It won't be long before your young reader is reciting all seventy Spanish words. You'll find a glossary in the back. There are two sequels: *Say Hola to Spanish at the Circus* and *Say Hola to Spanish, Otra Vez (Again)*.

★ Sing a Song of Popcorn: Every Child's Book of Poems

POETRY ANTHOLOGY

EDITOR: Beatrice Schenk deRegniers • ILLUSTRATOR: Various
HC: Scholastic
THEMES: weather; animals; rhyme; scary poems and stories; artists

If you are looking for a wide selection of poetry for your permanent collection, this is it. If you find it handy to have them placed in sections—"Mostly Animals, Spooky Poems, Mostly People, Mostly Nonsense . . ." and so forth—you'll find those, illustrated by nine Caldecott Medal artists.

Somewhere in the World Right Now

PICTURE BOOK

AUTHOR/ILLUSTRATOR: Stacey Schuett
PB: Knopf
THEMES: geography; time; comparisons

Tour around the world via lushly painted maps and lyrical writing, and learn about the concept of time zones. It's practical, and you don't even have to pack!

Take Me Out of the Bathtub and Other Silly Dilly Songs

PICTURE BOOK

AUTHOR: Alan Katz • ILLUSTRATOR: David Catrow
HC: Simon & Schuster
THEMES: songs; rhyme; parodies; humor

Betcha can't sing just one! Here are ridiculous new lyrics to tunes most everyone knows. Kids and adults alike howl with laughter at the inspired silliness of the combination of Katz's words and never-fail illustrator Catrow's insane pictures. Guaranteed to become a classic, as will the sequel, *I'm Still Here in the Bathtub: Brand New Silly Dilly Songs*.

Tell Me a Picture

AUTHOR/ILLUSTRATOR: Quentin Blake
HC/PB: Millbrook Press
THEMES: art; artists; paintings; imagination

Quentin Blake has chosen twenty-six paintings and drawings—by very different artists—from the National Gallery in London and found a winning way to introduce them to children. His characters announce the artist, allowing the reader to see the picture with the turn of the page. Each painting tells its own story, often coming to life in the imagination of the reader. To help him along, Blake follows each "art" page with one of his characters posing questions like "Did you notice that man who had fallen over? I hope they don't fall through that hole in the ice." This of course forces you to go back to the painting and look more closely. For details about the pictures, check the introductions at the back of the book.

It's amazing. When I go through this book with a child at my side, with each consecutive painting the child takes more time to look at details. Blake is brilliant. Besides, his characters always make me laugh. Oftentimes when a child learns to read, we take away his art. After all, chapter books are a sign of advancement. But picture books? I'm afraid they are left for the younger set. Don't let that happen here.

What About Ladybugs?

AUTHOR/ILLUSTRATOR: Celia Godkin
PB: Little Brown
THEMES: gardening; nature; ladybugs; insects

Interfering with the balance of nature can cause disastrous results. When a well-meaning gardener decides to get rid of the "bad" insects, he almost ruins his beautiful garden. A ladybug saves the day and children see how each insect has a job. Vibrant close-up illustrations add color to this important lesson.

Look Closely

Here are other books that send your child on a quest for details hidden in celebrated works of art.

ART UP CLOSE FROM ANCIENT TO MODERN
From Egyptian art in 1300 B.C. to Jackson Pollock in 1948, here's an invitation to scrutinize each oversized page for details pictured next to each masterpiece. Find lift-the-flap answers at the back along with fascinating stories about the artworks and the artists who created them.

DAN'S ANGEL: A DETECTIVE'S GUIDE TO THE LANGUAGE OF PAINTINGS
Amateur detective Dan figures out what is going on in a painting by using sleuthing techniques. Young readers are challenged to follow his lead in solving the mysteries in some of the world's greatest paintings.

CAN YOU FIND IT?
Can you find one chandelier, a man in a white wig, a chair in the air? This search-and-find book invites readers to look closely at nineteen great works of art by hunting for details listed along side each painting.

NO ONE SAW: ORDINARY THINGS THROUGH THE EYES OF AN ARTIST
Appropriate for any age, this quiet, beautiful book illustrates the unique way artists look at familiar items. Each page pairs a work of art with a statement, "No one saw flowers like Georgia O'Keeffe," or "No one saw stars like Vincent Van Gogh," and ends with the encouraging words, "Artists express their own point of view. And nobody sees the world like you."

PART TWO

Books for
Very Young Children

A Brilliant Idea from a Reader

"The clothes you give at a baby shower will last
three weeks, but Valerie & Walter's book is a
much more practical present—it will last forever."

Listening/Interest Level: Babies to Preschool (P)/ Reading Level: Early Elementary (E)

This section features books for babies, toddlers, and preschoolers that can be read by an early reader. Often these will be the kinds of books a very young child will sit and "read" to himself.

Barnyard Dance!

BOARD BOOK

AUTHOR/ILLUSTRATOR: Sandra Boynton
BB: Workman
THEMES: animals, farm; barns; birthdays; monsters; numbers; counting

One of four hilarious board books that show off Boynton at her funniest. Great to read aloud, and the slightly larger format makes good use of the bold colors in the illustrations. The other titles are *Birthday Monsters, Oh My Oh My Oh Dinosaurs!,* and *One, Two, Three.*

Blue Hat, Green Hat

BOARD BOOK

AUTHOR/ILLUSTRATOR: Sandra Boynton
BB: Little Simon
THEMES: color; humor; mistakes; dressing

Boynton's running refrain of a turkey making silly mistakes will delight the youngest child. He will ask you to read it over for the opportunity to go "Oops" with you. Great fun! Also read the other titles in this marvelous board book series: *A to Z* (alphabet); *But Not the Hippopotamus* (feeling left out); *The Going to Bed Book* (bedtime, night); *Doggies: A Counting and Bark-*

ing Book (dogs, counting); *Horns, Toes, and In-Between* (human body); *Moo, Baa, La La La* (singing); and *Opposites* (opposites).

Bubba and Beau, Best Friends

PICTURE BOOK

AUTHOR: Kathi Appelt • ILLUSTRATOR: Arthur Howard
HC: Harcourt Brace
THEMES: babies; dogs; blankets; comfort; baths

> Sure to become beloved family favorites, the adventures continue in *Bubba and Beau Go Night-Night* and *Bubba and Beau Meet the Relatives.*

It was a sad day in Bubbaville when Bubba and Beau's favorite blanket got washed. Would it ever be the same? Here are five short chapters about one perfect baby, one faithful hound, two best friends; and a lot of commotion. Just the thing for young listeners still attached to their security blankets or pacifiers.

Cold Little Duck, Duck, Duck

PICTURE BOOK

AUTHOR: Lisa Westberg Peters • ILLUSTRATOR: Sam Williams
HC: Greenwillow
THEMES: repetition; ducks; winter; spring; seasons; rhyme; determination

A cold little duck returns too early to her pond on a "miserable and frozen spring" and her feet freeze to the ice, "stuck stuck stuck." She tucks her head under her wing and begins to imagine warmer weather, "blades of grass in squishy mud, snack snack snack." Charming watercolors fill the pages, and the bold, repetitive text makes this a perfect selection for children beginning to notice words. We suggest you read this cold little duck's salute to positive thinking aloud.

Fuzzy Yellow Ducklings

NOVELTY

AUTHOR/ILLUSTRATOR: Matthew Van Fleet
HC: Dial
THEMES: animals; concepts; touch; senses

No lie, this is the *cutest* book of this type since that touch-and-feel classic *Pat the Bunny*. Textures, shapes, colors, and animals intermingle on the pages, culminating in a three-foot-long foldout free-for-all at the end.

Gossie

PICTURE BOOK

AUTHOR/ILLUSTRATOR: Olivier Dunrea
HC: Houghton Mifflin
THEMES: geese; shoes; sharing; friendship; searches

Gossie is a small, yellow gosling who loves her red boots. She wears them every day when she rides and hides and walks and plays. But one day she can't find them anywhere. This pocket-size gem—with a lesson in sharing—is simple enough for the youngest set and fun enough to be enjoyed by their older siblings.

Olivier Dunrea has created a not-to-be-missed quartet for toddlers and preschoolers. After reading *Gossie*, try *Gossie & Gertie, Ollie the Stomper*, and *Ollie*.

I Can   BOARD BOOK
AUTHOR/ILLUSTRATOR: Helen Oxenbury
BB: Candlewick
THEMES: babies; concepts; independence

One of four little books, just right for pretoddlers ready to take on the world. Oxenbury's light touch makes these early concept books inviting, and they stand up to countless readings. Other titles are *I Hear, I See,* and *I Touch,* and all four can be found in *Helen Oxenbury's Little Baby Books.*

I Wonder (Green Light Readers)   EARLY READER
AUTHOR/ILLUSTRATOR: Tana Hoban (photographs)
HC/PB: Harcourt Brace
THEMES: curiosity; concepts; guessing

A near-perfect beginning reader, featuring wonderful photography carefully paired with simple words—the effect is sublime. All early readers should be this good, and the nice thing is, many of the titles in the *Green Light Reader* series are.

Jesse Bear, What Will You Wear?   PICTURE BOOK
AUTHOR: Nancy White Carlstrom • ILLUSTRATOR: Bruce Degen
HC/BB: Simon & Schuster • PB: Aladdin
THEMES: dressing; rhyme; language

A great book to have on hand when the time comes to let your toddler dress himself. Jesse is a bear children will love and identify with. His understanding and loving parents give the right mix of support and guidance.

Maisy Goes Swimming

NOVELTY

AUTHOR/ILLUSTRATOR: Lucy Cousins
HC: Little Brown
THEMES: swimming; dressing; clothing

Other titles include *Better Not Get Wet, Jesse Bear; How Do You Say It Today, Jesse Bear; It's About Time, Jesse Bear; Happy Birthday, Jesse Bear; Let's Count It Out, Jesse Bear.*

Lucy Cousins's cheerful mouse has worked her way into the hearts of preschoolers. Her popular stories with their brilliant colors have Maisy doing regular kid things, like getting ready for bed or changing her clothes for a swim. Sturdy, with bright primary colors, this series offers preschoolers a chance to lift flaps and play peekaboo, while Maisy Mouse goes about her daily routine. Titles include *Maisy Goes to the Playground, Maisy's ABC, Maisy Goes to School, Maisy Goes to Bed,* and the *Maisy Lift the Flap Activity Books.*

Mrs. Mustard's Baby Faces

BOARD BOOK

AUTHOR/ILLUSTRATOR: Jane Wattenberg (photographs)
BB: Chronicle
THEMES: babies; faces; humor; emotions

Great photographs of baby faces in an accordion format—one side happy, one side sad. Adults will howl with laughter at some of the photos, but baby will stare with fascination.

The New Baby

PICTURE BOOK NONFICTION

AUTHOR: Fred Rogers • ILLUSTRATOR: Jim Judkis
    (photographs)
HC: Putnam • PB: Paperstar
THEMES: siblings; babies; jealousy; new baby

A sampling of other books found in Mr. Roger's *First Experience Books* for toddlers: *Going to the Dentist, Going to the Hospital, Going to the Potty, Making Friends,* and *Going to Daycare.*

"You were once a new baby. You had a special place in your family then—and you still have a special place in your family now . . ." Warm, direct, and reassuring, Mr. Rogers talks to toddlers about their feelings concerning the new baby in their homes.

Of Colors and Things

PICTURE BOOK

AUTHOR/ILLUSTRATOR: Tana Hoban (photographs)
PB: Mulberry
THEMES: color; concepts; toys; food; guessing

Hoban's genius is also evident in her board books, especially her black-and-white ones. See: *White on Black* (page 91).

Each colorful page shows four close-up photographs of food, toys, and other common objects grouped in squares according to color. Hoban cleverly reserves one of the squares as a simple guessing game for the young child learning to identify colors.

Pat the Bunny
NOVELTY

AUTHOR/ILLUSTRATOR: Dorothy Kunhardt

HC: Golden

THEMES: touch; peek-a-boo; senses

We don't know why it works, but it does. First published in 1940, this touch, smell, look, and feel book continues to be one of the most popular choices for baby's first books. Fond memories of the buyer's own childhood reading may be the reason, or perhaps it is the book's simplicity. Line drawings encourage a child to play peekaboo, see her own reflection, scratch daddy's beard, and experience five other activities. There are numerous competitors that never quite match up to this classic.

Peekaboo Kisses
BOARD BOOK

AUTHOR/ILLUSTRATOR: Barney Saltzberg

BB: Red Wagon

THEMES: peek-a-boo; touch; senses

Flaps, squeakers, and colorful textures combine for a peekaboo board book that will delight toddlers. Along with Saltzberg's *Animal Kisses* and *Baby Animal Kisses,* this book is a celebration of sensations for the touch-and-feel set.

Piggies
PICTURE BOOK

AUTHOR: Don and Audrey Wood • ILLUSTRATOR: Don Wood

HC/PB: Harcourt Brace

THEMES: fingerplay; counting; rhyme

A delightful riff on the old finger-counting games popular with toddlers. This imaginative romp, with wonderful art, will hold the average two-year-old captive, then leave him giggling when you're finished.

Quiet Night
PICTURE BOOK

AUTHOR: Marilyn Singer • ILLUSTRATOR: John Manders

HC: Clarion

THEMES: animal sounds; camping; night; counting; animals; repetition

"The moon is big. The moon is bright. A frog bar-rums on a quiet night."
Children will repeat the frog's *bar-rum* as the turn of each color-filled page
presents new animals and their sounds: two owls, three geese, and a concert
finale of raucous animal sounds.

Someone Says
PICTURE BOOK

AUTHOR: Carole Lexa Schaefer • ILLUSTRATOR: Pierr Morgan
HC: Viking
THEMES: preschool; imagination; cooperation; creativity

"Spring-boink, spring-sproink" children leapfrog into their classroom. They
are prancing ponies, swooping birds, and slurping tigers in this colorful ode
to imaginative movement for the preschool set.

Time for Bed
PICTURE BOOK

AUTHOR: Mem Fox • ILLUSTRATOR: Jane Dyer
HC/BB: Gulliver
THEMES: animals; rhyme; bedtime; comfort; animal babies

As darkness falls, parents and their young prepare for bed. Mice, horses,
fish, sheep, birds, bees, and other critters add a comforting thought to each
page until the last child's "good night." It's meant to be read quietly, slowly,
with emphasis—to let the reader or listener stop and ponder each illustration. A perfect bedtime book.

Tumble Bumble
PICTURE BOOK

AUTHOR/ILLUSTRATOR: Felicia Bond
HC: Front Street • PB/BB: HarperCollins
THEMES: friendship; animals; bugs

Sweet and bouncy, this tale in rhyme of a bug going for a walk is full of surprises. Along the way, he is joined by ten new friends, among them a bee, a
bear, and a pig. Perfect read-aloud for two- and three-year-olds.

Wake Up, Big Barn!
PICTURE BOOK

AUTHOR/ILLUSTRATOR: Suzanne Tanner Chitwood
HC: Scholastic
THEMES: barns; farm animals; animal sounds; onomatopoeia; rhyme; farms

Sing this before-bed rhyme and marvel at the torn-paper collage pictures.
You'll find be-bop frogs, chugga-ching wheels, and "Owls's on the night
shift, shooby, hooby, hoo!" Have fun!

White on Black

BOARD BOOK

AUTHOR/ILLUSTRATOR: Tana Hoban
BB: Greenwillow
THEMES: babies; comparisons; shapes

One of a pair of board books with sharp, high-contrast, black-and-white illustrations. Perfect for birth to nine months, when a baby's ability to see color is limited. Your child will gravitate toward these if you put them near her, as the bold images are attractive and easy to see. The companion title, *Black on White*, offers the same delights.

Who Hops?

PICTURE BOOK

AUTHOR/ILLUSTRATOR: Katie Davis
HC/BB: Harcourt
THEMES: animals; characteristics; humor; guessing

A delightful game of a book wherein a child gets to be right in the face of the book (or adult reading it to her), getting it wrong over and over. Simple and direct art provides incorrect examples. "Cows do not hop," your child will say, even before you turn the page to find out she was right, and the embarrassed look on the cow's face is funny enough to get you through the numerous times you will surely be requested to read this to your child. A sequel, *Who Hoots?*, creates fun with animal sounds.

Listening/Interest Level: Babies to Preschool and Early Elementary (P/E)/ Reading Level: Early Elementary (E)

This listening level, containing the largest number of entries, features books for older preschoolers through third graders, many of whom will be able to read them aloud.

1 Is One   PICTURE BOOK
AUTHOR/ILLUSTRATOR: Tasha Tudor
HC: Simon & Schuster
THEMES: rhyme; numbers; counting

Tudor's charming verse, along with illustrations of numbers from one through twenty, make counting a pleasure with this award-winning picture book. Another Tudor book we enjoy is *A Time to Keep: The Tasha Tudor Book of Holidays*.

123 Follow Me!   BOARD BOOK
AUTHOR/ILLUSTRATOR: Philippe Dupasquier
BB: Candlewick
THEMES: numbers; counting; farm animals

From numbers one to ten, sturdy, brightly colored number-shaped pages reveal a new animal with each turn. It's a farmyard chase with a surprise ending bound to cheer the youngest child.

26 Letters and 99 Cents
PICTURE BOOK

AUTHOR/ILLUSTRATOR: Tana Hoban (photographs)
HC: Greenwillow • PB: Mulberry
THEMES: alphabet; math; counting; money

A clever introduction to money, counting, and the alphabet, illustrated with Hoban's stunning photographs.

★ Abiyoyo
PICTURE BOOK

AUTHOR: Pete Seeger • ILLUSTRATOR: Michael Hays
HC: Simon & Schuster • PB: Aladdin
THEMES: cultural diversity; giants; music; songs; magicians; South Africa;
    magic; fathers and sons

This giant tale should be in every library!

 One of my all-time favorite read- (or sing-) alouds. I first heard this story on a Pete Seeger album. Then I told it so often over the years, it became mine. When I discovered a book was being published I was afraid it would never match my vision. I was wrong. It even includes the songs and music.

Abuela
PICTURE BOOK

AUTHOR: Arthur Dorros • ILLUSTRATOR: Elisa Kleven
HC: Dutton • PB: Puffin
THEMES: grandmothers; flying; imagination; Spanish; bilingual

Rosalba wonders what it would be like to fly and finds herself soaring into the sky, her *abuela* by her side. This imaginative story of a girl and her grandmother is interspersed with Spanish words much like in any conversation with someone whose primary language is not the one spoken. Cheery art and a glossary at the back.

Alexander \ the Terrible, Horrible, No Good, Very Bad Day
PICTURE BOOK

AUTHOR: Judith Viorst • ILLUSTRATOR: Ray Cruz
HC: Simon & Schuster • PB: Aladdin
THEMES: self-respect; change; bad days

A beloved classic. And a spot-on depiction of what it feels like at any age to have a day spin out of your control. Children laugh, but the laughter comes from identifying with poor Alexander. Two sequels follow: *Alexander, Who Used to Be Rich Last Sunday,* and *Alexander, Who's Not (Do You Hear Me? I Mean It!) Going to Move.* Each captures major childhood events with the same humor. All three Alexander books are also available in one volume, *Absolutely, Positively Alexander.*

Amelia Bedelia
EARLY READER

AUTHOR: Peggy Parish • ILLUSTRATOR: Fritz Siebel
HB: HarperCollins
THEMES: wordplay; humor; jobs; communication; misunderstanding; mistakes

Irrepressible Amelia is the star of this wonderful series that delights beginning readers! Every six-year-old can identify with Amelia's mistakes—better still, they can be smarter than she is and see the error first. Because she takes every instruction literally (when asked to "dress the chicken" for cooking, she makes a little outfit for it to wear), her mishaps are wildly comical, and throughout these books she often inadvertently saves the day, her good intentions and her wonderful fresh-baked cookies always getting her out of trouble. There is an Amelia Bedelia book for most any occasion, so pick one and enjoy.

★ Anansi and the Moss-Covered Rock
PICTURE BOOK

AUTHOR: Eric A. Kimmel • ILLUSTRATOR: Janet Stevens
HC/PB: Holiday House
THEMES: trickster tales; rocks; folklore; magic; repetition

Also by Kimmel and Stevens: *Anansi Goes Fishing, Anansi and the Magic Stick,* and *Anansi and the Talking Melon.*

A prize—this ridiculous story and the hilarious art are perfectly matched. Anansi, the famous trickster, discovers a moss-covered rock that has the power to knock anything flat on its back. All he has to do is say, "Isn't this a strange moss-covered rock?" Stevens's two-page spread of four jungle animals passed-out is worth the price of the book. Need a play for kids to act out, sheets for curtains? Try this one.

And to Think That I Saw It on Mulberry Street
PICTURE BOOK

AUTHOR/ILLUSTRATOR: Dr. Seuss
HC: Random House
THEMES: imagination; rhyme; tall tales

Dr. Seuss's first book, published in 1937, is a delightful tale that pushes imagination into high gear. When told by his father to "see what you can see,"

Dr. Seuss

Seuss has written more books than we can review here. These are some of our favorites:

Horton Hatches the Egg
Horton Hears a Who!
The Lorax
The 500 Hats of Bartholomew Cubbins
How the Grinch Stole Christmas
Green Eggs and Ham
The Cat in the Hat
One Fish, Two Fish, Red Fish, Blue Fish
Hop on Pop

Marco decides to make his story more interesting. "That can't be my story. That's only a start. I'll say that a ZEBRA was pulling that cart!" Dr. Seuss allows Marco the pleasure of keeping his soaring imagination to himself.

Angus and the Cat   PICTURE BOOK

AUTHOR/ILLUSTRATOR: Marjorie Flack
PB: Farrar, Straus & Giroux
THEMES: dogs; curiosity; cats; getting along

This delightful trilogy of books about a *very* curious Scottie dog has delighted children and adults for years. The other titles are *Angus and the Ducks* and *Angus Lost*.

Animal Dads   PICTURE BOOK NONFICTION

AUTHOR: Sneed B. Collard III • ILLUSTRATOR: Steve Jenkins
HC/PB: Houghton Mifflin
THEMES: fathers; child care; animals; science; babies

Animal dads do lots of things human dads do. In this fascinating look at fish, beavers, gorillas, prairie voles, birds, even isopods, young readers see how the males of different species care for their young.

Are You My Mother?   EARLY READER

AUTHOR/ILLUSTRATOR: P. D. Eastman
HC: Random House
THEMES: mothers; lost; searches

A classic easy-to-read book about the search for a mother. Not by Seuss, as many think, but almost as good. See also *Go, Dog. Go!* (page 112).

Arrow to the Sun   PICTURE BOOK

AUTHOR/ILLUSTRATOR: Gerald McDermott
HC: Viking • PB: Puffin
THEMES: Native American; pueblo; sun; teasing; folklore

McDermott's bold graphics reveal the power of the Pueblo sun in this myth of how an unhappy boy brought the Lord of the Sun to the world of men.

Arthur's Camp-Out EARLY READER

AUTHOR/ILLUSTRATOR: Lillian Hoban
HC/PB: HarperCollins
THEMES: camping; fear; bats; snakes; humor

While his sister goes camping with friends, Arthur goes into the woods alone. But there are scary creatures and sounds in the woods, and Arthur soon learns that venturing out alone is not much fun, even for a chimp.

As the Crow Flies: A First Book of Maps PICTURE BOOK

AUTHOR: Gail Hartman • ILLUSTRATOR: Harvey Stevenson
PB: Aladdin
THEMES: geography; animals; point of view; maps; imagination; journeys

"As the rabbit hops . . . A path winds around a farmhouse, past a shed, to a garden where the sweet greens grow." The Rabbit's Map, along with ones from the perspectives of an eagle, crow, horse, and seagull allow youngsters to follow simple journeys and to see how handy a map can be.

Aunt Eater Loves a Mystery EARLY READER

AUTHOR/ILLUSTRATOR: Doug Cushman
HC/PB: HarperCollins
THEMES: mystery; mistakes

A funny, easy-to-read series of mysteries featuring intrepid Aunt Eater, who sees trouble and clues in almost everything. Though she makes mistakes, she is usually proven correct at the end of the story, and the child reader has the satisfaction of being smarter than Aunt Eater is.

A Baby Sister for Frances PICTURE BOOK

AUTHOR: Russell Hoban • ILLUSTRATOR: Lillian Hoban
HC/PB: HarperCollins
THEMES: new baby; sisters; siblings; family; celebrations; friendship

A new baby has arrived and Frances jumps from jealousy to happiness and back again. Hoban is right on target when it comes to showing how children can feel.

A sampling of others in the series are: *Arthur's Loose Tooth* (teeth; sisters; courage), *Arthur's Pen Pal* (pen pals; friendship; writing; karate; drums; gender roles), *Arthur's Honey Bear* (growing up), *Arthur's Christmas Cookies* (Christmas; baking; gifts).

Other mystery titles by Cushman include *Aunt Eater's Mystery Christmas*, *Aunt Eater's Mystery Vacation*, and *The ABC Mystery*.

Other Frances books include *A Birthday for Frances* (jealousy; sisters; siblings; birthdays; gifts), *A Bargain for Frances* (friendship; playing tricks; tea parties), *Bedtime for Frances* (bedtime; family), *Best Friends for Frances* (friendship; family; neighbors), and *Bread and Jam for Frances* (food; eating).

The Baker's Dozen: A Saint Nicholas Tale

PICTURE BOOK

AUTHOR: Aaron Shepard • ILLUSTRATOR: Wendy Edelson
HC: Atheneum • PB: Aladdin
THEMES: U.S. History, Colonial America; bakers; magic; traditions;
    generosity; food; folklore; baking; Christmas; Dutch; New York

Van Amsterdam, the baker, gives his customers exactly what they request, not more, not less. One Saint Nicholas Day an old woman asks for a dozen cookies. When the baker counts out twelve, she demands thirteen. When he refuses to give her more, she casts a spell that leads the baker to poverty. Saint Nicholas and his gift of generosity set things right and bring us the origin of the baker's dozen. Enchanting, detailed art along with Shepard's well-told tale make this a perfect addition to the winter holiday library.

Bark, George

PICTURE BOOK

AUTHOR/ILLUSTRATOR: Jules Feiffer
HC/PB: HarperCollins
THEMES: dogs; mothers and sons; veterinarians; humor

"Bark, George," says George's mother, and George says, "Meow," which is a problem because George is a dog. He also says, "Quack, quack," which doesn't work either. So his mother calls a vet, who opens George's mouth and starts pulling out an array of fascinating animals. Children love this story, but their parents get the biggest kick out of the last page.

Barn Dance!

PICTURE BOOK

AUTHORS: Bill Martin Jr. and John Archambault •
    ILLUSTRATOR: Ted Rand
HC/PB: Henry Holt
THEMES: barns; music; dance; rhyme; animals, farm;
    country life

The full moon's shining and a skinny kid sneaks out to the barn in time for a raucous dance led by the fiddle-playing Scarecrow. "Out came the skinny kid, a-tickin' an' a-tockin' An' a hummin' an' a-yeein' an' a-tockin' an' a-sockin'." Rand's full-page watercolors and the rhythmic writing team have created a perfect blend for the eyes and ears, barnyard style.

Benny's Pennies

PICTURE BOOK

AUTHOR: Pat Brisson • ILLUSTRATOR: Bob Barner
PB: Dell
THEMES: math; counting; sharing; family; money; numbers

"Benny McBride had five new pennies. 'What should I buy?' he asked." In a simple tale that also provides an introduction to addition and subtraction, Benny's journey is complemented by Bob Barner's beautiful cut-paper art.

The Big Red Barn

PICTURE BOOK

AUTHOR: Margaret Wise Brown • ILLUSTRATOR: Felicia Bond
HC/PB/BB: HarperCollins
THEMES: barns; farm; animals; rhyme; daytime; night; counting

"By the big red barn in the great green field, there was a pink pig who was learning to squeal." There were also horses and cows and hens and other animals of the farm doing what they do during the day. Simple in rhyme and art; after the first or second reading, it's what a young child will choose to "read" to you!

Billywise

PICTURE BOOK

AUTHOR: Judith Nicholls • ILLUSTRATOR: Jason Cockcroft
HC: Bloomsbury
THEMES: owls; rhyme; mothers and sons;
            encouragement; courage; readiness

Reassuring verse is repeated throughout this gentle book, in which a baby owl is encouraged to leave the nest. "You will grow, you will prowl, you will glide through the air . . ." The illustrations are so beautiful they will make you whisper the story again and again.

Another version of this tale, Phoebe Gilman's *Something From Nothing*, features young Joseph and his tattered old baby blanket. In this version, Joseph's grandpa saves the day by performing miracles with his snipping and stitching until nothing

Bit by Bit

PICTURE BOOK

AUTHOR: Steve Sanfield • ILLUSTRATOR: Susan Gaber
PB: Paperstar
THEMES: clothing; sewing; problem solving; folklore;
    Russia; repetition; Yiddish; cumulative story; change;
    recycling

Sanfield tells his story in the rich tradition of a true storyteller, letting the reader/listener in on a personal tale. Gaber's rich folk-style full-color art is the perfect blend to this cumulative story about Zundel the tailor, who makes the most of his old, worn winter coat.

Some stories, like Bit by Bit *by Steve Sanfield, make me want to gather youngsters under a tree and tell them the story as if I'm sharing something from my own personal memory. In my children's preschool days, I did just that. Sometimes I'd simply pluck a tired leaf off a tree, look closely at it as if I were reading a secret message, then announce, "It looks like it's time for a story!" I like telling better than reading because I can connect with listeners as though in a conversation. When illustrations in a book are as important as the ones in* Bit by Bit, *I would take the book out afterward with excitement and say, "Look, pictures that go with this story!" I am certain Steve Sanfield wouldn't mind my introducing his story to a clutch of preschoolers in this fashion. After all, that's how most stories get passed down. Besides, when the children begin reading on their own, what delight they'll find in rediscovering Steve Sanfield's stories.*

is left, except a final treat from Joseph. Yet another version can be found in Sims Taback's Caldecott Medal winner *Joseph Had a Little Overcoat*, which features die-cut holes in the pages and an imaginative blend of visual and verbal storytelling.

Bootsie Barker Bites

PICTURE BOOK

AUTHOR: Barbara Bottner • ILLUSTRATOR: Peggy Rathmann
HC: Putnam • PB: Paperstar
THEMES: courage; strong girls; conflict; bullies; comeuppance

What a comfort this book can be! Any young child who is terrorized by a playmate but cannot get an adult to understand will identify with this tale of how horrible, biting Bootsie gets her comeuppance. The little girl in the story endures Bootsie's torments for as long as she can, but when faced with the prospect of Bootsie coming over to spend the night, she has to be resourceful and learns that big problems require big solutions. Hilarious to read aloud.

A Boy, a Dog, and a Frog

PICTURE BOOK

AUTHOR/ILLUSTRATOR: Mercer Mayer
HC: Dial • PB: Puffin
THEMES: wordless; dogs; frogs; friendship

A boy and his dog run into wet trouble when they try to catch a frog. But when at last they give up, the frog follows them home. This cheery, wordless series will have young ones telling the tale without missing a word. Also *A Boy, a Dog, a Frog and a Friend* and *Frog on His Own*.

Brave Irene

PICTURE BOOK

AUTHOR/ILLUSTRATOR: William Steig
HC/PB: Farrar, Straus & Giroux
THEMES: courage; strong girls; snow; storms; determination; illness; good
    deeds; perseverance

There is a raging snowstorm outside and Irene's mother can't deliver the
dress she has sewn for the duchess to wear to the ball, so Irene offers to take
it to her. The wind warns her to "GO HO—WO—WOME . . . or else," but Irene
perseveres. Steig's art shows the strength of the storm as well as the full
force of one determined, duty-bound young girl.

Bread Is for Eating

PICTURE BOOK

AUTHOR/ILLUSTRATOR: David Gershator
HC/PB: Henry Holt
THEMES: food; jobs; Spanish; songs; music; bread; bilingual

In honor of bread and all the steps that bring it to our plate, a young boy and
his mother thank the seed, earth, sun, and rain for the grain, and sing a celebration refrain in Spanish. Words and melody are found in the back of the
book.

Bringing the Rain to Kapiti Plain

PICTURE BOOK

AUTHOR: Verna Aardema • ILLUSTRATOR: Beatriz Vidal
PB: Puffin
THEMES: Africa; cumulative story; rain; weather; animals, general; drought

". . . These are the cows, all hungry and dry, Who mooed for the rain to fall
from the sky . . ." And this is Kapiti Plain, in serious need of water, where Ki-
pat, in charge of the herd, finds a way to bring down the rain. Appealing
folk-art illustrations and catchy "This Is the House That Jack Built" rhythm
make this a popular read-aloud.

★ Brown Bear, Brown Bear, What Do You See?

PICTURE BOOK

AUTHOR: Bill Martin Jr. • ILLUSTRATOR: Eric Carle
HC/BB: Henry Holt
THEMES: cumulative story; repetition; color; animals

Make a place for *Brown Bear* in your toddler's library. First published in
1967, this colorful classic with its bold art and soothing, repetitive rhyme, is

the first of a trio of call-and-response picture books by Carle and Martin. While *Brown Bear* is about seeing, *Polar Bear, Polar Bear, What Do You Hear?* is about hearing and *Panda Bear, Panda Bear What Do You See?* is about observing animals in action while introducing young children to ten of the world's endangered animals.

The Bug Cemetery
PICTURE BOOK

AUTHOR: Frances Hill • ILLUSTRATOR: Vera Rosenberry
HC: Henry Holt
THEMES: death; grief; loss; funerals; neighbors

"When I found a dead ladybug one day, my sister, Wilma, buried it for me . . . Then Wilma gave a moving speech about the dead ladybug's life while I pretended to cry for it." It's natural for children to pretend. Here siblings and their neighbors gather together to create bug funerals with much pretend crying. Then a pet cat dies, and it's no longer make-believe. This book deals with grief in a way children understand, using experiences familiar to them.

Bugs! Bugs! Bugs!
PICTURE BOOK

AUTHOR/ILLUSTRATOR: Bob Barner
HC: Chronicle Books
THEMES: bugs; insects; butterflies

Here's a cheery first look at bugs. There is even a clever Bug-O-Meter included that charts the characteristics of the eight featured. In addition to this, Barner has created a series of playful picture books with vivid color collages, lively rhymes, and eye-catching shapes with a great deal of young child appeal. Some of these include *Fish Wish; Dinosaur Bones;* and *Stars! Stars! Stars!*

Busy Buzzing Bumblebees and Other Tongue Twisters
EARLY READER

AUTHOR: Alvin Schwartz • ILLUSTRATOR: Paul Meisel
PB: HarperCollins
THEMES: tongue twisters; humor; wordplay; alliteration

Kids love tongue twisters. This I Can Read book offers early readers the chance to try tripping across these.

Can't You Sleep, Little Bear?
PICTURE BOOK

AUTHOR: Martin Waddell • ILLUSTRATOR: Barbara Firth
HC: Candlewick
THEMES: fear of dark; bedtime; fathers and sons; comfort; moon

Comfort. Reassurance. That's what you'll find here. Little Bear is afraid of the dark. "I don't like the dark," said Little Bear. Big Bear tries to show him that dark is nothing to be afraid of, but Little Bear isn't convinced. And then Big Bear remembers the bright moon and twinkly stars. This is the story night-shy youngsters will want to read over and over.

Caps for Sale: A Tale of a Peddler, Some Monkeys, and Their Monkey Business
PICTURE BOOK

AUTHOR/ILLUSTRATOR: Esphyr Slobodkina
HC/PB: HarperCollins
THEMES: hats; monkeys; peddlers; mischief; folklore; teasing

This book, published more than fifty years ago, offers proof that a good tale has lasting power. Children still laugh when the peddler loses his hats to a treeful of teasing monkeys.

The Carrot Seed
PICTURE BOOK

AUTHOR: Ruth Krauss • ILLUSTRATOR: Crockett Johnson
HC/PB: HarperCollins
THEMES: carrots; gardening; perseverance; patience; self-respect; gardeners; individuality

One naysayer after the other warns a young gardener "... It won't come up!" But his patience and perseverance prove that belief in one's own possibilities can be worth the wait.

Chicka Chicka Boom Boom
PICTURE BOOK

AUTHORS: Bill Martin Jr. and John Archambault • ILLUSTRATOR: Lois Ehlert
HC/PB/BB: Simon & Schuster
THEMES: alphabet; rhyme; trees; rhythm

Chants can be contagious, so be prepared for this one to bounce around your brain awhile. "Chicka chicka boom boom! Will there be enough room? Here comes H up the coconut tree..." And what better way to learn the ABCs than with a lively rhyme that sends youngsters up one side of the alphabet and down the other?

 Read-aloud alert! This is a tricky one if you have not practiced it beforehand. The first two pages set a tempo that can easily get away from you, so don't go too fast or you will really be sorry right around the letter *J*.

Cleversticks

AUTHOR: Bernard Ashley • ILLUSTRATOR: Derek Brazell
PB: Dragonfly
THEMES: chopsticks; self-respect; school; cultural diversity; readiness;
comparisons; Chinese

Lin Sung was ready to give up on school. He couldn't tie his shoes, write his name, or button his coat like other kids in class. Then he discovered what he could teach them—eating with chopsticks.

Colors Everywhere

AUTHOR/ILLUSTRATOR: Tana Hoban (photographs)
HC: Greenwillow
THEMES: color; wordless; concepts; comparisons

Tana Hoban has snatched up everyday colors to create a visual matching game. There isn't a word of text. There's no need. The columns of color on each page will have children shouting out their own color words as they match—color for color—each brilliant photograph.

Counting Crocodiles

AUTHOR: Judy Sierra • ILLUSTRATOR: Will Hillenbrand
HC/PB: Harcourt Brace
THEMES: counting; math; monkeys; crocodiles; cleverness

Judy Sierra's skill at verse shines in two other books; *Monster Goose* and *Antarctic Antics: A Book of Penguin Poems.*

A rhythmic, read-aloud text and wonderful illustrations make this a counting book that will hold up to the dozens of readings your children will surely request. They will love to watch the clever monkey use her counting skill to outwit the crocodiles and get the delicious bananas from the faraway island. Great for early math education.

The Country Bunny and the Little Gold Shoes

AUTHOR: Du Bose Heyward • ILLUSTRATOR: Marjorie Flack
PB: Sandpiper
THEMES: mothers; Easter; Easter bunny; strong women; single parents;
kindness; jobs; wisdom; yearnings

An Eastertime classic, this bunny makes all mothers proud. She is smart, organized, tidy, loving, thoughtful, and quick on her feet. For her bravery,

Grandfather Bunny honors her with the title "Gold Shoe Easter Bunny." Bring this out in springtime to show that there is no telling what good can happen to a child who learns to be "wise, and kind, and swift."

The Cow That Went Oink

PICTURE BOOK

AUTHOR/ILLUSTRATOR: Bernard Most
HC/PB: Harcourt Brace
THEMES: farms; animals, farm; diversity; language; problem solving; bilingual; communication; teasing; friendship; individuality; animal sounds

Children who are teased at school, have difficulty with the language, or simply see themselves as not fitting in are bound to find relief in this tale about a cow who oinks and a pig who moos.

Curious George

PICTURE BOOK

AUTHOR/ILLUSTRATOR: H. A. Rey
HC/PB: Houghton Mifflin
THEMES: curiosity; monkeys; adventure

George is one famous monkey. But much of his appeal is lost on us as adults. Oh, we read the stories as children and later to our own children, and we acknowledge the fact that they delight. But we are at a loss to explain why they are popular. Is it just that George's curiosity dovetails perfectly with the developmental stage when youngsters find out the consequences of their own? Is it nostalgia for simpler times, when a man in a big yellow hat taking a monkey from the jungle could be looked upon fondly and not as a poacher? Or is it that George is simply beloved, period, and we just don't get it? Whatever the reason for our hesitation to wholeheartedly recommend these titles, do not let us stop you from making up your own mind, as there is certainly plenty of George to go around. His tales are available in a variety of formats, including a big hardcover volume called *The Complete Adventures of Curious George.*

Dance, Tanya

PICTURE BOOK

AUTHOR: Patricia Lee Gauch • ILLUSTRATOR: Satomi Ichikawa
HC: Philomel • PB: Paperstar
THEMES: dance; siblings; ballet; strong girls

Other Tanya books are *Bravo, Tanya* and *Tanya and Emily in a Dance for Two.*

Tanya is too young to go with her sister to ballet class, so she copies the moves her sister learns. One day she puts on a special recital and shows she's ready to pack her slippers and go for a lesson of her own. Younger siblings will like Tanya's spunk, and whether they are interested in dance or marbles, they will learn a thing or two about determination.

The Day the Babies Crawled Away

AUTHOR/ILLUSTRATOR: Peggy Rathmann
HC: Putnam
THEMES: babies; picnics; rescue; rhyme

"Remember the day the babies crawled away?" The picnickers were eating pies and the babies saw some butterflies, and off they crawled heading for the trees. Fortunately, a young boy followed them past the trees, through a bog, inside a cave, and over the edge of a cliff and saved the day by bringing them all safely back to their cheering parents. Hooray for Peggy Rathmann! Her original story with pictures of black silhouettes against color-filled skies will delight youngsters who will pause at the turn of every page to notice each charming detail!

Did You See What I Saw?: Poems About School

POETRY COLLECTION

AUTHOR: Kay Winters • ILLUSTRATOR: Martha Weston
HC: Viking • PB: Puffin
THEMES: school; new experiences; playing; friendship; cooperation

Schoolchildren stand in line, get the chicken pox, and swing and slide in these poems about new experiences. Weston's illustrations add just the right touch.

Do You See a Mouse?

PICTURE BOOK

AUTHOR/ILLUSTRATOR: Bernard Waber
HC/PB: Houghton Mifflin
THEMES: mice; hotels; hiding; searching game

Everyone at the posh Park Snoot Hotel insists, "No, no, no, there is no mouse here." But the reader can find one hiding on each page. Great fun for the young detective.

Don't Laugh, Joe

PICTURE BOOK

AUTHOR/ILLUSTRATOR: Keiko Kasza
HC: Putnam • PB: Puffin
THEMES: opossums; humor; mothers and sons; bears

Mother Possum worries that her son Joe will never learn to play dead properly. He can't stop laughing. Children know what it's like to get the giggles, and this story makes them contagious.

Dream Dancer

PICTURE BOOK

AUTHOR: Jill Newsome • ILLUSTRATOR: Claudio Munoz
HC: HarperCollins
THEMES: dance; hope; handicaps; mishaps; patience; dolls, perseverance;
   determination; ballet

Lilly loved to dance, even in her dreams. But when she had a bad fall and couldn't dance until her leg healed, Lilly depended on perseverance, a small wooden doll, and her imagination. Swirls of motion fill the paintings, and the spare text reminds us that situations can arise that interfere with plans and force us to wait for what we want.

Each Peach Pear Plum

PICTURE BOOK

AUTHOR/ILLUSTRATOR: Janet and Allan Ahlberg
HC/BB: Viking • PB: Puffin
THEMES: rhyme; searching game; folktale variations; peek-a-boo

"Each Peach Pear Plum I spy Tom Thumb." Nursery book characters hide on the pages, waiting to be found by "I Spy" squealing children. One of the best of its kind.

Earl's Too Cool for Me

PICTURE BOOK

AUTHOR: Leah Komaiko • ILLUSTRATOR: Laura Cornell
PB: HarperCollins
THEMES: self-respect; comparisons; rhyme; friendship; humor; envy; judging

"Earl's got a bicycle made of hay. He takes rides on the Milky Way. Earl's too cool for me." Kids understand this story about wishing to be more like someone else. Komaiko's rhyme and Cornell's art warm the reader with the notion that when it comes to true friends, cool doesn't count.

Easter Egg Artists

PICTURE BOOK

AUTHOR/ILLUSTRATOR: Adrienne Adams
PB: Aladdin
THEMES: rabbits; artists; Easter; eggs; color; travel; decorating

It seems that just about anything can use a bit of decoration, and the Easter egg artists prove it's true. All it takes is paint and positive reinforcement. Read this bunny tale before decorating eggs.

Eating the Alphabet: Fruits and Vegetables From A to Z

PICTURE BOOK

AUTHOR/ILLUSTRATOR: Lois Ehlert
HC/BB/PB: Harcourt Brace
THEMES: alphabet; fruit; vegetables; vocabulary

Bananas, beans, beets, blueberries, broccoli, and brussels sprouts blossom in brilliant color on the *B* page. Each letter of the alphabet introduces youngsters to a variety of fruits and vegetables. A glossary at the end offers additional information. Have you ever eaten a xigua?

Farfallina & Marcel

PICTURE BOOK

AUTHOR/ILLUSTRATOR: Holly Keller
HC: Greenwillow
THEMES: caterpillars; geese; friendship; change; separation; growth

Farfallina was a caterpillar whose best friend was a gosling named Marcel. They played often together and were caring the way good friends are. When they played hide-and-go-seek, "Farfallina hid under a fern close to the ground because she knew that Marcel couldn't climb." When it was his turn, Marcel "... hid right behind the tree because he knew that Farfallina moved slowly." But one day they were separated and did not meet again until they had grown. Adults who read this will remember their old friends who came again into their lives, and children will see that even after a long separation, best friends can again be close.

Farmer Duck

PICTURE BOOK

AUTHOR: Martin Waddell • ILLUSTRATOR: Helen Oxenbury
HC/PB: Candlewick
THEMES: animals, farm; community; farms; jobs;
  laziness; friendship

"Reading opens children up to a whole new world—that of other people's lives, thoughts, and experience. Picture books are a stepping stone to learning to read and the pleasure that this embraces."
—*Helen Oxenbury, author/illustrator of* the Tom and Pippo *books*

Poor Duck! He has to do all the work while the lazy farmer stays in bed all day. It's up to the other animals to right the situation, and in a satisfying conclusion they drive the farmer away and save the day. Though the story can be viewed as a socialist parable about the need for revolution and the good of the collective versus the evil of the despotic, capitalistic tyrant, children will most likely see it only as a great story.

The First Thing My Mama Told Me

PICTURE BOOK

AUTHOR: Susan Marie Swanson • ILLUSTRATOR: Christine Davenier
HC: Harcourt Brace
THEMES: names; characteristics; self-respect; grandfathers and
    granddaughters

When she was born, the first thing Lucy's mama told her was her name. When she was one, her grandpa wrote *Lucy* in yellow frosting on her birthday cake. When she was three, she scribbled her name on the floor with an orange crayon. She's seven now and Lucy loves her name. Here's a story to delight children who have just learned to write their name, or for any children to celebrate the moniker with which they'll be identified throughout their lives.

Five Minutes' Peace

PICTURE BOOK

AUTHOR/ILLUSTRATOR: Jill Murphy
PB: Putnam
THEMES: mothers; baths; family; quiet; noise; solitude; meals

Look for *A Quiet Night In, A Piece of Cake*, and *Peace at Last* for further exploits of the Large family.

Follow the adventures of the Large family (elephants, of course) as the mother tries desperately to get some solitude and is thwarted by all three of her children. Funny and true to life, this will have little ones identifying with the plight of parents who need just a tiny break from the routine, and that is not a bad thing at all.

Flora McDonnell's ABC

PICTURE BOOK

AUTHOR/ILLUSTRATOR: Flora McDonnell
HC/PB: Candlewick
THEMES: animals; alphabet

Grand-scale paintings fill the pages with ants on alligators, bears and butterflies, cats in convertibles—from A to Z. We particularly like the fact that each letter is illustrated twice—once as a capital and once as a lower-case letter. Colorful, bright. If your preschool must limit its number of alphabet books, be sure to include this one. Kindergartners and first graders who are practicing their letters will find this helpful as well.

Frederick

PICTURE BOOK

AUTHOR/ILLUSTRATOR: Leo Lionni
HC/PB: Knopf
THEMES: mice; dreams; color; imagination; storytelling; poets

While the other mice collect and store food to prepare for winter, Frederick sits and gathers warmth, colors, and words, preparing in his own way. And when the food runs out, Frederick's imaginative gatherings ease the difficult times. This is a tale of the value of different personalities and the power of words. There is also a sequel, *Frederick's Fables*, containing author Lionni's favorite stories.

Freight Train   PICTURE BOOK

AUTHOR/ILLUSTRATOR: Donald Crews
BB/PB: HarperCollins
THEMES: trains; railroad; color; vocabulary; transportation

Gondola, trestles, hopper car, red, orange, yellow: few words, bright colors, and a train moving through tunnels and cities blend in this delightful, simple story about a train that comes, then goes.

Friends   PICTURE BOOK

AUTHOR/ILLUSTRATOR: Helme Heine
HC: McElderry • PB: Aladdin
THEMES: friendship; dreams; diversity

Charlie Rooster, Fat Percy the pig, and Johnny Mouse are the best of friends and constant companions. Of course they have to learn that friends cannot do *everything* together, and so the book ends with them dreaming in their separate beds of more adventures. A perfectly delightful book about friendship, rendered in Heine's droll style, this one will hold up under the dozens of readings your children will request. When you need another visit, read *Friends Go Adventuring*.

Frog and Toad Are Friends   EARLY READER

AUTHOR/ILLUSTRATOR: Arnold Lobel
HC/PB: HarperCollins
THEMES: friendship; swimming; mail

Arnold Lobel knew how to create lovable, lasting characters in an early reader series. Frog and Toad are timeless, and they are no-fail. Linked short stories about these two give new readers the sense of a first chapter book with the humor and warmth that will move them on with enthusiasm to their next reading level. Sit back and listen while your child reads them to you.

Froggy Gets Dressed

PICTURE BOOK

AUTHOR: Jonathan London • ILLUSTRATOR: Frank Remkiewicz
HC: Viking • PB: Puffin
THEMES: snow; dressing; mothers and sons; humor; lessons; repetition; clothing

Froggy has more adventures in his other books: *Let's Go Froggy*, *Froggy Learns to Swim*, *Froggy Goes to School*, *Froggy's First Kiss*, and *Froggy's Best Christmas*.

A terrific hit with preschoolers, but Froggy's popularity stretches to second and third grade. Perfectly paced and just repetitive enough, it has a payoff that sends kids into wild gales of laughter. It's silly, and that's the point.

 Performing *Froggy* can be a real highlight for me, regardless of the age of the audience. The book has become popular with the kindergarten set, so many kids already know it and are eager to shout out parts with me. Any book with the word *underwear* in it is bound to be a hit!

From Head to Toe

PICTURE BOOK

AUTHOR/ILLUSTRATOR: Eric Carle
HC: HarperCollins
THEMES: exercise; animals; pretending

Expanding the range of the traditional picture book has been a hallmark of Carle's work. Look for his *Papa, Please Get the Moon for Me* to see how he imaginatively addresses the phases of the moon.

With questions, answers, and oversize colored collages, Carle encourages youngsters to exercise by imitating the movements of a cat, penguin, giraffe, buffalo, seal, and other animals.

Galimoto

PICTURE BOOK

AUTHOR: Karen Lynn Williams • ILLUSTRATOR: Catherine Stock
HC: Lothrop • PB: Mulberry
THEMES: Africa; toys; cars; crafts; determination; collecting; playing

Kondi is only seven years old, but he wants to make a *galimoto* (toy) out of wire. Set in an African village, this story shows the value of persistence and the pride in creating something of your very own.

The Ghost-Eye Tree

PICTURE BOOK

AUTHORS: Bill Martin Jr. and John Archambault • ILLUSTRATOR: Ted Rand
HC/PB: Henry Holt
THEMES: fear of the dark; ghosts; siblings; trees; spooky stories

It's a full moon night and a boy and his sister must pass the ghost-eye tree on their way to town to fetch a pail of milk. Read this tale aloud, especially if you like playing with voices and sounds. The authors originally wrote it to be performed as theater.

Ginger   PICTURE BOOK
AUTHOR/ILLUSTRATOR: Charlotte Voake
HC/PB: Candlewick
THEMES: cats; babies; sharing; curiosity; siblings

Ginger the cat fits fine in his snuggly wicker basket. Life for him is just about purrfect—and then "they" bring home a kitten. Cat lovers will recognize what happens when a cat not used to sharing deals with a curious kitten who is here to stay. Read this aloud to young children who have a new baby living in the house.

The Gingerbread Boy   PICTURE BOOK
AUTHOR/ILLUSTRATOR: Richard Egielski
HC/PB: HarperCollins
THEMES: folklore; teasing; baking; chases; cities

Hilarious paintings show a flat, overconfident gingerbread boy teasing his way through big city streets. Pursued by his creators, a rat, some construction workers, street musicians, and a policeman, he meets his final demise in the mouth of a fox. Here's a new telling of an old tale with lots of humorous downtown detail.

The Girl Who Loved Caterpillars:
A Twelfth Century Tale, From Japan   PICTURE BOOK
AUTHOR: Jean Merril • ILLUSTRATOR: Floyd Cooper
PB: Paperstar
THEMES: caterpillars; Japan; determination; strong girls; gifted child;
    folklore; gender roles; individuality; nature

Izumi isn't interested in the pastimes of the ladies in the Emperor's court. She prefers spending her time with creatures of nature, like toads, worms, and caterpillars. Cooper's radiant art illuminates the individuality of this determined twelfth-century Japanese girl.

★ Go Away, Big Green Monster!

NOVELTY

AUTHOR/ILLUSTRATOR: Ed Emberley
HC: Little Brown
THEMES: monsters; change

Irresistible graphics! Children follow along as with each turn of the page this monster grows and gets smaller right before their eyes. They'll have it memorized by the second time through.

Go, Dog. Go!

EARLY READER

AUTHOR/ILLUSTRATOR: P. D. Eastman
HC: Random House
THEMES: dogs; cars; parties; comparisons

Dogs on the go and occasionally resting, dogs of all shapes and colors, dogs at work and play, all add up to a book that will make a child say, as one dog says in the book, "Go around again!"

Goldilocks and the Three Bears

PICTURE BOOK

AUTHOR/ILLUSTRATOR: Jan Brett
HC Putnam • PB: Paperstar
THEMES: lost; bears; concepts; folklore; comparisons

Some of our favorite Jan Brett art can be found in this classic nursery tale. A mouse family keeps busy in its own story tucked in the borders, but it's the detailed Scandinavian costumes and the close-up of staring bears that give the reader a clear understanding of why Goldilocks jumped out the window never to return. Scary? Not really. The bears seem more baffled by the trespasser than ready to eat her.

Goodbye Mousie

PICTURE BOOK

AUTHOR: Robie H. Harris • ILLUSTRATOR: Jan Ormerod
HC: Simon & Schuster
THEMES: loss; grief; pets; comfort

Harris's understanding of children is well known—her *It's Perfectly Normal* is arguably the best book for children on the subject of sex. Here she shows an even greater sensitivity as she trods the well-worn territory of that first picture book on death and loss. Combined with Ormerod's gentle illustrations, which show as great an understanding of a young child's feelings and responses as the text, this is as good, honest, and straightforward a look at the topic as we have ever seen.

Good Night, Gorilla
PICTURE BOOK

AUTHOR/ILLUSTRATOR: Peggy Rathmann

HC/BB: Putnam

THEMES: mischief; repetition; surprises; zoos; escape; night; playing tricks

Gleefully funny and a guaranteed delight to read aloud at bedtime or anytime. Follow the path of the zookeeper as he says good night to the animals. Follow also the path of the gorilla, who comes right behind him with the purloined key, letting all the animals out of their cages, only to follow the sleepy zookeeper home and crawl unnoticed into his bedroom to sleep. It takes his wife to set things right, but the gorilla has the last laugh, which he shares with you and your child, who will most likely clamor to have it read again. Good thing it's so funny.

★ Goodnight Moon
PICTURE BOOK

AUTHOR: Margaret Wise Brown • ILLUSTRATOR: Clement Hurd

HC/BB/PB: HarperCollins

THEMES: bedtime; night; balloons

This is the classic first book for babies. It was published in 1947 and is the stand-out bestseller for babies still. We didn't trust its powerful magic until we had children of our own. It works. Ask any child.

Growing Colors
PICTURE BOOK

AUTHOR/ILLUSTRATOR: Bruce McMillan (photographs)

HC: Lothrop • PB: Mulberry

THEMES: gardens; vegetables; fruit; color

Often the only encounter a child has with a fruit or vegetable is in the grocery story or on the table. Oranges piled in bins along with tomatoes, carrots, squash, and other garden treats offer no clue as to how and where they grow. McMillan uses vibrant color photographs close-up and at a distance—of the entire plant—to solve the mystery.

Guess How Much I Love You
PICTURE BOOK

AUTHOR: Sam McBratney • ILLUSTRATOR: Anita Jeram

HC/BB: Candlewick

THEMES: fathers and sons; love; family; comparisons

It's hard to measure feelings, and every time Little Nutbrown Hare tries to show how much he loves Big Nutbrown Hare, Big Nutbrown Hare shows that he can love him even more. "'I love you as high as I can reach.' That is very high, thought Little Nutbrown Hare. I wish I had arms like that." In this cozy tale, Big Hare can represent Dad, a brother, or an older friend.

Gus and Grandpa

EARLY READER

AUTHOR: Claudia Mills • ILLUSTRATOR: Catherine Stock
HC/PB: Farrar, Straus & Giroux
THEMES: friendship; grandfathers and grandsons

Here is an utterly charming book for beginning readers, and the first of several books in this series about a young boy's loving relationship with his grandpa. Other titles include *Gus and Grandpa and the Christmas Cookies*, *Gus and Grandpa Ride the Train*, and *Gus and Grandpa at Basketball*.

Hairy Maclary from Donaldson's Dairy

PICTURE BOOK

AUTHOR: Lynley Dodd
PB: Tricycle Press
THEMES: dogs; cumulative story; cats; rhyme

"Out of the gate and off for a walk went Hairy Maclary from Donaldson's Dairy and Hercules Morse as big as a horse." They were joined by "Bitzer Maloney all skinny and bony," and "Muffin McLay like a bundle of hay. . . ." Even more dogs join this cumulative canine crew. You don't have to be a dog lover to be enchanted by Hairy Maclary. A hit in New Zealand and the U.K.; over four million copies have sold in the English-speaking world. Enjoy the language, the art, and the fun your child has with each turn of the page. When you're ready for others, *try Hairy Maclary's Bone* and *Hairy Maclary Scattercat*.

Happy Birth Day

PICTURE BOOK

AUTHOR: Robie H. Harris • ILLUSTRATOR: Michael Emberley
HC/PB: Candlewick
THEMES: babies; birth; hospitals; new baby

If you're a sucker for babies, this book, with its oversize close-up illustrations, will warm your heart. It reminds us of our newborns, just as loved and certainly as gorgeous as the infant here. Read this delightful story about one baby's first day of life to young children and give it to new parents to cherish.

Harley

AUTHOR: Star Livingstone • ILLUSTRATOR: Molly Bang
HC/PB: Seastar
THEMES: llamas; fitting in; work; sheep

For the more assured beginner, *Harley* has everything a great early reader requires: a compelling central character (a fascinating, ill-tempered llama who doesn't seem to fit in), a well-paced narrative with just the right sense of a controlled vocabulary, and terrific illustrations by Caldecott honoree Bang. Kids will love reading about Harley and how he develops his special talents into a calling that is both perfect for him and helpful to his community.

Harold and the Purple Crayon

AUTHOR/ILLUSTRATOR: Crockett Johnson
HC/PB: HarperCollins
THEMES: drawing; imagination; art; crayons; creativity

Harold doesn't require a full spectrum of color to hold his interest, and neither will young readers. Crockett's character draws simple pictures with his crayon and then steps magically into the drawing, becoming a part of his own creation. Offer this one up with crayon and paper and let imaginations soar! Preschoolers looking for simple stories and children in early stages of reading will enjoy this.

Harvey Slumfenburger's Christmas Present

AUTHOR/ILLUSTRATOR: John Burningham
HC/PB: Candlewick
THEMES: Christmas; determination; jobs; Santa Claus; promises; repetition

After a long night of delivering presents to the boys and girls of the world, and after putting the reindeer to bed, Santa Claus discovers he has forgotten to deliver Harvey Slumfenburger's present. The epic journey that ensues will warm the heart of any adult and assure even the most skeptical child of the faithfulness of Santa. Never sickly-sweet, and told in a repetitive style that encourages children to join in the telling, this one is a modern masterpiece by one of our favorite authors.

Hattie and the Fox

PICTURE BOOK

AUTHOR: Mem Fox • ILLUSTRATOR: Patricia Mullins
HC/PB: Simon & Schuster
THEMES: courage; animals, farm; repetition; cumulative story; farms;
   communication; survival; triumph

If it's written by Mem Fox, you can count on catchy rhythm and a repeatable tale. In this cumulative story, Hattie the hen spots danger but the other farm-yard animals don't seem to care. Young children will ask you to read about Hattie outsmarting Fox over and over.

Henny Penny

PICTURE BOOK

AUTHOR/ILLUSTRATOR: Paul Galdone
HC/PB: Clarion
THEMES: folklore; farms; cumulative story; animals

"Goodness gracious me!" said Henny Penny. "The sky is falling! I must go and tell the King." And so begins this famous tale of a hen who, along with Cocky Locky, Ducky Lucky, Goosey Loosey, and Turkey Lurkey, goes off to warn the king. Ah, but foolish, quickly made observations prove to be the downfall of this well-meaning quintet. Fat Foxy Loxy and Mrs. Foxy Loxy and their seven little foxes can attest to that.

> If you are looking for a classic nursery tale, look for Paul Galdone. His simple, expressive illustrations and to-the-point tellings do the job every time. A sampling of his titles: *The Little Red Hen*, *The Teeny-Tiny Woman*, *The Elves and the Shoemaker*, *The Three Little Kittens*, *The Gingerbread Boy*, and *The Three Billy Goats Gruff*.

Henry and Mudge

EARLY READER

AUTHOR: Cynthia Rylant • ILLUSTRATOR: Sucie Stevenson
HC: Simon & Schuster • PB: Aladdin
THEMES: friendship; dogs

Rylant perfectly captures the friendship of a boy and his very large dog in a delightful series. She proves that early readers do not have to suffer through boring text just because the vocabulary is limited. Here's an example, from *Henry and Mudge and the Happy Cat*: "Sitting on the steps was the shabbiest cat Henry had ever seen. It had a saggy belly, skinny legs, and fur that looked like mashed prunes." Rylant's writing is vivid. Her humor makes us laugh. Try any of the books in this series—the titles all begin *Henry and Mudge*.

> When you run out of *Henry and Mudge* books, do not despair. Rylant's charming style is also to be found in another early reader series, *Mr. Putter and Tabby*.

Here Comes Henny

PICTURE BOOK

AUTHOR: Charlotte Pomerantz • ILLUSTRATOR: Nancy Winslow Parker

PB: Mulberry

THEMES: cooperation; wordplay; mothers; picnics; manners

Irresistible because of its catchy, silly language, this is one kids will want to learn by heart. Adults will appreciate the message—it's not wise to be too picky.

Hey! Get Off Our Train

PICTURE BOOK

AUTHOR/ILLUSTRATOR: John Burningham

PB: Dragonfly

THEMES: environment; fables; trains; dreams; animals, endangered; humor

It may be a dream, but when a boy and his railroad engineer dog speed along the tracks picking up endangered animals, the message is wide-awake clear. Without a lecture, Burningham uses his signature humor to create an entertaining story with a conscience.

A Hole Is to Dig: A First Book of First Definitions

PICTURE BOOK

AUTHOR: Ruth Krauss • ILLUSTRATOR: Maurice Sendak

HC/PB: HarperCollins

THEMES: vocabulary; definitions; humor

Arms are for hugging and ears are for wiggling, and these "first definitions" will delight young children who will practice new words as they wiggle and giggle at Sendak's characters.

Home Sweet Home

PICTURE BOOK

AUTHOR: Jean Marzollo • ILLUSTRATOR: Ashley Woolf

PB: HarperCollins

THEMES: nature; animals; prayer; quiet

Looking for a book for the quiet times—one with a gentle message and beautiful art? This simple prayer for the planet and its inhabitants, with lovely art by Ashley Woolf, is just the thing.

Hooray, a Piñata!

PICTURE BOOK

AUTHOR/ILLUSTRATOR: Elisa Kleven

HC: Dutton • PB: Puffin

THEMES: birthdays; celebrations; piñatas; Mexico; parties; pets; friendship; traditions

Piñatas add a festive touch to parties. They're decorative and create a focus children look forward to. That is, unless that child is Clara, the birthday girl, who has gotten attached to her piñata and doesn't want it broken. Colorful, lively pictures add to the festivities in this story of friendship, family, and finding a perfect solution to a sensitive situation.

Hooray for Me   PICTURE BOOK

AUTHOR: Remy Charlip • ILLUSTRATOR: Vera Williams
HC: Tricycle Press
THEMES: self-respect; family; neighbors; pets; relatives

> Remy Charlip has a tremendous understanding of how children respond to books, and we love him for his imagination and willingness to thrill readers with it. For other doses of originality read Charlip's *Arm in Arm, Peanut Butter Party*, and *Why I Will Never Have Enough Time to Read This Book*.

Third cousin, great-uncle, stepbrother, nephew. There are lots of responses to "What kind of me are you?" Charlip's cheery shouts of pride show how we relate to our family, friends, and even pets. Williams adds the color to this feel-good book.

Hotshots   PICTURE BOOK NONFICTION

AUTHOR/ILLUSTRATOR: Chris L. Demarest
HC: McElderry
THEMES: firefighters; teamwork; fire; heroes

> Demarest's other books on the heroes include *Firefighters A to Z; Smokejumpers One to Ten*; and *Mayday! Mayday! A Coast Guard Rescue*.

Blazes of orange and yellow blow across the pages as the hotshots are called to battle. ". . . With drip-torches and fusees, 'shots race through scrub grass. A 'four-fifteen' bucks through thick smoke on a pass." Volunteer firefighter Demarest fuses stunning art and rhyming text in this introduction to the "hotshots," fire-fighting men and women trained to fight out-of-control fires. Includes information about their equipment, a bibliography, and web sites.

A House for Hermit Crab   PICTURE BOOK

AUTHOR/ILLUSTRATOR: Eric Carle
HC/PB: Simon & Schuster
THEMES: crabs; science; nature; moving; animals, sea; fear of new things; friendship; neighbors; change

Hermit Crab is frightened when he becomes too big for his first shell house and must find a new one. When he moves into his empty, dull new shell, neighbors come along to help him decorate. Children often worry about change, and Carle's brilliant collages and Hermit's undersea community show that change can be the perfect move.

★ A House Is a House for Me   PICTURE BOOK

AUTHOR: Mary Ann Hoberman • ILLUSTRATOR: Betty Fraser
HC: Viking • PB: Puffin
THEMES: houses; rhyme; repetition; habitats; animals; architecture; dwellings; Native American; diversity; comparisons; imagination

"A hill is a house for an ant, an ant. A hive is a house for a bee. A hole is a house for a mole or a mouse. And a house is a house for me." So begins this incredible rhyme about dwellings. But don't think Hoberman has limited the subjects to animals. Young readers will delight in learning about houses for airplanes, teabags, cookies, jackets, and many more.

How Do Dinosaurs Get Well Soon?   PICTURE BOOK

AUTHOR: Jane Yolen • ILLUSTRATOR: Mark Teague
HC: Blue Sky Press
THEMES: dinosaurs; illness; doctors; manners

"What if a dinosaur catches the flu? Does he whimper and whine in between each Atchoo?" The combination of Yolen's rhymes and Teague's larger-than-life pictures will bring cheer—even to the child who's feeling a bit under the weather. A companion to this book is *How Do Dinosaurs Say Goodnight?*, the duo's ode to good bedtime behavior.

How Many Bugs in a Box?   POP-UP

AUTHOR/ILLUSTRATOR: David A. Carter
HC: Simon & Schuster
THEMES: bugs; counting; numbers

Kids who relish the thought of peeking, sneaking, comical bugs will find them popping out, in, over, and under colorful boxes in a sturdy pop-up form. Carter is one of the masters of the pop-up, and his bugs can be found in numerous titles, including *Alpha Bugs*, *Bed Bugs*, and *Peekaboo Bugs*.

How My Parents Learned to Eat

PICTURE BOOK

AUTHOR: Ina R. Friedman • ILLUSTRATOR: Allen Say
HC/PB: Houghton Mifflin
THEMES: traditions; Japan; USA; England; eating; chopsticks; manners;
    cultural diversity

A young girl explains that in her house "some days we eat with chopsticks and some days we eat with knives and forks." After her American father and Japanese mother met and fell in love in Japan, each learned how to use the other's eating utensils. Cultural differences in eating styles are served up here, with a taste of humor and a touch of insight into our differences and similarities.

Hunting the White Cow

PICTURE BOOK

AUTHOR: Tres Seymour • ILLUSTRATOR: Wendy Anderson Halperin
HC/PB: Orchard
THEMES: farms; cows; animals, farm; family; cooperation; problem solving

A young girl tells this tale about folks working together. Everyone's trying to figure out a way to catch the white cow. She is "one tough dude" and manages to elude all attempts. From the farmhouse to the general store to the meadows beyond, the full-page pencil-and-watercolor art delightfully depicts the relaxed life on this farm.

Hush, Little Ones

PICTURE BOOK

AUTHOR/ILLUSTRATOR: John Butler
HC: Peachtree
THEMES: animal babies; bedtime

Sing this to the tune of "Hush Little Baby" or just whisper it. The soft color pencil drawings of animal parents with their babies, along with the gentle verse, add up to a cozy before-sleep story.

I Love You as Much . . .

PICTURE BOOK

AUTHOR: Laura Krauss Melmed • ILLUSTRATOR: Henri Sorensen
HC/PB/BB: HarperCollins
THEMES: mothers; love; rhyme; lullabies; animal babies

Said the mother goat to her child, "I love you as much as the mountain is steep." Said the mother whale to her child, "I love you as much as the ocean is deep." This tender gathering of mother animals and their babies is a perfect sleep send-off.

I Stink!

PICTURE BOOK

AUTHOR: Kate McMullan • ILLUSTRATOR: Jim McMullan
HC: HarperCollins
THEMES: recycling; trucks; New York; humor

This macho New York City garbage truck is hungry and loud. "Know what I do while you're asleep?" he asks. "Eat your TRASH." With a "BURRRP!" he announces he's ready for "alphabet soup." He then gulps down apple cores, dirty diapers, puppy poo, and more. Have fun imitating the voice of a ravenous garbage truck as you read this one aloud. And when you're finished, move on to the McMullan's *I'm Mighty!* and discover a "mighty" little tugboat who can pull even the biggest ships to shore.

I Went Walking

PICTURE BOOK

AUTHOR: Sue Williams • ILLUSTRATOR: Julie Vivas
HC/PB/BB: Gulliver
THEMES: animals; cumulative story; repetition; color

Just as *Brown Bear, Brown Bear, What Do You See?* asks questions and answers with cheery, oversize animals, so does this, but there's room on our shelves for both. On every page a hint of an animal appears at the next turn, allowing the child to guess what's coming. Vivas's fanciful paintings add a lively touch of humor.

★ I Wish I Were a Butterfly

PICTURE BOOK

AUTHOR: James Howe • ILLUSTRATOR: Ed Young
HC/PB: Harcourt Brace
THEMES: self-respect; crickets; spiders; gardens; ponds; friendship;
    insects; butterflies

The littlest cricket in Swampswallow Pond won't come out to sing with the others. He wants to be a butterfly, not an ugly cricket. But with the help of a wise spider he learns—along with young listeners—to appreciate himself. The ending is perfect (we won't ruin it). If you are looking for a lesson in self-acceptance, or simply a warm and reassuring story, this is for you.

I'll Fix Anthony

PICTURE BOOK

AUTHOR: Judith Viorst • ILLUSTRATOR: Arnold Lobel
PB: Aladdin
THEMES: brothers; siblings; dreams; revenge

It is tough being Anthony's little brother. Here is a catalog of all the things Anthony's younger brother will do when he is six, and bigger at last than Anthony, gleefully told with spite and malice. This is a sibling book where the sibs never get along—Anthony is as mean to his brother at the end as he is at the beginning. Fantasizing along with the narrator about ways to "fix" Anthony may provide some comfort for put-upon youngsters who have to stay the youngest.

If You Give a Mouse a Cookie   PICTURE BOOK
AUTHOR: Laura Numeroff • ILLUSTRATOR: Felicia Bond
HC/PB: HarperCollins
THEMES: mice; cumulative story; predictable

The kind of book that children want to hear again and again, this cumulative tale goes full circle from the introduction of a young boy and a mouse and the gift of a cookie. Bond's clever details add much to the story, making it a delight to read aloud with a child on your lap, noticing the visual elements and how well they complement the words. There have been many spinoffs of this successful tale, featuring a moose, a pig, and a bear, as well as several return visits from the mouse, all using the same circular formula.

 A sequel or two can work. They don't necessarily match the fun or excitement found in the first book, but still I often look forward to the next. But four? Five? I think it takes the punch out of the story that started the whole process.

 Why? When children clamor to have a beloved book read to them repeatedly? When sales of a sequel surpass those of the original? If the market demands more books, why should publishing be different from other industries? Give the people what they want!

 Really, Walter . . .

If You Were Born a Kitten   PICTURE BOOK NONFICTION
AUTHOR: Marion Dane Bauer • ILLUSTRATOR: JoEllen McAllister Stammen
HC: Simon & Schuster • PB/BB: Aladdin
THEMES: animal babies; birth; babies; comparisons; nature

Welcome twelve animal babies, popping, pecking, nudging, and poking their way into the world. The finale? A human baby. Extraordinary full-page illustrations fill each enchanting page. Read this when you and your child could use a snuggly, feel-good, learn-a-bit moment in your lives.

In Enzo's Splendid Gardens

PICTURE BOOK

AUTHOR/ILLUSTRATOR: Patricia Polacco
HC: Philomel
THEMES: restaurants; rhyme; cumulative story; bees; mishaps

"This is the bee that stopped on a tree in Enzo's splendid gardens . . ." A boy drops his book to look at the bee, and the waiter trips on the book and tips his tray, and the pandemonium begins.

 Enzo's Restaurant really did exist in Oakland, California. And the ladies ". . . foo-foo and shee-shee, who lost their balance and spilled their tea, bumped by the matron, all dressed in pink" are real too. I know that, because one of them is me.

In the Desert

PICTURE BOOK NONFICTION

AUTHOR: David M. Schwartz • ILLUSTRATOR: Dwight Kuhn (photographs)
PB: Creative Teaching Press
THEMES: desert; animals; cactus; nature

"Is this leg hairy enough for you? If not, there are seven more hairy legs where this one came from." The *Look Once, Look Again* science series by David Schwartz gives young children a close-up look at part of an animal with just enough words to hint what it might be. A turn of the page shows the answer with a brief explanation: "Tarantulas are the world's biggest spiders. Some are so large that they can eat lizards, small birds, and mice . . ." Dwight Kuhn's photo images get close enough to keep the pages turning on this guessing game. Others in the series include *At the Pond, In the Forest, At the Seashore, Among the Flowers,* and *In a Tree.*

In the Night Kitchen

PICTURE BOOK

AUTHOR/ILLUSTRATOR: Maurice Sendak
HC/PB: HarperCollins
THEMES: dreams; kitchens; bakers; baking; milk; cake

Do not attempt to analyze or make sense of this wonderful, dreamlike romp—it would spoil the fun. Mickey discovers the secret behind the cake that gets baked in time for breakfast every morning and even helps out the three identical bakers, who look just like Oliver Hardy! Magical illustrations and a fun read-aloud rhythm make this a great toddler book, but it's been known to enthrall older children and adults as well.

In the Tall, Tall Grass

PICTURE BOOK

AUTHOR/ILLUSTRATOR: Denise Fleming
HC/PB: Henry Holt
THEMES: grass; caterpillars; fireflies; rhyme; nature; animals; bees; sound

From the warmth of a sunny sky "crunch, munch, caterpillars lunch" to the cool shades of night "stop, go, fireflies glow," critters do what they do from a toddler's view in bright, bold, award-winning color collages. Also: *In the Small, Small Pond* (ponds, frogs).

Is This a House for Hermit Crab?

PICTURE BOOK

AUTHOR: Megan McDonald • ILLUSTRATOR: S. D. Schindler
HC/PB: Orchard
THEMES: nature; sea; science; crabs; home; change; moving; habitats

Hermit Crab tries a variety of places in his search for a new home. Not until a wave carries him far out to sea does he find the perfect place, a discarded snail's shell. A delightful story matched by Schindler's sandy, speckled pictures provides an entertaining balance between science and fiction.

Is Your Mama a Llama?

PICTURE BOOK

AUTHOR: Deborah Guarino • ILLUSTRATOR: Steven Kellogg
HC/BB/PB: Scholastic
THEMES: llamas; predictable; rhyme; guessing; bats; swans; seals; kangaroos; cows

With whimsy and rhyme, animals give hints to a llama who asks them, "Is your mama a llama?" Readers guess what everyone's mama really is and discover the answer with the turn of the page. Read this to one child or a group. We guarantee you'll get enthusiastic participation.

It's Snowing

PICTURE BOOK

AUTHOR/ILLUSTRATOR: Olivier Dunrea
HC: Farrar, Straus & Giroux
THEMES: winter; snow; mothers; babies; playing

With precise rhythm, clipped dialogue, and a circular storytelling style, Dunrea's text tells of a mother's delight in sharing a snowy evening with her baby. The art's glorious depiction of the transformation from barren to snowy wonderland adds the crowning touch. Like Uri Shulevitz's *Snow* and

Ezra Jack Keats's *The Snowy Day*, this is a wonderful portrayal of the delights that snow can bring.

Just Enough and Not Too Much   PICTURE BOOK
AUTHOR/ILLUSTRATOR: Kaethe Zemack
HC: Arthur A. Levine Books
THEMES: collecting; gifts; friendship; musicians; parties; generosity; greed;
    music; sharing

"Simon the fiddler had a cozy little house and everything he needed." And then one day, Simon decided he didn't have enough. So Simon began to gather more chairs and hats and toys and . . . it wasn't long before Simon decided he had too much! This delightful tale will strike a chord with many in our world of excess. It may even be step one in preparing a give-away party.

 This is the book for every one of us who has said, "Where did I get all this junk?" Adults are bound to be giving this book to each other.

Just Like My Dad   PICTURE BOOK
AUTHOR: Tricia Gardella • ILLUSTRATOR: Margot Apple
PB: Boyds Mills
THEMES: fathers and sons; horses; ranches; cowboys

There is something heartwarming about a son following in the footsteps of his father. Dad's a ranch hand, and his son accompanies him as we watch them go through their daily routine. Margot Apple's warm illustrations portray the details of this rugged life alongside Gardella's simple and perfect story.

Just Me and My Dad   PICTURE BOOK
AUTHOR/ILLUSTRATOR: Mercer Mayer
PB: Golden
THEMES: fathers and sons; camping; fishing; confidence; mischief

Little Critter is a typical four-year-old full of mischief, confidence, and the inability to admit he can't do everything. In this book, as in its companion, *Just Me and My Mom,* Little Critter spends some time alone with one very patient parent. This inexpensive series maintains its popularity well into elementary school.

Bye-bye Dick and Jane:
Beginning-to-Read Series

Parents encounter a lot of confusion when choosing books within the category variously named "Easy to Read," "Beginning to Read," "Early Chapter Books," etc. Many publishers have specific lines of books aimed at the child just venturing into solo reading. These will range from titles with no more than six words on a page to books with full pages of text and pictures every third page or so.

How are you to make sense of the labels, color codes, levels, and recommendations that shout at you from the covers? Many families find a series that works for them and stick with it. The most popular ones are the *I Can Read* (HarperCollins) series and *Step into Reading* (Random House). These series have well-thought-out and easy-to-understand guidelines for parental use. Each one divides its list of titles into levels designed to take a child from the letter-recognition stage all the way to chapter books. Other series that we like are:

Start to Read series (School Zone)
DK Readers (DK Publishing)
Green Light Readers (Harcourt Brace)
Reading Rainbow Readers (Seastar)
See More Readers (Seastar)

Whatever books or series you choose, we recommend that the child, the parent, and the child's teacher work together to select titles that will teach both the skill and the joy of reading. And remember this as you choose: a book that has fewer and simpler words does not have to be boring nor is it excused from telling a good story. Examples of excellence in this genre include classic stories like *Danny and the Dinosaur* by Syd Hoff and *Harry the Dirty Dog* by Gene Zion, and more recent books such as *The Bravest Dog Ever: The True Story of Balto* by Natalie Standiford, *Iris and Walter* by Elissa Haden Guest, and *Dust for Dinner* by Ann Turner. There are also outstanding extended series like *Junie B. Jones* by Barbara Park and *The Kids of the Polk Street School* by Patricia Reilly Giff that provide familiar characters children will want to read about over and over, building reading confidence along the way.

Many books, regardless of size, series, or format, will fit the bill when you are looking for enchanting first reads. Do not limit yourself to a publisher's preselected list, a library or bookstore's beginning reader section, or even our advice. Sit down with your child and a selection of books—both picture books and others that interest you. Many families have given birth to readers without the help of a beginning reader program.

★ King Bidgood's in the Bathtub

PICTURE BOOK

AUTHOR: Audrey Wood • ILLUSTRATOR: Don Wood

HC/PB: Harcourt Brace

THEMES: kings; baths; queens; cleverness; repetition; resourcefulness

King Bidgood's having too much fun in his bath to get out. So he invites all the members of his court to join him. This one is a winner. Its imploring refrain—"King Bidgood's in the bathtub, and he won't get out! Oh, who knows what to do?"—causes children to demand a repeat performance. You might mention that the Queen is the spitting image of Audrey Wood. And the Page? Their son Bruce is much older now, but that is definitely he!

Last Night I Dreamed a Circus

PICTURE BOOK

AUTHOR: Maya Gottfried • ILLUSTRATOR: Robert Rahway Zakanitch

HC: Knopf

THEMES: circus; animals; acrobatics; dreams; performers

Dazzling watercolor paintings on a stark black background spotlight circus clowns, horseback riders, acrobats, lion tamers, and other performers in a style more reminiscent of Cirque du Soleil than the classic Ringling Brothers circus. It's a pleasure to turn each brilliant page.

Leo the Late Bloomer

PICTURE BOOK

AUTHOR: Robert Kraus • ILLUSTRATOR: Jose Aruego

HC/PB: HarperCollins

THEMES: self-respect; mothers and sons; fathers and sons; readiness

We've all met Leo. He's not reading yet. He's having trouble writing. Leo is not ready. This reassuring tale shows late bloomers that, in time, they too will take off.

Let's Be Enemies

PICTURE BOOK

AUTHOR: Janice May Udry • ILLUSTRATOR: Maurice Sendak

HC/PB: HarperCollins

THEMES: friendship; disagreements; sharing

Unready

Sometimes kids are just not ready to try something new, like an overnight at a friend's, learning to swim, or starting school. Rosemary Wells has written a three-book series that reminds children and their parents that things take longer for some than for others: *Edward Unready for a Sleep Over*, *Edward Unready for Swimming*, and *Edward Unready for School.*

Being unready is not limited to the preschool set, nor is it confined to the reluctant child. Judith Viorst's *Earrings!* shows the frustrations a child can feel when she thinks she is ready (to have her ears pierced) and her parents don't. Viorst is just plain funny. And these are times when a laugh is good medicine.

Sometimes friends don't get along, but it doesn't have to be the end of the world. John has had it with James. A friend shouldn't always want to be the boss, or throw sand, or take all the crayons. But friends work things out, and Udry and Sendak know how to get this across without being too sweet.

Let's Talk About It: Adoption

PICTURE BOOK NONFICTION

AUTHOR: Fred Rogers • ILLUSTRATOR: Jim Judkis (photographs)
HC: Putnam • PB: Paperstar
THEMES: adoption; family; diversity

In spare text accompanied by color photographs, *Let's Talk About It* books offer Mr. Rogers's characteristic straightforward, reassuring responses to questions children have about various issues: "Being in a family means belonging . . . belonging because you are loved and cared for—and because you give love and give care, too." By simply turning pages, parents can bring up issues that may be on their child's mind. Others in the series: *Let's Talk About It: Divorce, Let's Talk About It: Stepfamilies.*

A Lion Named Shirley Williamson

PICTURE BOOK

AUTHOR/ILLUSTRATOR: Bernard Waber
HC/PB: Houghton Mifflin
THEMES: lions; zoos; names; animals; jealousy

Lions Goobah, Poobah, and Aroobah are not happy with Shirley Williamson, the newest lion at the zoo. After all, she gets special treatment. ". . . Seymour, the zookeeper, served Shirley her meals on a tray. 'But what am I to do?' said Seymour, 'I just couldn't shove food at her—not at someone named Shirley Williamson.'" Waber, who also wrote and illustrated the tales of Lyle the Crocodile, is his typically silly self in this delightful tale in which a worrisome situation ends with a happy solution.

Little Bear

EARLY READER

AUTHOR: Else Holmelund Minarik • ILLUSTRATOR: Maurice Sendak
HC/PB: HarperCollins
THEMES: family; bears

Other Little Bear stories: *A Kiss for Little Bear, Little Bear's Friend, Father Bear Comes Home,* and *Little Bear's Visit.*

 Hicklebee's doors first opened in 1979. Little Bear was on the shelf. The simple, tender stories with Sendak's art continue to be a popular classic for beginning readers.

Other excellent books to explore when you want to know more about how colors work are *Mouse Paint* (see page 135), *Who Said Red* by Mary Serfozo, Ruth Heller's *Color* (see page 432), *Hailstones and Halibut Bones* (see page 327), and *The Gift of Driscoll Lipscomb* (out of print, but listed on page 432 in The Out-of-Print Hall of Shame).

Little Blue and Little Yellow
PICTURE BOOK

AUTHOR/ILLUSTRATOR: Leo Lionni

PB: Mulberry

THEMES: color; concepts; friendship; family; change; diversity; belonging

When a little blue spot and a little yellow spot give each other a big hug, they turn green. This deceptively simple book offers an opportunity to discuss issues of diversity in the guise of a primer on mixing colors.

The Little House
PICTURE BOOK

AUTHOR/ILLUSTRATOR: Virginia Lee Burton

HC/PB: Houghton Mifflin

THEMES: change; cities; country life; houses; home; environment

Delightfully old-fashioned, yet no other book on this topic has gotten it so right. A house in the country is, over time, gradually surrounded by the city. The child reading this book gets a sense of the passage of the years and the changes wrought on once pristine land. A classic.

The Little Mouse, the Red Ripe Strawberry, and the Big Hungry Bear
PICTURE BOOK

AUTHORS: Don and Audrey Wood • ILLUSTRATOR: Don Wood

HC/PB: Child's Play Ltd.

THEMES: bears; mice; strawberries; fear; cleverness

Wood's oversize illustrations draw the reader nose to nose with the character. The story begins with a voice asking a little mouse what he is doing. And then the voice says, "But, little Mouse, haven't you heard about the big, hungry Bear?" This isn't scary. It's funny and exciting and will capture your preschooler's attention. But be prepared; he'll want you to read it again, and may even want a strawberry to go with it. A sequel, *Merry Christmas, Big Hungry Bear,* is set at holiday time and offers similar delights.

Little Toot
PICTURE BOOK

AUTHOR/ILLUSTRATOR: Hardie Gramatky

HC: Putnam • PB: Paperstar

THEMES: boats; courage; fear; determination

Little Toot is terrified of stormy seas, but he musters up his courage when an ocean liner is in trouble. The story of this now famous tugboat was first pub-

Look at *The Little Red Ant and the Great Big Crumb* (page 176) for another take on someone who is ready despite thinking he's not.

lished in 1939, and continues to entertain children encouraged by the little guy who saves the day.

Livingstone Mouse

PICTURE BOOK

AUTHOR: Pamela Duncan Edwards • ILLUSTRATOR: Henry Cole

HC/PB: HarperCollins

THEMES: mice; geography; habitats; humor; wordplay; searches

Livingstone mouse is searching for China. He can't find it in a cupboard, a sneaker, a picnic basket, or a lamppost. Young readers will like recognizing Livingstone's silly mistakes, but may need some help with the play-on-words ending.

Louella Mae, She's Run Away!

PICTURE BOOK

AUTHOR: Karen Beaumont Alarcon • ILLUSTRATOR: Rosanne Litzinger

HC/PB: Henry Holt

THEMES: lost; searching game; pigs; family; rhyme; predictable

A rollicking chase around the farmyard gears up young listeners to wonder where Louella Mae has gone. "Round up the horses! Hitch up the team! Hop in the buckboard and look by the . . ." They'll shout out their guesses but will have to wait till you turn the page for an answer.

Madeline

PICTURE BOOK

AUTHOR/ILLUSTRATOR: Ludwig Bemelmans

HC: Viking • PB: Puffin

THEMES: Paris; rhyme; school; strong girls; travel; orphans; illness; gifts; hospitals; jealousy; mischief

"In an old house in Paris that was covered with vines lived twelve little girls in two straight lines." And one of them was spunky Madeline, who woke one night with an attack of appendicitis and was rushed to the hospital. Empathy and jealousy come lightly into play here, but they take a backseat to a fun sense of mischief and togetherness.

Madeline's adventures have delighted young children since this classic was first published in 1939. Other adventures about this small, spirited heroine are *Madeline and the Bad Hat*, *Madeline and the Gypsies*, *Madeline's Rescue*, *Madeline's Christmas*, and *Madeline in London*.

The Maggie B.

PICTURE BOOK

AUTHOR/ILLUSTRATOR: Irene Haas

HC: McElderry • PB: Aladdin

THEMES: sailing; boats; wishes; siblings; sea; strong girls; brothers; sisters; yearnings

We've wished on our share of stars, but when Margaret Barnstable did, she woke to find herself in the cabin of her very own ship, the *Maggie B.*, and with her for company was her dear baby brother, James. Luscious watercolor paintings show Maggie's ship filled with flowers, chickens, a goat, a toucan, and just about anything else a self-reliant sailor needs.

The Magic Fan
PICTURE BOOK

AUTHOR/ILLUSTRATOR: Keith Baker
HC: Harcourt Brace • PB: Voyager
THEMES: Japan; self-respect; magic; folklore; creativity

Yoshi was a boy who loved to build things: wagons, fences, houses, stairs, tables, and walls—everything that was needed in his village by the sea. But one day, with the help of a magic fan, he built something that had never been built before and used it to save the people in his village. Baker's brilliant paintings have their own magic in the shape of fan cutouts that allow the reader to discover answers to Yoshi's difficult questions.

Mama Don't Allow
PICTURE BOOK

AUTHOR/ILLUSTRATOR: Thacher Hurd
HC/PB: HarperCollins
THEMES: music; swamps; bands; family; cleverness; triumph; songs

Miles plays his saxophone a little too loudly for people's taste, and his bandmates are the only ones in town who appreciate his talents, so they go down to the swamp to play. Of course, the alligators in the swamp just love their music and invite the swamp band to play for them, and then be their dinner! This charming story has rhythm, cleverness, and a lot of heart. You will love reading—or even singing—this aloud to your family.

Math Start Series
PICTURE BOOK

AUTHOR: Stuart J. Murphy • ILLUSTRATOR: Various
HC/PB: HarperCollins
THEMES: math; counting; numbers; comparisons; time; problem solving

Stuart Murphy might have liked math when he was a kid if only it had been explained differently. He thinks people understand things best when they can see them, so he has come up with a series of his own math storybooks illustrated by well-known artists. There are three levels:

1: Counting, ordering, patterning, and comparing sizes, ages three and up (*The Best Bug Parade*, Holly Keller)

2: Adding, subtracting, time lines, estimating, and fractions, ages six and up (*Elevator Magic*, G. Brian Karas)

3: Multiplying, dividing, equations, problem solving, ages seven and up (*Too Many Kangaroo Things to Do!*, Kevin O'Malley)

Max

PICTURE BOOK

AUTHOR/ILLUSTRATOR: Rachel Isadora
PB: Aladdin
THEMES: dance; baseball; ballet; humor; gender roles; gentle boys

Max discovers that his sister's ballet class is a perfect place for him to improve his baseball skills. An enlightening story for young male athletes.

May I Bring a Friend?

PICTURE BOOK

AUTHOR: Beatrice Schenk deRegniers • ILLUSTRATOR: Beni Montresor
HC: Simon & Schuster • PB: Aladdin
THEMES: manners; humor; kings; queens; comparisons; tea parties; friendship; diversity

When one has a daily invitation for tea from the king and queen, it makes sense to bring a friend. This fun Caldecott Medal winner shows how unusual friends can be.

Mean Soup

PICTURE BOOK

AUTHOR/ILLUSTRATOR: Betsy Everitt
HC: Harcourt Brace • PB: Voyager
THEMES: problem solving; bad days; emotions; mothers and sons

Get ready to throw your whole body into this read-aloud. Sometimes when you feel crabby, you don't want to talk about it. Horace feels so mean at the end of a bad day that his mother helps him vent by making Mean Soup. This is not only fun on the good days, but perfect for letting out the mean stuff on bad ones.

Millions of Cats

PICTURE BOOK

AUTHOR/ILLUSTRATOR: Wanda Gag
HC: Putnam • PB: Paperstar
THEMES: cats; loneliness; pets; repetition; fighting

"Hundreds of cats, Thousands of cats, Millions and billions and trillions of cats" is what the old man brought home when his wife sent him off to find one pet to keep them company. That was far too many to feed, so the cats had to choose which one would stay. Gag's classic tale, first published in

1928, has the rhythm and repetition you find in a tune and it bounces around in your mind. Prepare for your child to request this one repeatedly.

Minerva Louise at School   PICTURE BOOK
AUTHOR/ILLUSTRATOR: Janet Morgan Stoeke
HC: Dutton • PB: Penguin
THEMES: school; chickens; wordplay; misunderstanding; humor; curiosity

We enjoy finding books in which the child gets the joke before the character in the story does. Minerva Louise is one of those characters. This feather-brained hen who mistakes a school for a barn and cubbies for nesting boxes will keep young readers in stitches. Other titles include *Minerva Louise* and *A Hat for Minerva Louise*.

Mirette on the High Wire   PICTURE BOOK
AUTHOR/ILLUSTRATOR: Emily Arnold McCully
HC: Putnam • PB: Paperstar
THEMES: friendship; teachers; talent; strong girls; courage

When Mirette sees one of her mother's boarders walking on the clothesline, she is enchanted. Young readers, too, will be captivated by Bellini's skill as well as by the lessons learned by a teacher and his young student.

Miss Bindergarten Gets Ready for Kindergarten   PICTURE BOOK
AUTHOR: Joseph Slate • ILLUSTRATOR: Ashley Wolff
HC: Dutton
THEMES: school; kindergarten; teachers; diversity; new experiences; rhyme; alphabet

> Miss Bindergarten and her class have more adventures in several sequels, including *Miss Bindergarten Celebrates the 100th Day of Kindergarten.*

A perfect starter for any child about to begin kindergarten or preschool. Every other two-page spread shows students at home: "Adam Krupp wakes up. Brenda Heath brushes her teeth," and their teacher "Miss Bindergarten gets ready for kindergarten." They'll recognize familiar activities as students prepare for school, and will be intrigued and perhaps comforted to see some of what their teacher does when she's not with them.

Mole and the Baby Bird   PICTURE BOOK
AUTHOR/ILLUSTRATOR: Marjorie Newman
HC: Bloomsbury
THEMES: birds; responsibility; grandfathers; moles; pets; freedom

Little Mole has found a baby bird that has fallen out of its nest. When no one comes to claim it, he takes it home to be his pet. Although his parents protest, Mole feeds it and builds a wooden cage. It isn't until his grandfather takes him to the top of a hill where Mole sees birds flying free that he decides to release it. This tender story of a loving family shows that a child can make the right decision even if it makes him sad.

The Monster at the End of This Book   PICTURE BOOK

AUTHOR: Jon Stone • ILLUSTRATOR: Mike Smollin
PB: Golden
THEMES: anticipation; surprises; monsters; humor; embarrassment; frustration

Lovable, furry old Grover stars in this Little Golden Book based on the character from *Sesame Street*. Warning the reader that scares lie ahead, Grover tries in vain to convince the reader not to turn the page, as it will bring her closer to "the monster at the end of this book." As your giggling child reader turns the pages anyway, Grover becomes more and more frustrated, trying more elaborate methods to stop the inevitable. With a desperate plea, he makes a final stand on the next-to-last page, only to have it revealed that *he* is the monster. This is an example of how you cannot judge a book by format or price—good stories can be found anywhere.

Mordant's Wish   PICTURE BOOK

AUTHOR/ILLUSTRATOR: Valerie Coursen
PB: Henry Holt
THEMES: moles; wishes; turtles; connections

Mordant Mole wishes his cloud were a real turtle and that it was his friend. From a wish to a dandelion puff to a bike rider to a snow cone drip, a chain of events ultimately makes two wishes come true.

★ More, More, More, Said the Baby: 3 Love Stories   PICTURE BOOK

AUTHOR/ILLUSTRATOR: Vera Williams
HC/BB/PB: Greenwillow
THEMES: babies; fathers; grandmothers; mothers; love; affection; cultural diversity

Here's a baby love story in three parts. Daddy, Grandma, and Mama show their affection with hugs, chases, tosses, swings, tastes of toes, and a tuck into bed. Williams's cheery paintings capture the warmth of these babies imploring, "More, More, More!" in a perfect bedtime book.

Mouse Paint
PICTURE BOOK

AUTHOR/ILLUSTRATOR: Ellen Walsh
HC/PB: Harcourt Brace
THEMES: color; mice; art; paint; concepts; change

Three white mice find three jars of paint: red, yellow, and blue. They think it's mouse paint and climb right in. Now there are three colored mice who puddle and mix and come up with other colors. Cheery, bold collages mix with humor to make this a fine choice for young ones experimenting with their own colors.

Mr. Rabbit and the Lovely Present
PICTURE BOOK

AUTHOR: Charlotte Zolotow • ILLUSTRATOR: Maurice Sendak
HC/PB: HarperCollins
THEMES: gifts; mothers and daughters; birthdays; color; imagination

A matter-of-fact conversation between a rabbit and a young girl searching for the perfect birthday gift for her mother makes up this long-loved tale.

Mr. Willowby's Christmas Tree
PICTURE BOOK

AUTHOR/ILLUSTRATOR: Robert Barry
HC: Doubleday
THEMES: Christmas; recycling; rhyme; trees; sharing; connections

The ultimate book on recycling the Christmas tree! Mr. Willowby's tree is too tall for the space intended, so the top gets lopped off. What to do? As the treetop shrinks, it gets passed on to another person, then another, finally winding up in the home of a mouse family. An endearing family read-aloud that holds up year after year.

Muncha! Muncha! Muncha!
PICTURE BOOK

AUTHOR: Candace Fleming • ILLUSTRATOR: G. Brian Karas
HC: Atheneum
THEMES: rabbits; gardening; vegetables; cleverness

Mr. McGreely's dream of planting a vegetable garden is ruined by three hungry bunnies. Everything he does to protect his garden fails so he builds a fortress. Alas, even that doesn't keep out those clever bunnies. Repeated sound effects make this a fun read-aloud, and young listeners will surely chant along. Be sure to let them look carefully at the fifth page from the end to catch the bunnies as they sneak into Mr. McGreely's basket.

My House Has Stars

PICTURE BOOK

AUTHOR: Megan McDonald • ILLUSTRATOR: Peter Catalanotto
HC/PB: Orchard
THEMES: houses; cultural diversity; stars; geography; dwellings; nature

As night falls, children all over the world describe their houses and their stars. "My house rocks me to sleep at night. I hear the water lapping the sides of our boat, lapping the sides, lapping the sides." ". . . the sky looks like a blue bowl filled with popcorn." A map is included on the last page for geography buffs, but the point here is the children: the differences in where they live, the similarities in the warmth of their families.

My Pony

PICTURE BOOK

AUTHOR/ILLUSTRATOR: Susan Jeffers
HC: Hyperion
THEMES: horses; pets; imagination; patience

Often young children rely on their imagination to conjure up what they can't have. Here a young girl imagines ponies. Soft pastel paintings show the ponies of every child's dreams.

★ My Very First Mother Goose

PICTURE BOOK

EDITOR: Iona Opie • ILLUSTRATOR: Rosemary Wells
HC/BB: Candlewick
THEMES: rhyme; Mother Goose

Destined to be a classic: more than sixty nursery rhymes chosen by Iona Opie, illustrated in oversize full-color art by Rosemary Wells. Nothing scary here; these are rhymes to comfort. Pay attention to Wells's pictures; she sneaks in an occasional surprise, as on page 14. We all know the story of Humpty Dumpty, but look closely: Ah, now we know why he fell in the first place! There is a second volume, featuring more rhymes, as well as individual board books of some of the best-known rhymes.

Mother Goose

Like the choice of a family dictionary, Bible, or general cookbook, your favorite Mother Goose collection may be different from ours. Lucky for us all there are plenty to go around. Most major illustrators get around to doing Mother Goose sooner or later, and the traditional versions continue to be in print. While we believe in the power of the rhymes themselves, we realize that most people will make their choices based upon the artists.

Take heed: it is a common practice to reshape, edit, and even rewrite Mother Goose's rhymes to suit a particular point of view.

My favorite Mother Goose rhyme is: "Snail, snail come out of your hole, or else I'll beat you black as coal/ Snail, snail stick out your head, or else I'll beat you till you're dead." This does not show up very often in modern Mother Goose collections. Mother Goose in the original version was not the namby-pamby stuff we think of today. Peter Peter Pumpkin Eater, The Old Woman In the Shoe, and Georgie Porgie are all edgy. I don't approve of removing them from Mother Goose entirely.

Walter, You are proof that Mother Goose is not just for preschoolers. I'm certain you were that rotten boy who terrified us all during recess.

The following is a list of recommended titles that show the many sides of Mother Goose—and just a sampling of what you'll find on bookstore and library shelves.

The Arnold Lobel Book of Mother Goose by Arnold Lobel
Brian Wildsmith's Mother Goose by Brian Wildsmith
The Jessie Willcox Smith Mother Goose: A Careful and Full Selection of the Rhymes by Jessie Willcox Smith
Michael Foreman's Mother Goose by Michael Foreman
Mother Goose: The Original Volland Edition by Eulalie Osgood Grover (Editor)
My Very First Mother Goose by Iona Archibald Opie (Editor), Rosemary Wells (Illustrator)
The Real Mother Goose by Blanche Fisher Wright
Richard Scarry's Best Mother Goose Ever by Richard Scarry
Sylvia Long's Mother Goose by Sylvia Long
Tomie dePaola's Mother Goose by Tomie dePaola
James Marshall's Mother Goose by James Marshall

For a delightfully macabre interpretation, very much in the spirit of the original rhymes, look for *The Charles Addams Mother Goose* by Charles Addams.

AUTHOR SPOTLIGHT ON
TOMIE dePAOLA

*"If you know how and love to read, you can find out
anything about everything and everything about anything."*
—Tomie dePaola

No one brings more whimsy and heart to their books than Tomie dePaola! A master storyteller and a gifted illustrator, dePaola has lent his talents to a wide variety of outstanding books for young children. Whether writing about his beloved Italy, retelling legends and stories of long ago, illustrating stories from the Bible, or putting his own personal spin on classics like Mother Goose, Tomie's work is always of high quality and a welcome addition to bookshelves.

Here are our favorites:

The Art Lesson
Bill and Pete
The Clown of God
Days of the Blackbird: A Tale of Northern Italy
Fin M'Coul, the Giant of Knockmany Hill
The Legend of the Bluebonnet
The Legend of the Poinsettia
Oliver Button Is a Sissy
Pancakes for Breakfast
Patrick, Patron Saint of Ireland
The Popcorn Book
Strega Nona (and the sequels *Strega Nona Meets her Match; Big Anthony and the Magic Ring;* and *Strega Nona: Her Story*)
Tony's Bread
Tomie dePaola's Book of Bible Stories

We want to make special mention of Tomie's *26 Fairmont Avenue* books. These early chapter books are autobiographical accounts of Tomie's childhood, and the writing is clear, engaging, and just right for young readers looking to branch out into longer, more involved books. Titles include *26 Fairmount Avenue, Here We All Are!, On My Way,* and *What a Year.* After years of acclaim as an illustrator and creator of picture books, dePaola, with this series, has earned recognition for his writing, reminding us that good picture books begin and end with the words.

We have treasured Tomie's writing as well as his art for years, and include some of his earlier autobiographical picture books (*Tom,* and especially *Nana Upstairs & Nana Downstairs*) among our most beloved. There are so many wonderful books by Tomie that writing about them could fill up many pages we cannot spare here. Thankfully, Barbara Elleman has already done it. To gain a fuller appreciation of Tomie's books, look for her *Tomie dePaola: His Art & His Stories,* a thorough look at the life and work of one of the treasures of the children's book world.

Nana Upstairs & Nana Downstairs

PICTURE BOOK

AUTHOR/ILLUSTRATOR: Tomie dePaola
HC: Putnam • PB: Puffin
THEMES: family; death; grandmothers; loss; comparisons

Tommy loves his Sunday visits with his grandmother, who lives downstairs, and his great-grandmother, who lives upstairs. When ninety-four-year-old Grandmother Upstairs dies, Tommy's family helps him adjust to her death and to understand that life's natural process is to start out young, grow old, perhaps very old, then die. For a warm, comforting story that shows young children that it is possible to cope with loss from death, this one is among the best.

★ The Napping House

PICTURE BOOK

AUTHOR: Audrey Wood • ILLUSTRATOR: Don Wood
HC/BB: Harcourt Brace
THEMES: rhyme; cumulative story; bedtime; grandmothers; pets; naps

It's nap time, and in this house you'll find a cozy bed with a snoring granny, a dreaming child, a dozing dog, a pile of sleepy pets, all snuggled for a nap—until a tiny wakeful flea enters the picture. Notice how Wood's paintings go from sleepy blues to wake-up yellows.

Nate the Great

EARLY READER

AUTHOR: Marjorie Weinman Sharmat • ILLUSTRATOR: Marc Simont
PB: Dell
THEMES: mystery; dogs; gifted child; community; cleverness

> If you'd like another series on the same reading and interest level that will further delight your mystery lover, look for the *Cam Jansen* books by David Adler.

A must for the reader just beginning to read chapter books. This is the first book in an outstanding series featuring the exploits of the smartest detective around, Nate the Great, and his dog, Sludge, as they uncover and solve mysteries in their neighborhood.

Nine-In-One Grr! Grr!: A Folktale from the Hmong People of Laos

PICTURE BOOK

AUTHOR: Blia Xiong • ILLUSTRATOR: Nancy Hom
PB: Children's Book Press
THEMES: Hmong; tigers; birds; trickster tales; Laos; folklore

It takes a smart bird to trick a tiger. And this colorful book, which shows off the Hmong folk art tradition of appliquéd story cloths, offers up a trick clever enough to limit the tiger population to one every nine years.

No, David!

PICTURE BOOK

AUTHOR/ILLUSTRATOR: David Shannon
HC: Blue Sky Press
THEMES: mothers and sons; manners; discipline; consequences; misbehaving

> If you'd like more David, try *David Gets in Trouble* and *David Goes to School.*

Read this to a four- or five-year-old and watch him giggle uncontrollably—it never fails. We have presented to family groups where children have spontaneously moved to the front of the room to get closer to the pictures. When Shannon was five years old, he wrote an autobiographical story of a little kid who broke all his mother's rules. "No, David," his mother would repeat throughout her day. Here it is, fine-tuned but still exquisitely childlike. Negative? We don't think so. Children hear "No!" all day long and revel in the familiarity. Besides, the ending is sweet.

No Fighting, No Biting!

PICTURE BOOK

AUTHOR: Else Holmelund Minarik • ILLUSTRATOR: Maurice Sendak
HC/PB: HarperCollins
THEMES: siblings; fighting; disagreements

Simple to read and a must to have ready for those times when the children's quarreling gets out of hand. You can read it to them or they can read it to you. Either way there is sure to be peace and quiet, at least while reading the book.

★ Noisy Nora

PICTURE BOOK

AUTHOR/ILLUSTRATOR: Rosemary Wells
HC: Dial • PB: Puffin
THEMES: new baby; jealousy; frustration; family; rhyme; siblings

Nora's a middle child. Her older sister gets to do all the fun things and her baby brother needs constant attention, so Nora has to wait. "First she banged the window, then she slammed the door, Then she dropped her sister's marbles on the kitchen floor."

 This was a favorite in our house, and I didn't even have a middle child.

 (Although I suppose the fact that you are the fourth of five children has no bearing on your liking this . . .)

AUTHOR SPOTLIGHT ON
ROSEMARY WELLS

Rosemary Wells gets it. There is no better writer today who can home in on the emotional, sometimes funny, sometimes not, concerns of very young children. *Noisy Nora* arrived with a "monumental crash!" showing that Wells understands about being a middle child. There are not always advantages to being the youngest either, so Wells provided Morris and his "disappearing bag" (*Morris' Disappearing Bag*).

No matter where they fit in a family, children are sometimes just not ready, so Edward was created to comfort children who need a bit more time (*Edward in Deep Water, Edward Unready for School, Edward's Overwhelming Overnight*). And then there are Max and Ruby; Max knows exactly what he wants, but so does his older sister, Ruby. *Max's Dragon Shirt, Bunny Cakes,* and the delightful *Bunny Money,* in which Wells uses the endpapers of the book to show us who she thinks ought to be on our money, are just a few examples of Wells's mastery of droll humor derived from sibling situations. Wells also knows that board books do not have to be boring, so she uses them as a hilarious stage for Max and Ruby in *Max's Bath, Max's Bedtime, Max's Birthday,* and *Max's Ride.*

Although Wells's work frequently combines her talents as author and illustrator, she does not always illustrate her own books. Richard Igielski's illustrations for *The Small World of Binky Braverman* perfectly capture Wells's wistful writing and quirky characters. She teamed with artist Susan Jeffers in several outstanding ventures, including a retelling of Eric Knight's *Lassie Come Home; Forest of Dreams,* a poem that celebrates nature; and McDuff (*McDuff and the Baby, McDuff Comes Home, McDuff Moves In*), an irresistible dog who looks a good deal like the pets of both Jeffers and Wells. Her Depression-era tale of deferred dreams and aerial derring-do, *Wingwalker,* benefits greatly from the muted illustrations of Brian Selznick.

Wells's range is astonishing. She has stretched the picture-book format to include families touched by war in *Waiting for the Evening Star* and *The Language of Doves,* as well as provided warm and whimsical illustrations for Rodgers and Hammerstein's songs for the musical theater in *Getting to Know You.* Her books *Yoko* and *Yoko's Paper Cranes* reveal a delicacy of style in both writing and illustration that are a perfect fit for the Japanese-American subject matter.

Two of Wells's works deserve special mention: Her illustrations for Iona Opie's *My Very First Mother Goose* showcase her talents as an artist at their most endearing and perfectly match Opie's selections of rhymes; and Wells surely deserves a place in heaven for the three-book collection *Voyage to the Bunny Planet.* Through work that is poignant, humorous, and understanding, Rosemary Wells is a child's best friend. She shares children's concerns and lovingly brings them to their parents' attention.

Just a few more we can't resist mentioning: *Hazel's Amazing Mother, Fritz and the Mess Fairy,* and *Emily's First 100 Days of School.* And we know there's more wonder to come, so don't stop where this list does, by any means.

★ Nutshell Library

PICTURE BOOK BOXED SET

AUTHOR/ILLUSTRATOR: Maurice Sendak
HC: HarperCollins
THEMES: alphabet; alligators; seasons; soup; months; counting; misbehaving; mischief

Sheer perfection! Contained in one little box are four tiny hardcover books: *Chicken Soup with Rice* is a guide to the months and seasons, each one a better occasion than the last for eating that wholesome comfort food, chicken soup with rice; *Pierre* is a cautionary tale in which a boy who says only, "I don't care!" gets eaten by a lion and learns to care; *Alligators All Around* is an alphabet book; and *One Was Johnny* is a counting book of considerable mischief. Sendak's illustrations match the subject matter perfectly, and the tiny size is just right for young hands. Individual paperback editions are available of the four titles.

 "Free, free, free. Libraries are free!" I told you I was going to keep saying it! Been to the library this week?

The Old Man & His Door

PICTURE BOOK

AUTHOR: Gary Soto • ILLUSTRATOR: Joe Cepeda
HC: Putnam • PB: Paperstar
THEMES: misunderstanding; Spanish; humor; wordplay; Mexico

"La puerta. El puerco. There's no difference to el Viejo!" The door. The pig. There's no difference to the old man! Soto's tale of an old man who is very good at working in his garden but not so good at listening to his wife offers the same kind of silly situations found in Jewish tales of Chelm. Have fun with these, and learn some Spanish words while you're at it. A glossary is included.

On Market Street

PICTURE BOOK

AUTHOR: Arnold Lobel • ILLUSTRATOR: Anita Lobel
HC: Greenwillow • PB: Mulberry
THEMES: alphabet; shopping; rhyme; markets; food; imagination

Inspired by seventeenth-century French trade engravings, Lobel's fascinating paintings are of shopkeepers composed entirely of his or her wares. *A* represents *apple* and *B, books* as we journey through this marvelous alphabetical fete of artistry.

On Mother's Lap

PICTURE BOOK

AUTHOR: Ann Herbert Scott • ILLUSTRATOR: Glo Coalson
HC/PB/BB: Clarion
THEMES: new baby; jealousy; Inuit; sisters; siblings

Michael learns there is plenty of room on mother's lap for his new baby sister, his boat, dolly, puppy, reindeer blanket, and himself.

Once There Was a Bull . . . (Frog)

PICTURE BOOK

AUTHOR: Rick Walton • ILLUSTRATOR: Greg Hally
HC/PB: Gibbs Smith
THEMES: wordplay; animals; guessing; humor; connections

From the three-year-old who will get a kick out of the pictures to the second-grader who can't wait to outsmart grown-ups, this play on words—and pictures—will delight anyone who likes active participation in stories. Frog has lost his hop. He looks for it under a toad. . . . (stool), behind a dog . . . (house) and under a hedge . . . (hog). Make this into a guessing game, and prepare yourself for a surprise at each turn of a page.

One Dark Night

PICTURE BOOK

AUTHOR: Lisa Wheeler • ILLUSTRATOR: Ivan Bates
HC: Harcourt Brace
THEMES: mice; moles; bears; animals, general; fear; friendship; rhyme

"In a wee little house, in a wee little hole, lived a wee little mouse and a wee little mole." One dark night they left their cozy home and trudged through the mush-mucky swamp and the marsh-misty wood and heard *some*thing coming! Young listeners will find themselves on the edge of their seats when a grumpy, hungry bear comes along and growls, "YOU'RE LATE!" (He had been waiting for his animal friends to join him for dinner.) Here's a suspenseful read-aloud for young ones, who will be delighted by the oversize pictures, beasty growl sounds, and surprise ending to this not-too-scary tale.

One Leaf Rides the Wind

PICTURE BOOK POETRY

AUTHOR: Celeste Davidson Mannis • ILLUSTRATOR: Susan Kathleen Hartung
HC: Viking
THEMES: Japan; counting; numbers; gardens; haiku

In one simple, beautifully illustrated book you'll find objects found in a Japanese garden—one to ten, an introduction to haiku, and interesting facts about Japanese culture.

Our Granny

PICTURE BOOK

AUTHOR: Margaret Wild • ILLUSTRATOR: Julie Vivas
HC/PB: Houghton Mifflin
THEMES: grandmothers; comparisons; humor; diversity

> For a look at one wildly untraditional granny, search your library for the sadly out-of-print *My Grandma Has Black Hair* by Mary Hoffman.

Wild's words and Vivas's hilarious art add up to a very funny comparison of today's grannies, old and young, short and tall, traditional and non. No matter how she stacks up, you know your granny is the best, and the subtle encouragement to appreciate folks for who they are won't be missed.

Owl Babies

PICTURE BOOK

AUTHOR: Martin Waddell • ILLUSTRATOR: Patrick Benson
HC/BB: Candlewick
THEMES: owls; mothers; animal babies; fear of separation

"What's all the fuss?" Owl Mother asked. "You knew I'd come back." These comforting words are just what owl babies need. And this reassuring story is the perfect antidote for youngsters who worry when their parents leave.

Ox-Cart Man

PICTURE BOOK

AUTHOR: Donald Hall • ILLUSTRATOR: Barbara Cooney
HC: Viking • PB: Puffin
THEMES: oxen; jobs; U.S.A., New England; U.S. history, 19th century;
    seasons; markets; family

A family makes mittens, a shawl, birch brooms, candles, and shingles. They gather goose feathers, honey, and wool. One working-together family creates enough to sell at Portsmouth Market to buy what they need to begin the cycle again. Look back at life in nineteenth-century New England with a simple turn of each beautifully illustrated page.

Pete's a Pizza

PICTURE BOOK

AUTHOR/ILLUSTRATOR: William Steig
HC/PB: Harper
THEMES: playing; fathers and sons; pizza; imagination; bad days

A winning story of a father who joshes his son out of a bad mood by pretending to make him into a pizza, with checkers for the pepperoni and talcum powder for the flour. Funny, warm, and inventive, this imaginative romp will captivate children and adults alike.

 Oh, how I wish someone had made me into a pizza when I was a kid!

 This story, with the parents looking like grandparents from the fifties, shows such warmth and humor you just feel good reading it.

Peter's Chair   PICTURE BOOK
AUTHOR/ILLUSTRATOR: Ezra Jack Keats
PB: HarperCollins
THEMES: siblings; new baby; brothers; sisters;
    jealousy; African American

> For another book on the same topic, but with a girl protagonist, see *Julius, the Baby of the World.*

Life isn't easy for Peter with that new baby sister, but he comes around. Keats's collages combine with a common theme to keep this classic popular.

The Philharmonic Gets Dressed   PICTURE BOOK
AUTHOR: Karla Kuskin • ILLUSTRATOR: Marc Simont
PB: HarperCollins
THEMES: orchestras; music; dressing; diversity; cities;
    musical instruments; readiness

> A first concert, like many new experiences, may require some preparation for young listeners. We are big fans of reading a story or two to a child before a major event, and *The Philharmonic Gets Dressed* fits the bill nicely. For more preconcert reads, look for Leah Komaiko's *I Like the Music* and Ann Hayes's *Meet the Orchestra.*

They clean themselves, put on their clothes, and travel to the concert, all 105 members of the orchestra. How Kuskin thought to find fascination in the different ways people get ready, we don't know, but it's there. It's fun, and it allows a child a glimpse into what goes on behind the scenes.

A Pillow for My Mom   PICTURE BOOK
AUTHOR: Charissa Sgouros • ILLUSTRATOR: Christine Ross
HC: Houghton Mifflin
THEMES: illness; worry; mothers and daughters

A useful book for dealing with grief and illness that gets into the feelings of a small child, concerned about her mother's serious illness. The focus is not on the illness itself, but rather on allowing the child to come to terms with things out of her control by feeling useful.

The Piñata Maker/El Piñatero
PICTURE BOOK NONFICTION

AUTHOR/ILLUSTRATOR: George Ancona (photographs)
HC/PB: Harcourt Brace
THEMES: Mexico; piñatas; celebrations; bilingual

Here's a bilingual, photographic glimpse of life in a Mexican village. From the initial gathering of paper to the final breaking at the end, we're given a complete tour of the art of making a piñata.

Possum Magic
PICTURE BOOK

AUTHOR: Mem Fox • ILLUSTRATOR: Julie Vivas
HC: Gulliver • PB: Voyager
THEMES: magic; Australia; grandmothers; food; snakes; opossum

Mem Fox takes some of her own storytelling magic and gives it to Hush's grandmother, who could make "wombats blue and kooka burras pink. She made dingoes smile and emus shrink. But the best magic of all was the magic that made Hush invisible." But when Grandma Poss forgets the magic that makes her visible again, she and Hush set out across Australia to find the needed blending of food. Magic, new foods, and a glossary of Australian words are just the right mix.

Pretend You're a Cat
PICTURE BOOK

AUTHOR: Jean Marzollo • ILLUSTRATOR: Jerry Pinkney
PB: Puffin
THEMES: rhyme; pretending; acting; animals

"Can you climb? Can you leap? Can you stretch? Can you sleep? Can you hiss? Can you scat? Can you purr like a cat?" What else can you do? Snort. Run. Dig. Leap. Make room, this picture book will get your youngster moving.

> "Why read to very little ones? Because it's more fun than anything else . . . and relaxing too."
> —Don Wood, *illustrator of* Heckedy Peg *and* King Bidgood's in the Bathtub

Quick as a Cricket
PICTURE BOOK

AUTHOR: Audrey Wood • ILLUSTRATOR: Don Wood
HC/PB/BB: Child's Play Ltd.
THEMES: comparisons; self-respect; wordplay; parts of speech

"I'm as tough as a rhino, I'm as gentle as a lamb. I'm as brave as a tiger, I'm as shy as a shrimp . . ." A celebration of "all I can be," this cheery, colorful collection of comparisons continues to be a hit.

The Quilt Story
PICTURE BOOK

AUTHOR: Tony Johnston • ILLUSTRATOR: Tomie dePaola
HC: Putnam • PB: Paperstar
THEMES: quilts; moving; art; pioneers; mothers and daughters; crafts

A pioneer mother stitched a quilt to keep her daughter warm. Many years later, a young girl discovers the quilt and makes it her own. DePaola's folk-art style and Johnston's warm telling make this a cozy, wrap-up-in-a-quilt-and-listen story.

The Rainbabies
PICTURE BOOK

AUTHOR: Laura Krauss Melmed • ILLUSTRATOR: Jim LaMarche
HC: Lothrop
THEMES: parents; magic; moon; wishes; adoption; little folk

Kids love the idea of having tiny people of their own to play with. Rainbabies offers up a whole handful, twelve to be exact. This fantasy with its touch of moon magic shows that loyal, loving caretakers can have their own dreams come true. If you see the cover of this book you will be compelled by the luminous art to open it!

 Not me! I thought books like this were creepy when I was a kid. Don't even get me started on *Stuart Little*!

 How about Jim LaMarche's <u>The Elves and the Shoemaker</u>? *His classic version is not only stunning, but the characters are so sweet that I can't imagine anyone being afraid of them. After all, in the end, goodness is rewarded and everyone lives happily ever after!*

Trickster tales are wonderful to hear, and McDermott has retold several of them in his books. His *Coyote* is from the American Southwest, and his *Jabuti the Tortoise* is from the South American rain forest. All feature his distinctive story-telling voice and vibrant artwork.

Raven: A Trickster Tale from the Pacific Northwest
PICTURE BOOK

AUTHOR/ILLUSTRATOR: Gerald McDermott
HC/PB: Harcourt Brace
THEMES: ravens; birds; Native American; trickster tales; sun; U.S.A., the Pacific Northwest

Raven feels sorry for those who have to live in a dark world, and when he discovers it's the Sky Chief who has hoarded all the light, he moves into action.

McDermott's award-winning illustrations—brilliant colors with bold graphic characters—prove that some of our finest art is found on the pages of children's books.

Richard Scarry's Best Word Book Ever

AUTHOR/ILLUSTRATOR: Richard Scarry
HC: Golden
THEMES: words; vocabulary

REFERENCE

You have seen Richard Scarry's books everywhere from bookstores to supermarkets to gas station gift shops. His popularity comes from his ability to combine detail with cute in a way that kids love and parents can stand. His busy picture books are ideal for the ages of two to five, and this word book is one of our favorites. Of the seemingly millions of his other titles, the others we strongly admire are *Richard Scarry's Busy Town* (towns; cities; home; jobs; community), *Richard Scarry's Cars and Trucks and Things That Go* (cars; trucks; airplanes; trains; buses; transportation; motorcycles), and *Richard Scarry's What Do People Do All Day* (jobs; careers).

The Runaway Bunny

PICTURE BOOK

AUTHOR: Margaret Wise Brown • ILLUSTRATOR: Clement Hurd
HC/PB/PB: HARPERCOLLINS
THEMES: mothers and sons; love; patience; faith; imagination; connections;
     comfort; running away

Children can't help but be comforted by this mother, steadfast in showing her son that she will be there for him, regardless of how far his imagination takes him. First published in 1942; generations of readers have been reassured by its loving message.

The Salamander Room

PICTURE BOOK

AUTHOR: Anne Mazer • ILLUSTRATOR: Steve Johnson
HC: Knopf • PB: Dragonfly
THEMES: salamanders; pets; nature; environment; gentle boy

Kids want to take in critters, which might be all right for the child but not so good for the critter. This is the book to help explain to a child that every living thing has its proper place. Told in a gentle, cumulative style, the message of the story is accompanied by astounding art that brings you right inside the book.

Scared Silly

PICTURE BOOK

AUTHOR/ILLUSTRATOR: Marc Brown

HC/PB: Little Brown

THEMES: humor; monsters; courage

It may be "a book for the brave," but with Brown's silly illustrations it's clear that the theme in this collection of poems and stories is not to frighten children but to help them replace fear with humor.

Seven Blind Mice

PICTURE BOOK

AUTHOR/ILLUSTRATOR: Ed Young

HC: Philomel • PB: Paperstar

THEMES: India; elephants; folklore; blindness; rhyme; mice; color; senses;
point of view

"Knowing in part may make a fine tale, but wisdom comes from seeing the whole." Ed Young's moral comes at the end of his version of the old story "The Blind Men and the Elephant." Each extraordinary page again shows that some of our country's most striking art is found in picture books.

Sheep in a Jeep

PICTURE BOOK

AUTHOR: Nancy Shaw • ILLUSTRATOR: Margot Apple

HC/PB: Houghton Mifflin

THEMES: Jeeps; rhyme; mishaps; sheep

Other adventures include *Sheep in a Shop*, *Sheep on a Ship*, *Sheep Out to Eat*, *Sheep Take a Hike*, and *Sheep Trick or Treat*.

An irresistible series of picture books featuring a hapless group of sheep, all told in a few carefully chosen rhyming words. Not only side-splittingly funny but a great example of how to get the most story out of the fewest words, especially if there's a clever illustrator like Margot Apple to assist.

"Slowly, Slowly, Slowly," said the Sloth

PICTURE BOOK

AUTHOR/ILLUSTRATOR: Eric Carle

HC: Philomel

THEMES: time; sloths; jungles; animals; Amazon; rain forest

Why are we always in a hurry? Rush. Rush. Rush. We scurry from here to there. We play computer games and then—quick! Click!—we watch TV. We eat fast food . . . Eric Carle's solution? This book. He hopes we can learn a little from the gentle sloth who moves slowly, slowly, slowly. Take the time to read this . . . slowly. You and your youngster will enjoy it.

 This book reminds me of watching Mr. Rogers slowly, slowly, slowly removing each button on his sweater. It wasn't until I had toddlers that I appreciated him and got the importance of taking time, putting on shoes, unbuttoning sweaters. Eric Carle does that here, except he adds his spectacular art.

Snow
PICTURE BOOK

AUTHOR/ILLUSTRATOR: Uri Shulevitz
HC: Farrar, Straus & Giroux
THEMES: snow; change; faith; patience

A lovely presentation in a simple, poetic style of one boy's faith in the power of snow to transform the world. Shulevitz's art received a well-deserved Caldecott Honor for this book.

The Snowy Day
PICTURE BOOK

AUTHOR/ILLUSTRATOR: Ezra Jack Keats
HC/BB: Viking • PB: Puffin
THEMES: snow; African American; weather; playing; city life; solitude

Keats's bold, Caldecott Medal–winning art shows a young boy enveloped in the quiet magic of the first snowfall. The fact that the child is African American was groundbreaking in 1963, but the story has lost none of its power to portray the possibilities snow offers a child's imagination.

 This was one of my favorites as a very young child. I responded to the urban landscapes and the look of the whiteness covering the familiar streets and pavement of my childhood, far different from the depiction of country snowfall that was so prevalent at the time.

Somebody Loves You, Mr. Hatch
PICTURE BOOK

AUTHOR: Eileen Spinelli • ILLUSTRATOR: Paul Yalowitz
HC: Simon & Schuster • PB: Alladin
THEMES: friendship; love; mail carrier; mail; self-respect; Valentine's Day;
    celebrations; neighbors; community; change

"Mr. Hatch was tall and thin and he did not smile." That is, until he got an anonymous valentine with a message that read "Somebody loves you." It's amazing how a person changes when he feels loved. It can change the whole neighborhood, which is exactly what happens in this story. A warm valentine for the entire year.

Picture Book Collections for Children: Several Books in One Volume

We like the fact that books can be put together as a value to the consumer. It allows readers access to books and characters they might not discover. But collections are not the same as holding a single favorite story in your hands. When an individual story becomes a child's favorite, help her to find her own copy of it in the library or bookstore.

There appears to be an endless number of children's collections popping up each season. How does one work better than another? Here are some things we consider:

The power of a picture book lies in turning the page when the text and pictures work in harmony to create anticipation in young readers. Look for collections that avoid condensing illustrations or putting several on a single page to preserve space.

Collections often include only part of the original story, or a condensed version, leading youngsters to believe they've read the whole book when they have not. Look for unabridged collections. However, when a selection catches your child's interest, we suggest you find it in its original form for him to enjoy.

Right off the bat I'll admit that I worked on _The HarperCollins Treasury of Picture Book Classics,_ but I would have been as enthusiastic about it even if I had not been involved. I think it is an excellent example of how a good collection can work. (Okay, it weighs five pounds, but it is designed for parents' laps.) Featuring twelve complete stories (_Goodnight Moon, Harold and the Purple Crayon, William's Doll, Pete's a Pizza, If You Give a Mouse a Cookie, Caps for Sale, From Head to Toe, Baby Says, Leo the Late Bloomer, George Shrinks, Crictor,_ and _A Baby Sister for Frances_), reproduced in their original size and print method, it has kept the integrity of each story's rhythm and author's intent — to keep the reader anticipating, guessing, and imagining — and it satisfies our above-mentioned considerations. It's diverse in selection and style and the stories are classics, as children have requested them for generations.

Here are others we recommend.

Big Bear's Treasury: A Children's Anthology
The Complete Adventures of Curious George
Corduroy & Company: A Don Freeman Treasury
A Family Treasury of Little Golden Books: 46 Best-Loved Stories
Garth Williams Treasury of Best-Loved Golden Books
George and Martha: The Complete Stories of Two Best Friends
James Herriot's Treasury for Children
Keats's Neighborhood: An Ezra Jack Keats Treasury
Mad About Madeline: The Complete Tales by Ludwig Bemelmans
Mike Mulligan and More: A Virginia Lee Burton Treasury
Ready, Set, Read—And Laugh!: A Funny Treasury for Beginning Readers
The 20th-Century Children's Book Treasury: Picture Books and Stories to Read Aloud

Splash!

AUTHOR/ILLUSTRATOR: Ann Jonas
HC: Greenwillow • PB: Mulberry
THEMES: math; concepts; ponds; animals; comparisons

Bright colors dazzle the young reader, who soon finds out that keeping track of the critters hopping in and out of the pond is the trick.

Stone Soup

PICTURE BOOK

AUTHOR/ILLUSTRATOR: Marcia Brown
PB: Aladdin
THEMES: soldiers; trickster tales; soup; food; hunger; change; cleverness; fear
    of strangers; community

"Such men don't grow on every bush" is the moral in this classic tale. Three tired, hungry soldiers arrive in a village seeking food and a place to sleep. The villagers claim they have neither, for they fear strangers. But the clever soldiers create a feast for all from stones and a few offerings from the folks in the village. This is great fun for children who like "getting it" when the characters in the story don't.

The Story About Ping

PICTURE BOOK

AUTHOR: Marjorie Flack • ILLUSTRATOR: Kurt Wiese
HC: Viking • PB: Puffin
THEMES: ducks; adventure; family; rivers; boats; danger; China; independence

Ping does not want to get the spank always given the last duck to board Master's boat. So he hides, and far from the safety of his family his adventures begin. First published in 1933, and set against the background of China's Yangtze River, this tale of a duckling that thinks for himself is also a reminder not to stray too far away from the security of family.

The Story of Ferdinand

PICTURE BOOK

AUTHOR: Munro Leaf • ILLUSTRATOR: Robert Lawson
HC: Viking • PB: Puffin
THEMES: bulls; peace; individuality; gentle boys; bullies; teasing

Ferdinand, whose story was first published in 1936, is known worldwide as the bull who would just as soon smell the flowers as fight. This is not just for bullies and children on the receiving end, it's also for any child who chooses to be different.

A String of Beads

PICTURE BOOK

AUTHOR: Margarette S. Reid • ILLUSTRATOR: Ashley Wolff
HC: Dutton
THEMES: beads; cultural diversity; diversity; vocabulary; math; Native
   American; concepts; comparisons; vegetables; minerals; jewelry;
   crafts

Grandma agrees that it's the hole that makes a bead a bead. But it's not just beads that makes this book worthwhile. Comparing sizes, shapes, textures, colors, and a touch of history, a young girl and her grandmother explore beads and where they come from. It would be great fun to make beads from Wolff's dazzling art, but we suggest you simply follow instructions at the back for making some of your own.

Suddenly!

PICTURE BOOK

AUTHOR/ILLUSTRATOR: Colin McNaughton
HC: Harcourt Brace
THEMES: wolves; pigs; chases; humor; surprises

Preston the pig is completely unaware that a toothy, mean-looking wolf is stalking him. But each time the wolf starts to pounce, Preston changes direction—outsmarting him. Children can't help laughing in relief as danger lurks at the turn of every page. A close look at the pictures is required, so limit your reading aloud to smallish groups.

★ Sylvester and the Magic Pebble

PICTURE BOOK

AUTHOR/ILLUSTRATOR: William Steig
HC: Simon & Schuster • PB: Aladdin
THEMES: magic; wishes; fear; rocks; problem solving; family; change;
   loneliness

It's one thing when you've been frightened by a lion to find a magic pebble and wish yourself into a rock. It's another thing altogether to have to figure out how to get hold of that much needed magic pebble when you're stuck as a rock. This isn't simply a lesson in planning ahead, it's a much loved tale perfect for reading aloud.

Tacky the Penguin

PICTURE BOOK

AUTHOR: Helen Lester • ILLUSTRATOR: Lynn Munsinger
HC/PB: Houghton Mifflin
THEMES: individuality; penguins; community; friendship; triumph

"Tacky was/wasn't an odd bird." His companions were graceful, he wasn't. But when hunters come around looking for pretty penguins, it is Tacky's individuality that saves the day. Choose this tale for the child (or adult) who moves to the beat of his own drum: There are sequels, including *Three Cheers for Tacky*, that are also great fun.

The Tale of Peter Rabbit

PICTURE BOOK

AUTHOR/ILLUSTRATOR: Beatrix Potter
HC/PB: Warner
THEMES: rabbits; vegetables; farmers; farms; family; disobeying; consequences; adventure

> Along with *The Tale of Peter Rabbit*, the following make up the first ten of the original twenty-three Peter Rabbit Books: *The Tale of Squirrel Nutkin*, *The Tailor of Gloucester*, *The Tale of Benjamin Bunny*, *The Tale of Two Bad Mice*, *The Tale of Mrs. Tiggy-Winkle*, *The Tale of Tom Kitten*, *The Tale of Mr. Jeremy Fisher*, *The Tale of Jemima Puddle-Duck*, and *The Tale of the Flopsy Bunnies*.

The story of Peter Rabbit and his close escape from Mr. McGregor was first published in 1902. Poor Peter is a curious, naughty little rabbit who does not follow his mother's instructions. That can lead to real trouble, which Peter soon discovers. Children love Peter and his escapades, along with the other delightful creatures (rodents, felines, waterfowl, and more) created by Potter.

Tell Me Again About the Night I Was Born

PICTURE BOOK

AUTHOR: Jamie Lee Curtis • ILLUSTRATOR: Laura Cornell
HC/PB: HarperCollins
THEMES: babies; adoption; birth; family; love; humor

A young girl asks her mother and father to retell the tale of her birth night. "Tell me again how the phone rang in the middle of the night and they told you I was born. Tell me again how you screamed." Not just for adopted children, this love story will please any youngster, who will ask then about the day he was born. Curtis and Cornell are an apt match of sweetness and humor.

The Tenth Good Thing About Barney

PICTURE BOOK

AUTHOR: Judith Viorst • ILLUSTRATOR: Erik Blegvad
HC: Atheneum • PB: Aladdin
THEMES: death; cats; loss; pets; grief

A child whose cat has just died wonders about death. This sensitive story from a child's perspective confronts the questions and feelings of loss that come with the death of a loved one.

There's a Nightmare in My Closet

PICTURE BOOK

AUTHOR/ILLUSTRATOR: Mercer Mayer
HC: Dial • PB: Puffin
THEMES: fear of monsters; nightmares; monsters; self-respect; fear of the
dark; problem solving

If children begin to see monsters in their closets and require lights on at night, bring out this gem in the light of day. Monsters are in the closet, but they are terrified—just like the boy who takes things into his own hands and finally gets some sleep.

This Is the Rain

PICTURE BOOK NONFICTION

AUTHOR: Lola M. Schaefer • ILLUSTRATOR: Jane Wattenberg
HC: Greenwillow
THEMES: water; rain; cumulative; clouds; rhyme

Wattenberg's illustrations from photographs and original art create a brilliant collage of the journey of water from clouds to creeks and rivers, and finally to the sea. Schaefer's cumulative rhyme, "This is the ocean, blue and vast, that holds the rainwater from the past . . ." will be fun to memorize. The scientific content is a bonus.

Through Moon and Stars and Night Skies

PICTURE BOOK

AUTHOR: Ann Turner • ILLUSTRATOR: James Graham Hale
HC/PB: HarperCollins
THEMES: adoption; Asia; love; travel; airplanes; memory; cultural diversity

A young boy remembers his flight across the world to his new family in America. This tender tale will pull the heartstrings of adults who have adopted and offer loving reassurance to youngsters who are learning about adoption.

Tight Times

PICTURE BOOK

AUTHOR: Barbara Shook Hazen • ILLUSTRATOR: Trina Schart Hyman
HC: Viking • PB: Puffin
THEMES: family; jobs; city life; cats; hardship; pets; change; choices

A family is going through some financial hardship—"tight times" the parents call it—and the young narrator is having trouble understanding why this will prevent them from getting a dog. Told with honesty and love, this story will resonate with many families who have experienced similar problems. Hyman's black-and-white art skillfully evokes the emotion on the characters' faces.

Time to Sleep

PICTURE BOOK

AUTHOR/ILLUSTRATOR: Denise Fleming
HC/PB: Henry Holt
THEMES: winter; animals; hibernation; bears; snails; ladybugs; skunks;
    turtles; connections; woodchucks

Things come full circle in this chain of events that starts with a sniffy bear who smells winter in the air. Off he goes to tell Snail, who must tell Skunk, who must tell Turtle. Each animal puts off sleep till the Ladybug wakes up Bear to tell him the news. Cozy, grand, colorful pictures and animal friends make a just-right bedtime story.

To & Fro, Fast & Slow

PICTURE BOOK

AUTHOR/ILLUSTRATOR: Durga Bernhard
HC: Walker
THEMES: divorce; change; comparisons; concepts

The role of place and time are explored in this look at a young girl's routine as she splits her life between the two different homes she shares with her divorced parents. The text is very simple, using only opposites, but the outstanding art and design show the differences between life with Dad and life with Mom. An excellent book for children of divorce.

To Market, to Market

PICTURE BOOK

AUTHOR: Anne Miranda • ILLUSTRATOR: Janet Stevens
HC/PB: Harcourt Brace
THEMES: rhyme; humor; animals; vegetables; shopping; food; soup

Vegetarians one and all, here's a book full of laughs for you. Starting with the rhyme "To market, to market, to buy a fat pig," the narrator tries over and over to bring animals home from the store—the pig, a hen, goose, trout, lamb, cow, duck, and a goat. But this unruly bunch interferes with the cooking of lunch until there is a change in the menu. Stevens's black-and-white photos combined with brilliant, zany paintings will make you howl, especially if you know legendary storyteller Coleen Salley, whose image shines throughout.

Miz Salley takes the reins herself and retells the old story of Epamimondas in her collaboration with Janet Stevens, *Epossumondas*, and the delights are many. Stevens wisely chooses to again use her incomparable depiction of Coleen, this time as the mother of the tale's imprudent possum protagonist, and the running refrain "You ain't got the brains you were born with" will have audiences giggling and joining the fun.

Tough Boris

PICTURE BOOK

AUTHOR: Mem Fox • ILLUSTRATOR: Kathryn Brown
HC/PB: Harcourt Brace
THEMES: pirates; death; loss; grief

Tough Boris has the elements of Fox's other successes: language best read aloud, suspense, invitations for child participation, and a lesson. Boris Von der Borch is a tough pirate, but even tough guys cry when they lose someone they love.

A Tree Is Nice

PICTURE BOOK

AUTHOR: Janice May Udry • ILLUSTRATOR: Marc Simont
HC/PB: HarperCollins
THEMES: trees; nature

"Trees are very nice. They fill up the sky. They go beside the river and down the valleys. They live up on the hills." Udry lists the reasons trees are so nice, and children will want to come up with a few of their own.

Tree of Cranes

PICTURE BOOK

AUTHOR/ILLUSTRATOR: Allen Say
HC/PB: Houghton Mifflin
THEMES: Japan; Christmas; mothers and sons; cultural diversity; traditions; origami

The spirit of Christmas comes through in this tender story of a young Japanese boy whose mother tells him how she celebrated Christmas in America. "You give and receive, child. It is a day of love and peace. Strangers smile at one another. Enemies stop fighting. We need more days like it." Poignant. Simple. Say knows how to touch a reader's heart, with affecting words and radiant art.

★ The Very Hungry Caterpillar

PICTURE BOOK

AUTHOR/ILLUSTRATOR: Eric Carle
HC/BB: Putnam
THEMES: caterpillars; cocoons; hunger; butterflies; change; concepts; eating

Here is one famous caterpillar. Millions of copies of this modern classic have been sold, and Carle's tale has been translated into over a dozen languages. It begins with a hungry caterpillar that pops out of a tiny egg. As he searches for food, young readers learn the days of the week, and numbers one to ten, and by peeking through die-cut pages they see the caterpillar's metamorphosis into a brightly colored butterfly. Carle's *The Very Busy Spider* and *The Very Quiet Cricket* are also marvels of book engineering and worth checking out.

We Are a Rainbow

AUTHOR/ILLUSTRATOR: Nancy Maria Grande Tabor
PB: Charlesbridge
THEMES: comparisons; cultural diversity; moving; friendship; prejudice; Spanish

"You say sol. I say sun. But no matter how we say it, it is the same one." Simple paper cutouts and comparisons celebrate personal similarities while showing that even with our differences we are "so much the same."

Welcoming Babies

PICTURE BOOK

AUTHOR: Margy Burns Knight • ILLUSTRATOR: Anne Sibley O'Brien
HC/PB: Tilbury House
THEMES: babies; love; songs; new baby; celebrations; cultural diversity; gifts; traditions; ritual

Every day babies are born all over the world. This salute to life and diversity shows that there are many ways to celebrate their arrivals. The text is simple and straightforward. "We Sing" tells about the women near Afam's house who sing, at the sound of his first cry, "Beautiful one, beautiful one, welcome!" An informative glossary can be found at the end of the book.

Alphabet books: Food and Flowers

Pete ate his share, but if you're hungry for more alphabet books to satisfy your appetite, try: *A is for Salad, The Accidental Zucchini, Alison's Zinnia, The Flower Alphabet Book, Eating the Alphabet, The Spice Alphabet,* and *The Victory Garden Vegetable Alphabet Book.*

What Pete Ate from A to Z

PICTURE BOOK

AUTHOR/ILLUSTRATOR: Maira Kalman
HC: Putnam
THEMES: alphabet; zany; dogs; eating

An utterly wonderful treat for Kalman lovers, but a simpler, more accessible book than many of her others. An alphabetical romp through the rampaging appetite of a mischievous and very hungry dog that "devours a myriad of items which he should not." Great fun.

When Bluebell Sang

PICTURE BOOK

AUTHOR/ILLUSTRATOR: Lisa Campbell Ernst
HC: Simon & Schuster • PB: Aladdin
THEMES: cows; farmers; farms; singing; songs; fame

When Farmer Swenson discovers how well his cow Bluebell can sing, he takes her to town for a taste of show business. It doesn't take long for crafty Big Eddie, a talent agent with dollar bills on his mind, to sign her up. Fortunately, he underestimates the clever duo, who outsmart him and end up right back home where they belong.

When I Was Little: A Four-Year-Old's Memoir of Her Youth

PICTURE BOOK

AUTHOR: Jamie Lee Curtis • ILLUSTRATOR: Laura Cornell

HC/PB: HarperCollins

THEMES: growing up; babies; memories; comparisons; childhood

"When I was little, I kissed my mom and dad good night every night. I still do, but only after they each read me a book and we play tickle torture." A spunky four-year-old compares being a baby with now. Read this to a child who's got a new baby in the house, or when you both can use a good laugh. Curtis is that rare celebrity who knows how to write stories for children, and illustrator Cornell's hilarious watercolors perfectly match her words. Be sure to check for details in everything from shoes to toothpaste tubes.

When I'm Sleepy

PICTURE BOOK

AUTHOR: Jane Howard • ILLUSTRATOR: Lynne Cherry

HC/BB: Dutton

THEMES: bedtime; animals; sleep; habitats; imagination

Guaranteed to induce pleasant drowsiness. A young girl imagines sleeping with all sorts of animals in their habitats. Cherry's art adds splendid detail that makes this a book for learning as well as for bedtime.

Where's My Teddy?

PICTURE BOOK

AUTHOR/ILLUSTRATOR: Jez Alborough

HC/PB: Candlewick

THEMES: teddy bears; bears; rhyme; fear; forests; stuffed animals

A boy named Eddie has lost his teddy and goes searching for it in the woods. A gigantic bear with a similar problem meets him face-to-face. Just scary enough to be requested repeatedly. Have fun with your voice while reading this one.

Where's Spot?

AUTHOR/ILLUSTRATOR: Eric Hill
HC: Putnam • PB: Puffin
THEMES: dogs; hiding; animals; guessing; searches

Children love to peek and hide, and Spot is the perfect pup to play with. Each page shows a dog searching for Spot, the hiding puppy. "Is he behind the door?" "No," responds a honey-slurping bear who can be seen when the door flap is opened. Fortunately, many books in this popular series are available, because your child will want to "read" Spot, again and again.

Who Is the Beast?

PICTURE BOOK

AUTHOR/ILLUSTRATOR: Keith Baker
HC/PB: Harcourt Brace
THEMES: tigers; self-respect; fear; jungle

Poor tiger. He is confused to find that he is the beast the other animals fear. Beautiful in art and message, this tender tale encourages a look at the whole picture before being quick to judge.

William's Doll

PICTURE BOOK

AUTHOR: Charlotte Zolotow • ILLUSTRATOR: William Pene Du Bois
HC/PB: HarperCollins
THEMES: gentle boys; fathers; brothers; gender roles; self-respect; toys; grandmothers and grandsons; dolls

William wants a doll to hold, to tuck in, to feed, and to kiss good night. His father gives him a basketball. He gets good at playing ball, but William still wants a doll. His father gives him an electric train. He enjoys playing with it, but William still wants a doll. His grandmother buys a doll for William and explains that now he can practice being a father. In the story the boy next door chants, "Sissy, sissy," but there is nothing "sissy" about this gentle message.

Would You Rather . . . ?

PICTURE BOOK

AUTHOR/ILLUSTRATOR: John Burningham
HC: North-South
THEMES: imagination; journeys

Not a story but a series of questions posed to the young listener: "Would you rather an elephant drank your bath water, an eagle stole your dinner, a pig tried on your clothes, or a hippo slept in your bed?" Burningham's simple, clever illustrations show the possible result of each choice the child could make. Some questions are scary, some are silly, but the child is always the one in control, doing the choosing. This valuable book can be used in a variety of situations, from long car trips to getting-to-know-each-other sessions at preschools.

The Year at Maple Hill Farm

PICTURE BOOK

AUTHOR/ILLUSTRATOR: Alice and Martin Provensen
PB: Aladdin
THEMES: farms; animals, farm; seasons; weather

The activities change from season to season in this beautifully illustrated look at farm life. When viewed along with the companion book, *Our Animal Friends at Maple Hill Farm*, children who have never seen a farm get a good look at rural life.

Listening/Interest Level: Babies to Preschool and Early Elementary (P/E)/
Reading Level: Early to Middle Elementary (E/M)

Beginning readers may be challenged by the vocabulary and the size of the print in some of these books, but good, strong early readers will be able to read them to their younger siblings.

A Is for Africa   PICTURE BOOK NONFICTION
AUTHOR/ILLUSTRATOR: Ifeoma Onyefulu (photographs)
PB: Puffin
THEMES: Africa; alphabet; family; traditions; folk art

Onyefulu uses stunning photographs taken in Nigeria to illustrate her favorite images of the Africa she knows. Each letter represents warm family ties and life in a traditional village.

The Adventures of Taxi Dog   PICTURE BOOK
AUTHORS: Debra and Sal Barracca • ILLUSTRATOR: Mark Buehner
PB: Puffin
THEMES: dogs; taxicabs; New York; rhyme; friendship

Maxi the dog and his owner, Jim, are best friends. They go everywhere and do everything together, and meet all sorts of interesting people, mostly in the streets of New York in Jim's taxi. Kids love reading about their adventures, so we are lucky that there are more of them, including *Maxi the Hero* and *Maxi the Star*.

All the Places to Love

AUTHOR: Patricia MacLachlan • ILLUSTRATOR: Mike Wimmer
HC/PB: HarperCollins
THEMES: farms; family; diversity; individuality; comparisons

Everyone in Eli's family has his or her own favorite place, as different as their personalities and ages might be. Gentle text and lovely paintings show the simple pleasures of life on a farm.

Alphabet Under Construction

PICTURE BOOK

AUTHOR/ILLUSTRATOR: Denise Fleming
HC: Henry Holt
THEMES: alphabet; mice; anticipation

> *Arches to Zigzags: An Architecture ABC* is another book for would-be builders.

Brilliant paintings created from paper pulp show a mouse working his way through the alphabet. He airbrushes the *A*, buttons the *B*, carves the *C*. . . . While preschoolers enjoy the mouse's antics, early elementary readers can anticipate what the mouse will do with each letter.

And the Dish Ran Away with the Spoon

PICTURE BOOK

AUTHORS: Janet Stevens and Susan Stevens Crummel • ILLUSTRATOR: Janet
    Stevens
HC: Harcourt Brace
THEMES: rhyme; cats; cows; dogs; maps; running away; Mother Goose

". . . and the dish ran away with the spoon." Every night when the rhyme gets read, they run away, and every night they return. But one night they don't come back, and Cat, Cow, and Dog must find them before the next reading of their rhyme. This oversize pun-filled picture book, bursting with hilarious watercolor pictures, adds characters such as Miss Muffet and the Big Bad Wolf. Children will be laughing to see such sport, unless they don't know their Mother Goose.

Angelina Ballerina

PICTURE BOOK

AUTHOR: Katherine Holabird • ILLUSTRATOR: Helen Craig
HC: Pleasant Company
THEMES: dance; ballet; school; determination; friendship; humor

Other stories in the Angelina series include *Angelina's Birthday Surprise*, *Angelina and the Princess*, and *Angelina on Stage*.

A dream-come-true story of a tutu-clad, slippered, light-as-a-feather mouse who can't seem to stop dancing. Angelina tales will delight young dancers as well as those preoccupied with music, art, sports, or hobbies.

Babushka Baba Yaga   PICTURE BOOK

AUTHOR/ILLUSTRATOR: Patricia Polacco
HC: Philomel
THEMES: witches; grandmothers; loneliness; Russia; disguises

In this telling of the legendary Baba Yaga, Babushka Baba feels lonely and disguises herself as an old woman so that she too can know the joys of being a grandmother.

★ Badger's Parting Gifts   PICTURE BOOK

AUTHOR/ILLUSTRATOR: Susan Varley
HC: Lothrop • PB: Mulberry
THEMES: death; animals; community; loss; grief; friendship; memories; gifts;
    wisdom

Mole, Frog, Fox, and Rabbit are stunned by their loss when old Badger dies. He had been their friend, helpmate, and adviser. But when they begin to remember the different things he taught them, memories ease their mourning. There are numerous books on the subject of death, but when it comes to expressing feelings of loss, this is our favorite for young children.

The Bear Snores On   PICTURE BOOK

AUTHOR: Karma Wilson • ILLUSTRATOR: Jane Chapman
HC: McElderry
THEMES: sleep; animals; bears; mice; storms; caves

". . . They nibble and they munch with a CHEW-CHOMP-CRUNCH! But the bear snores on." A cheery refrain is repeated throughout as a mouse, hare, badger, mole, wren, and raven find their way into a bear's cave to seek refuge from a storm. The bear does sleep on until the delightful end, when the others start to snooze. Chapman's cozy paintings show why these animals have picked a perfect shelter.

 Read it aloud. This story has a catchy rhythm throughout that will have your child chanting ". . . and the bear snores on." Be sure to pause so she will know it's her turn.

Bill Peet

Bill Peet has created a beloved menagerie of delightful animal characters who find themselves in all sorts of human situations. *Chester the Worldly Pig* would like to join the circus; *Cock-A-Doodle Dudley* is a rooster who thinks he causes the sun to rise every morning; *Cowardly Clyde* is a horse who wishes he were braver; *Eli* is a feeble lion who learns a lesson about friendship; *Encore for Eleanor* is about an artistic elephant who has retired from the circus and has begun a new career as the resident artist in the city zoo; and *Fly, Homer, Fly* is about a farm pigeon who learns that life in the city is not all it's made out to be.

Big Bad Bruce

PICTURE BOOK

AUTHOR/ILLUSTRATOR: Bill Peet
HC/PB: Houghton Mifflin
THEMES: bullies; lessons; fantasy; witches

Children who have been bullied love to read about Bruce, the big bad bear bully. He never picks on anyone his own size until he gets a taste of his own medicine from a small but clever witch.

Bugs

PICTURE BOOK NONFICTION

AUTHOR: Joan R. Wright • ILLUSTRATOR: Nancy Winslow Parker
HC: Greenwillow • PB: Mulberry
THEMES: science; bugs; insects; slugs; spiders; dragonflies; centipedes

Humor, plus a perfect blending of facts, equals this Bug encyclopedia. There's just enough creepy-crawly to pique attention and information to make a young child want a closer look at insects. *Frogs, Toads, Lizards, and Salamanders* offers Parker and Wright's look at the world of slimy reptiles and amphibians.

Bus-A-Saurus Bop

PICTURE BOOK

AUTHOR: Diane Z. Shore • ILLUSTRATOR: David Clark
HC: Bloomsbury
THEMES: buses; dinosaurs; rhyme; humor; monsters

"Early in the mornin' when the sun is done a-snorin', the boppin' bus-a-saurus comes a-rippen' and a-roarin'." Imagine this school bus—a green and orange monster—that gobbles up students, takes them to school, and delivers them in one huge burp to the front steps. It's fun to read aloud and a guaranteed hit with the silly set.

Cherries and Cherry Pits

PICTURE BOOK

AUTHOR/ILLUSTRATOR: Vera B. Williams
HC: Greenwillow • PB: Mulberry
THEMES: art; imagination; fruit; drawing; creativity

Also look for Williams's remarkable *A Chair for My Mother*, a Caldecott Honor book.

Bidemmi loves to draw. She also likes to tell stories. Here, she combines the two and includes delicious cherries and cherry pits in each story she makes. Williams, too, clearly likes to combine bright, cheery art with her story. Read this to a creative child and watch her imagination soar.

Click Clack Moo: Cows That Type

PICTURE BOOK

AUTHOR: Doreen Cronin • ILLUSTRATOR: Betsy Lewin
HC: Simon & Schuster
THEMES: farm animals; farms; activism; determination; writing; change

For another look at activism on the farm, see *Farmer Duck* (page 107) or go to the library in search of the wonderful *Ornery Morning*.

What happens when a bunch of cows get hold of a type-writer? They start making demands. "The barn is very cold at night. We'd like some electric blankets." When Farmer Brown refuses to give them what they want, they go on strike and bring the hens and ducks along with them. Clearly to be read aloud, this early lesson in political organizing will have teachers and students howling—and mooing and quacking.

A Cool Drink of Water

PICTURE BOOK NONFICTION

AUTHOR: Barbara Kerley • ILLUSTRATOR: Various (photographs)
HC: National Geographic Society
THEMES: water; cultural diversity; environment

Water is scooped from the river, drawn from the well, caught as it drips from the roof. It is carried in buckets, brass pots, plastic jugs, and caravan cans. Extraordinary full-page color photos show people by the sea and in deserts, rich and poor, old and young, from all over the world, with a cool drink of water. At the back you'll find a map and interesting information about the photographs. There is also a note on water conservation.

The Cozy Book

PICTURE BOOK

AUTHOR: Mary Ann Hoberman • ILLUSTRATOR: Betty Fraser
HC/PB: Harcourt Brace
THEMES: rhyme; senses; friendship; comfort

 If it's cozy, it's in this book. Cozy people, cozy beds, cozy smells, cozy sounds, and cozy rhymes that remind young children about life's comforts.

 . . . and if you say the word *cozy* one more time, I'll scream. This pushes my limit for cute and quiet. Maybe for others, but not for me!

Day of the Dead

Look for these books to further explore this fascinating holiday:

Day of the Dead: A Mexican-American Celebration by Diane Hoyt-Goldsmith, Lawrence Migdale (Illustrator)
Pablo Remembers: The Fiesta of the Days of the Dead by George Ancona
The Spirit of Tio Fernando: A Day of the Dead Story by Janice Levy, Morella Fuenmayor (Illustrator)

Day of the Dead   PICTURE BOOK

AUTHOR: Tony Johnston • ILLUSTRATOR: Jeanette Winter
HC/PB: Harcourt Brace
THEMES: Day of the Dead; Mexico; celebrations; dance; singing; memories; traditions; rituals

Black borders frame brilliantly colored scenes of a family preparing for the Day of the Dead. This under-sized book is perfect for the little hands of a child, who will learn a few Mexican words along with how family and community work together, then dance, sing, and share memories of their loved ones in celebration of this annual holiday.

Did You Hear Wind Sing Your Name?: An Oneida Song of Spring   PICTURE BOOK

AUTHOR: Sandra De Coteau Orie • ILLUSTRATOR: Christopher Canyon
HC/PB: Walker
THEMES: Native American; nature; seasons; spring

Lovely and lyrical, this is an English translation of a joyous ode to spring, sung by the Oneida people. The art is breathtaking, and it serves to show how strongly this tribe is connected to the seasons.

Dinosaurs Divorce   PICTURE BOOK

AUTHORS: Marc Brown and Laurie Krasny Brown • ILLUSTRATOR: Marc Brown
HC/PB: Little Brown
THEMES: divorce; family; emotions; change

The Browns and their family of dinosaurs take on issues of health and safety in *Dinosaurs Alive and Well!* and *Dinosaurs, Beware!*

A helpful guide to the breakup of a marriage, as seen from the point of view of a family of dinosaurs. The distancing that the dinosaurs provide offers the child reader some room to sort out his own feelings. Useful without overstepping the bounds into preachiness, this is as good a book as any to help a young child deal with one of life's biggest disappointments.

Do Not Open

AUTHOR/ILLUSTRATOR: Brinton Turkle
PB: Puffin
THEMES: strong women; monsters; courage; cleverness; storms

Miss Moody has weathered some pretty strong storms, safe in the knowledge that her sturdy house was built to last and that storms bring treasures to the beach in their aftermath. But when one of those treasures releases a horrid being capable of causing terrible things, she and her cat, Capt. Kidd, work together to defeat it in a tale that has a wonderfully satisfying ending.

Duck on a Bike

PICTURE BOOK

AUTHOR/ILLUSTRATOR: David Shannon
HC: Scholastic
THEMES: bicycles; farm animals; ducks

David Shannon makes us laugh. And this hilarious romp is no exception. Duck spies an abandoned bike near the farmyard and decides to take a ride. When the other animals see him, they each respond politely while their private thoughts range from ridicule to jealousy. Cow thinks it's the silliest thing he has ever seen, and Horse says, "You're still not as fast as me, Duck!" But when there is a variety of bikes for all, the animals change their tunes. The double page spread of each animal on a bike is worth the price of the book. Notice the details, like who is riding the ten-speed and who has the training wheels. Priceless!

The Everything Book

PICTURE BOOK

AUTHOR/ILLUSTRATOR: Denise Fleming
HC: Henry Holt
THEMES: variety; alphabet; counting; shapes; seasons

Bright paper collages are the stars in this collection of words, rhymes, ABCs, numbers, colors, seasons, and images of a child's world. Fleming has created what young children like in this delightful book for babies and toddlers.

The Eyes of Gray Wolf

PICTURE BOOK

AUTHOR: Jonathan London • ILLUSTRATOR: Jon Van Zyle
PB: Chronicle
THEMES: wolves; nature; animal, endangered

London describes the grace and dignity of wolves and Van Zyle enhances the description with spectacular art. Detailed facts and a list of organizations dedicated to preserving wolves can be found in the back of the book.

Fire Race: A Karuk Coyote Tale About How Fire Came to the People
PICTURE BOOK

AUTHOR: Jonathan London • ILLUSTRATOR: Sylvia Long
HC/PB: Chronicle
THEMES: Native American; coyotes; cooperation; wasps; fire; animals; folklore; trickster tales

Inspired by an ancient Native American legend of the Karuk people, this California tale explains how fire came to the people. Coyote, a trickster in many Native American stories, comes up with a plan that will work only with help from his friends. The focus is cooperation, and there's a bonus . . . learn how the yellowjacket got its stripes.

★ Fishing in the Air
PICTURE BOOK

AUTHOR: Sharon Creech • ILLUSTRATOR: Chris Raschka
HC: HarperCollins
THEMES: fishing; fathers and sons; imagination

"We're going on a journey," my father said. "To a secret place. We'll catch the air! We'll catch the breeze!" This isn't only a story about a father and son going fishing; it's a tale of togetherness, imagination, and the gift of time. In perfect synch, Creech and Raschka have matched their talents and created a book in which the words provide a sense of joy, the pictures cause the reader to pause for another look before turning the page, and the tenderness makes her keep this gem within distance to pick up again. Soon.

Gingerbread Baby
PICTURE BOOK

AUTHOR/ILLUSTRATOR: Jan Brett
HC: Putnam
THEMES: gingerbread; chases; teasing; folklore; snow; baking

"Catch me if you can . . ." is the familiar refrain from the mouth of this gingerbread baby, which is what jumped out of the oven when Matti was too impatient to wait till it was done. The sassy Gingerbread Baby teases his way through the snow-covered Swiss town and is the subject of the classic chase. Matti, though, has stayed home to bake a gingerbread house for baby's escape. Detailed paintings combine with colorful borders that tell their own story in this delicious tale for the younger set.

Grandmother's Nursery Rhymes/Las Nanas De Abuelita

POETRY COLLECTION

AUTHOR: Nelly Jaramillo • ILLUSTRATOR: Elivia Savadier
HC/PB: Henry Holt
THEMES: bilingual; Spanish; grandmothers; rhyme; riddles; rhythm

Sounds, rhythm, and riddles are wonderful ways to introduce language to young children. This bilingual collection works in both English and Spanish.

Hello Benny! What It's Like To Be A Baby

PICTURE BOOK

AUTHOR: Robie H. Harris • ILLUSTRATOR: Michael Emberley
HC: Simon & Schuster
THEMES: babies; siblings; growing up

Growing Up Stories is a new series that offers fascinating facts and charming tales about the first five years of life. *Hello Benny* is the first and celebrates his first year. This oversized full-color picture book is perfect to read to an older sibling or to any child who wonders about what he was like as a baby.

Here Is the Tropical Rain Forest

PICTURE BOOK NONFICTION

AUTHOR: Madeleine Dunphy • ILLUSTRATOR: Michael Rothman
HC/PB: Hyperion
THEMES: rain forest; plants; animals; environment; rain

The plants and animals of the rain forest are celebrated with a familiar rhythm. "Here is the eagle who hunts the sloth that hangs from the tree, which holds the bromeliad that shelters the frog who bathes in the rain . . ." The last page shows line drawings of rain forest animals and includes the address of the National Wildlife Federation for the child who wants to learn more about protecting the rain forests.

The House That Drac Built

PICTURE BOOK

AUTHOR: Judy Sierra • ILLUSTRATOR: Will Hillenbrand
HC/PB: Harcourt Brace
THEMES: rhyme; haunted houses; Halloween; spooky stories; cumulative story; monsters; bats; vocabulary; repetition

"This is the cat that bit the bat that lived in the house that Drac built." This is a tale with a familiar rhythm, spooky at first until the children come and set things straight for the monsters, werewolves, fiends, and more who inhabit the house that Drac built. Just what they'll want for Halloween reading.

How I Became a Pirate

PICTURE BOOK

AUTHOR: Melinda Long • ILLUSTRATOR: David Shannon
HC: Harcourt
THEMES: pirates; treasure; journeys; manners

Shiver me timbers, Braid Beard the pirate takes a wrong turn at Bora Bora and lands with his crew on North Beach where Jeremy Jacob is making sand castles. Young Jeremy is a fine digger, so he joins the pirate crew (after all, he doesn't have soccer practice until tomorrow) to help them dig a hiding place for their treasure chest. Filled with fun pirate expressions and buccaneer Shannon's action-packed art, this not-too-scary adventure is a wonderful introduction to pirates.

Hungry Hen

PICTURE BOOK

AUTHOR: Richard Waring • ILLUSTRATOR: Caroline Jayne Church
HC: HarperCollins
THEMES: chickens; foxes; patience; anticipation; humor; surprises

"There once was a very hungry little hen, and she ate and ate, and grew and grew, and the more she ate, the more she grew." Up on the hill lived a fox, who watched her grow and waited till just the right time to pounce. Few words, hilarious pictures, and anticipation at the turn of every page lead readers to a laugh-out-loud surprise ending.

I Hate English

PICTURE BOOK

AUTHOR: Ellen Levine • ILLUSTRATOR: Steve Bjorkman
HC/PB: Scholastic
THEMES: immigration; Chinese; self-respect; school; frustration; teachers;
    language, learning

Sometimes it is easier to remain silent than to chance making a fool of yourself while learning a new language. A Chinese girl refuses to speak English until a sympathetic teacher helps her out, and the result is something many newcomers to English will recognize.

I Love Saturdays y Domingos

PICTURE BOOK

AUTHOR: Alma Flor Ada • ILLUSTRATOR: Elivia Savadier
HC: Atheneum
THEMES: grandparents; Mexican Americans; Spanish language; cultural
    diversity; family

On Saturdays a young girl visits Grandpa and Grandma. They are her father's parents. She says, "Hi, Grandpa! Hi, Grandma!" She spends *los domingos* with Abuelito y Abuelita. She says to them, "Hola, Abuelito! Hola, Abuelita! This story of a girl who enjoys the similarities and differences between her English- and Spanish-speaking grandparents will ring true for the many children who grow up in bilingual families. It will also spark an interest in children who are curious about their own families and ethnic backgrounds.

Imani's Music   PICTURE BOOK
AUTHOR: Sheron Williams • ILLUSTRATOR: Jude Daly
HC: Atheneum
THEMES: music; grasshoppers; slavery; storytelling; gifts; Africa

Every so often Grandfather beckons the children to him with a knobby hand and they all come running. He tells stories of the land of Used-to-Be and begins those tales with "Used to be a time when there was no music on the planet . . ." Only a grasshopper named Imani was blessed with music. Complemented by Daly's stunning art, this is a story of Africa, the New World, a storyteller, and how a grasshopper gave the gift of music to the world.

Into the A, B, Sea   PICTURE BOOK
AUTHOR: Deborah Lee Rose • ILLUSTRATOR: Steve Jenkins
HC: Scholastic
THEMES: alphabet; sea; vocabulary; language

This visual adventure offers a glimpse into life under the sea. From anemones to zooplankton, an alphabet of sea creatures clings, stings, prances, preys, dives, and thrives. Jenkins's amazing paper collages fill each page with marine animals and plants. Rose's simple, rhyming text is followed by a glossary, which tells readers more about umbrellamouths, viperfish, and other critters they discover. The same team journeys into the sea again in *Into the Nighttime Sea*.

It's a Spoon, Not a Shovel   PICTURE BOOK
AUTHOR: Caralyn Buehner • ILLUSTRATOR: Mark Buehner
PB: Puffin
THEMES: manners; family; friendship; humor

Children laugh out loud as they choose the right answers to multiple-choice politeness quizzes that test one's consideration of others.

Jack's Garden

AUTHOR/ILLUSTRATOR: Henry Cole
HC: Greenwillow • PB: Mulberry
THEMES: gardening; flowers; bugs; insects; connections; cumulative story;
plants; gardens

"This is the garden that Jack planted. These are the seeds that fell on the soil that made up the garden that Jack planted . . ." Against the rhythm of the familiar cumulative verse, readers can watch a garden grow from seed to bloom. Cole's realistic pictures include birds, bugs, and butterflies familiar to gardeners.

Jethro Byrd Fairy Child

AUTHOR/ILLUSTRATOR: Bob Graham
HC: Candlewick
THEMES: fairies; imagination; family; siblings

Annabelle finds a boy the size of her thumb moving in the cement and weeds. "Who are you?" she asked. ". . . He hitched up his jeans, flew onto a leaf, and wiped his nose on the back of his sleeve. 'Jethro,' he said. 'Jethro Byrd . . . I'm a *Fairy Child*.'" The wonder of tiny thumb-size people living nearby never fails to intrigue youngsters. And this tale, with Graham's marvelous, oversized pictures, will not disappoint.

John Henry

AUTHOR: Julius Lester • ILLUSTRATOR: Jerry Pinkney
HC: Dial • PB: Puffin
THEMES: folklore; tall tales; storytelling; heroes; railroad; jobs; change;
determination

On the day he was born, John Henry "grew until his head and shoulders busted through the roof which was over the porch. John Henry thought that was the funniest thing in the world. He laughed so loud, the sun got scared." Lester writes for reading aloud. Jerry Pinkney's watercolors burst with John Henry's energy.

Jojo's Flying Side Kick

AUTHOR/ILLUSTRATOR: Brian Pinkney
PB: Aladdin
THEMES: African American; martial arts; strong girls; grandfathers; courage

It's surprising how much braver Jojo is after her tae kwon do class; not even the big tree in the front yard scares her anymore.

The Jolly Postman, or Other People's Letters

NOVELTY

AUTHORS: Janet and Allan Ahlberg • ILLUSTRATOR: Allan Ahlberg
HC: Little Brown
THEMES: communication; fairy tales; mail; rhyme; folktale variations; mail carrier

The Jolly Postman delivers mail to fairy-tale characters. It's great fun to imagine what Goldilocks has sent to the Three Bears, or whom the wedding announcement is from. Each envelope actually opens, and tiny, readable letters, invitations, and even junk mail are found inside.

The Jupiter Stone

PICTURE BOOK

AUTHOR/ILLUSTRATOR: Paul Owen Lewis
HC: Tricycle Press
THEMES: rocks; space; science; planets; evolution

"A small striped stone tumbled in the vastness of space . . . until it crossed the path of one planet among many . . . and joined countless other stones there." Millions of years later a boy finds it and sees that it is sent away "to tumble again in the vastness of space. Until one day . . ." Extraordinary acrylic paintings and few words tell the story of one small, striped stone and its journey through the universe. The unexpected ending is bound to promote discussion.

The King of Capri

PICTURE BOOK

AUTHOR: Jeanette Winterson • ILLUSTRATOR: Jane Ray
HC: Bloomsbury
THEMES: greed; kings and queens; wind; generosity; fairy tales; Italy; cats

When the tempest blows in across the sea there is a great reversal of fortune. It blows the wigs off the ladies-in-waiting and all the milk out of the cows, and everything that belongs to the greedy king, including his breeches and shirt, and ends up across the bay in poor Mrs. Jewel's backyard. This delightful tale offers laugh-out-loud images, a bit of magic, and a touch of romance. Read it aloud.

Kogi's Mysterious Journey

PICTURE BOOK

AUTHOR: Elizabeth Partridge • ILLUSTRATOR: Aki Sogabe
HC: Dutton
THEMES: art; artists; inspiration; nature; fish; Japan; folklore; change; point of view

Kogi—the artist—paints waterfalls, mountains, trees, and fish, but no matter how hard he tries, he can't capture the graceful beauty that inspires him. Not until he walks deep into a lake and transforms into a fish does he experience the joy of plunging down into the lake's depths, pushing through weedy forests, experiencing a freedom he had never imagined.

Here is the story of a painter who wants to know first hand the spirit of nature so he can create the art he desires. And here is a book with cut-paper art that is so stunning that there is no doubt that the artist, Sogabe, has reached that goal.

Let's Eat

PICTURE BOOK

AUTHOR: Ana Zamorano • ILLUSTRATOR: Julie Vivas
PB: Scholastic
THEMES: meals; family; new baby; manners; food

A warm book about a Spanish family and mealtime. Each evening a different member of the family misses the dinner Mama has worked hard to prepare because of something else they have to do. When Mama is the one absent, it is to deliver her new baby, who joins the entire family at the next meal. Terrific art by Julie Vivas. This book makes us hungry.

 Sorry, but more than hungry, it makes me frustrated, because when someone fixes you dinner, you don't ignore mealtime because it's inconvenient. And if you can't be there, you don't just not show up!

 Well, sure, you grew up in a family where they put tongue on the table and you had to eat it. I think you're projecting a little bit here, sort of, "If I had to stay at the table, no way am I gonna be happy about anyone else getting away!"

The Library

PICTURE BOOK

AUTHOR: Sarah Stewart • ILLUSTRATOR: David Small
HC/PB: Farrar, Straus & Giroux
THEMES: books; reading; humor; strong girls; rhyme; obsession

Is there a book nut in your life? This story in rhyme of the life of Elizabeth Brown makes a perfect gift for any reading fanatic: "Books were piled on top of chairs, And spread across the floor. Her shelves began to fall apart, As she read more and more."

 "Free, free, free. Libraries are free!" Just a reminder . . .

★ Lilly's Purple Plastic Purse

AUTHOR/ILLUSTRATOR: Kevin Henkes
HC: Greenwillow • PB: Mulberry
THEMES: school; teachers; anger; strong girls; regret; consequences;
    conscience; taking action; forgiveness

Kevin Henkes's characters usually make us laugh. Lilly makes us howl. She represents our fears, our hopes, our frustrations, and our guilt. When her favorite teacher, Mr. Slinger, takes away her purple plastic purse for the day, Lilly's stomach lurches. Then she becomes sad. And then angry. And when she's angry she takes action against Mr. Slinger. Youngsters and the adults fortunate enough to read this aloud will find themselves or someone they know in this funny, strong-willed, vulnerable character.

Listen to the Desert (Oye El Desierto)

PICTURE BOOK

AUTHOR: Pat Mora • ILLUSTRATOR: Francisco X. Mora
HC/PB: Clarion
THEMES: desert; bilingual; Spanish; animals; sound

Sounds of the desert are described in this simple poem in two languages. It invites children to participate in both Spanish and English, and offers a chance for them to pipe in with sounds of their own.

Little Old Big Beard and Big Young Little Beard: A Short and Tall Tale

PICTURE BOOK

AUTHOR: Remy Charlip • ILLUSTRATORS: Remy Charlip and Tamara
    Rettenmund
HC: Marshall Cavendish
THEMES: cowboy; cows; lost and found; humor

When Little Old Big Beard and Big Young Little Beard discover their cow, Grace, is gone, they head down and around and around their favorite hill to search for her. After all, ". . . as you know, you can't be a cowboy unless you have a cow." Fresh, fun humor makes this a fine read-aloud.

AUTHOR SPOTLIGHT ON
KEVIN HENKES

One of our most insightful observers of childhood, Kevin Henkes writes and illustrates picture books that celebrate the painful and joyful transitions of early school–age children. His charming mouse community has served to remind us just how seriously children take issues like names, blankets, little brothers, belonging to a group, and being special, in books such as *Chester's Way; Chrysanthemum; Julius, the Baby of the World; Lilly's Purple Plastic Purse*; and *Owen*. Lilly has become his superstar: A strong-willed little mouse who is not afraid to speak her mind, she has moved completely to center stage after being introduced in *Chester's Way*, and her exploits serve to remind us of the fragile feelings that lie at the heart of even the strongest of our children. Henkes's portrayal of a fretful young mouse in *Wemberly Worried* offers humorous insight into the fears of our more sensitive children.

He has added board books to his impressive repertoire, and *Owen's Marshmallow Chick* and *Sheila Rae's Peppermint Stick* stand out as welcome introductions to the youngest child of his delightful characters.

Henkes does not always illustrate his own work, sometimes collaborating instead with artists, including Nancy Tafuri (*Biggest Boy*), Marisabina Russo (*Good-Bye Curtis*), and Victoria Chess (*Once Around the Block*) on picture books that have their own delights, even if Lilly isn't in them.

He is also an accomplished novelist, and among his works for middle readers are *Sun and Spoon, Protecting Marie, The Birthday Room, Words of Stone*, and *Olive's Ocean*. They are books of grace and wonder that deal with older children's concerns and are written with his customary sensitivity, though they lack the side-splitting quality he brings to his picture books. These make excellent bridges from middle-grade fiction to young adult novels.

In his young career, Kevin Henkes has done much to remind us of how much care our children's souls require, sometimes with humor, sometimes with sadness, and always with lyrical writing and an eye for truth. We look forward to new insights he will share in works to come.

The Little Red Ant and the Great Big Crumb– A Mexican Fable

PICTURE BOOK

AUTHOR: Shirley Climo • ILLUSTRATOR: Francisco X. Mora
HC/PB: Clarion
THEMES: Mexico; ants; folklore; Spanish language; animals; self-respect

A small red ant finds a piece of cake in a Mexican cornfield. It's all she'd need to feed herself through the winter, but she doesn't feel strong enough to move it on her own. She asks other animals to help her, but has no luck until she learns, "You can do it if you think you can." Climo adds some Spanish words to the mix. A glossary is included.

Madlenka
PICTURE BOOK

AUTHOR/ILLUSTRATOR: Peter Sis
HC: Farrar, Straus & Giroux
THEMES: neighbors; community; teeth; cultural diversity; jobs; friendship

For another romp around Madlenka's block, read *Madlenka's Dog*, a salute to the imagination. Madlenka longs for a dog, but will she get one? Discover surprises in the lift-up flaps and peek-through windows.

Based on Sis's daughter, Madlenka is a delight. She has discovered her tooth is loose and wants the whole neighborhood to know. Down her stairs she runs for a trip around her multiethnic New York block, where Mr. Gaston, the French baker, as well as the Indian news vendor, the Italian ice-cream man, the Latin American grocer, and other neighbors cheer her on. Sis's art will take your breath away as you peek through die-cut windows and peer at his surprises as this city block takes you on a trip around the world.

The Magic Hat
PICTURE BOOK

AUTHOR: Mem Fox • ILLUSTRATOR: Tricia Tusa
HC: Harcourt Brace
THEMES: hats; magic; wizards; rhyme; anticipation; repetition

"Oh, the magic hat, the magic hat! It moved like this, it moved like that! It spun through the air (It's true! It's true!) And sat on the head of a . . ." "Kangaroo!" your youngster will exclaim and urge you to turn to the next page. This is a fanciful story of a wizard's hat that blows into town and changes people into different animals when it lands on their heads.

 This story begs to be turned into an acting game. Begin with a hat and a few children. Let them chant the repeated verses a few times. As you read the story aloud, place the hat on a different child's head each time a new animal appears. He will then "become" that animal, with the sounds and gyrations to match.

Mama, Do You Love Me?
PICTURE BOOK

AUTHOR: Barbara M. Joosse • ILLUSTRATOR: Barbara Lavallee
HC/BB: Chronicle
THEMES: love; mothers; Arctic; whales; wolves; puffins; comfort

A little girl asks, "Mama, do you love me?" "Yes I do, Dear One." "How much?" And Mother responds by comparing her love to the animals of the Arctic. "I'll love you until the umiak flies into the darkness, till the stars turn to fish in the sky, and the puffin howls at the moon." Beautifully illustrated, this warm, reassuring story goes perfectly with a hug during quiet time.

Margaret and Margarita   PICTURE BOOK
AUTHOR/ILLUSTRATOR: Lynn Reiser
HC: Greenwillow • PB: Mulberry
THEMES: comparisons; bilingual; Spanish language; communication

Reiser writes: "Words can be a bridge; or a barrier. In this bilingual book the adults immediately respond to differences. Their words make a barrier. The children recognize similarities." Her visuals show body language, her words, a delightful merging of languages and a great way to teach basic words, including colors.

Max   PICTURE BOOK
AUTHOR/ILLUSTRATOR: Bob Graham
HC: Candlewick
THEMES: heroes; families; readiness; teasing; flying

The son of legendary heroes Captain Lightning and Madam Thunderbolt, he too is destined to become a superhero. But unlike his parents, Max is slow in learning to fly. Prodding and teasing doesn't speed up the process. It's when flying is required to save a helpless creature that Max shows his pluck. This oversized, brightly colored picture book offers hope to other late bloomers.

Meet the Orchestra   PICTURE BOOK
AUTHOR: Ann Hayes • ILLUSTRATOR: Karmen Thompson
HC/PB: Harcourt Brace
THEMES: musical instruments; music; orchestras; musicians; animals

Animal musicians gather for their evening performance. All of their instruments have an important role in the orchestra, and young readers are introduced to each with a rollicking rhythm and lively watercolor close-ups. For a romp with a marching band, try Hayes's *Meet the Marching Smithereens.*

The Mitten   PICTURE BOOK
AUTHOR/ILLUSTRATOR: Jan Brett
HC/PB/BB: Putnam
THEMES: folklore; Ukraine; clothing; animals; lost; snow; winter

It's difficult to see a white mitten in the snow, so the boy doesn't even know it's missing. But it's soon discovered by a mole, rabbit, badger, and other animals. Pay attention to Brett's details. She often creates an entire story in her borders, and this book is no exception.

More Than Anything Else   PICTURE BOOK

AUTHOR: Marie Bradby • ILLUSTRATOR: Chris K. Soentpiet
HC/PB: Orchard
THEMES: biography; African American; reading; writing; literacy

A testament to the power of reading and the need for books in all children's lives. On the last page you find out that this is about Booker T. Washington, but you do not need to know that to enjoy the story.

Mud Pies and Other Recipes: A Cookbook for Dolls   NONFICTION

AUTHOR: Marjorie Winslow • ILLUSTRATOR: Erik Blegvad
HC/PB: Walker
THEMES: cooking; dolls; mud; fantasy; playing; recipes; tea parties

Absolutely straightforward without a hint of condescension, this book is just as the title claims—a collection of recipes for that doll tea party in the backyard.

 Remember, boys make mudpies, too! Though I didn't feed them all genteel-like to dolls. I tried to cram them down my stuffed elephant's throat. I can see uses for this book with both sexes and am putting in my plea not to leave the boys out of the fun.

My Little Sister Ate One Hare   PICTURE BOOK

AUTHOR: Bill Grossman • ILLUSTRATOR: Kevin Hawkes
HC: Crown • PB: Dragonfly
THEMES: cumulative story; hunger; counting; humor, gross; connections; repetition; eating

This is a story we knew at first glance would cause children to howl in hysterics. It does. It is absurd, silly, and repeats "We thought she'd throw up then and there" on almost every page. Try it before lunch or after school. We do not recommend it for bedtime. It is not calming.

My Mama Says There Aren't Any Zombies, Ghosts, Vampires, Creatures, Demons, Monsters, Fiends, Goblins, or Things

PICTURE BOOK

AUTHOR: Judith Viorst • ILLUSTRATOR: Kay Chorao
HC: Atheneum • PB: Aladdin
THEMES: monsters; fear of monsters; humor; imagination; mothers

Judith Viorst is very funny. Here she manages to keep up the hilarity as young Nick worries about whether his mom is right when she says that monsters do not exist. She often makes mistakes, and those monsters look mighty real. Fears of what could be lurking in the closet or behind a door are very real, too, but have fun with this one.

My Visit to the Zoo

PICTURE BOOK NONFICTION

AUTHOR/ILLUSTRATOR: Aliki
HC/PB: HarperCollins
THEMES: animals, endangered; birds; zoos; habitats; nature; geography; insects; comparisons

Based on several real zoos, Aliki's journey takes young readers through a rambling parklike enclosure designed to preserve its inhabitants. Interesting information fills each page. "You can tell where a monkey comes from by its nose." ". . . the thick-skinned rhinoceros (has been) hunted to near extinction for its long horns . . ." A map at the end shows where endangered and vulnerable animals exist in the world.

 I find zoos to be among the more depressing places on earth. Anthony Browne knows what I mean—his book *Zoo* gives the animals' point of view. Aliki addresses this issue well, making this a zoo book even for people who don't like zoos.

Old Black Fly

PICTURE BOOK

AUTHOR: Jim Aylesworth • ILLUSTRATOR: Stephen Gammell
HC/PB: Henry Holt
THEMES: alphabet; family; humor; flies

Funny enough to make you laugh at the flies during hot, buggy, summer days. When a fly pesters each member of the family in this unorthodox ABC book, Baby decides she's had enough. Ayelsworth's catchy refrain encourages kids to chant along.

Old Devil Wind

PICTURE BOOK

AUTHOR: Bill Martin Jr. • ILLUSTRATOR: Barry Root
HC: Harcourt Brace
THEMES: Halloween; cumulative story; spooky stories

Martin is a master of rhythm, and this spooky tale offers language that builds suspense and inspires exaggeration in sound and the imagination. This is just what many children want at Halloween time. Root's dark and stormy illustrations add to the fun.

Olivia

PICTURE BOOK

AUTHOR/ILLUSTRATOR: Ian Falconer
HC: Simon & Schuster
THEMES: pigs; brothers; independent; strong girl

> Other Olivia books include, *Olivia . . . and the Missing Toy* and *Olivia Saves the Circus.*

This is Olivia.
She is good at lots of things.
She is *very* good at wearing people out.

 Pay attention to Olivia. I'm certain she will be in our lives for years to come. Falconer has created a treasure: spare text, black, white, and red drawings, and spunky Olivia, a theatrical pig with a clear sense of herself.

 This isn't a children's book! It's a book with decidedly adult sensibilities masquerading as one. So what if the main character is a cute little pig? I think it's derivative of *Eloise* (which, though I love it, is soooo much more for the grown-ups than the children). And though I am certain thousands of adults just love Olivia because they know a little girl just like her, I imagine there are thousands of kids who politely endure the repeated readings without ever seeing the story with quite the enthusiasm of Mummy, Daddums, or Auntie.

★ Owen

PICTURE BOOK

AUTHOR/ILLUSTRATOR: Kevin Henkes
HC/PB: Greenwillow
THEMES: growing up; comfort; family; busybodies; problem solving;
    neighbors; readiness

Owen is not ready to give up his fuzzy yellow blanket. "Fuzzy goes where I go," says Owen. He loves it with all his heart. After all, he's had it since he was a baby. This is for the youngest schoolchild who understands the difficulties of growing up, and for the parents who could use a good laugh when faced with their side of the struggle.

Byrd Baylor

When it was time to cull titles in this edition to make room for newer books, we decided we could drop a couple of Byrd Baylor's titles. After all, we'd included a lot of them. But when we asked friends to choose their favorites, we got as many answers as we did people we asked. Her subject is nature, her words poetic, and her writing brings to the reader the soothing wonder of nature. Choose any—or all—of the following:

Amigo (illustrated by Garth Williams): Francisco is lonely and longs for a pet, a friend to keep him company in the desert. Amigo is a prairie dog who finds a boy. And this heartwarming story shows how wishes can come true.

Everybody Needs a Rock (illustrated by Peter Parnall): Here you'll find Baylor's rules on finding the perfect rock: "... if your rock is going to be special it should look good by itself in the bathtub." That's just one. A perfect book for any collector—child or adult.

Hawk, I'm Your Brother (illustrated by Peter Parnall): Rudy Soto wants to soar across the sky like a hawk, so he captures one in the hopes that their friendship will bring him closer to flying. Here you'll find the power of freedom and a young boy's lesson learned.

One Small Blue Bead (illustrated by Ronald Himler): A small blue bead hidden in the grass takes the reader back ten thousand years to those who once inhabited the desert.

I'm in Charge of Celebrations (illustrated by Peter Parnall): Byrd Baylor celebrates the extraordinary events of nature: meteors, rainbows, the quick movement of an animal.

The Other Way to Listen (illustrated by Peter Parnall): This quiet gem uses few words in a conversation between an old man and a boy who talk about the virtues of taking the time to listen.

When Clay Sings (illustrated by Tom Bahti): Baylor steps back into history through ancient pots and shards found in the deserts of America's Southwest. She tells how some pieces were made and how others were used.

The Painter

PICTURE BOOK

AUTHOR/ILLUSTRATOR: Peter Catalanotto
HC/PB: Orchard
THEMES: family; home; artists; fathers and daughters; jobs; paintings

When your office is in your home, it is frequently frustrating to loved ones that you are so near and yet so unavailable. Catalanotto's clever, touching story about a father who paints and a daughter who is inspired by him offers a solution for the increasing number of families dealing with this arrangement.

Why doesn't this guy ever get mentioned when the awards are given out? Many of his books have gone out of print, too. Folks, listen up—especially you librarians lucky enough to have his books on your shelves. Peter Catalanotto is one of the best illustrators in the business! Please look at his books and share them with everyone you can.

★ Possum Come A-Knockin'   PICTURE BOOK
AUTHOR: Nancy Van Laan • ILLUSTRATOR: George Booth
HC: Knopf • PB: Dragonfly
THEMES: opossums; humor; rhyme; rhythm; family; playing tricks

Caution! This book will skip a rap rhythm through your mind all day. Raucous and wild, it begs to be read aloud. "Brother was untanglin' all the twiny line for fishin' while Sis was tossin' Baby and Pappy was a-whittlin' and Pa was busy fixin' and Ma was busy cookin' and Granny was a-knittin' when a possum come a-knockin' at the door." Pay attention to the possum. He has an entire routine going on all by himself.

This is the book that taught me there is no "right" way to tell a story. I heard banjos picking in my head the first time I read it, and I perform it at a fast clip, but I have seen it read sing-songy slow, and it works just fine.

Promises   PICTURE BOOK
AUTHOR: Elizabeth Winthrop • ILLUSTRATOR: Betsy Lewin
HC: Clarion
THEMES: illness; mothers and daughters; hospitals; hope; promises

Sarah's mother is ill and spends much of her time in the hospital. Her treatments seem to make her sicker, and before long she loses her hair. After a time she begins to feel better. It's then that Sarah asks her to promise that she'll never get sick again. In the hopeful—and moving—end to the story, Sarah's mother tells her that she can't promise not to get sick again, but that there are other promises she can make. This gentle story with watercolor pictures is perfect for any child whose family must face serious illness.

Rain   PICTURE BOOK
AUTHOR/ILLUSTRATOR: Manya Stojic
HC: Crown
THEMES: Africa; animals; rain; storm; weather; vocabulary; drought

In this book with bold, bright images of the African savanna, animals use all their senses to track a storm. The porcupine smells rain, the zebras see lightning, and other animals hear, feel, and taste the storm. This parade of verbs, with thunder booming and rivers gushing and gurgling, invites readers to experience the effects of a wet storm on parched land.

Snow Ponies   PICTURE BOOK

AUTHOR: Cynthia Cotton • ILLUSTRATOR: Jason Cockcroft
HC: Henry Holt
THEMES: winter; snow; horses; forests; animals; change

Old Man Winter releases his snow ponies across the wide openness of the countryside, where everything they touch turns white with snow. Cockcroft's enchanting paintings in blues, grays, and brown add a chill to Cotton's otherwise warm winter tale.

Stellaluna   PICTURE BOOK

AUTHOR/ILLUSTRATOR: Janell Cannon
HC: Harcourt Brace
THEMES: courage; new experiences; bats; mothers; solitude; change; birds; adoption; comparisons; searches

Bats are not often thought of as cute or soft. Stellaluna has changed all that. Cannon tells a heartwarming story about a young bat separated from her mother. Her art makes you pick up the book, and the feeling shown in the face of its bat heroine causes you to read it through. Each page will delight you. If you'd like to see a similarly sweet snake, look for Cannon's *Verdi*.

Swamp Angel   PICTURE BOOK

AUTHOR: Anne Isaacs • ILLUSTRATOR: Paul O. Zelinsky
HC: Dutton • PB: Puffin
THEMES: tall tales; strong women; bears; folklore

Feisty Angelica Longrider could hold her own against any varmint, including Thundering Tarnation, the "low down pile of pelts" bear that was making everybody miserable. Read this original tall tale aloud, and be sure to share the incredible pictures. Caldecott honor artist Zelinsky's oil-on-wood paintings offer up a fun folk-art view of the tall-tale characters in the Tennessee wilderness.

The Tale of Rabbit and Coyote

PICTURE BOOK

AUTHOR: Tony Johnston • ILLUSTRATOR: Tomie dePaola
HC: Putnam • PB: Paperstar
THEMES: trickster tale; folklore; Mexico; Spanish words; coyotes; rabbits

Johnston and dePaola look to the folklore of Oaxaca, Mexico, for this trickster tale. Rabbit outsmarts coyote and readers discover why coyotes howl at the moon. A glossary of Spanish expressions is included.

That's Mine, Horace

PICTURE BOOK

AUTHOR/ILLUSTRATOR: Holly Keller
HC: Greenwillow
THEMES: theft; worry; choices; problem solving

Horace knows that the toy truck he finds on the playground belongs to his classmate, but he keeps it anyway. The next day he is too "sick" to go to school. This topic is not often found in picture books; use it to discuss how it feels to make a bad choice and what can be done about it.

Throw Your Tooth on the Roof

PICTURE BOOK NONFICTION

AUTHOR: Selby B. Beeler • ILLUSTRATOR: G. Brian Karas
HC/PB: Houghton Mifflin
THEMES: teeth; folklore; traditions; superstitions; cultural diversity

For a rollicking true story about teeth falling out, read *George Washington's Teeth* by Deborah Chandra and Madeleine Comora. It will leave you in stitches.

Tooth lore and customs from all over the world are presented in a visually appealing style. Perfect to have on hand when teeth fall out.

Tiger, Tiger

PICTURE BOOK

AUTHOR: Dee Lillegard • ILLUSTRATOR: Susan Guevara
HC: Putnam
THEMES: jungle, imagination, tigers, independence, courage

Books like *Tiger, Tiger*; *Where the Wild Things Are* (pg 31); the sadly out-of-print *Delphine* (pg 430); and *Castle Builder* (pg 429) offer terrific portrayals of children using solo play and their imagination to master their fears.

Pocu, a young boy living on the edge of the jungle, finds a feather and uses it in a game that tests the limits of his imagination and courage. What does anyone living near a jungle fear most? A tiger. And Pocu creates one that threatens to get out of his control. This is a satisfying look at a child's solo play and the games we often use to test our own fears.

Tom Finger
PICTURE BOOK

AUTHOR: Gillian McClure
HC: Bloomsbury
THEMES: hope; faith; witches; fairies; magic; cats; siblings

"There was once a little girl called Queenie who had a dear tabby cat. One winter Queenie's tabby cat died of old age. Every day Queenie called her tabby; sadly she called her dear old tabby. But Queenie's brother Ben said, 'Stop calling your tabby, he won't come back!'"

In the language of an ancient fairy tale, this is the story of a child who's longing for her cat and summons up the appearance of another Tabby: young, tall, blue-eyed Tom Finger. Queenie, in contrast to her suspicious brother, holds on to hope and curiosity and in the end is rewarded.

When I read the first lines of this story I was entranced. It reminded me of old stories read to me when I was a child. The ending, though, left me uncertain about who summons Tom Finger and Queenie. Here is a chance to ask what your youngster thinks. There isn't necessarily a right answer in a magical tale, nor, in my opinion, does there need to be.

Town Mouse, Country Mouse
PICTURE BOOK

AUTHOR/ILLUSTRATOR: Jan Brett
HC/PB: Putnam
THEMES: individuality; home; mice; cats; owls; diversity; lessons; city life;
    country life; comparisons

Brett's rendition of this classic tale includes two mice couples that agree to swap homes and a cat and owl that stalk them. Lush country scenes and an elegant Victorian town house are the backdrops of an adventure that reminds us things are not always greener on the other side.

When Winter Comes
PICTURE BOOK

AUTHOR: Nancy Van Laan • ILLUSTRATOR: Susan Gaber
HC: Atheneum
THEMES: winter; snow; wind; rhyme; animals

". . . when winter comes and the cold winds blow," what happens to flowers, field mice, caterpillars, and other living things? Van Laan's rhyming text offers the answers while Gaber's luminous paintings show the thrill of the first snow and the chill as it whitens the ground by the end of the day.

Why Mosquitoes Buzz in People's Ears

PICTURE BOOK

AUTHOR: Verna Aardema • ILLUSTRATORS: Leo and Diane Dillon
HC: Dial • PB: Puffin
THEMES: Africa; mosquitoes; folklore; sound

Why do mosquitoes buzz in people's ears? You'll get the answer here, along with award-winning graphics, a menagerie of tattletales, and a story teeming with personalities and sound effects to match.

★ The World of Christopher Robin: The Complete When We Were Very Young and Now We Are Six

POETRY COLLECTION

AUTHOR: A. A. Milne • ILLUSTRATOR: Ernest H. Shepard
HC: Dutton
THEMES: rhyme; family; friendship; fantasy; animals

 If you were to make me choose one can't-do-without title, one book that can be read again and again and be worth its weight in gold, this is the one. I read it for myself. I read it for my children. When I cautioned them against straying too far from the house they repeated James James Morrison Morrison Weatherby George Dupree's verse, "You must never go down to the end of the town, if you don't go down with me." We loved Jonathan Jo who had ". . . a mouth like an 'O' And a wheelbarrow full of surprises." When they caught cold, we'd wonder along with Christopher Robin ". . . If wheezles could turn into measles, if sneezles would turn into mumps . . ." and we'd laugh at the prospect of visiting the zoo where ". . . There are biffalo-buffalo-bisons, and a great big bear with wings." It's all here. And how can you get your small child interested in a novel-size book with small black-and-white illustrations and mostly words? Easy. Start her young. Share your delight in the words. Memorize your favorites. The complete texts of <u>When We Were Very Young</u> and <u>Now We Are Six</u> are found in this remarkable volume. You can also find them separately.

The World of Pooh: The Complete Winnie the Pooh and The House at Pooh Corner

COLLECTION

AUTHOR: A. A. Milne • ILLUSTRATOR: Ernest H. Shepard
HC: Dutton
THEMES: bears; honey; bees; animals; childhood; imagination; friendship; community; kangaroos; stuffed animals

"Here is Edward Bear, coming downstairs now, bump, bump, bump, on the back of his head, behind Christopher Robin. It is, as far as he knows, the only way of coming downstairs, but sometimes he feels that there really is another way, if only he could stop bumping for a moment and think of it." This is how Winnie the Pooh is first introduced to readers, pulled down the stairs by Christopher Robin, who has hold of his arm. Milne is a master storyteller. But Pooh has been sold as a book for babies, Disneyfied, turned into coloring books and pop-ups and flaps and every possible sales tie-in. The writing has been left somewhere on a back shelf to be accidentally discovered. Discover it! Open it to any page and delight in its images. Read it to a five- or six-year-old. Laugh with it. Don't for a minute think that the Disney or spin-off books are Milne's Pooh. They portray a completely different breed of bear. The complete texts of *Winnie the Pooh* and *The House at Pooh Corner* are in this wonderful volume. You can also find them in separate volumes.

Zin! Zin! Zin! A Violin   PICTURE BOOK

AUTHOR: Lloyd Moss • ILLUSTRATOR: Marjorie Priceman
HC/PB: Simon & Schuster
THEMES: music; musical instruments; vocabulary; counting; math

A trombone is playing alone. Soon a trumpet makes a duet, a french horn a trio, and the music continues until a full orchestra "soars, implores, with notes galore that causes the audience to shout, Encore!" Moss's rhythmic verse not only introduces the orchestra but stretches vocabulary, too.

Retellers

Retellings of folklore from the world's cultures and traditions are at the heart of children's literature. Whether classic fairy tales, sacred stories of indigenous peoples, or secular folklore, the passing down of tales has been in the hands of the world's storytellers for as long as there have been stories to tell. Every child needs to have the privilege of hearing and reading the world's great tales, and building a library of titles can be a daunting task. Here are some writers whose work stands as examples of the very best in their field, with a few representative titles to get you started.

JOE BRUCHAC

The Great Ball Game: A Muskogee Story
The First Strawberries: A Cherokee Story

SHIRLEY CLIMO

The Korean Cinderella
Atalanta's Race: A Greek Myth
Magic & Mischief: Tales from Cornwall

VIRGINIA HAMILTON

In the Beginning: Creation Stories From Around the World
A Ring of Tricksters: Animal Tales From North America, the West Indies, and Africa

JOE HAYES

Here Comes the Storyteller
A collection of eight stories, each illustrated with photos of the storyteller at work and full of hints on how to tell.
Pájaro Verde / The Green Bird

NINA JAFFE

The Uninvited Guest & Other Jewish Holiday Tales
While Standing on One Foot: Puzzle Stories and Wisdom Tales from the Jewish Tradition (with Steve Zeitlin)

STEVEN KELLOGG

Jack and the Beanstalk
Sally Ann Thunder Ann Whirlwind Crockett (and others)

The intense visual approach that is a hallmark of Kellogg's picture books serves the tall tale very well.

ERIC KIMMEL

Anansi and the Talking Melon
Brother Wolf, Sister Sparrow: Stories About Saints and Animals

DEBORAH NOURSE LATTIMORE

Punga, the Goddess of Ugly
Arabian Nights: Three Tales

JAMES MARSHALL

Turning his eye to fairy-tale retellings, Marshall, with his sly humor and sure hand, produced some of his best work, and the best modern versions of these tales to be found.

Hansel & Gretel
Old Mother Hubbard and Her Wonderful Dog
The Three Little Pigs
Goldilocks and the Three Bears

RAFE MARTIN

The Eagle's Gift
The Shark God

MARY POPE OSBORNE

Mermaid Tales From Around the World
New York's Bravest

NEIL PHILIP (EDITOR)

Stockings of Buttermilk: American Folktales
American Fairy Tales, from Rip Van Winkle to the Rootabaga Stories

ROBERT D. SAN SOUCI

Folklorist San Souci has amassed a body of story retellings that set the standard for solid research (he always includes fascinating notes about where he found the stories and how he chose to adapt them), as well as spirited retellings that affect the flavor of the culture he is portraying. There are too many to mention here, but his collaborations with award-winning illustrator Jerry Pinkney deserve special mention:

The Hired Hand: An African-American Folktale
The Talking Eggs

San Souci is fortunate to collaborate also with Jerry Pinkney's son, Brian, on a number of retellings:

The Faithful Friend
Sukey and the Mermaid

And last, but perhaps most special to him, is the fact that he has the opportunity to collaborate with his talented brother, artist Daniel San Souci, on a number of books:

Sootface: An Ojibwa Cinderella Story
Two Bear Cubs: A Miwok Legend from California's Yosemite Valley
The Legend of Sleepy Hollow

GEORGE SHANNON

Stories to Solve (and *More Stories to Solve*)
True Lies: 18 Tales for You to Judge

The truth is not always clear-cut and often depends on your point of view. These stories, from a variety of sources, are perfect for reading and discussing.

AARON SHEPARD

Master Man: A Tall Tale of Nigeria
The King o' the Cats

JUDY SIERRA

Nursery Tales Around the World
Can You Guess My Name?

JANET STEVENS

Tops and Bottoms
The Tortoise and the Hare

JANE YOLEN

Not One Damsel in Distress: World Folktales for Strong Girls
Sleeping Ugly

This book in particular is one of the best examples of how to take a well-known story and twist it into something new and fresh. The title lets you know what to expect, but it is Yolen's skill as a writer that makes this concept into an original and entertaining tale.

PAUL O. ZELINSKY

Rapunzel
Rumpelstiltskin

Zelinsky's extraordinary oil paintings often obscure the fact that he writes as well as he illustrates, making him the author we would most like to illustrate all our favorite fairy tales.

PART THREE

Books for Children of Reading Age

Listening/Interest Level: Early Elementary (E)/ Reading Level: Early Elementary (E)

Not to say that the books in earlier sections aren't for readers also, but here begins the list of titles that we like to use best with children of reading age. Either because of subject matter or complexity of the story, these books work better with children five and up, and can serve as excellent choices for you to read together.

A Is for Salad   PICTURE BOOK

AUTHOR/ILLUSTRATOR: Mike Lester
PB: Puffin
THEMES: alphabet; puzzle; guessing

Here's a guessing game with a twist.

> A is for salad.
> B is for Viking.
> C is for hot dog.

A isn't for salad. It's for the alligator eating a bowl of mixed greens. And *B*? That stands for the beaver wearing a Viking helmet. *C* is for the cat eating a hot dog. Children will get the joke. The fun is in the *"No it isn't!"* they cry out with their corrected answer at the turn of every page.

Emma's Magic Winter   EARLY READER

AUTHOR: Jean Little • ILLUSTRATOR: Jennifer Plecas
PB: HarperCollins
THEMES: friendship; shyness; magic; winter

Perfect in tone, sacrificing none of the power of the story to accommodate the controlled vocabulary, this is an example of an early reader that transcends the format and becomes a great book. Emma's friendship with the new girl next door sets the stage for a winter of changes. Is it magic, or is Emma finally finding her confidence? A sequel, *Emma's Yucky Brother*, is just as good.

How Many, How Many, How Many?   PICTURE BOOK

AUTHOR: Rick Walton • ILLUSTRATOR: Cynthia Jabar
HC/PB: Candlewick
THEMES: rhyme; numbers; riddles

These number riddles are filled with rollicking verse and depend on a child's familiarity with nursery rhymes. "Spiders like to steal her seat, How many things does Muffett eat?" Two (curds and whey).

Museum ABC   PICTURE BOOK NONFICTION

AUTHOR: Metropolitan Museum of Art • ILLUSTRATOR: Various
HC: Little Brown
THEMES: alphabet; art; paintings; artists; museums

On each captivating spread you'll find four images of art by ancient to contemporary artists representing a different letter of the alphabet. This is an excellent opportunity to see how artists portray the same subjects. There is inconsistency in presentation. The letter Y uses the color yellow rather than an image representing Y, and the letter X presents a problem.

 I have a certain set of standards that I apply to ABC books. Nitpicky though it may be, I feel that every letter of the alphabet must get an equal depiction. If the concept of the ABC book is a clever one, but doesn't yield a good X or Q, those letters receive a forced depiction that doesn't work. For example, books that use words with X in the middle of a word to show X drive me crazy. I know it's hard to come up with twenty-six good ideas to fit an ABC book concept ("X is for Xylophone—because X is always for Xylophone," from *Uncle Shelby's ABZ Book* by Shel Silverstein), but it's my opinion that if you can't make all the letters work you shouldn't do the book in the first place.

 Okay, Walter, I agree—for the most part. But Museum ABC has twenty-five pages that work for me. I'd even point out to the child, "Whoa! Look here at what they did with the Y. How is it different from the other pages?" Besides, the emphasis here is comparing works of art rather than on the alphabet, and it does that well.

It sends a message to the child that getting twenty-five out of twenty-six is close enough. I was taught that close enough counts only in horseshoes.

My Great-Aunt Arizona

PICTURE BOOK

AUTHOR: Gloria Houston • ILLUSTRATOR: Susan Condie Lamb
HC/PB: HarperCollins
THEMES: U.S.A., Appalachia; teachers; aunts; family

A heartwarming tribute to teaching. Read about this lively, dedicated lady from Appalachia, and then give the book away to a teacher or your favorite aunt. It will be a perfect gift.

One Hundred Hungry Ants

PICTURE BOOK

AUTHOR: Elinor Pinczes • ILLUSTRATOR: Bonnie Mackain
HC/PB: Houghton Mifflin
THEMES: numbers; math; ants; picnics; rhyme

> Pinczes tackles other early math topics in her picture books *Inchworm and a Half*, *A Remainder of One*, and *Arctic Fives Arrive*.

One hundred hungry ants hurry to their picnic, but marching single file seems too slow for a hundred empty tummies. The youngest ant suggests they travel in two rows of fifty, four rows of twenty-five . . . and the division begins. This will tickle the funnybone as children learn basic principles of division in rhyme.

Poppleton

EARLY READER

AUTHOR: Cynthia Rylant • ILLUSTRATOR: Mark Teague
HC/PB: Blue Sky Press
THEMES: friendship; truth; reading; libraries; books

Our favorite thing about Poppleton the pig is his love of reading. If there were only one adventure—"The Library"—it would be enough to make this early reader worthwhile, but you get three! Better still, emerging readers can enjoy more stories about Poppleton and friends in the series of books bearing his name.

Three Stories You Can Read to Your Dog

EARLY READER

AUTHOR: Sara Swan Miller • ILLUSTRATOR: True Kelley
HC/PB: Houghton Mifflin
THEMES: humor; dogs; reading

Miller offers this advice in her introduction: "When you feel bored, you can read a book. But dogs can't read. Here's a good way to make your dog happy. You can read these stories out loud. Your dog will like them. They are about the things that dogs understand best." Burglars, bones, and running free—all from a dog's point of view! This hits the spot for an easy chuckle, and offers a child the chance to read aloud to an audience that won't intimidate him as many adults would. The companion book *Three Stories You Can Read to Your Cat* is equally fun.

Yesterday I Had the Blues

PICTURE BOOK

AUTHOR: Jeron Ashford Frame • ILLUSTRATOR: R. Gregory Christie
HC: Tricycle Press
THEMES: family; love; colors; emotions; African American

Moods can take over when we least expect them, like "The hold a pillow, wish it was tomorrow blues," or the ". . . write a poem that don't rhyme indigos." Here's a rhythmic read-aloud that features Father's grays, Gram's yellows, and Mama's reds (look out!) in a changing spectrum of colors used to illustrate feelings.

Listening/Interest Level: Early Elementary (E)/ Reading Level: Early Elementary to Middle Elementary (E/M)

While this section interests children in their early elementary years, the books challenge beginning readers and are best read by ones that are more confident.

Apple Pie 4th of July
PICTURE BOOK

AUTHOR: Janet S. Wong • ILLUSTRATOR: Margaret Chodos-Irvine
HC: Harcourt Brace
THEMES: Fourth of July; food; cooking; Chinese American; family; tradition

Americans do not eat Chinese food on the Fourth of July. At least that is what this Chinese American child thinks as her parents prepare a feast of chicken chow mein, sweet-and-sour pork, and more, to sell in their store for the holiday. A fusion of culinary cultures results when the young girl sees how many people do order Chinese takeout on this holiday. At day's end, she joins her family to eat apple pie and watch the celebratory fireworks.

Bravo Maurice!
PICTURE BOOK

AUTHOR/ILLUSTRATOR: Rebecca Bond
HC: Little Brown
THEMES: jobs; family; community; comparisons

Ever since he can remember, Maurice's family has wondered what he will be when he grows up. Will he be a baker like Papa or a writer like his mom? Will he drive a taxi like Uncle Eddie or be a gardener like his grandmother? Children who are compared with one relative or another will identify with Maurice and have their own reasons to shout, "Bravo, Maurice!" as the last page turns.

Dear Mrs. Larue: Letters From Obedience School
PICTURE BOOK

AUTHOR/ILLUSTRATOR: Mark Teague
HC: Scholastic
THEMES: dogs; letters; school; camp; pets

"Dear Mrs. LaRue, How could you do this to me? This is a PRISON, not a school!" So begins the first of many letters from Ike, a dog who implores his master to release him from obedience school. Teague's paintings in joyful color (representing reality) and black and white (Ike's point of view) add even more humor to this already hilarious tale. A perfect book to share at the beginning of the school year or just after a vacation.

Everybody Cooks Rice
PICTURE BOOK

AUTHOR: Norah Dooley • ILLUSTRATOR: Peter Thornton
HC/PB: Lerner
THEMES: neighbors; rice; cultural diversity; food; cooking; meals; community; eating; recipes

At dinnertime a child goes to several neighbors' homes in search of his younger brother. He learns about various cultures by seeing the different ways rice is prepared for each family. Recipes are included.

Fairy Wings
PICTURE BOOK

AUTHORS/ILLUSTRATORS: Lauren Mills and Dennis Nolan
HC/PB: Little Brown
THEMES: fairies; friendship; wings; comparisons; trolls

Lovely flitting fairies with gossamer wings up against an ugly troll—this is what a reader looks for when she's intrigued with fairies. Fia, the heroine, was born without wings and teased by other fairies. But she is a good friend to the earthy creatures in the forest and to Kip, the boy fairy who adds a slight touch of romance. When you finish this, try the sequel: *Fia and the Imp.*

Finding Providence: The Story of Roger Williams
EARLY READER

AUTHOR: Avi • ILLUSTRATOR: James Watling
PB: HarperCollins
THEMES: Rhode Island; U.S. history, Colonial America; biography

An excellent, easy-to-read biography, perfect for introducing younger readers to colonial America or for a reluctant reader who needs to do a book report (but is not able to do one on a book 100 pages in length).

Ghost Wings

PICTURE BOOK

AUTHOR: Barbara Joosse • ILLUSTRATOR: Giselle Potter
HC: Chronicle
THEMES: Mexico; butterflies; migration; Day of the Dead; grandmothers and granddaughters

This is a heartwarming tale of a young girl and her close, warm relationship with her grandmother. It takes place in Mexico during the monarch butterflies' annual migration and during the celebration of the Day of the Dead. A study guide is included in the back that describes both.

Gooney Bird Greene

EARLY READER

AUTHOR: Lois Lowry • ILLUSTRATOR: Middy Thomas
HC: Houghton Mifflin
THEMES: storytelling; strong girl; school; diversity; teachers; individuality

Gooney Bird Greene, second-grader, is the star of this early chapter book. She likes to be "right smack in the middle of everything" and that's a good thing since her personality, imagination, and storytelling skills are so adept that her classmates clamor for more of her tales. Young readers will learn concepts and techniques of telling stories through the voice of this exceptional young girl, who dances to the beat of her own drummer.

The Journey of Oliver K. Woodman

PICTURE BOOK

AUTHOR: Darcy Pattison • ILLUSTRATOR: Joe Cepeda
HC: Harcourt
THEMES: journeys; travel; dolls; letters; U.S.A.

Uncle Ray can't spend time with Tameka this summer, so he builds a life-size wooden doll named Oliver K. Woodman to visit her instead. Oliver starts his journey perched on a rock at the side of a road in Rock Hill, South Carolina, with a note that begins, "Dear Traveler, I am going to see Tameka Schwartz, 370 Park Avenue, Redcrest, California . . ." His journey across America is told with postcards and letters from the colorful characters who help him on his way. Cepeda's bright, bold paintings show off the countryside and include a map of Oliver's travels.

The Eleven Most Important Rules About Reading and Children... Not!

Rule #1

They say:

Always choose a book to fit the age of the child.

We say:

There is no such thing as a "nine-year-old" book. Age can be used as a guide, not the determining factor in choosing a book.

Rule #2

They say:

Children's books should enrich as well as inform.

We say:

Lighten up! Children need first of all to read for pleasure. Enrichment and information is a bonus. Once they develop a love of reading, a lifetime of learning will follow.

Rule #3

They say:

Never skip pages.

We say:

Anyone who has read to a two-year-old knows the value of page skipping. When children get antsy it's a perfect time to move more quickly through the pages. Of course, once your child has memorized the story, you'll never get away with it! One of the things about reading is that you can do it your own way. If you get bogged down in a story, skipping pages or some of the text is a good way to get through it.

Rule #4

They say:

Some children are simply too old for picture books.

We say:

We live in a society where children are rewarded for reading by having the art taken away. Some children need visuals to help them through a story. Others simply enjoy the pleasure of a good picture book—much like the ones found on their parents' coffee tables.

Rule #5

They say:

Make sure what you read to your child is appropriate.

We say:

What is suitable for one child or for another can be very different. Worry less about what is appropriate. Instead, offer up a sampling of all kinds of writing on a variety of subjects. They'll learn to make the choices best for them.

Rule #6

They say:

Comic books are a lesser form of reading.

We say:

Some of the best writing today can be found in comics, though often the subject matter requires a mature reader. A comic-book reader can experience a world of masterly storytelling, sophisticated vocabulary, and complex imagery. The reader will choose his favorites. Comics are not for everyone, and, like books, they range in quality, but they can be a vital and creative form of reading for those who choose them.

Rule #7

They say:

Certain books for children really aren't very well written and you should avoid these titles.

We say:

How are we going to teach them the difference between good writing and bad writing if we don't let them sample the latter?

Rule #8

They say:

The best time to read to children is just before bedtime.

We say:

Bedtime is a terrific opportunity for reading in a lot of households. But it isn't the only time. Look for moments in your day when stories will fit. It's more important that you do it every day than at a particular time.

Rule #9

They say:

Children should be encouraged to read a certain number of pages a day.

We say:

Children should be encouraged to read at their own pace, not at somebody else's.

Rule #10

They say:

Girls will always read books about boys. Boys will never read books about girls.

We say:

We don't think so.

Rule #11

They say:

Growing up is difficult enough; children don't need books that show unpleasant situations.

We say:

You have to make a lot of hard decisions as a parent. We have never found that soft-pedaling an issue has worked with our kids, and we have been grateful for books that were available to help us explain some of life's difficulties.

The Lotus Seed

PICTURE BOOK

AUTHOR: Sherry Garland • ILLUSTRATOR: Tatsuro Kiuchi

HC/PB: Harcourt Brace

THEMES: Vietnam; war; hope; grandmothers; family; immigration; plants; refugees

Grandmother Ba has come all the way from Vietnam with only one memento from home, a lotus seed. This poignant story of war, loss of homeland, and life in a new country ends with a ray of hope.

Martha Speaks

PICTURE BOOK

AUTHOR/ILLUSTRATOR: Susan Meddaugh

HC/PB: Houghton Mifflin

THEMES: dogs; language; humor; soup; alphabet; family; pets

> Other Martha books: *Martha Calling*, *Martha Blah Blah*, and *Martha Walks the Dog.*

The whole idea of a dog learning to speak English because of its diet of alphabet soup is silly enough. Add Meddaugh's pictures with the ballooned dog comments, and you have a runaway hit.

Patsy Says

PICTURE BOOK

AUTHOR/ILLUSTRATOR: Leslie Tryon

HC: Atheneum

THEMES: manners; school; change; behavior; friends

Patsy Pig is under pressure to teach Ms. Klingensmith's first-grade class how *not* to be rude. Open House for parents is on Friday, and if they don't change their behavior in time, it will be a disaster. This book about manners is not your usual "please" and "thank you." Instead it covers meeting and greeting guests, introducing yourself and others, serving and making pleasant conversation.

Stand Tall, Molly Lou Melon

PICTURE BOOK

AUTHOR: Patty Lovell • ILLUSTRATOR: David Catrow

HC: Putnam

THEMES: school; bullies; self-respect; grandmothers

Molly Lou Melon is the shortest girl in the first grade. She doesn't mind. Her grandma has told her, "Walk as proudly as you can and the world will look up to you." So she does, even when a bully picks on her the first day at her new school. By the fifth day, buck-toothed, short, fumble-fingered, artistic Molly Lou has made friends, including that bully, Ronald Durkin. The art will make young readers laugh, and this feisty character will make them want to stand tall like Molly Lou Melon.

There's a Zoo in Room 22
POETRY

AUTHOR: Judy Sierra • ILLUSTRATOR: Barney Saltzberg
HC: Harcourt
THEMES: school; animals; alphabet; pets; rhyme

> Please don't ask to feel
> Our electric eel,
> Because, if you bug him,
> We cannot unplug him.

Fish tanks in classrooms and a hamster or two aren't unusual. But when Miss Darling's students ask for a pet, they get one in poetic form for every letter in the alphabet.

Listening/Interest Level: Early and Middle Elementary (E/M)/ Reading Level: Early Elementary (E)

This section boasts a wide selection of picture books, evenly distributed between fiction and nonfiction, that will interest E- and M-level listeners.

Allison
PICTURE BOOK

AUTHOR/ILLUSTRATOR: Allen Say
HC: Houghton Mifflin
THEMES: adoption; dolls; Japan; anger; frustration; family; cats; cultural
diversity; fitting in; comparisons; solitude; problem solving

When Allison realizes she looks more like her Japanese doll than her parents, she becomes confused and angry. While there are several good books that deal with adoption—with being loved and being part of a family—few confront the feelings a child may have with physical differences in an interracial family. Say captures heart-tugging expressions with his watercolors and the need for belonging with his words.

Annie and the Old One
PICTURE BOOK

AUTHOR: Miles Miska • ILLUSTRATOR: Peter Pamall
HC/PB: Little Brown
THEMES: death; Native American; nature; grandmothers and granddaughters

Annie cannot control the passage of time, even if it means that her grandmother will soon "... go to mother earth." A sensitive story in which a young girl, through the voice of her Navajo grandmother, learns the concept of death.

At the Crossroads

PICTURE BOOK

AUTHOR/ILLUSTRATOR: Rachel Isadora
PB: Mulberry
THEMES: South Africa; fathers; mines; jobs; patience; yearning; anticipation; miners

Zola, Sipho, and Nomsa play their rhythm instruments and sing, "Our fathers are coming home!" Today is the day the fathers return from their months of work at the mines. Mr. Sisulu closes his store and people from the town come to wait. They wait and they wait. Soon it gets dark and folks go home to sleep, except for children, who won't go home till their fathers arrive. This sweet South African tale makes you want to weep with tired delight when finally the children are able to play and sing, "Our fathers are home!"

Barefoot: Escape on the Underground Railroad

PICTURE BOOK

AUTHOR: Pamela Duncan Edwards • ILLUSTRATOR: Henry Cole
HC/PB: HarperCollins
THEMES: courage; animals; African American; feet; Underground Railroad; U.S. history, pre–Civil War; slavery; adventure; chases

Dark, close-up images with slight suggestions of light creep through the forest, all from the perspective of eyes close to the ground. An escaped slave searches for safety while the "Heavy Boots" close in. The animals watch and ease the way to his shelter. Historical fiction and a touch of fantasy merge in this stunning picture book suggesting nature's role on the pathways leading from one "safe house" to another as slaves escaped northward to freedom.

Barn

PICTURE BOOK

AUTHOR/ILLUSTRATOR: Debby Atwell
HC/PB: Houghton Mifflin
THEMES: U.S. history; barns; change

Two hundred years of history is told from the perspective of a barn. A barn? Yes, and it works. From the late eighteenth century to the present day the barn stands as its owners fight for their living in a changing world.

A Chocolate Moose for Dinner

PICTURE BOOK

AUTHOR/ILLUSTRATOR: Fred Gwynne
PB: Aladdin
THEMES: language; wordplay; parts of speech; humor

Fred Gwynne was an actor whose love of wordplay shines in several humorous books. Look for his others: *The King Who Rained*, *A Little Pigeon Toad*, and *The Sixteen Hand Horse*.

A young girl visualizes the things her parents talk about. "At the ocean Daddy says watch out for the under toe," and "Daddy says lions pray on other animals." Here's a perfect way to laugh at our crazy language. Have fun thinking up other homonyms.

Company's Coming

PICTURE BOOK

AUTHOR: Arthur Yorinks • ILLUSTRATOR: David Small
HC/PB: Hyperion
THEMES: aliens; diversity; judging; flying saucers; humor; gifts; anticipation

A ridiculous story that turns the reader into a real ham, *Company's Coming* is one of our favorites. "On the day Shirley had invited all of her relatives to dinner and Moe, her husband, was pleasantly tinkering in the yard, a flying saucer quietly landed next to their toolshed." Try a monotone voice for the aliens. It's perfect (and it's easy).

 In writing workshops, I read this aloud up to the moment when Shirley is about to open her gift. "It's a . . . it's a . . ." Close the book and ask, "What do you think it is?" They'll beg you to read on!

The Dot

PICTURE BOOK

AUTHOR/ILLUSTRATOR: Peter H. Reynolds
HC: Candlewick Press
THEMES: art; school; individuality; creativity; frustration; talent; teachers; encouragement; confidence

One small dot on an empty piece of paper marks the beginning of a delicate tale about the often hidden glimmer of creativity in us all. Whether you focus on the teacher who brilliantly frees the creative spark in a child who has given up, or the spirited child who pushes her own boundaries to success, this charming journey offers ample encouragement for budding artists.

 I came to the end, involuntarily clutched this small book to my chest, exhaled, and searched for someone to share it with.

Dragonfly's Tale

AUTHOR/ILLUSTRATORS: Kristina Rodanas

HC/PB: Clarion

THEMES: Native American; folklore; U.S.A., the Southwest; corn; dragonflies; nature; kindness; crafts; siblings

In this Zuni legend, a brother's kindness to his younger sister starts the process that brings life back to their starving village. Young readers discover where dragonflies come from and why they hum about the cornfield. Full-color art shows off the rich and vast landscape of the American Southwest.

Ed Emberley's Big Purple Drawing Book

PICTURE BOOK NONFICTION

AUTHOR/ILLUSTRATOR: Ed Emberley

HC/PB: Little Brown

THEMES: art; drawing

Ed Emberley's drawing books allow anyone to draw. From grapes to pirate ships and centipedes to swamp creatures, simple shapes result in subjects you can actually identify. Emberley offers a drawing alphabet: shapes that form pictures as letters form words. Easy and accessible, this book is a perfect solution for quiet times. There are numerous other titles in this series, all worthwhile.

Emma's Rug

PICTURE BOOK

AUTHOR/ILLUSTRATOR: Allen Say

HC: Houghton Mifflin

THEMES: art; talent; school; teachers; magic; self-respect; comfort; confidence; creativity

Who knows where an artist gets her creativity? Emma's may come from the small, shaggy rug someone gave her when she was a baby. Or maybe it's all in her mind. Allen Say takes on a new topic for children's books: artistic inspiration. And while the reader is left to some interpretation of her own, there is no question that Say himself is artistically inspired. Look at Emma's quiet pride on page 13 and recoil at her anguish on page 23.

Grandfather Tang's Story

PICTURE BOOK

AUTHOR: Ann Tompert • ILLUSTRATOR: Robert Andrew Parker

HC: Crown • PB: Dragonfly

THEMES: tangrams; origami; storytelling; art; folklore; shapes; math; puzzles; China

By arranging tangram pieces, Grandfather Tang tells Little Soo a story. Foxes, fairies, rabbits, dogs, squirrels, hawks, turtles, and other tangram creatures appear to help with the tale. A tangram and description of the puzzle game are included along with instructions on paper folding and shadow art.

The Handmade Alphabet
PICTURE BOOK NONFICTION

AUTHOR/ILLUSTRATOR: Laura Rankin
HC: Dial • PB: Puffin
THEMES: alphabet; sign language; communication; wordless; cultural diversity; deafness

Realism and imagination merge as colored pencil drawings fill pages with hand shapes representing the twenty-six letters of the American Sign Language alphabet. Words are not needed as hands do all the talking; a gloved hand forms the letter *G*, fingers dipping into a palette of paint form the letter *P*, and an X-rayed hand offers up the *X*. A perfect guide for the curious as well as the proficient.

Homeplace
PICTURE BOOK

AUTHOR: Anne Shelby • ILLUSTRATOR: Wendy Anderson Halperin
HC/PB: Orchard
THEMES: social studies; U.S. history; farms; family; relatives; genealogy; family history; change; grandparents

From the time her great-great-great-great-grandpa built the house in which the family still lives, a child traces almost two hundred years of family history. Over 150 softly rendered pictures detail generations of change. Don't try to see it all in one reading. Read the story aloud once, then set it aside for perusal.

I'll See You in My Dreams
PICTURE BOOK

AUTHOR: Mavis Jukes • ILLUSTRATOR: Stacey Schuett
HC: Knopf
THEMES: illness; daydreams; problem solving; flying; strong girls; uncles; loss; airplanes; hospitals

When painful and difficult situations come up—even death—good books help. Jukes's story is about a young girl traveling to visit her critically ill uncle. It's about the worry of saying good-bye, and the daydreams that accompany that fear.

Judy Moody
FICTION

AUTHOR: Megan McDonald • ILLUSTRATOR: Peter Reynolds
HC/PB: Candlewick
THEMES: school; brothers; bad days; friends; family; emotions

Judy Moody's in a bad mood. It's the first day of third grade and nothing is going right. But Judy's sparkly self won't let that mood last long. Besides, her teacher has just assigned a project that encourages her to concentrate on herself. Judy is a lively, likable character, and McDonald has captured the middle elementary years so well, kids cannot help but identify.

When your child finishes the first book, be ready with the next ones: *Judy Moody Gets Famous!; Judy Moody Saves the World!;* and *Judy Moody Predicts the Future.*

Judy Moody fits snuggly between Junie B. Jones and Ramona Quimby in terms of reading level, and is more than a match for either in terms of personality.

Komodo
PICTURE BOOK

AUTHOR/ILLUSTRATOR: Peter Sis
HC: Greenwillow
THEMES: dragons; maps; Indonesia; Komodo dragon; lizards

When you read a Peter Sis book, take time for the illustrated details. *Komodo* has few words on each page but it may take you ten minutes to find this dragon-loving boy, who sets off with his parents to Indonesia in search of a real monitor lizard—the last living dragon. Facts mix with imagination in this simple tale.

Luke's Way of Looking
PICTURE BOOK

AUTHOR: Nadia Wheatley • ILLUSTRATOR: Matt Ottley
HC: Kane/Miller
THEMES: art; diversity; artists; school; museums; comparisons

A boy with real artistic ability breaks free of the bonds of an unappreciative world and a stodgy teacher to look at the world his own way. What he sees will amaze you, and it is great fun to spot the references to artists such as Henry Moore, Andy Warhol, El Greco, Caravaggio, and half a dozen others throughout the illustrations.

Many Luscious Lollipops

PICTURE BOOK NONFICTION

AUTHOR/ILLUSTRATOR: Ruth Heller
PB: Sandcastle Books
THEMES: parts of speech; language; rhyme

> The others in this extraordinary series include *A Cache of Jewels and Other Collective Nouns; Up, Up and Away: A Book About Adverbs; Merry-Go-Round: A Book About Nouns; Kites Sail High: A Book About Verbs; Behind the Mask: A Book About Prepositions;* and *Mine, All Mine: A Book About Pronouns.*

To have had this book and its companions when we were learning grammar would have been a stimulating experience. Alas, they weren't available then. But children today can learn about adjectives with astonishing, colorful art, and poetic descriptions. "An adjective's terrific when you want to be specific. It easily identifies by number, color, or by size. Twelve large, blue, gorgeous butterflies." Memorize them. Enjoy them again and again.

Marvin Redpost: Alone in His Teacher's House

EARLY READER

AUTHOR: Louis Sachar • ILLUSTRATOR: Barbara
     Sullivan
HC/PB: Random House
THEMES: teachers; dogs; pets; school; friendship;
     responsibility; humor

Marvin is excited when his teacher asks him to dog-sit Waldo while she is away for a week. But things don't go well for Marvin, or for Waldo. Sachar can find a kid's funny bone as readily as he can identify what worries kids most, and combine them with ease. Look for others in this popular series of chapter books.

Masai and I

PICTURE BOOK

AUTHOR: Virginia Kroll • ILLUSTRATOR: Nancy Carpenter
PB: Aladdin
THEMES: social studies, cultural diversity; comparisons; Africa; African
     American; imagination

Linda is a city girl who learns about the Masai people in school and wonders what life would be like for her if she were Masai. "If I were Masai preparing for a celebration, I'd rub my skin with cows' fat mixed with red clay so that my skin would shine." As Linda goes through her day's routine she compares her simple tasks with those of the Masai. A fascinating way to learn about another culture.

Don't Underestimate The Power of A Wordless Book

Books aren't the bad guys. But reading them can create problems. Sometimes the frustrations of learning to read cause children to "hate" books. Offer them one that is wordless. If that seems "babyish," try Ward's *Silver Pony*—a chapter book without words—and watch them get pulled in. Or, show a child *Zoom* by Istvan Banyai. Adults often request that one for themselves. Sometimes frustrated children need a break from words. But don't let them take it out on books.

Wordless books allow a child's imagination to soar. Without interruptions or intrusions, children come up with words of their own. It's impossible to read *Clown* by Blake without "hearing" the words. Children who like to follow detail will be engrossed by books like David Wiesner's *Free Fall* (page 22).

When my daughter Kaela was five years old, she showed her frustration at not being able to read well by chirping noisily while her older sister, Laura, read aloud. Wordless books solved our problem. Kaela took her turn reading those books aloud—from the front to the back page, night after night, using the same words.

Miss Nelson Is Missing! PICTURE BOOK
AUTHOR: Harry Allard • ILLUSTRATOR: James Marshall
HC/PB: Houghton Mifflin
THEMES: school; teachers; mystery; substitute teachers;
    misbehaving; mischief

The creators of The Stupids deliver another hilarious character in the person of Miss Viola Swamp, the meanest teacher in the whole world. The alter ego of the title character, though only the reader is allowed to know that, Viola Swamp whips a class of unruly and disruptive kids into shape in no time. We suspect that most teachers have a little of Miss Swamp in them, and that's why this book, and the sequels *Miss Nelson Is Back* and *Miss Nelson Has a Field Day,* have become classroom favorites.

The Patchwork Quilt PICTURE BOOK
AUTHOR: Valerie Flournoy • ILLUSTRATOR: Jerry Pinkney
HC: Dial
THEMES: quilts; grandmothers; illness; family; storytelling;
    memories; family history; African American

Each piece grandmother stitches on her quilt comes with a memory, and Tanya loves hearing the stories. When Grandma becomes ill, Tanya takes on the job of finishing the magnificent heirloom. When read aloud, this heartwarming story of a bond across generations offers a perfect chance to share your own family stories. There is a sequel, *Tanya's Reunion.*

The Recess Queen PICTURE BOOK
AUTHOR: Alexis O'Neill • ILLUSTRATOR: Laura Huliska-Beith
HC: Scholastic
THEMES: friendship; bullies; new experiences; schools

"Mean Jean was Recess Queen and nobody said any different." Nobody swung, kicked, or bounced until she did. Then a new kid came to school and changed things around. This story in rhyme shows readers—who will recognize the playground dynamics—that even bullies can become friends.

The Red Wolf

PICTURE BOOK

AUTHOR/ILLUSTRATOR: Margaret Shannon

HC: Houghton Mifflin

THEMES: fairy tales; princesses; knitting; kings; wolves; strong girls; freedom

Forced to live in a tower by her overprotective father, seven-year-old Princess Roselupin longs to venture out into the forest below. When she receives a mysterious box of wool with a note that reads "Knit what you want," she knits a magical red wolf suit, climbs into it, and grows and grows till she breaks through the walls of her tower and romps through the woods to freedom. Start with a modern fairy tale, add a dose of Sendak's *Wild Things*, and you have this delightful story with a surprise ending.

★ The Silver Pony

PICTURE BOOK

AUTHOR/ILLUSTRATOR: Lynd Ward

PB: Houghton Mifflin

THEMES: wordless; horses; farms; fantasy; friendship; good deeds; geography; cultural diversity

Moving and suspenseful, this chapter book has no words. Pictures in shades of black and white tell the story of a farm boy's adventure with a powerful winged horse. Start at the front and don't skip pages. You will be mesmerized.

 I like it as a read-by-yourself book, but was happy to have my children point out parts I'd missed, like clues given by weather vanes.

Sit on a Potato Pan, Otis!

PICTURE BOOK

AUTHOR/ILLUSTRATOR: Jon Agee

HC: Farrar, Strauss & Giroux

THEMES: palindromes; wordplay; vocabulary; language; humor

Wow! Looking for more books about palindromes? Agee's *So Many Dynamos!*; *Go Hang a Salami! I'm a Lasagna Hog!*; and *Palindromania!* are must-reads.

Exercise your vocabulary. More than sixty palindromes— ". . . a word, verse or sentence which reads the same backward and forward"—are depicted in this humorous look at one of the marvels of language. This will give readers a workout.

Some Things Are Scary

PICTURE BOOK

AUTHOR: Florence Parry Heide • ILLUSTRATOR: Jules Feiffer

HC: Candlewick

THEMES: fear; anxiety; humor

Not everyone is afraid of the same thing, and this list covers many possibilities: "Holding on to someone's hand that isn't your mother's when you thought it was" or "Getting a shot" or "Skating downhill when you haven't learned to stop." It's hard not to laugh out loud at Feiffer's pictures, but some children may want to talk seriously about what frightens them. Whether it's anxiety over new happenings in a child's life, or Halloween looming in the shadows, use this book for conversation about the scary things and an opportunity to approach them with a dose of humor.

The Stupids Step Out   PICTURE BOOK

AUTHOR: Harry Allard • ILLUSTRATOR: James Marshall
HC/PB: Houghton Mifflin
THEMES: humor; family; comparisons; opposites; point of view; fools

Meet the Stupids! In story after story, Allard and Marshall delight readers and listeners of all ages with the adventures of the dumbest family in all of literature. Not only are they clueless, but they excel at doing exactly the opposite of what the reader would do in any given situation, frequently resulting in the comment, "Man, they are really stupid!" And that is the point. Look for these other titles: *The Stupids Have a Ball, The Stupids Take Off,* and *The Stupids Die.*

Read *Fishing in the Air* (page 169) by Sharon Creech for another look at father and son who fish together.

Today I'm Going Fishing with My Dad   PICTURE BOOK

AUTHOR: N. L. Sharp • ILLUSTRATOR: Chris Demarest
PB: Boyds Mills
THEMES: comparisons; gentle boys; fishing; fathers and sons; preferences

A young boy does not like fishing . . . or the buzzing mosquitoes, or the wiggly worms, or the smelly fish, or eating them. But he loves spending time with his dad. A fine book for discussing that even when we don't feel the same way about things that others do, we can still participate at our own level.

Tomorrow's Alphabet   PICTURE BOOK

AUTHOR: George Shannon • ILLUSTRATOR: Donald Crews
PB: Mulberry
THEMES: alphabet; puzzle

Full-page illustrations stretch the imagination as children guess answers to this alphabet puzzle:

A is for seed . . . tomorrow's APPLE.
B is for eggs . . . tomorrow's BIRDS.

We suggest you cover the right-hand page of each spread with a blank piece of paper. While the left page reads "C is for milk" cover up the right until the children have guessed tomorrow's CHEESE. There is challenge enough here to keep your child thinking and possibilities enough to keep him happy.

Working Cotton

PICTURE BOOK

AUTHOR: Sherley Anne Williams • ILLUSTRATOR: Carole Byard
HC/PB: Harcourt Brace
THEMES: migrant farm workers; African American; jobs; California

They get to the fields early, before it's even light. The bus comes for them again when it's almost dark. In between, the migrant families pick cotton in central California. Shelan is too young to carry her own sack so she piles cotton in the middle of the row for her mama to collect. Byard's luminous paintings earned her a Caldecott Honor.

The Z Was Zapped: A Play in Twenty-Six Acts

PICTURE BOOK

AUTHOR/ILLUSTRATOR: Chris Van Allsburg
HC: Houghton Mifflin
THEMES: alphabet; plays; guessing; vocabulary

 That tingly moment again—opening up a gem that shines beyond its concept. Van Allsburg presents the alphabet as a twenty-six-act play. Each letter is one act, one image:

Act I: The A . . . was an Avalanche.
Act II: The B . . . was badly bitten.

First you see the image and then you turn the page to read Van Allsburg's clever twist on each black-and-white letter. In front of a classroom of fourth-graders, I discovered the creative potential in this drama. Holding up the *D* page, I asked, "The *D* was . . . ?" Hands went up and the children hollered, "Dipped!" "Dunked!" "Drowned!" "Dead!" "Dripping!" "Destroyed!" "My," I thought, ". . . all this excitement over a *D*—over a letter in the alphabet."

Listening/Interest Level: Early and Middle Elementary (E/M)/ Reading Level: Early to Middle Elementary (E/M)

As the reading level rises, the experiences offered in this selection of mostly picture books are more in-depth, offering some great opportunities for reading that will provoke reflection and discussion afterward.

The 500 Hats of Bartholomew Cubbins
PICTURE BOOK

AUTHOR/ILLUSTRATOR: Dr. Seuss
HC: Random House
THEMES: hats; courage; respect; kings; wisdom; counting

A wonderful, magical tale of the boy who could not take his hat off to show respect for the King, as there was always another, more elaborate one underneath it. Wise men and wizards are confounded and the King orders Bartholomew's execution, but the executioner cannot chop off his head unless he removes his hat. Longer, more storybook Seuss than his other books, and only in two colors, but how splendid he makes the hats look!

A for Antarctica
PICTURE BOOK NONFICTION

AUTHOR/ILLUSTRATOR: Jonathan Chester (photographs)
HC: Tricycle Press
THEMES: alphabet, Antarctic, photographs

A minimum amount of text, loaded with information and eye-catching photographs, take readers into Antarctica. Each page shows a letter with one or more corresponding words and photographs. "*A is for Albatross and Aurora*

Australis." This photo journal is bound to have young readers clamoring for more information about one of the most wild and endangered places on earth.

A My Name Is Alice
PICTURE BOOK

AUTHOR: Jane Bayer • ILLUSTRATOR: Steven Kellogg
PB: Puffin
THEMES: rhyme; animals; jumping rope; alliteration; alphabet

"A my name is Alice and my husband's name is Alex. We come from Alaska and we sell ants" (Alice is an APE. Alex is an ANTEATER). Twenty-six verses of this jump-rope rhyme take the reader through the alphabet. The natural next step is for children to make up their own verses. Take time to enjoy the details in Kellogg's very funny drawings.

The Adventures of Captain Underpants
FICTION

AUTHOR/ILLUSTRATOR: Dav Pilkey
HC: Blue Sky Press • PB: Scholastic
THEMES: adventure; humor, adolescent; friendship; playing tricks

In the previous edition of our book, we wrote, "This one is going to delight every boy from seven to seventy." How right we were. This silly series about two best friends who hypnotize their principal into believing he is that great, nearly unclothed super hero, Captain Underpants, has become one of children's publishing's biggest successes. Irreverent, crudely drawn, and full of toilet humor, is there any wonder why boys who resist reading clamor for the next volume?

 Girls clamor, too!

 When my son was eight he thought this was the funniest book he had ever read. He's a teenager now, but he still looks forward to the next adventure.

Albert
PICTURE BOOK

AUTHOR: Donna Jo Napoli • ILLUSTRATOR: Jim LaMarche
HC: Harcourt Brace
THEMES: birds; habitats; friendship; fear; patience; change

Albert can't seem to muster the courage to leave his home. There are good noises outside (children giggling), but there are also bad ones (the rumble of garbage trucks). Albert is content with keeping himself busy inside and occasionally sticking his hand out the window to check the weather. Then one day a cardinal drops a twig into his open hand, builds a nest, and lays eggs. Albert is patient. Pulling his arm back in through the window would cause the nest to fall, so he keeps it outside—for weeks—until the fledglings hatch and are able to fly away. Marche's radiant color-pencil art will cause you to pick up this book, and Albert's personal transition will keep you turning pages till the end.

 This is a story where fantasy is "dressed up" as reality. I've talked to readers, who say, "This couldn't happen; when does Albert go to the bathroom?" And I find myself wondering why a man standing at the window long enough for birds to hatch and fly away—as well as birds willing to build a nest in his hand—isn't enough to show that this tale doesn't pretend to be real.

Alphabet Books: People and Places

f *The Alphabet Atlas* intrigues you, ook for these books and their take on a geographical alphabet: *A Is for Africa; A is for Antarctica; Alphabet City; Big City ABC; C is for City; Caribbean Alphabet; A Northern Alphabet; On Market Street; A Prairie Alphabet; Young Adventurers Guide to Everest; Ashanti to Zulu; D is for Doufu; Gathering the Sun: An Alphabet in Spanish and English; Play Mas! A Carnival ABC;* nd *The Farmer's Alphabet.*

The Alphabet Atlas
PICTURE BOOK NONFICTION
AUTHOR: Arthur Yorinks • ILLUSTRATORS: Adrienne Yorinks
and Jeanyee Wong
HC: Winslow Press
THEMES: alphabet; quilts; geography; cultural diversity; crafts

Vibrant quilt illustrations are the highlight here, utilizing textiles from twenty-six countries, and combined with calligraphy in this unique alphabetical look at the world's countries.

The Always Prayer Shawl
PICTURE BOOK
AUTHOR: Sheldon Oberman • ILLUSTRATOR: Ted Lewin
HC: Boyds Mills • PB: Puffin
THEMES: traditions; Jews; Russia; Judaism; grandfathers and grandsons; immigration; war; change; faith

"Some things change. And some things don't," says Adam's grandfather. He then gives Adam the Prayer Shawl he received from *his* grandfather. When Adam has to leave Russia for America, he knows that there is one thing he can count on: "I am always Adam and this is my Always Prayer Shawl. That won't change." Ted Lewin's paintings, from black and white to full color, illuminate this tender tale of family tradition. Compare this to Patricia Polacco's *The Keeping Quilt* and use it to discuss the traditions in your own family.

Amber Brown Is Not a Crayon

FICTION

AUTHOR: Paula Danziger • ILLUSTRATOR: Tony Ross
HC: Putnam • PB: Scholastic
THEMES: strong girls; humor; family; school; friendship

A delightful series of books about an irrepressible young girl and her adventures. For all those kids who love Pippi Longstocking and Ramona the Pest, the Amber books are written on a reading level that will encourage readers who are not yet ready for long chapter books. There are many other titles, including beginner-level readers that are every bit as enjoyable.

Amber on the Mountain

PICTURE BOOK

AUTHOR: Tony Johnston • ILLUSTRATOR: Robert Duncan
HC: Dial • PB: Puffin
THEMES: friendship; reading; books; strong girls; comparisons; literacy;
    mountains; country life

Isolated on the mountain where she lives, Amber meets a girl from the city who gives her the determination to read and write. A good book about friendship and the power of the written word.

Amelia and Eleanor Go for a Ride

PICTURE BOOK

AUTHOR: Pam Muñoz Ryan • ILLUSTRATOR: Brian Selznick
HC: Scholastic
THEMES: flying; U. S. History, the Depression;
    Washington, D.C.; U.S. presidents; biography;
    women, independent

For another picture book biography from this talented author/illustrator team, read *When Marian Sang: The True Recital of Marian Anderson*, a portrayal of a lady with grace and dignity who was one of our country's greatest singers.

Based on a true event. Ryan tells a story of Amelia Earhart and Eleanor Roosevelt flying over the nation's capital after a dinner party in 1933. With a bit of fact-bending to set her tale aloft, Ryan's picture book celebrates the friendship and spirit of two great Americans. Wonderful you-are-there text, and Selznick's black-and-white illustrations (with just a dash of color, here and there) make this "herstory" come vibrantly to life.

Angelo

PICTURE BOOK

AUTHOR/ILLUSTRATOR: David Macaulay
HC: Houghton Mifflin
THEMES: architecture; buildings; birds; rescue; friendship; Rome; Italy

As Angelo begins his work restoring a once glorious old church in Rome, he discovers an injured pigeon. Finding no place to safely leave her, he takes her home and helps her back to health. This tender story of the friendship of an old man and a pigeon has an added bonus: Macaulay's architectural renderings seen from various angles throughout the book.

Baseball Saved Us   PICTURE BOOK

AUTHOR: Ken Mochizuki • ILLUSTRATOR: Dom Lee
HC/PB: Lee & Low
THEMES: suspicion; U.S. history, World War II; prejudice; baseball; Japanese
    American; self-respect; captivity; family

Shorty and his family had to leave their home and move to a Japanese internment camp during World War II. It was hard living, but when his dad built a baseball field, Shorty started to gain the confidence he would need when he left the heat, dust, and staring eyes of the guards at the camp. Young readers may ask questions about this time in our history. An Author's Note has some of the answers.

The Black Snowman   PICTURE BOOK

AUTHOR: Phil Mendez • ILLUSTRATOR: Carole Byard
PB: Scholastic
THEMES: African American; snow; self-respect; storytelling; folklore; slavery;
    poverty; African culture; anger; pride

Jacob hates being poor and he hates being black. He doesn't want to build a snowman out of the watery black snow people have trampled on. But he does, and when the snowman comes to life he helps Jacob discover the beauty of his African heritage and pride in himself.

The Bracelet   PICTURE BOOK

AUTHOR: Yoshiko Uchida • ILLUSTRATOR: Joanna Yardley
HC: Philomel • PB: Paperstar
THEMES: captivity; friendship; U.S. history, World War II; memory; prejudice;
    Japanese American

Emi, a Japanese American in the second grade, is sent with her family to an internment camp during World War II. Her best friend gives her a bracelet as a farewell gift. When Emi loses her precious gift, she learns that she does not need a physical reminder of friendship.

The Brocaded Slipper and Other Vietnamese Tales

FOLKLORE COLLECTION

AUTHOR: Lynette Vuong • ILLUSTRATOR: Vo-Dinh Mai
PB: HarperCollins
THEMES: Vietnam; folklore; fairy tales; folktale variations

Cinderella, Thumbelina, and *The Frog Prince* are part of this collection of Vietnamese fairy tales. Here's a fine way to show that folklore is universal and that while we think of many of these old stories as ours, they belong to children across the world.

Brown Honey in Broomwheat Tea

POETRY COLLECTION

AUTHOR: Joyce Carol Thomas • ILLUSTRATOR: Floyd Cooper
PB: HarperCollins
THEMES: African American; self-respect; family; individuality

Another collection by Thomas and Cooper, *Gingerbread Days,* offers a poem each month and is also a treasure.

This collection of poems by Joyce Carol Thomas, illustrated with Floyd Cooper's glowing paintings, is about family, individuality, and pride of heritage. "I sprang up from mother earth. She clothed me in her own colors. I was nourished by father sun. He glazed the pottery of my skin. I am beautiful by design. The pattern of night in my hair. The pattern of music in my rhythm. As you would cherish a thing of beauty. Cherish me."

The Buck Stops Here: Presidents of the United States

PICTURE BOOK NONFICTION

AUTHOR/ILLUSTRATOR: Alice Provensen
PB: HarperCollins
THEMES: U.S. presidents; government; U.S. history; politics; rhyme

It's a rap, and children who learn it will remember a bit about each one of our country's presidents. "Harding, Twenty-nine, no doubt should have cleaned his Cabinet out." Illustrations, including interesting details of each president's tenure, fill the oversize pages. Teachers: This book begs to introduce a project. Have students research the rap details to explain their meaning.

Buddha

PICTURE BOOK BIOGRAPHY

AUTHOR/ILLUSTRATOR: Demi
HC: Henry Holt
THEMES: biography; India; Buddhism; religion; coming of age

A picture book introduction to the life of Buddha told with sensitivity and reverence as well as with Demi's usual glowing art. If you are hungry for more of the Buddha's teachings, check out Demi's retellings of ten key stories of the Buddha in her picture book *Buddha Stories*.

Burnt Toast on Davenport Street

PICTURE BOOK

AUTHOR/ILLUSTRATOR: Tim Egan
HC/PB: Houghton Mifflin
THEMES: wishes; magic; marriage; fantasy

Egan's trademark whimsy and social commentary (see: *Metropolitan Cow*) are dosed with a bit of magic, courtesy of a fly that grants three wishes to Arthur Crandall, a dog with a life that is already pretty good. Though the fly gets the wishes fouled up, the outcome serves to illustrate one of the finest, most time-honored traditions in all of children's literature: There's no place quite like your own home. Sly, humorous touches abound in this unique tale.

The Butter Battle Book

PICTURE BOOK

AUTHOR/ILLUSTRATOR: Dr. Seuss
HC: Random House
THEMES: war; weapons; deadlocks; rhyme; comparisons

A parable for the nuclear age that had many up in arms upon its publication. "It's a portrait of hopelessness," cried some, "and children cannot live without hope." "It is a portrait of reality," cried others, "and we all must come to terms with reality, even the children." Both sides missed the point. We feel this is an opportunity for discussion, a chance to read a book that really leaves you hanging and almost forces you to decide what happens after the story is over. Whichever answer you and your child come to will be a "right" one.

Calling the Doves/El Canto De Las Palomas

PICTURE BOOK BIOGRAPHY

AUTHOR: Juan Felipe Herrera • ILLUSTRATOR: Elly Simmons
HC/PB: Children's Book Press
THEMES: bilingual; Spanish language; Mexico; rhyme; poets; farms; migrant
    farmworkers; family; biography; storytelling; California; Mexican

Herrera tells of his migrant farmworker childhood in the fields of California: his father's stories, his mother's poems, their different homes, their meals together. Love for the land and for each other set the foundation for young Herrera's future. "... I knew one day I would follow my own road. I would let my voice fly the way my mother recited poems, the way my father called the doves." We are all richer for it.

Captain Abdul's Pirate School
PICTURE BOOK

AUTHOR/ILLUSTRATOR: Colin McNaughton
HC/PB: Candlewick
THEMES: pirates; strong girls; humor; school; mail

A rollicking account of the only school where the children get good grades by defying their teachers. The school is run by bona fide pirates, which lead to some hilarious adventures, not the least of which is a mutiny in which the students take charge. A surprise ending—the ringleader turns out to be a girl—will catch a few readers off guard.

The Cherokees
PICTURE BOOK NONFICTION

AUTHOR: Virginia Driving Hawk Sneve • ILLUSTRATOR: Ronald Himler
HC/PB: Holiday House
THEMES: Native American; creation; rituals; U.S. history; maps; folklore;
    celebrations; traditions

Beginning with a creation story, Sneve explains the history and migration of each tribe in the series. If you are looking for a straightforward introduction to the first Americans, this is it. Interesting facts combined with Himler's beautifully detailed paintings make this series a must for children interested in Native American life. Others in *The First Americans* series include *The Cheyennes, The Hopis, The Iroquois, The Navajos, The Nez Perce, The Seminoles,* and *The Sioux.*

Cinderella's Rat
PICTURE BOOK

AUTHOR/ILLUSTRATOR: Susan Meddaugh
HC/PB: Houghton Mifflin
THEMES: magic; siblings; surprises; rats; change; secrets; folktale variation

"I was born a rat. I expected to be a rat all my days. But life is full of surprises." From the unique perspective of one of the rats turned into a coachman by Cinderella's fairy godmother, a new twist to this old tale. Meddaugh's animated art and wild imagination ensure laughs, so sit down with your child and read it aloud for a spell.

Fractured Fairy Tales*

Once upon a time there were the basic fairy tales of childhood: Cinderella, Little Red Riding Hood, The Three Little Pigs, etc. Every child knew them. Every parent loved them. Every teacher taught them. Everyone should have been happy. But no! Though we cannot credit them with the initial idea of turning traditional tales on their ear (for gifted storytellers have been doing this for generations), two madmen by the names of Jon Scieszka and Lane Smith created a publishing revolution with the 1989 release of their now classic *The True Story of the Three Little Pigs by A. Wolf.* Their zany, irreverent approach to this genre set a standard to which dozens of authors have aspired. Now, a season doesn't go by without an abundance of fairy-tale retellings that are fractured, skewed, or otherwise toyed with. Some are more successful than others. Here follows a list of our favorites. Please note that we are not talking about versions of stories from other cultures, but new tellings inspired by traditional versions.

Be certain your child knows the classic fairy tales. If she doesn't have the foundation of the original story, then the effect of the fracture is lost on her. Besides, classic characters are referred to throughout our lives and it's best if our children recognize them.

FRACTURED VERSIONS OF *THE THREE LITTLE PIGS*
The Three Little Javelinas by Susan Lowell
The Three Little Wolves and the Big Bad Pig by Eugene Trivizas
The Three Pigs by Barry Moser
The Three Pigs by David Wiesner
The True Story of the Three Little Pigs by Jon Scieszka and Lane Smith
Wait! No Paint! by Bruce Whatley
Yo, Hungry Wolf! by David Vozar (also contains fractured versions of *Little Red Riding Hood* and *The Boy Who Cried Wolf*)

FRACTURED VERSIONS OF *CINDERELLA*
Cinder Edna by Ellen Jackson
Cinderella Skeleton by Robert San Souci
Cinderella's Rat by Susan Meddaugh
Fanny's Dream by Caralyn Buehner
I Was a Rat! by Phillip Pullman
Prince Cinders by Babette Cole

FRACTURED VERSIONS OF *THE GINGERBREAD MAN*
The Matzah Man: A Passover Story by Naomi Howland
The Runaway Rice Cake by Ying Chang Compestine
The Runaway Tortilla by Eric Kimmel

*Jay Ward, creator of the cartoon series *Rocky and Bullwinkle*, coined this phrase.

OTHER FRACTURED VERSIONS TO LOOK FOR

Alice Nizzy Nazzy, the Witch of Santa Fe by Tony Johnston (Baba Yaga)

Goldilocks Returns by Lisa Campbell Ernst (The Three Bears)

Henny Penny by Jane Wattenberg

The Jolly Postman, or Other People's Letters by Janet and Allan Ahlberg (several in one)

Kate and the Beanstalk by Mary Pope Osborne (Jack and the Beanstalk)

Little Lit: Folklore and Fairy Tale Funnies by Art Spiegelman, editor (several in one)

Look Out Jack! The Giant Is Back! by Tom Birdseye (Jack and the Beanstalk)

The Princess Tales (*Princess Sonora and the Long Sleep; Cinderellis and the Glass Hill; The Fairy's Return; For Biddle's Sake; The Fairy's Mistake; The Princess Test*) by Gail Carson Levine (various princesses)

The Seven Dwarfs by Etienne Delessert (Snow White)

Sleeping Ugly by Jane Yolen (Sleeping Beauty)

Somebody and the Three Blairs by Marilyn Tolhurst (The Three Bears)

The Stinky Cheese Man and Other Fairly Stupid Tales by Jon Scieszka and Lane Smith (several in one)

A Telling of the Tales by William J. Brooke (several in one)

The Very Smart Pea and the Princess to Be by Mini Grey (The Princess and the Pea)

Yours Truly, Goldilocks (and others) by Alma Flor Ada (several in one)

Cloudy with a Chance of Meatballs

PICTURE BOOK

AUTHOR: Judi Barrett • ILLUSTRATOR: Ron Barrett
HC: Atheneum • PB: Aladdin
THEMES: wordplay; food; weather; storytelling; change; fantasy

Grandpa tells the story of a town called Chewandswallow where there were no food stores. "They didn't need any. The sky supplied all the food they could possibly want . . . Whatever the weather served, that was what they ate." It rained soup and juice. It snowed mashed potatoes, and a big storm could blow in hamburgers. Tweak imaginations with this tall tale and watch the children come up with their own food fantasies.

★ The Clown of God

PICTURE BOOK

AUTHOR/ILLUSTRATOR: Tomie dePaola
HC/PB: Harcourt Brace

THEMES: juggling; folklore; Italy; history, the Renaissance; gifts; aging; jobs; faith; religion

Sweetly told, with beautiful, Renaissance-style illustrations, dePaola's version of the story of the juggler and his gift to God is one of his best books. Giovanni starts out as a poverty-stricken youth, but through his juggling ability he becomes a famous entertainer. When times grow hard and he returns to his boyhood home, Giovanni gives one last performance before a statue of The Madonna and Child. Moving and unforgettable.

The Crow and the Pitcher
PICTURE BOOK NONFICTION

AUTHOR/ILLUSTRATOR: Stephanie Gwyn Brown
HC: Tricycle Press
THEMES: birds; water; perseverance; science; science experiments; fables; problem solving

A thirsty crow half dead from the desert heat finds a pitcher of water, but his beak is too short, the pitcher too narrow, and the water too low for him to take a drink. He almost gives up hope when—drawn from information and inspiration—he gets an idea. Brown's version of Aesop's classic fable tackles Crow's problem through scientific method—from question to communication. Brightly colored pictures fill the pages with Crow's scientific discoveries. Readers will think, laugh, and learn a thing or two.

Dakota Dugout
PICTURE BOOK

AUTHOR: Ann Turner • ILLUSTRATOR: Ronald Himler
PB: Aladdin
THEMES: pioneers; dwellings; home; U.S. history, frontier life; U.S.A., the prairie; U.S. history, Westward movement; family

Beautifully rendered black-and-white drawings with little text describe prairie life in a sod house from the voice of a woman who remembers.

Dawn
PICTURE BOOK

AUTHOR/ILLUSTRATOR: Molly Bang
HC: Seastar
THEMES: folklore; strong girls; boats; geese; change; patience; artists; secrets

A powerful retelling of the Japanese folktale "The Crane Wife" set in New England. A poor shipbuilder saves a goose's life and meets a beautiful young woman, a sailmaker of magical origin. Bang's marvelous art, alternating between black-and-white and color, adds depth to the tale, offering clues to the observant as to the true nature of the sailmaker.

The Day Jimmy's Boa Ate the Wash

PICTURE BOOK

AUTHOR: Trina Hakes Noble • ILLUSTRATOR: Steven Kellogg
HC: Dial • PB: Puffin
THEMES: farms; snakes; humor; field trips

This cleverly constructed tale is told in flashback by a young girl who is relating what happened on a field trip. Using the usual blasé style that kids have of telling about their day to contrast with the highly outrageous goings on at the farm, Noble creates a story whose pages we can't wait to turn, and she is ably assisted by Kellogg's outstandingly detailed illustrations.

A Day with Wilbur Robinson

PICTURE BOOK

AUTHOR/ILLUSTRATOR: William Joyce
HC/PB: HarperCollins
THEMES: humor; family; grandfathers; friendship; fantasy; zany

Wilbur Robinson must be the envy of every young reader. He lives in an enormous house with a wacky family, unusual pets, and wild servants. Each time we open this book, we find something we'd missed—even grandfather's teeth, which had been the subject of an all-day search. If you don't like zany, don't read this. Save it for a kid who does.

A Day's Work

PICTURE BOOK

AUTHOR: Eve Bunting • ILLUSTRATOR: Ronald Himler
HC/PB: Clarion
THEMES: truth; jobs; Spanish words; conscience; problem solving; Mexican; grandfathers and grandsons; responsibility; cooperation

This tale begins in a parking lot with men lined up hoping a truck or car will appear with a driver looking for workers. Francisco is there with his grandfather, who doesn't speak English. Francisco knows they need the work, so he lies about their experience with gardening—which results in a lot more work than he'd planned on and a lesson in honesty.

Dear Willie Rudd

PICTURE BOOK

AUTHOR: Libba Moore Gray • ILLUSTRATOR: Peter Fiore
PB: Aladdin
THEMES: African American; U.S.A., the South; memories; civil rights; taking action; prejudice; regret; mail; writing

Many of us have had an adult in our life we later wish we had told how much we loved. With a child's longing and an adult's regret, Miss Elizabeth sits on the porch of her house one afternoon, remembering Willie Rudd, the "colored" woman who took care of her when she was a child. Wishing more than anything that she could go back and right the wrongs of the past, she comes up with a remarkably simple and healing solution. Though it deals with a specific relationship, the story's theme is universal and is told with a great deal of love.

Dogzilla

PICTURE BOOK

AUTHOR/ILLUSTRATOR: Dav Pilkey
HC/PB: Harcourt Brace
THEMES: humor; dogs; monsters; parodies; puns

One of the funniest books we've encountered in years. This parody of the famous Japanese monster movie is illustrated in a photocollage style, with the author's dog playing the monster and his pet mice standing in for the terrified population of "Mouseopolis." Full of atrocious puns that will have adults groaning and kids rolling in the aisles, this is one of the best books for enticing an older boy into reading, especially if he thinks he is too cool to be bothered.

For another outrageous adventure, be sure to get a copy of Pilkey's *Kat Kong*.

The Dragonling

FICTION-FANTASY

AUTHOR: Jackie French Koller • ILLUSTRATOR: Judith Mitchell
PB: Aladdin
THEMES: adventure; community; courage; rituals; traditions; family;
    friendship; dragons; fantasy; prejudice

Collected in two volumes, this series of books provides a terrific stepping-stone from early readers to longer chapter books. Set in a world where people and dragons are enemies, this series tells the story of a boy who befriends a dragon pup and raises him, despite the fears and prejudices of his community and family. What elevates the books above the pack is author Koller's ability to wrestle with big moral issues in a way that is both appropriate and understandable to a seven-year-old, without losing sight of the fact that the story needs to come first. The first volume includes *The Dragonling, A Dragon in the Family*, and *Dragon Quest*, and the second volume contains *The Dragons of Krad, Dragon Trouble*, and *Dragons and Kings*.

AUTHOR SPOTLIGHT ON
EVE BUNTING

Eve Bunting is a writer of a wide range, both in the types of books she writes (folktale retellings, picture books, and novels for all ages of reader) and in the range of topics she covers. Her interests are seemingly boundless, and each year brings at least one new picture book examining an aspect of the human condition in her characteristically caring and strongly felt style. Bunting's desire to shed light on some of the more disturbing aspects of life often results in books that stir up our feelings, many of them uncomfortable, about the issues at hand.

Issues like homelessness (*Fly Away Home*), urban riots (the Caldecott-winning *Smoky Night*), illiteracy (*The Wednesday Surprise*), divorce (*Some Frog,*) adoption (*Jin Woo*), and the Vietnam War (*The Wall*) are explored with compassion in picture-book format. Bunting's books often make the perfect introduction to discussions of these hard topics. This author does not always offer solutions but allows a means to discuss these issues with our children so that they can grow up to find the solutions that have eluded us.

But Eve Bunting is not only a writer of issue-oriented books. Our delight in her work stems chiefly from the way she can move between genres, from a funny, contemporary look at a sixth-grade class learning the burdens of parenthood (*Our Sixth Grade Sugar Babies*), to a gripping account of loss and false heroism (*Blackwater*), to a stunning look at ancient Egypt through the eyes of one of its residents (*I Am the Mummy Heb-Nefert*), from holiday-oriented books aimed at younger readers (*St. Patrick's Day in the Morning*, *The Valentine Bears*, and *A Turkey for Thanksgiving*) to picture books illuminating the injustice embedded in the American way of life (*Cheyenne Again* and *Train to Somewhere*), to her creepy books about gargoyles (*Night of the Gargoyles*) and owls (*The Man Who Could Call Down Owls*).

Bunting is at heart an Irish storyteller, a Shanachie, who, in more than 100 books spanning forty years of creative fertility has transcended her roots to become one of America's best-loved and most thoughtful writers for children. Her concern for the lives of children shines on the pages of every story she tells.

Earrings!

PICTURE BOOK

AUTHOR: Judith Viorst • ILLUSTRATOR: Nola Langner Malone
HC: Antheneum • PB: Aladdin
THEMES: yearning; family; jewelry; comparisons

She wants to have her ears pierced. Her parents want her to wait a couple of years. She tells them, "I'm the only girl in my class, in my school, in the world, in the solar system whose mom and dad won't let her have pierced ears." This is for every child who knows she or he is the only one who can't have "it" or do "it." It's also for the rotten parents.

Eight Hands Round: A Patchwork Alphabet
PICTURE BOOK
AUTHOR: Ann Whitford Paul • ILLUSTRATOR: Jeanette Winter
HC/PB: HarperCollins
THEMES: quilts; crafts; alphabet; folk art; symbols; U.S. history

An ABC of patchwork quilts, in which each letter introduces a pattern and its history, starting with *A* for Anvil. The page shows an anvil design and explains that "Two hundred years ago most towns had a blacksmith. An anvil always sat on a flat stump in his shop . . ." *B*? is for Buggy Wheel, *C* is for Churn Dash, and patterns proceed through the alphabet to "Zigzag," the symbol for lightning. A fascinating way to learn history and respect for the folk art tradition.

El Chino
PICTURE BOOK BIOGRAPHY
AUTHOR/ILLUSTRATOR: Allen Say
HC/PB: Houghton Mifflin
THEMES: jobs; yearning; cultural diversity; Chinese American; Spain; bullfighting; biography; determination

Billy Wong wants to learn the art of bullfighting. He is a Chinese American in Spain and his chances are slim. He studies hard, practices, and one day finds faith in himself: "And as I stared in the mirror, a strange feeling came over me. I felt powerful. I felt that I could do anything I wished—even become a matador!" Say's watercolor paintings make this book a treasure to hold and his account of the true story of Billy Wong will encourage young readers who have dreams of their own.

Hanukkah and Christmas

In addition to *Elijah's Angel*, here are three books about the relationship between Jews and Gentiles at holiday time:

My Two Grandmothers by Effin Older, Nancy Hayashi (Illustrator)
The Trees of the Dancing Goats by Patricia Polacco
The Rugrats' Book of Chanukah by Sarah Wilson, Barry Goldberg (Illustrator)

★ Elijah's Angel: A Story for Chanukah and Christmas
PICTURE BOOK
AUTHOR: Michael J. Rosen • ILLUSTRATOR: Aminah Brenda Lynn Robinson
HC/PB: Harcourt Brace
THEMES: religion; friendship; cultural diversity; Christmas; Judaism; Chanukah; artists; symbols; comparisons; elderly and children

A story for Chanukah and Christmas. Michael worries about how his parents will feel if he brings home the beautiful Christmas Angel his friend Elijah has carved for him. After all, it is a forbidden graven image. Rosen sensitively handles the problems that can occur during holiday times when religions and personal beliefs differ.

Encyclopedia Brown Series

FICTION-MYSTERY

AUTHOR: Donald Sobol
PB: Bantam
THEMES: detectives; clues; mystery

Leroy Brown is the son of the chief of police in Idaville. No one except his parents and an occasional teacher calls him Leroy. He is known far and wide as Encyclopedia Brown, the smartest and most observant young sleuth in the world. This wonderful series is perfect for enticing beginning readers to become more confident. Have your kids read all the Nate the Greats and Cam Jansens? Then it's time to introduce them to these. Each book contains multiple short mysteries and encourages sleuthing on the part of the reader. The clues are all there, allowing the reader to match wits with "the Sherlock Holmes in sneakers." There are many titles in this series, and they all begin with *Encyclopedia Brown*.

The Faeries' Gift

PICTURE BOOK

AUTHOR: Tanya Robyn Batt • ILLUSTRATOR: Nicoletta Ceccoli
HC: Barefoot Books
THEMES: fairies; folklore; wishes; family; magic

Once upon a magical time, there was a poor woodcutter who lived in the forest with his wife and parents. One day he saved the life of a faerie and was granted one wish. But what should he wish for? His wife wanted a child, his mother her sight, and his father requested gold. Young readers will be delighted when he comes up with one wish to satisfy everyone. Ceccoli's acrylic and oil pictures add luster to this magic read-aloud.

 If you are someone who likes to have fun with your read-aloud listeners, here is a perfect tale for pausing before the final pages to let them figure out what might happen.

Fanny's Dream

PICTURE BOOK

AUTHOR: Caralyn Buehner • ILLUSTRATOR: Mark Buehner
HC: Dial • PB: Puffin
THEMES: change; marriage; family; strong women; folktale variations; yearning

Sometimes you give up your dreams and learn to make the best of what you have. And sometimes your prince is right there under your nose. Taking a page from the Cinderella story and setting it in the pioneer days, this funny and bittersweet tale is a terrific way to introduce children to the concept of lifelong commitment between a couple that is based on reality, not fantasy.

Festivals

POETRY COLLECTION

AUTHOR: Myra Cohn Livingston • ILLUSTRATOR: Leonard Everett Fisher
HC: Holiday House
THEMES: holidays; festivals; celebrations; cultural diversity

Organized chronologically, here are fourteen poems, each a look at important days around the world combining a balance of cultures and festivals. Livingston's style of poetry varies from page to page, matching the spirit of each festival.

Fireboat: The Heroic Adventures of the John J. Harvey

PICTURE BOOK

AUTHOR/ILLUSTRATOR: Maria Kalman
HC: Putnam
THEMES: boats; firefighters; disaster; New York;
    September 11; heroes

Another Kalman book that would make a great read in conjunction with a visit to New York is *Grand Central Station*—be sure to check out her murals in the train station the next time you have the chance.

A strong story of a boat, its owners, and its role on September 11, told with Kalman's off-kilter style and deep love of New York City. The best book about New York's response to September 11 we have seen.

Flight

PICTURE BOOK BIOGRAPHY

AUTHOR: Robert Burleigh • ILLUSTRATOR: Mike Wimmer
PB: Paperstar
THEMES: flying; Charles Lindbergh; U.S. history, early 20th century;
    airplanes; navigation; trailblazing; heroes; biography

"It is 1927, and his name is Charles Lindbergh. Later they will call him the Lone Eagle. Later they will call him Lucky Lindy. But not now. Now it is May 20, 1927. And he is standing in the still-dark dawn." The reader gazes between Lindbergh's boots at the *Spirit of St. Louis* parked in the distance. Wimmer's incredible close-up perspectives fuse with Burleigh's text to create an outstanding account of Lindbergh's famous flight.

Fly Away Home

AUTHOR: Eve Bunting • ILLUSTRATOR: Ronald Himler

HC: Clarion

THEMES: homelessness; airports; courage; fathers and sons; home; yearning; poverty; jobs; single parents

A boy and his dad live in an airport, striving to remain unnoticed. This is a devastating look at the effects of homelessness, rendered in Bunting's usual poignant style.

From Head to Toe: The Amazing Human Body and How It Works

PICTURE BOOK NONFICTION

AUTHOR: Barbara Seuling • ILLUSTRATOR: Edward Miller

HC: Holiday House

THEMES: bones; human body; brain; science experiments; cumulative

Parts of the human body, including bones, muscles, joints, the brain, and others, are covered with lively text, bright illustrations, and easy-to-do experiments. Conversational language, along with a design that utilizes bullet points, sidebars, and humorous asides, makes this an inviting volume for the curious.

From Pictures to Words: A Book About Making a Book

PICTURE BOOK NONFICTION

AUTHOR/ILLUSTRATOR: Janet Stevens

HC/PB: Holiday House

THEMES: authors; illustrators; writing; books; creativity

How a Book Is Made by Aliki (page 292) offers another look at this topic.)

Stevens takes us on the journey an author takes to write and illustrate a book. Her characters intrude, comment, and generally get in the way, but the reader gets a solid understanding of the process.

Geography from A to Z: A Picture Glossary   PICTURE BOOK NONFICTION

AUTHOR: Jack Knowlton • ILLUSTRATOR: Harriett Barton

HC: HarperCollins

THEMES: geography; glossary; alphabet

From "archipelago" to "zone," this colorful glossary of geographic terms is a perfect resource for young geographers.

George Hogglesberry, Grade School Alien

PICTURE BOOK

AUTHOR: Sarah Wilson • ILLUSTRATOR: Chad Cameron

HC: Tricycle Press

THEMES: new experiences; fitting in; school; comparisons; family; aliens;
  plays; diversity; friendship; self-confidence; self-respect

"Before George Hogglesberry went into his new class, he put a nose on his face." George is different; there is no doubt about it. He walks on the ceiling, can't maneuver the drinking fountain, and changes shapes without warning—oh, and then there's the nose. He has trouble fitting in at school. George probably doesn't feel all that different from your child on the first day as the new kid. In this salute to diversity, George's parents, teacher, and classmates all lend a hand in helping him become a beloved member of the class. A funny and satisfying story that will find its home on many bookshelves.

David Wisniewski

David Wisniewski was an artist who must have had incredible patience to work his craft with such precision. Children are often fascinated with the pictures in his books and will stare at them for long periods of time. To see more of his amazing folklore retellings, get a copy of *Rain Player*, *The Wave of the Sea Wolf*, or *Sundiata: Lion King of Mali*. Then, for a different treat, see how his cut-paper illustrations work to make his hilarious *The Secret Knowledge of Grownups* a favoite with kids of all ages.

Golem

PICTURE BOOK

AUTHOR/ILLUSTRATOR: David Wisniewski

HC: Clarion

THEMES: folklore; Jews; Prague; monsters; creation;
  magic; Judaism; fathers and sons; clay

Four hundred years ago, the story goes, a rabbi plunged his hands into an enormous lump of clay, shaped it into a giant man, and brought him to life to watch over the Jews. This Caldecott-winning rendition of one of the most gripping stories in Jewish tradition serves not only as a good scary story, but also as an introduction to cut-paper illustrations. Isaac Bashevis Singer's *The Golem* is a longer retelling of the folktale and an excellent book to turn to if the picture-book adaptation whets the appetite for more.

★ Grandfather's Journey

PICTURE BOOK

AUTHOR/ILLUSTRATOR: Allen Say

HC: Houghton Mifflin

THEMES: Japan; immigration; grandfathers and grandsons; journeys;
  Japanese American; cultural diversity; war; comparisons; memories

Master craftsman Say offers a poignant look at how it feels to be raised in two cultures. Beautifully rendered, with a perfect combination of art and text, this masterpiece illuminates the joys and conflicting emotions many bicultural people feel. As the narrator says, "The funny thing is, the moment I am in one country, I am homesick for the other." There is a piece of the author's heart on every page.

Grass Sandals: The Travels of Basho

PICTURE BOOK BIOGRAPHY

AUTHOR: Dawnine Spivak • ILLUSTRATOR: Demi
HC: Atheneum
THEMES: Japan; poets; biography; writing; journeys

Rich, descriptive writing brings the famed Japanese poet Basho to life, and Demi's art adds the perfect touch. Basho's adventures will motivate young writers.

The Great White Man-Eating Shark: A Cautionary Tale

PICTURE BOOK

AUTHOR: Margaret Mahy • ILLUSTRATOR: Jonathan Allen
PB: Puffin
THEMES: lessons; disguises; sharks; swimming; dreaming; playing tricks

Hilarious! In the tradition of Victorian cautionary tales, here is the story of Norvin, who looks like a shark and uses this fact to wreak havoc in the peaceful waters of Caramel Cove. Pretending to be a shark in order to frighten the other swimmers away gives him great satisfaction and results in his having the waters all to himself. He learns his lesson when a real shark mistakes him for a potential mate. A stitch to read aloud!

Hairdo! What We Do and Did to Our Hair

PICTURE BOOK NONFICTION

AUTHOR: Ruth Freeman Swain • ILLUSTRATOR: Cat Bowman Smith
HC: Holiday House
THEMES: hair; fashion; history

Did you know . . .

there are about 100,000 hairs on our heads?
that your hair grows about half an inch a month?
that in eighteenth-century Europe, some women's hairdos rose to more than two feet high and were coated with lard and flour?

Chinese New Year

Here are our favorite titles about this holiday:

Celebrating Chinese New Year by Diane Hoyt-Goldsmith, Lawrence Migdale (Illustrator)
The Dancing Dragon by Marcia K. Vaughan, Stanley Wong Hoo Foon (Illustrator)
Lion Dancer: Ernie Wan's Chinese New Year by Kate Waters and Madeline Slovenz-Low, Martha Cooper (Illustrator)
My Chinatown: One Year in Poems by Kam Mak (Illustrator)
The Runaway Rice Cake by Ying Chang Compestine, Tungwai Chau (Illustrator)
Sam and the Lucky Money by Karen Chinn, Cornelius Van Wright and Ying-Hwa Hu (Illustrators)
This Next New Year by Janet S. Wong, Yangsook Choi (Illustrator)

These are just samples of the hairy bits of history from all over the world that you'll find in this informative and entertaining book.

Happy New Year! Kung-Hsi Fa-Ts'ai!

PICTURE BOOK NONFICTION

AUTHOR/ILLUSTRATOR: Demi

PB: Dragonfly

THEMES: Chinese New Year; Chinese culture; traditions; food; celebrations; social studies; dragons

Demi's cheery, colorful paintings and straightforward text present the Chinese New Year. Children learn about the animal zodiac, parades, dances, dragons, and how families prepare for the holiday, making this a perfect book for sharing in January or February when the celebration takes place.

★ Hershel and the Hanukkah Goblins

PICTURE BOOK

AUTHOR: Eric Kimmel • ILLUSTRATOR: Trina Schart Hyman

HC/PB: Holiday House

THEMES: Hanukkah; cleverness; courage; candles; monsters; spooky stories; faith; folklore; Jews; traditions

Kimmel's retelling of the story of Hershel of Ostropol and how he restores Hanukkah to a town where goblins reign supreme is outstanding. Match his words with Caldecott Honor–winning illustrations by Hyman and you have a treasure that stands up to countless readings every holiday season. There is much humor here, as well as cleverness, scares, and heartwarming faith.

How Big Is a Foot?

EARLY READER

AUTHOR/ILLUSTRATOR: Rolf Myller

PB: Dell

THEMES: math; measurement; kings; queens; gifts; beds

A simple, fun tale with lots of math application. A king wants to build a bed for his queen, but first he has to figure out how big it is to be. How big *is* a foot, he wonders, and his journey of discovery, with the aid of almost everyone in the kingdom, will delight children

---

Hanukkah and Other Holidays of the Jewish Tradition

Not that there aren't other writers who do fine tales for this special season, but we are partial to Eric Kimmel's holiday retellings when we want a dose of Hanukkah folklore. In addition to *Hershel and the Hanukkah Goblins*, look for *The Magic Dreidels, When Mindy Saved Hanukkah, A Hanukkah Treasury*, and *Zigazak! A Magical Hanukkah Night*.

Kimmel has also written a terrific tale for Rosh Hashanah, *Gershon's Monster: A Story for the Jewish New Year*.

For Passover, we like *Matzah Man: A Passover Story* by Naomi Howland, and *Miriam's Cup: A Passover Story* by Fran Manushkin, Bob Dacey (Illustrator).

For Shavuot, look for *A Mountain of Blintzes* by Barbara Diamond Goldin, Anik McGrory (Illustrator)

For Sukkott, Patricia Polacco offers a moving tale of a lost cat, a devastating fire, and a miracle in *Mrs. Katz and Tush*.

just coming to terms with the twelve inches in a foot and the three feet in a yard.

How Much Is a Million?   PICTURE BOOK NONFICTION
AUTHOR: David Schwartz • ILLUSTRATOR: Steven Kellogg
HC: Lothrop • PB: Mulberry
THEMES: math; numbers; counting; measurement; concepts; comparisons

An outstanding counting book that goes beyond 1-2-3 and gives concrete examples of the enormity of big numbers. Many children become obsessed with numbers, the bigger the better. In this book, Schwartz and Kellogg bring to life the concepts of million, billion, and beyond in ways that contribute greatly to children's understanding. For example: "If you sat down to count from one to one billion . . . you would be counting for 95 years." Great fun, with detailed explanations at the back of the book from the author, and clever touches throughout by the illustrator.

> Schwartz and Kellogg team up for a look at money (*If You Made a Million*) and measurements (*Millions to Measure*), and the books are every bit as wonderful as their first.

How to Eat Fried Worms   FICTION
AUTHOR: Thomas Rockwell • ILLUSTRATOR: Emily Arnold McCully
HC: Franklin Watts • PB: Dell
THEMES: worms; dares; wagers; humor, gross

Short, funny chapters and one of the best titles ever make this one of a handful of books we suggest confidently for boys who say they don't like reading. Billy's bet that he can eat fifteen worms gets him into all kinds of squirmy, gross, disgusting situations. Those fifteen worms get eaten. And the reader is there for every one of them.

How to Make an Apple Pie and See the World   PICTURE BOOK
AUTHOR/ILLUSTRATOR: Marjorie Priceman
HC: Knopf • PB: Dragonfly
THEMES: geography; baking; travel; recipes; pies

A young baker leads the reader around the world gathering ingredients for making an apple pie. Sound interesting to you? Probably not. So how come this is one of our picks? Priceman's sense of humor prevails on every page, delivering facts and fun along the way. Maps are found on the end papers, as well as the recipe for the pie. Yum!

I Pledge Allegiance

PICTURE BOOK

AUTHORS: Bill Martin Jr. and Michael Sampson • ILLUSTRATOR: Chris
   Raschka
HC: Candlewick
THEMES: flag, patriotism, U.S. history

A word-by-word explanation of the famous pledge, originally written as a
children's poem. Facts abound and Raschka comes up with various clever
and insightful uses of the colors red, white, and blue.

If You Find a Rock

PICTURE BOOK NONFICTION

AUTHOR: Peggy Christian
HC: Harcourt Brace
THEMES: rocks; poetry; comparisons; nature

Skipping, splashing, climbing, wishing—rocks have lots of uses, and some
work well as a tool for drawing on a sidewalk. Poetic text and hand-tinted
photographs transform common stones into prized possessions. This quiet
gem invites young readers to ponder the possibilities.

Into the Sea

PICTURE BOOK NONFICTION

AUTHOR: Brenda Z. Guiberson • ILLUSTRATOR: Alix Berenzy
HC/PB: Henry Holt
THEMES: animal; life cycles; turtles; sea; science; nature

From the "tap, tap, scritch" of the tiny hatchling to the "thump, scrape,
whoosh, wheeze" of the hardworking turtle returned to lay her eggs, young
readers learn the life cycle of the sea turtle. The pictures are rich and colorful
and the words read like a story. A perfect blend of fiction and nonfiction.

★ Julius, the Baby of the World

PICTURE BOOK

AUTHOR/ILLUSTRATOR: Kevin Henkes
HC: Greenwillow • PB: Mulberry
THEMES: jealousy; new baby; humor; brothers; family; change; strong girl

The definitive book on sibling jealousy, told in a side-splitting manner. Lilly
will win you over in spite of her outrageous behavior, and if you can't get
enough of her, she returns in *Lilly's Purple Plastic Purse*.

Jumanji

PICTURE BOOK

AUTHOR/ILLUSTRATOR: Chris Van Allsburg

HC: Houghton Mifflin

THEMES: games; magic; mystery; jungles; animals; boredom; problem
solving; consequences

We need to stress *forget the movie!* This is a simple and terrifying tale of
what happens to two children who play a board game without fully understanding the rules. Creepy black-and-white illustrations and a spare text
make this a book that beckons the reader inside over and over again. A
sequel, *Zathura,* offers more of the same.

The Last Dragon

PICTURE BOOK

AUTHOR: Susan Nunes • ILLUSTRATOR: Chris Soentpiet

HC/PB: Clarion

THEMES: dragons; community; aunts; neighbors; Chinese
American; Chinese culture

Peter does not want to spend the summer with his great-
aunt in a small apartment above a noodle factory—until he
sees a dragon in the window of the Lung Fung Trading
Company. The unique culture of Chinatown is celebrated in
this story where neighbors rally to restore a dragon for a
young boy who learns a thing or two about community.

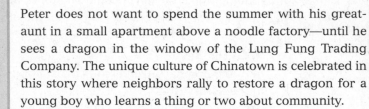

Julie (Andrews) Edwards

Writing under her married name,
Julie Andrews has been providing
children of all ages with reading
adventures for nearly as long as she
has been a star. Books about Little
Bo are for beginning readers, while
Dumpy and the Big Storm (part of a
series of picture books about a
dump truck created with daughter
Emma Walton) offers delights for
preschoolers. Also written with her
daughter and stunningly illustrated
by Grennady Spirin is *Simeon's Gift,*
a musician's tale for the early elementary set. Her two novels, *Mandy*
and *The Last of the Really Great
Whangdoodles,* have found comfortable homes on library shelves as
beloved classics and are read and
enjoyed by each new generation of
third- to sixth-graders.

Little Bo in France: The Further Adventures of Bonnie Boadicea

PICTURE BOOK

AUTHOR: Julie Andrews Edwards • ILLUSTRATOR: Henry
Cole

HC: Hyperion

THEMES: France; Paris; friends; cats; travel

In this sequel to *Little Bo,* the heroine cat and her sailor
friend make their way to Paris. There they visit the Eiffel
Tower and Montmartre. Cole's gentle oil paintings combine
with French words sprinkled throughout to offer a young
reader a glimpse into one of the world's most beautiful
countries.

Little Gold Star/Estrellita de Oro

PICTURE BOOK

AUTHOR: Joe Hayes • ILLUSTRATORS: Gloria Osuna Perez
and Lucia Angela Perez
HC: Cinco Puntos Press
THEMES: bilingual; Cinderella; folktale variation; magic;
transformation

Here is a Southwest version of the Cinderella story, accompanied by acrylic paintings by El Paso artist Gloria Osuna Perez and her daughter, Lucia Angela Perez, who stepped in to finish the project after her mother's death. This reads aloud well in both languages and is a perfect book to use for storytelling in schools with a high population of Hispanic children.

★ Liza Lou and the Yeller Belly Swamp

PICTURE BOOK

AUTHOR/ILLUSTRATOR: Mercer Mayer
PB: Aladdin
THEMES: monsters; swamps; opossums; witches; strong girls; folktale
variations; cleverness; triumph

 It was a read-aloud hit for my daughters' kindergarten, first- and second-grade classrooms—and years later is still a guaranteed no fail. Clever Liza Lou has the spunk kids like. Her story has swamp haunts, witches, devils, gobblygooks, repeatable poems, "how's she gonna get out of this mess" intrigue, and a possum who has a page to page wordless story all of his own. Liza Lou is a must read!

 Hey folks, if there are those among you who like a real storytelling workout, this is a good one to try. There are ten different voices to use and a mess of southern/swamp dialects to try out. Have fun!

Many people read Dr. Seuss's work and think they know something about how to make a children's book. He made it look too easy, especially with his topical subjects and simple rhyme. But what most people fail to realize is that he was a genius, a truly gifted master of the word and the minds of children. His timeless appeal cannot be copied, as it would require a talent and a heart like his, the likes of which we will never see again. Other longer Seuss titles we like are *On Beyond Zebra*, *McElligott's Pool*, *Yertle the Turtle*, and *The Sneetches and Other Stories*.

The Lorax

PICTURE BOOK

AUTHOR/ILLUSTRATOR: Dr. Seuss
HC: Random House
THEMES: trees; environment; taking action; rhyme; nature

"I am the Lorax. I speak for the trees" . . . and someone sure has to. In this environmental fable, Seuss walks a perilous line between preaching and telling a good story, but such is his magic that he never crosses over into the realm where the message is the medium.

Teaching Poetry

Ever had a conversation with a class of fifth-graders about poems? I have, many times. At the mere mention of the word *poetry*, they begin to groan. Ask them if they like poetry and they say, "No!" However, ask them if they like rap music, Shel Silverstein, or Jack Prelutsky and they get excited! "What?" I say to them. "Didn't you know that rap is poetry?" They often have never thought of it in those terms. Though I have met and worked with some truly gifted educators, too often poetry is taught by teachers who are uncomfortable with it themselves. These are the folks in classrooms who, with no connection to the material they are *required* to teach, fall back on the syllabus or required texts and teach them in a manner that is more about getting the subject over with than inspiring the students to like a subject with which they themselves are unversed.

For many students, these classes are the turning point in their relationship with poetry, as they have "Evangeline" or "The Raven" stuffed down their throats in a distinctly unappetizing manner, forever disconnecting them from the joy that earlier poems once delivered. I've even seen classes who hated "Jabberwocky!" (How can anyone dislike "Jabberwocky"?)

Teaching children to analyze poetry and literature without ripping the joy right out of it is hard and requires delicacy, insight, and patience. One of the reasons I adore Sharon Creech's *Love That Dog* is because it so wonderfully portrays the dance between a gifted, patient teacher and a child who is intrigued but suspicious of the subject of poetry. Reading that book and watching the teacher patiently pull a poet from the depths of that boy's soul is a gift, I tell you. Worse things could happen than teachers using that book as a foundation upon which to build a love of poetry in their students.

★ **Love that Dog**   FICTION

AUTHOR: Sharon Creech
HC: HarperCollins
THEMES: poetry; dogs; school; teachers; pets; poets;

> *September 13*
> I don't want to
> because boys
> don't write poetry.
>
> Girls do.

This novel, written as a series of poems from Jack's point of view, packs a wallop. Jack's caring and inspired teacher, Miss Stretchberry, uses works by a variety of poets, including William Blake, Robert Frost, and Walter Dean Myers, to encourage him to write. The more he writes, the more Jack has to say. The more he has to say, the more riveted the reader becomes. We see Jack transformed into a lover of poetry before our eyes. This brilliant testament to the power of poetry is a novel of warmth, love, and loss and will stay in the minds of readers long after the last page has been turned.

Luka's Quilt
PICTURE BOOK

AUTHOR/ILLUSTRATOR: Georgia Guback

HC: Greenwillow

THEMES: Hawaii; traditions; grandmothers and granddaughters; compromise; disagreements; quilts; feelings, hurt

Luka's grandmother makes a traditional two-colored Hawaiian quilt for her, but Luka thinks it should have lots of colors, like the flowers in her garden. Each has a strong opinion of her own, and hurts the other's feelings. This is a story of compromise and of putting aside differences.

I didn't like Luka's response. I thought she should have been thrilled that her grandmother made her a quilt at all and eternally grateful she had a grandmother!

Mailing May
PICTURE BOOK

AUTHOR: Michael O. Tunnell • ILLUSTRATOR: Ted Rand

HC: Greenwillow • PB: HarperCollins

THEMES: railroad; mail; Idaho; fathers and daughters; cleverness; mail carrier; promises; problem solving

Based on the true tale of how young Charlotte May's father gets her delivered by the U.S. Postal Service to her grandma, seventy-five miles away. This is a charming and informative look at life in rural Idaho in 1914 and a tribute to the cleverness of a loving father.

Math Curse
PICTURE BOOK

AUTHOR: Jon Scieszka • ILLUSTRATOR: Lane Smith

HC: Viking

THEMES: school; math; humor; problem solving; zany; point of view

A rollicking look at the effects of math education on all aspects of a bewildered child's life. Great fun for even the most math-phobic. Another success-

ful collaboration from a team that delights in showing us new ways of looking at old subjects.

Meanwhile . . .

PICTURE BOOK

AUTHOR/ILLUSTRATOR: Jules Feiffer
HC/PB: HarperCollins
THEMES: imagination; comic-book style; adventure;
    cleverness; fantasy

> Feiffer's two novels, *A Barrel of Laughs, a Vale of Tears* and *The Man in the Ceiling*, offer similar fun for older readers.

Told in comic book style, these fun adventures culminate in
cliffhangers. Comic-book-obsessed Raymond has to get himself out of them, so he uses the time-honored device of changing the scene
with a "Meanwhile . . ." It works, up to a point, and then he has to use his
own ingenuity to get himself out of his final scrape. Great fun for the reluctant reader, but there is no reason why the rest should be deprived of the
enjoyment.

Meet Danitra Brown

POETRY COLLECTION

AUTHOR: Nikki Grimes • ILLUSTRATOR: Floyd Cooper
HC: Lothrop • PB: Mulberry
THEMES: friendship; strong girls; African American; bullies; self-respect

In thirteen lively poems, Zuri tells us about Danitra, her best friend. Warm,
sweet, and spunky—read this to a friend. When it is over, look for more
poems by Zuri in *Danitra Brown Leaves Town*.

Metropolitan Cow

PICTURE BOOK

AUTHOR/ILLUSTRATOR: Tim Egan
HC/PB: Houghton Mifflin
THEMES: prejudice; friendship; diversity; city life

A terrific piece of social commentary that never forgets how to tell a good
story, *Metropolitan Cow* tells of a city where there are upper-class cows and
working-class pigs. When cow Bennett Gibbons expresses a desire to jump
in the mud and play with the pigs, his parents make their disapproval quite
clear: "Don't be ridiculous. You know cows don't go in the mud. We're far too
dignified for such nonsense." But after Webster Anderson, the pig next door,
befriends him the temptation proves too great for Bennett. How Webster
and Bennett's families come together as friends is the heart of this charming
and whimsical tale of defeating class prejudice.

★ Miss Rumphius

PICTURE BOOK

AUTHOR/ILLUSTRATOR: Barbara Cooney

HC: Viking • PB: Puffin

THEMES: strong women; gardening; taking action; travel; independence; individuality; journeys; elderly and children; aging; self-respect; responsibility; friendship

This powerful recounting of the life of a woman who lives on her own terms and still remembers her responsibility to make the world more beautiful is one of our favorites. Its quiet strength and wisdom stay with the reader and listener long after the story has finished. We'd like our sons and daughters to think about Miss Rumphius when they make their own life decisions.

Mrs. Biddlebox

PICTURE BOOK

AUTHOR: Linda Smith • ILLUSTRATOR: Marla Frazee

HC: HarperCollins

THEMES: bad days; problem solving; baking; change

Frazee's spectacular art makes excellent use of the somber, limited palette of a bad day. Smith's poem of a woman who makes the best of things by baking the awful day into a cake and eating it is one of the most lively and inspiring "lemons into lemonade" tales we've encountered.

My Family Tree: A Bird's Eye View

NOVELTY

AUTHOR/ILLUSTRATOR: Nina Laden

HC: Chronicle

THEMES: family; relatives; genealogy; connections

"Maybe your grandparents came from another country, your uncle has five stepbrothers, or your second cousins once-removed are identical twins." Whatever the mix, this book includes a family-tree poster to fill out, as well as an illustrated explanation of who is who. It makes room for a variety of family connections—including stepfamilies—in a fun, easy-to-understand style.

My First Book of Proverbs/Mi Primer Libro De Dichos

PICTURE BOOK NONFICTION

AUTHORS/ILLUSTRATORS: Ralfka and Ana Gonzalez

HC: Childrens Book Press

THEMES: proverbs; wordplay; Mexican American; Spanish language; bilingual; Mexico

"Pig out while you have the chance" and "Experience is the Mama of Science" are only a couple in this playful, bilingual collection of Mexican American proverbs. Bright, colorful paintings capture Mexico's folk-art style.

★ The Mysteries of Harris Burdick   PICTURE BOOK
AUTHOR/ILLUSTRATOR: Chris Van Allsburg
HC: Houghton Mifflin
THEMES: mystery; magic; writing; storytelling; imagination; guessing

In a sequence of unrelated pictures, each accompanied by one tantalizing caption, Van Allsburg opens a world of possibilities to the reader. If you take him at his word, and we have no reason to disbelieve him, he has found these pictures unaccompanied by any writing except the sentences he includes, and he is offering them without editorial comment in the hopes that they will inspire some storytelling creativity on the part of the reader. We guarantee that children will have lots to say.

When my daughter Kaela was in the fourth grade, she reminded me that Harris Burdick was a very scary book and that I should warn parents when they bought it. Yet she had pored over the pages for hours the year before, never mentioning her concerns. His images force a reader response, and to Kaela they were frightening. Oh, the power of Van Allsburg, whose art can linger in the backs of our minds! I've used this incredible book for years during writing workshops with fascinating results. It lives permanently in our library.

The Mysterious Tadpole   PICTURE BOOK
AUTHOR/ILLUSTRATOR: Steven Kellogg
HC: Dial
THEMES: friendship; pets; frogs; monsters; Scotland; cleverness; triumph

Louis's uncle sends him a birthday surprise from Scotland—a tadpole that turns out to be related to the Loch Ness Monster. How Louis and his family cope with the growth and appetite of Alphonse and how the day is ultimately saved by a combination of boyish ingenuity and a deep-diving pet makes for a whopper of a tale. Kellogg's wonderful sense of humor is abundantly evident in all the details of the illustrations, from the names on the signs to the faces and clothes of the characters. A delight from beginning to surprising end.

Nathaniel Talking   POETRY COLLECTION
AUTHOR: Eloise Greenfield • ILLUSTRATOR: Jan Spivey Gilchrist
HC/PB: Black Butterfly
THEMES: gentle boys; African American; rhyme; love; family; loss; music; grief; rhythm; lessons

"One day I was dumb enough to let somebody bet me into a fight and then I was mad with two stupid boys—the one who was hitting me and the one who was hitting him." Nathaniel B. Free is a spirited nine-year-old who tells his story through rap and rhyme. Funny, poignant, strong, and sad, his poems will stay with you. Greenfield has included directions on how to write a twelve-bar blues poem at the back of the book.

The Other Side   PICTURE BOOK

AUTHOR: Jacqueline Woodson • ILLUSTRATOR: E. B. Lewis
HC: Putnam
THEMES: prejudice; friendship; change; problem solving

Clover lives where a fence separates the black side of town from the white. Her mother has warned her that it is not safe to climb over to the other side. When a white girl named Annie begins to sit on the fence, it doesn't take long for Clover to join her, and the fence is transformed from a divider to a resting place for children, black and white. In Woodson's story of the power of innocence over bigotry, the young girls are the activists, making change. Lewis's lifelike watercolor paintings draw the reader into each page.

 I wish they had eliminated the last page. It's as though we don't trust young readers (or listeners) to get the point. Children don't need this story explained.

Parents in the Pigpen, Pigs in the Tub   PICTURE BOOK

AUTHOR: Amy Ehrlich • ILLUSTRATOR: Steven Kellogg
PB: Puffin
THEMES: farms; animals; farms; barns; family; comparisons; zany

Hilarious fun, as the farm animals move into the house and the family moves into the barn. Kellogg's usual outstanding art takes Ehrlich's already funny story and makes it a laugh riot.

Peppe the Lamplighter   PICTURE BOOK

AUTHOR: Alisa Bartone • ILLUSTRATOR: Ted Lewin
HC: Lothrop • PB: Mulberry
THEMES: jobs; immigration; family; courage; taking action

Ted Lewin's paintings illuminate this story about a young boy who insists on taking a job when his immigrant father becomes ill. The lesson here is to take pride in your work, regardless of the job.

Piggybook

AUTHOR/ILLUSTRATOR: Anthony Browne
PB: Dragonfly
THEMES: gender roles; mothers; family; jobs; change; pigs; lessons

Mrs. Piggott has had quite enough of her horrid husband and her churlish children and their boorish behavior. They let her do all the housework and the cooking (in addition to her own job) and they lie around the house, taking her alarmingly for granted. Leaving a note saying only "You are pigs," she leaves them in the lurch, and—lo, and behold!—they turn into real pigs. With art that demands close inspection to catch all the story's hints and clues, Browne has created a funny and thought-provoking look at fairness in the home.

> Canadian Barbara Greenwood has several other books of merit that use this format of fact and fiction: *The Last Safe House: A Story of the Underground Railroad*; *A Pioneer Thanksgiving: A Story of Harvest Celebrations in 1841*; and *Gold Rush Fever: A Story of the Klondike, 1898*.

A Pioneer Sampler: The Daily Life of a Pioneer Family in 1840

PICTURE BOOK NONFICTION

AUTHOR: Barbara Greenwood • ILLUSTRATOR: Heather Collins
HC/PB: Houghton Mifflin
THEMES: pioneers; family; bees; U.S. history, frontier life; recipes

Facts blend with fiction in these stories about the Robertson family, which lives on a farm in the mid-1800s. One story that tells about the family's search for a bee tree is followed by several pages of interesting facts about bees, including why it was important for pioneer families to go to the trouble of finding them. Readers also learn what it was like to attend school, shear sheep, spin wool, and make cheese. Maps, recipes, crafts, a glossary, and an index are included in this fascinating introduction to life on the frontier.

Rechenka's Eggs

PICTURE BOOK

AUTHOR/ILLUSTRATOR: Patricia Polacco
HC: Philomel • PB: Paperstar
THEMES: Easter; eggs; festivals; Ukraine; folk art; miracles; artists; geese; creativity

Each year Old Babushka spends the long cold winter painting eggs. People everywhere know about their beauty and look forward to seeing them at the annual festival. So you can imagine what a shock it is for her when Rechenka, the goose whose life she saved, tipps over her basket of eggs and causes them to fall and shatter in pieces on the floor. Poor old Babushka. Thank goodness for miracles. This story of talent and compassion is filled with miracles, and makes a perfect springtime read-aloud.

AUTHOR SPOTLIGHT
CYNTHIA RYLANT

The power of words has no greater friend than Cynthia Rylant. Whether writing poetry, short stories and novels for every age, or picture books, she continually astounds us with her insight and gentle wisdom. Children who read a book by Rylant receive the gifts of her understanding voice and her ability to get directly to the heart of the concerns of childhood.

Her picture books have been illustrated by such masters as Peter Catalanotto, Barry Moser, and Stephen Gammell and include gems like *All I See, The Old Woman Who Named Things, When I Was Young in the Mountains, The Relatives Came,* and two Christmas books we feel will become classics, *An Angel for Solomon Singer* and *Christmas in the Country.* She has even taken to illustrating her own books on occasion, with her loving odes to departed pets, *Cat Heaven* and *Dog Heaven,* becoming must-haves for pet lovers.

Her insight into the lives of the young women of Appalachia, where she grew up, is evident in her novels *A Blue-Eyed Daisy* and the Newbery-winning *Missing May,* as well as her poetry collections *Waiting to Waltz: A Childhood* and *Something Permanent.* But she is perhaps more astounding when she crawls inside the minds of boys, displaying a cross-gender empathy that few writers possess, as in her gentle, easy-to-read novel in stories, *The Blue Hill Meadows,* or the Newbery Honor book *A Fine White Dust,* a novel of youthful religious fervor and heartbreaking betrayal. Some novels do not fit neatly into categories, such as her lovely ode to magic and believing in a small town, *The Van Gogh Café,* or her examination of heaven in short but powerful stories, *The Heavenly Village.* The *Henry and Mudge* series as well as the *Mr. Putter and Tabby* books and her *Poppleton* series have set new standards of excellence for books aimed at beginning readers; her short story collections *Every Living Thing* and *A Couple of Kooks and Other Stories About Love* are excellent in breadth and style; and her picture autobiography, *But I'll Be Back Again,* is a charming and informative account of childhood in the sixties. Rylant has even dared to fill in the two-year gap in the Laura Ingalls Wilder's Little House books and has written the best of the many sequels, *Old Town in the Green Groves.* In every area in which she chooses to shine her talent, her brilliant illuminations open the world of great literature to young readers.

★ **The Relatives Came**   PICTURE BOOK

AUTHOR: Cynthia Rylant • ILLUSTRATOR: Stephen Gammell
HC: Macmillan • PB: Aladdin
THEMES: family; travel; relatives; reunions; visits

Rylant's text and Gammell's art, both at the top of their form, make this a warm and lovely picture-book ode to visiting relatives, ripe summer fruit, and memories. Give this as a gift when you visit your relatives.

The Remarkable Farkle McBride   PICTURE BOOK

AUTHOR: John Lithgow • ILLUSTRATOR: C. F. Payne
HC: Simon & Schuster • PB: Aladdin
THEMES: music; musical instruments; gifted children; orchestra

A splendid read-aloud! Move over Jamie Lee Curtis, here's another celebrity children's book writer to admire instead of cringe at. Young Farkle McBride is a musical genius—he can play the violin, the flute, the trombone, and the drums with incredible skill. However, once having mastered an instrument, he sours on it. Luckily, Farkle finds a proper outlet for his talents (and his temperament) . . . as conductor of an orchestra! Payne's art helps bring Lithgow's precisely rhymed text to vivid life, and the double gatefold at the end of the book shows the entire orchestra, making this a terrific book to use when introducing musical instruments to young children.

 Farkle comes across as a real brat, and I found myself wishing his parents would take charge. Of course, his temperament does remind me of certain conductors I've known . . .

★ Riding the Tiger   PICTURE BOOK

AUTHOR: Eve Bunting • ILLUSTRATOR: David Frampton
HC: Clarion
THEMES: bullies; gangs; tigers; neighborhood

Some children are tempted to join a gang or to become bullies themselves. When a tiger comes along and asks ten-year-old Danny to ride on his back, he is moved by the power and excitement and jumps on. He soon notices people's fear and the tiger's wickedness as it swaggers through town. When the tiger turns on Danny for wanting to join a basketball game, and then hurts a homeless man, Danny chooses to separate himself from the beast. Frampton's woodcuts show the tiger at various angles revealing its evil through its eyes, bared teeth, and enormous size. Read this aloud for the children who have to make tough choices, and talk about ways to keep their distance from negative influences.

Rikki-Tikki-Tavi   PICTURE BOOK

AUTHOR: Rudyard Kipling • ILLUSTRATOR: Jerry Pinkney
HC: Morrow
THEMES: mongooses; cobras; India; cleverness; triumph

Rikki, a brave young mongoose, is the hero. Two cobras, Nag and Nagaina, are the villains, and Jerry Pinkney is the artist who adds his stunning full-page watercolors to Kipling's classic tale. Read this aloud. It will bring out voice inflection you didn't even know you had.

Riptide
PICTURE BOOK

AUTHOR: Frances Ward Weller • ILLUSTRATOR: Robert Blake
HC: Philomel • PB: Paperstar
THEMES: dogs; beaches; survival; swimming

A dog-in-jeopardy book where the dog does not die! Great art helps tug at your heart. The ending makes the whole thing tense, but finally okay.

★ A River Ran Wild: An Environmental History
PICTURE BOOK NONFICTION

AUTHOR/ILLUSTRATOR: Lynne Cherry
HC: Gulliver • PB: Voyager
THEMES: rivers; history; change; ecology; the environment; activism; taking action; making a difference

Thousands of years ago there were lush valleys and the water was pure in New Hampshire's Nashua River. Cherry's pictorial history shows the river's changes through industrialization the harmful effects of a paper mill, and then the healthy turn it takes following activist Marion Stoddart's actions in the 1960s. Colorful double-page spreads and informative borders help to bring home her message that getting involved in protecting the environment can make a difference.

> For another book on environmental activism, look for Molly Bang's *Nobody Particular: One Woman's Fight to Save the Bays* (page 371).

Rolling Harvey Down the Hill
POETRY COLLECTION

AUTHOR: Jack Prelutsky • ILLUSTRATOR: Victoria Chess
HC: Greenwillow • PB: Mulberry
THEMES: friendship; bullies; city life; competition

Gleefully told poems about the adventures of five boys, all friends, who endure the antics of bully Harvey up to a point, then finally roll him down the hill to teach him a lesson. A funny and irreverent portrait of urban boyhood.

Roxaboxen

AUTHOR: Alice McLerran • ILLUSTRATOR: Barbara Cooney

HC: Lothrop • PB: Puffin

THEMES: childhood; memories; playing; imagination; community; desert;
    U.S. history, early twentieth century

A wistful re-creation of a long-ago childhood and the imaginary town of Roxaboxen. This is an ode to children's fantasy play, where the rules of conduct and society mimic the adult world enough to be recognizable but have a logic that is more fitting for childhood. "In Roxaboxen you can eat all the ice cream you want." Any child who has ever picked up a stick and pretended it was something else knows Roxaboxen. A lovely book.

Ruby Mae Has Something to Say

AUTHOR/ILLUSTRATOR: David Small

HC: Crown • PB: Dragonfly

THEMES: United Nations; peace; determination; taking action; self-respect;
    speeches; communication

Ruby Mae Foote wants to deliver a message of universal peace and understanding at the United Nations. The problem is, she's tongue-tied. Her nephew Billy Bob comes up with a solution. The lesson here is that it's not how you say it, but what you have to say that's important.

Saint George and the Dragon

AUTHOR: Margaret Hodges • ILLUSTRATOR: Trina Schart Hyman

HC/PB: Little Brown

THEMES: dragons; knights; courage; England; folklore; fighting

The greatest dragon battle in all fiction is herein rendered by a suitably powerful pair of storytellers—Hyman, with her deservedly Caldecott Medal–winning illustrations, and Hodges, whose retelling of the epic fight exhausts and exhilarates.

Saving Sweetness

AUTHOR: Diane Stanley • ILLUSTRATOR: G. Brian Karas

HC: Putnam • PB: Puffin

THEMES: strong girls; orphans; U.S.A., the West; humor; running away;
    adoption; cleverness

Mrs. Sump is awfully mean for someone who runs an orphanage, so Sweetness, the littlest orphan—with more than her share of spunk—decides to run away to find a better life. That's when she comes across the sheriff, outsmarts him, and finds a firm foundation for herself and the others in the orphange. Read this aloud for fun and a taste of the Wild West.

The Sea Chest
PICTURE BOOK

AUTHOR: Toni Buzzeo • ILLUSTRATOR: Mary Grandpre
HC: Dial
THEMES: lighthouses; sea; sisters; loneliness; aunts; U.S.A., New England;
    storms; adoption; legends

"I was a solitary child, alone on Halley's Head Light for all my first ten years, with just my mama . . . and papa." Great-aunt Maita tells her niece the story of how her life changed following a fearsome storm, when a baby washed ashore inside a sea chest. Superbly written and illustrated with luminous oil paintings, this is a story of adventure, adoption, and a warm account of a beloved family member reliving a time in her childhood.

Sense Pass King: A Story from Cameroon
PICTURE BOOK

AUTHOR: Katrin Tchana • ILLUSTRATOR: Trina Schart Hyman
HC: Holiday House
THEMES: strong girl: gifted children; kings; jealousy; cleverness, folklore

Ma'antah was a brilliant girl. "By the time she was two she could speak the languages of all seven villages and communicate with animals." The folks in her village were so dazzled by her gifts that they called her Sense Pass King, because she had more sense than even the king. The jealous king did not share their enthusiasm; instead, he set out to do away with her. This portrait of a young girl's cleverness and a battle of wits—child against adult—will please young readers. Storyteller and extraordinary artist, this mother-and-daughter team have created a read-aloud that will keep listeners in suspense till the end.

Seven Brave Women
PICTURE BOOK

AUTHOR: Betsy Hearne • ILLUSTRATOR: Bethanne Andersen
HC: Greenwillow
THEMES: courage; genealogy; strong women; U.S. history; peace; family
    history

"In the old days, history books marked time by the wars that men fought. The United States began with the Revolutionary War. Then there was the War of 1812, the Civil War, the Spanish-American War . . ." Betsy Hearne has looked to her own history and found seven brave women who fought their share of battles—but never in a war. They cared for the sick, worked on farms, started hospitals, studied in men's schools, built their homes, and told their stories. This incredible book shows how brave, devout, and determined women have left their tracks through time.

 This book reminded me of my mother, who clipped photos from newspapers, tears in her eyes, to implant in us the faces of children in war. She also talked of women whose strength showed in their intellect and spirit. Use these stories to discuss the history makers in your child's past.

Slugs
PICTURE BOOK

AUTHOR: David Greenberg • ILLUSTRATOR: Victoria Chess
PB: Little Brown
THEMES: slugs; rhyme; revenge; humor, gross

> Swallow a slug by its tail or its snout
> Feel it slide down
> Feel it climb out.

Gleefully gross, and sure to induce shivers and squeals, this is one of our favorite "no redeeming value" books. There is nothing in *Slugs* that will cause adults to shove it at a child saying, "Read this. It's good for you!" Sure, it has an ending that could be interpreted as "Be nice to animals or else," but the kids know that it's there to placate the grown-ups. Try this book on any age child who flat-out refuses to listen to you read aloud and see if this doesn't grab some attention.

Sod Houses on the Great Plains
PICTURE BOOK NONFICTION

AUTHOR/ILLUSTRATOR: Glen Rounds
PB: Holiday House
THEMES: home; U.S.A., the prairie; U.S. history, frontier life; dwellings

The only building material for pioneers who moved onto the Great Plains was sod, taken from the prairie itself. Writer/illustrator Glen Rounds was born in a sod house so he is in the ideal place to show the clever and not-so-clever techniques used in building these shelters. Here you'll find a perfect mix of humor and information that will stick . . . like sod.

The Spice Alphabet Book: Herbs, Spices, and Other Natural Flavors

PICTURE BOOK NONFICTION

AUTHOR: Jerry Pallotta • ILLUSTRATOR: Leslie Evans
PB: Charlesbridge
THEMES: alphabet; spices; cooking; diversity; plants

Pallotta's Nature Alphabet series includes a wide variety of subjects. Some of them are *The Icky Bug Alphabet Book, The Desert Alphabet Book,* and *The Yucky Reptile Alphabet Book.*

Add some spice to your child's life with this colorful alphabet of herbs, flavors, and spices. A lot of information is covered in a easy-to-absorb style, making this a book for browsing, research, or just because you want to know what spice begins with *X.*

Spinky Sulks

PICTURE BOOK

AUTHOR/ILLUSTRATOR: William Steig
PB: Farrar, Straus & Giroux
THEMES: family; feelings; hurt; sulking; problem solving; anger

No matter how hard they try or what they offer him, Spinky refuses to forgive his family for their awful behavior. So he sulks. A lot. Until neither he nor anyone else is sure what exactly got him so mad in the first place, but by then he's almost too deep into it to find a graceful way out. But he does. This is a book for any child who has backed himself into an emotional corner, not sure what's supposed to happen next. And it's funny!

Spooky ABC

PICTURE BOOK

For another scary alphabet book, look for *The Absolutely Awful Alphabet* by Mordecai Gerstein.

AUTHOR: Eve Merriam • ILLUSTRATOR: Lane Smith
HC: Simon & Schuster
THEMES: spooky stories; alphabet; rhyme; Halloween

Originally published as *Halloween ABC*, these mayhem-filled rhymes coupled with eerie illustrations make this a perfect read-aloud for older children at Halloween time:

Icicle
An icy stabbing so swiftly done,
the victim scarcely felt it.
The police are baffled: "Where's the weapon?"
The sun shines down to melt it.

★ The Stinky Cheese Man and Other Fairly Stupid Tales

PICTURE BOOK

AUTHOR: Jon Scieszka • ILLUSTRATOR: Lane Smith
HC: Viking
THEMES: humor; fairy tales; folktale variations; zany

Scieszka's introduction pretty well sums it up: "The stories in this book are Fairly Stupid Tales. I mean, what else would you call a story like Goldilocks and the Three Elephants?" When Scieszka and Smith get together, there is sure to be riotous laughter, pathetic puns, ridiculous rewrites, and off-the-wall art that shatters every convention of traditional illustration. We get the results in zany tales like "Little Red Running Shorts" with nags from the Little Red Hen. ("Over fifty pages of nonsense and I'm only in three of them.") It will be over the heads of younger children, but this is the humor that infects third-graders and fifth-graders too.

> Other *Babar* titles we are fond of are *Babar and His Children*, *Travels of Babar* and *Babar the King*.

The Story of Babar the Little Elephant PICTURE BOOK
AUTHOR/ILLUSTRATOR: Jean deBrunhoff
HC/PB: Random House
THEMES: elephants; hunters; cities; friendship; family; cousins; kings; orphans

Little Babar runs away to the city after a hunter kills his mother. There he meets an old lady, who fits him in fine clothes and gives him a place to live. In this classic tale (published in 1933) Babar becomes a proper gentleman, finds a wife, and returns to the forest to be king of the elephants. Children love Babar. What a relief that such impossibly good things can happen to an orphaned elephant who has had his share of bad luck!

The Tale of Despereaux FICTION
AUTHOR: Kate DiCamillo • ILLUSTRATOR: Timothy Basil Ering
HC: Candlewick Press
THEMES: mice; princesses; music; wishes; castles; fairy tales

"This story begins within the walls of a castle, with the birth of a mouse. A small mouse." His name is Despereaux. He loves music, stories, and a princess—who is not a mouse—named Pea. It is also the story of a serving girl, rats, and dungeons. Would you like to know what happens? "Reader," challenges DiCamillo, ". . . it is your destiny to find out."

 Do find out! Kate DiCamillo has a talent for creating characters that stay with you, that make you smile.

Teammates PICTURE BOOK BIOGRAPHY
AUTHOR: Peter Golenbock • ILLUSTRATOR: Paul Bacon
HC/PB: Harcourt Brace
THEMES: baseball; prejudice; self-respect; athletes; taking action; friendship; cultural diversity; biography

When black players were not allowed in the major leagues, Jackie Robinson had to break down barriers to play ball. With the help of teammate Pee Wee Reese, he led the way for players who followed. This is the story of Reese and Robinson's friendship, illustrated in black-and-white photographs and full-color art.

That Summer

PICTURE BOOK

AUTHOR: Tony Johnston • ILLUSTRATOR: Barry Moser
HC: Harcourt
THEMES: illness; death; quilts; brothers; grief; family

Two brothers begin their summer like always, hooting and shouting, running into the sun, freed from school. Then one gets sick. What does a family do when faced with a terminal illness? Joey and his family sew together a quilt of memories to help them keep the small joys of each new day. Moser alternates his paintings, in black and white and then color, to represent past and present in this poignant story of a family's dealing with its grief. This is an important book that will most likely be saved for a time of crisis and loss. We suggest that books on difficult subjects not be limited to hard times. They can prepare children for when they learn about a crisis in anyone's life.

There's a Frog in My Throat: 440 Animal Sayings a Little Bird Told Me

PICTURE BOOK NONFICTION

AUTHORS: Loreen Leedy and Pat Street • ILLUSTRATOR: Loreen Leedy
HC: Holiday House
THEMES: language; animals; parts of speech; vocabulary; proverbs

Warning! Once you get started, you'll be hooked in two shakes of a lamb's tail. Similes, metaphors, idioms, proverbs—440 animal sayings with cheerful art to match will have you talking turkey. We wouldn't pull the wool over your eyes.

A Three Hat Day

PICTURE BOOK

AUTHOR: Laura Geringer • ILLUSTRATOR: Arnold Lobel
PB: HarperCollins
THEMES: hats; loneliness; love; obsession; friendship; individuality

An engaging story about eccentric R. R. Pottle the Third, who loves hats, and his search for happiness. Without preaching or being overly sweet, the message gets across—there is someone for everyone in this world.

The Three Little Javelinas

PICTURE BOOK

AUTHOR: Susan Lowell • ILLUSTRATOR: Jim Harris
HC: Northland
THEMES: folktale variation; pigs; deserts; Hispanic; cleverness; coyote;
   U.S.A., the Southwest

Javelinas are piglike creatures that roam the American desert southwest, and, boy, are they ugly! Using them as the main characters in this wild and funny retelling of *The Three Little Pigs* is a stroke of genius. You will love reading this aloud, and so will your kids.

Thunder at Gettysburg

FICTION

AUTHOR: Patricia Lee Gauch • ILLUSTRATOR: Stephen Gammell
HC/PB: Boyds Mills
THEMES: U.S. history, Civil War; war; coming of age;
   change; community

Tillie thinks it will be fun to see the Union soldiers beat the pants off the Rebels, and she plans to spend all day watching them from the attic window of her Gettysburg home. She is irrevocably changed as she finds herself right in the middle of the events of July 1–3, 1863, and a better introduction to the horrors of war we can't imagine. Gammell's stark black-and-white illustrations match Gauch's spare prose, making this a book not just for younger readers but for anyone interested in the Civil War.

Too Many Pumpkins

PICTURE BOOK

AUTHOR: Linda White • ILLUSTRATOR: Megan Lloyd
HC/PB: Holiday House
THEMES: pumpkins; gardening; cooking; baking;
   stubbornness; problem solving

Rebecca Estelle hates pumpkins. Stubborn and set in her ways, she refuses to acknowledge the pumpkin patch that is growing by accident in her front yard. When she can ignore it no longer, she is motivated to do some major baking, enough for the whole town to share. This fun read-aloud is great for fall and harvesttime.

Seeing Ourselves

If you want to give your child an understanding of cultural diversity, choose titles showing a variety of races and religions in situations with which he can identify. Imagine a child who has access only to books portraying people who look like him and live as he does. Imagine further that another child has books that only show people like him as exotic creatures of folklore and myth. Neither is a scenario we would want for our own children.

We are more than thirty-five years beyond "The All White World of Children's Books," as described by Nancy Larrick in her groundbreaking *Saturday Review* article, which served as a wake-up call to publishers regarding their lack of portrayal of African American children, and its effects are still being felt as other excluded groups work to become more visible in libraries and bookstores. This is not mere political correctness but an acknowledgment that the need to find oneself in a book walks hand in hand with the need to find others who are different yet similar. A balance of the two provides cultural empathy and allows a greater focus on that which unites us, rather than on *us* versus *them*.

Too Many Tamales

PICTURE BOOK

AUTHOR: Gary Soto • ILLUSTRATOR: Ed Martinez

HC: Putnam • PB:PAPERSTAR

THEMES: Christmas; Hispanic; family; cooking; Mexican
culture; cousins; conscience; consequences

Maria loses her mother's diamond ring in the masa when helping to prepare the Christmas tamales, so she makes her cousins eat the entire batch in search of it. Of course the ring isn't in them but on her mother's finger. This is a charming read-aloud at holiday time, full of humor and warmth.

Ug: Boy Genius of the Stone Age

PICTURE BOOK

AUTHOR/ILLUSTRATOR: Raymond Briggs

HC: Knopf

THEMES: history; inventions; pre-history; curiosity; fathers and sons; gifted
child; comic book style

In comic strip form, Briggs takes readers to the Stone Age where Ug, a curious young boy with inventor's aspirations, seeks to create a pair of pants made of something softer than stone. The subject is a familiar one—parents sticking to traditional ways while their child pushes the edges. But when you set it in the Stone Age and add Briggs's dry and amusing drawings, you have laughs all around.

Velcome!

PICTURE BOOK

AUTHOR/ILLUSTRATOR: Kevin O'Malley

HC/PB: Walker

THEMES: humor, adolescent; jokes; puns; spooky
stories; Halloween

The goofiest Halloween book ever! Full of silliness, outrageous puns, and a wacky sense of humor, this will delight many of the same kids who find *The Adventures of Captain Underpants* funny. O'Malley has outdone himself with this combination of horror and humor.

Visiting the Art Museum

PICTURE BOOK NONFICTION

AUTHORS: Laurie Krasny and Marc Brown •

ILLUSTRATOR: Marc Brown

PB: Puffin

THEMES: art; museums; paintings; family

> "The apple doesn't fall far from the tree. If you are an avid reader, your child will undoubtedly follow your lead. Make a child's own place for books as important as a place for toys. Find a cozy spot that's special for reading times. Make it a daily ritual. But above all, have fun reading to your child. Select books you can truly enjoy together."
>
> —*Marc Brown,*
> *author of the* Arthur *books*

Read this together before that first trip to a museum. The kids act like real kids, the paintings are presented in a way that will encourage discussion, and the experience is made to be something a child would be interested in. Useful and entertaining.

Waiting for the Whales
PICTURE BOOK

AUTHOR: Sheryl McFarlane • ILLUSTRATOR: Ron Lightburn
PB: Orca Books
THEMES: death; grandfathers and granddaughters; whales; aging; loneliness

An old man's life regains meaning with the birth of his granddaughter, and he passes on to her his love of the orcas who visit the shore once a year. When the old man dies, a new whale joins the pod, and a simple story of connections to nature and family gets a message of hope and rebirth. A great book to use in grief and loss situations.

The Way West: Journal of a Pioneer Woman
PICTURE BOOK BIOGRAPHY

AUTHOR: Amelia Stewart Knight • ILLUSTRATOR: Michael McCurdy
PB: Aladdin
THEMES: pioneers; journeys; U.S. history, frontier life; Native American; Oregon; diaries; strong women; determination; survival; U.S. history, Westward movement; hardship; storms

"Saturday, April 9, 1853. Started from home about eleven o'clock and traveled eight miles and camped in an old house; night cold and frosty." The story of Amelia Stewart Knight's journey in 1853 from Iowa to Oregon begins with these words. Filled with fascinating details—Mrs. Knight cooked with "buffalo chips" over fires and rolled her pie dough on the wagon seat—this authentic journal gives young readers a glimpse at the hardship and determination of one family of nine as they struggle west to a better life.

Whaling Days
PICTURE BOOK NONFICTION

AUTHOR: Carol Carrick • ILLUSTRATOR: David Frampton
HC/PB: Clarion
THEMES: whales; U.S. history, colonial America; environment; animals, endangered

We were not looking forward to reading a book that details the harpooning of a whale, but we have to admit there is an incredible history here and fascinating details. "A sperm whale head would be cut off and hauled onto the deck. Climbing into the case, a cavity in the upper part of the head, a man with a bucket bailed out the oil." Stunning woodcuts show the beauty and power of the whale. This history of whaling in America from colonial times to the present includes a glossary of whaling terms, an index, and a bibliography.

What About Me? PICTURE BOOK
AUTHOR/ILLUSTRATOR: Ed Young
HC: Philomel
THEMES: Sufis; folklore; Middle East; wisdom; fable

When a boy seeks knowledge, he goes to the Grand Master, who requests a carpet in exchange for his answer. The carpet man wants thread, the spinner woman needs goat hair . . . and so on. Like the tales of Aesop, this traditional Sufi folktale ends with a moral lesson. Whether or not young readers are looking for wisdom, Young's color collages, rich in texture, are reason enough to open the pages of this treasure.

What You Know First PICTURE BOOK
AUTHOR: Patricia MacLachlan • ILLUSTRATOR: Barry Moser
HC/PB: HarperCollins
THEMES: moving; change; U.S.A., the prairie; family

A stunning collaboration between a gifted writer and a master artist. Leaving the prairie to move to the ocean, the young narrator tells us in simple, affecting prose exactly how she feels about the prospect. Perfectly grasping the wrenching sadness of any childhood uprooting, as well as the specifics of this individual child's life, MacLachlan explains how we all are a part of where we've been, and how "What you know first stays with you." If you know of a child who is moving away, this book can be his salvation.

Who Sees the Lighthouse? PICTURE BOOK
AUTHOR: Ann Fearringon • ILLUSTRATOR: Giles Laroche
HC: Putnam
THEMES: lighthouse; counting; rhyme; beaches; light

"Who sees the light?" is the refrain in this counting book about a lighthouse. Items both large (whales and small (butterflies) are illustrated with distinctive cut paper following the beam of the Fresnel lens into space, giving children a glimpse of the infinite.

Wilma Unlimited: How Wilma Rudolph Became the World's Fastest Woman

PICTURE BOOK BIOGRAPHY

AUTHOR: Kathleen Krull • ILLUSTRATOR: David Diaz
HC/PB: Harcourt Brace
THEMES: sports; biography; African American; triumph; illness; polio;
   Olympics; athletes; track and field; strong women

Against all odds, Wilma Rudolph stopped wearing the leg brace she needed as a child and went on to become the first woman ever to win three gold medals in track in a single Olympics. This is her story, illustrated with a striking combination of paintings and photos by David Diaz.

The Worry Stone

PICTURE BOOK

AUTHOR: Marianna Dengler • ILLUSTRATOR: Sybil Graber Gerig
HC: Rising Moon
THEMES: loneliness; storytelling; friendship; elderly and children; folklore;
   Native American

Richly textured, with a story within a story within a story format, this tale of an old woman befriending a lonely boy in a park will comfort the most isolated among us. Beautiful illustrations that capture the faces of the characters help the tale to spring off the page.

Yonder

PICTURE BOOK

AUTHOR: Tony Johnston • ILLUSTRATOR: Lloyd Bloom
HC: Gibbs Smith
THEMES: farms; family history; life cycle; seasons; change; country life

With poetic language and folk art–style paintings, Johnston and Bloom portray the story of a family farm, from the planting of the first tree to the burial of the now aged farmer. Along the way we are shown the cycle of seasons and lifetime and given a lovely reminder of the power of renewal.

The ABCs of Feelings

Sometimes the cure for easing a difficult time is to discover you are not alone, that someone understands how you feel. Books can be the ointment that lessens the pain during these times. Other occasions may be zany, mischievous, happy ones, a perfect time for a wacky tale.

This list is only a starting point. Books don't have to be *about* a specific feeling to do the job. Here you'll find stories with characters who display feelings in situations children will recognize. There are tons of titles that can help you discuss feelings and concerns with your child. The important thing is to choose books you will enjoy sharing, that will communicate the feelings kids have in common.

Anxious: *Can't You Sleep Little Bear?* (Waddell)
Bashful: *Shy Charles* (Wells)
Competitive: *Don't Fidget a Feather* (Silverman)
Disagreeable: *Contrary Mary* (Jeram)
Embarrassed: *Airmail to the Moon.* (Birdseye)
Frustrated: *To Market to Market* (Miranda)
Gutsy: *Liza Lou and the Yeller Belly Swamp* (Mayer)
Hunger: *When Hunger Calls* (Kitchen)
Insecure: *I Wish I Were a Butterfly* (Howe)
Jealous: *Julius the Baby of the World* (Henkes)
Kind: *Brave Irene* (Steig)
Loving: *Guess How Much I Love You* (McBratney)
Mean: *Mean Soup* (Everitt)
Nervous: *Harriet's Recital* (Carlson)
Ornery: *Steamboat Annie and the Thousand Pound Catfish* (Wright)
Powerful: *Bootsie Barker Bites* (Bottner)
Quarrelsome: *Rat and the Tiger* (Keiko)
Regretful: *Lilly's Purple Plastic Purse* (Henkes)
Smug: *Some Smug Slug* (Edwards)
Teased: *The Cow That Went Oink* (Most)
Uncool: *Earl's Too Cool for Me* (Komaiko)
Vulnerable: *Lost* (McPhail)
Wishful: *Mordant's Wish* (Coursen)
Xenophobic: *The Araboolies Of Liberty Street* (Swope)
Yearning: *Earrings!* (Viorst)
Zany: *A Day with Wilbur Robinson* (Joyce)

Listening/Interest Level: Early and Middle Elementary (E/M)/ Reading Level: Middle Elementary (M)

These titles feature a vocabulary that matches the ability of M readers and offers a range of listening experiences that they and their younger siblings can enjoy together.

1,000 Years Ago on Planet Earth

PICTURE BOOK NONFICTION

AUTHOR: Sneed B. Collard • ILLUSTRATOR: Jonathan Hunt
HC: Houghton Mifflin
THEMES: cultural diversity; history, medieval times; change

A fascinating flashback describes how the planet has changed over the centuries and helps readers imagine what the future may be like. Discover what was happening in twelve different civilizations at the turn of the first millennium as you travel to Central America to explore the great pyramid at Chichen Itza; witness the acts of the bloodthirsty and adventurous Vikings in northern Europe; and learn about the fascinating innovations of the Chinese during the Sung Dynasty.

101 Ways to Bug Your Parents

FICTION

AUTHOR: Lee Wardlaw
PB: Dell
THEMES: family; humor; school; writing; inventions

A truly funny book that is sure to wind up on kids' lists of their favorites. A boy decides to spend his summer writing class creating a manual for other kids of time-tested ways to drive parents crazy. Fun situations and goofy characters abound, making this a good book for reluctant readers as well as those who just like a good laugh. The list at the end, summing up all 101 ways, is worth the price of the book alone.

Adopted by the Eagles: A Plains Story of Friendship and Treachery
PICTURE BOOK

AUTHOR/ILLUSTRATOR: Paul Goble
PB: Aladdin
THEMES: friendship; betrayal; Native American; hunters; birds

This Plains Indian story about friendship tells of treachery between two hunters when they are far from home, and birds who rescue them. Look also for Goble's books about Iktomi, the Plains Indian trickster, which are great examples of visual and written storytelling mastery, and funny, to boot.

The Adventures of Tintin
FICTION

AUTHOR/ILLUSTRATOR: Herge
HC/PB: Little Brown
THEMES: adventure; mystery; science fiction; comic-book style

This comic-book adventure series featuring the exploits of the world's greatest boy reporter, Tintin, and his dog, Snowy, has stood the test of time. Set in the first half of the twentieth century and possessed of that era's worldview, these are breathtakingly paced: Tintin goes around the world and has more adventures per book than the Hardy Boys and Nancy Drew combined. The comic-book style makes these books look deceptively easy to read. The vocabulary is not easy, but the reader has the visuals to fall back on. These find their way into lots of hands at various stages of reading development—third-graders who like adventure will devour these, yet so will fifth-and sixth-graders for whom reading is a chore. Great fun.

★ Airmail to the Moon
PICTURE BOOK

AUTHOR: Tom Birdseye • ILLUSTRATOR: Stephen Gammell
HC/PB: Holiday House
THEMES: family; strong girls; teeth; U.S.A., Appalachia; tooth fairy; humor

Ore Mae Cotton of Crabapple Orchard loses her first tooth and hunts down the no-good varmint who stole it from underneath her pillow. She hears a lot of conflicting information about the tooth fairy but can't seem to find out who stole her tooth. So funny it hurts!

All-of-a-Kind Family

FICTION

AUTHOR: Sydney Taylor • ILLUSTRATOR: Helen John

HC: Taylor • PB: Dell

THEMES: family; sisters; Judaism; New York; U.S. history, early 20th century; growing up; new baby; traditions

Here is a warm family series, old-fashioned without being stodgy, and perfect for younger kids who read at an accelerated level. The four hard-to-find sequels (check your library) are: *More All-of-a-Kind Family, All-of-a-Kind Family Uptown, All-of-a-Kind Family Downtown,* and *Ella of All-of-a-Kind Family.*

Ella, Henny, Sarah, Charlotte, and Gertie are five sisters, each two years older than the next, forming a human stairstep when they stand together, and earning themselves the name The All-of-a-Kind Family. As they grow up in New York's lower east side at the turn of the century in a loving Jewish family, we see them celebrating the festivals and holidays of their faith as well as universal experiences, such as going to the library, family members' birthdays, and the birth of a baby brother.

Alvin Ailey

PICTURE BOOK BIOGRAPHY

AUTHOR: Andrea Davis Pinkney • ILLUSTRATOR: Brian Pinkney

HC/PB: Hyperion

THEMES: dance; biography; African American; trailblazing; dancers

Swirling scratchboard drawings illustrate this lively biography of dancer and choreographer Alvin Ailey, who created his own modern dance company.

All the Lights in the Night

PICTURE BOOK

AUTHOR: Arthur A. Levine • ILLUSTRATOR: James E. Ransome

PB: Mulberry

THEMES: Hanukkah; escape; Israel; Jews; brothers; immigration; courage; faith; separation; journeys

Life has become intolerable for Russian Jews, so when brothers Moses and David have a chance to go to Palestine, their mother helps them escape. To stave off fear during their dangerous journey, they tell each other the ancient story of Hanukkah. Lustrous oil paintings dominated by blues and greens provide the backdrop for this moving story of faith and courage.

★ Amber Was Brave; Essie Was Smart

FICTION

AUTHOR/ILLUSTRATOR: Vera B. Williams

HC: Greenwillow

THEMES: poetry; sisters; family; poverty; courage; prison

With immense love and respect for her characters and an artistry of design that equals her best work (*A Chair for My Mother* and *"More, More, More!" said the Baby*), Williams offers us a look, in drawings and poems, at the life of two sisters living in urban poverty and depending on each other for support as they deal with the incarceration of their father. The details of their daily life and routine, the portrait they paint of their hardworking and often absent mother, and the artful rendering of the interdependence that siblings in a crisis can manifest make for a story that many children can recognize, if not from their own lives, then from those of their friends. A difficult subject handled with warmth, humor, style, and grace.

Amelia's Road   PICTURE BOOK
AUTHOR: Linda Jacobs Altman • ILLUSTRATOR: Enrique O. Sanchez
HC/PB: Lee & Low
THEMES: Mexican; change; moving; home; migrant farm workers; problem
     solving

A strong portrayal of the migrant farm worker life, and how a young girl comes to develop a sense of "home" despite all odds. Leaving behind mementos of her life and family ensure Amelia of something familiar upon her return to one of her many homes. A useful book on problem solving.

The American Girl Series   FICTION
AUTHOR: Various
PB: Pleasant Company
THEMES: U.S. history; strong girls; cultural diversity

The American Girl series has helped to make historical fiction accessible and popular, offering a glimpse of the past that will liven up any history lesson. Each girl in this popular series represents a different time in history and receives her own set of stories. The girls include: *Addy*: 1864—the Civil War; *Josefina*: 1824—Hispanic girl in New Mexico during the movement west; *Felicity*: 1774—colonial times; *Kirsten*: 1854—pioneer life; *Samantha*: 1904— raised by her Victorian grandmother; *Molly*: 1944—World War II; and *Kaya*: 1764—a member of the Nez Perce tribe.

Anastasia Krupnik   FICTION
AUTHOR: Lois Lowry
HC: Houghton Mifflin • PB: Dell
THEMES: family; gifted child; strong girls;
     siblings

Anastasia has gotten too old to be the star of a series of middle-grade novels, so thank goodness for her younger brother, Sam, who moved to center stage in the books *All About Sam*, *Attaboy, Sam!*, and *See You Around, Sam*. All the Anastasia books start with her name, so they are easy to find in the library or bookstore. Look for: *Anastasia Again*, *Anastasia at Your Service*, *Anastasia Has the Answers*, *Anastasia on Her Own*, and *Anastasia's Chosen Career*.

Irrepressible and too bright for her own good, Anastasia Krupnik is the star of a delightful series of books that will bring readers from the age of chapter books almost up to the age of the young adult novel. Full of fun and warm details about a charming and often hilarious family, these books are perfect family read-alouds when you are looking for a dose of contemporary as opposed to historical or fantasy fiction.

The Animal Family   FICTION

AUTHOR: Randall Jarrell • ILLUSTRATOR: Maurice
    Sendak
HC/PB: HarperCollins
THEMES: family; mermaids; hunters; bears; lynx;
    adoption

A lovely and quiet tale of a lonely hunter who makes his own family. This is a great read-aloud, especially for the chance to truly savor some of Jarrell's poetic writings by hearing them spoken. A meditation on what makes a family, told with humor and wisdom.

★ The Araboolies of Liberty Street   PICTURE BOOK

AUTHOR: Sam Swope • ILLUSTRATOR: Barry Root
PB: Farrar, Straus & Giroux
THEMES: taking action; bullies; cultural diversity; neighbors; prejudice;
    community; comeuppance

Such a wonderful tale! General Pinch and his wife have their entire street completely under their thumb, forcing their tastes upon everyone with threats to call in the army shouted through a bullhorn. But when the non-English-speaking, multicolored, glow-in-the-dark Araboolies move in right next door, with their huge family, large menagerie of animals, and unusual decorating ideas, the inspiration for a little rebellion is born in one of the neighborhood kids. Reading how the kids turn the tables on the bullying, bigoted Pinches makes for a terrific lesson in civil disobedience. And the art is great, too.

Babe, the Gallant Pig   FICTION

AUTHOR: Dick King Smith
HC: Crown • PB: Knopf
THEMES: animals, farm; pigs; sheep; farmers; farms; courage; competition;
    talent; triumph

There are few writers who can make animals come alive as well as Dick King Smith, and his best loved book is *Babe*. The story of the pig who becomes a sheepherder has been made into a successful movie and has created interest in other works by this remarkable author. These include *Harry's Mad; Ace: The Very Important Pig;* and *The School Mouse.*

Bard of Avon: The Story of William Shakespeare
PICTURE BOOK BIOGRAPHY

AUTHORS: Diane Stanley and Peter Vennema • ILLUSTRATOR: Diane Stanley
HC/PB: Morrow
THEMES: biography; Shakespeare; theater; England; poets; actors and acting

Stanley and Vennema have figured out that it's more fun to learn about history through story than through a listing of facts. Some parts of Shakespeare's life remain a mystery (like exactly when he was born), but by looking at the times in which he lived, gathering information left by his fellow writers and friends, and adding paintings, these authors have created a fascinating picture-book account of his life.

A Bear Called Paddington
FICTION

AUTHOR: Michael Bond • ILLUSTRATOR: Peggy Fortnum
HC/PB: Houghton Mifflin
THEMES: bears; trains; theater; shopping; beaches

"Please look after this bear. Thank you" is the sign hanging around the poor bear's neck. From Darkest Peru, he finds himself sitting in Paddington Railway Station in London. It's lucky for him that Mr. and Mrs. Brown come along to care for him, even though their lives will never be quite the same. Read this aloud. It's great fun, and if you enjoy exaggerated voices, you can try them here. There are at least ten other Paddington chapter books in this series. If you like this one, try another.

Because of Winn Dixie
FICTION

AUTHOR: Kate DiCamillo
HC/PB: Candlewick
THEMES: fathers and daughters; pets; community; diversity; dogs; librarians; Florida

Read this aloud or recommend it to anyone who could use a laugh and would like to spend time with an engaging, warm group of characters. Ten-year-old

India Opal Buloni has just moved to a new town with her father and she has no idea what is in store for her—least of all that she'd be adopting a big, ugly dog named after a supermarket. This novel brings alive a community of integrity and diversity, where evil does not lurk behind each stranger or unusual person.

The BFG

FICTION-FANTASY

AUTHOR: Roald Dahl • ILLUSTRATOR: Quentin Blake
HC: Farrar, Straus & Giroux • PB: Puffin
THEMES: giants; friendship; imagination; fantasy; adventure; good vs. evil; orphans; strong girls

It's a good thing it was The Big Friendly Giant who lifted Sophie (an orphan) from her bed and whisked her out the window. It would have been a different story if it had been Fleshlumpeater, Gizzardgulper, Bonecruncher, or any one of the other giants. They are disgusting and enjoy swallomping nice little "childers," whom Sophie and the BFG set out to save. Like many great writers, Dahl was never shy about inventing words when he needed them—his "giant language" of snozzcumbers, frobscottles, and whizzpoppers will leave young readers howling.

A Big Cheese for the White House: The True Tale of a Tremendous Cheddar

PICTURE BOOK NONFICTION

AUTHOR: Candace Fleming • ILLUSTRATOR: S.D. Schindler
HC: Farrar, Straus & Giroux
THEMES: community; competition; cleverness; U.S. History, Colonial America; food

For other pieces of history retold, look for Fleming's *The Hatmaker's Sign* and *Benjamin Franklin's Almanac: Being a True Account of the Good Gentleman's Life.*

Based on a true event, this is a story of civic pride and ingenuity set at the turn of the nineteenth century in a small New England town. The residents of Cheshire, Massachusetts, make the largest cheese anyone has ever seen and manage (with no small amount of effort) to get it to Thomas Jefferson's White House so that the president will be serving their cheese for a long, long time. Fleming makes history come vividly to life in this funny story.

Big Rain Coming

AUTHOR: Katrina Germein • ILLUSTRATOR: Bronwyn Bancroft
HC: Clarion
THEMES: Australia; aborigines; art; patience; rain; drought; dogs; frogs;
   children; vocabulary

In the Australian outback, everyone is waiting for rain. Old Stephen says it's
on its way, but still the dogs, frogs, and Rosie's kids have to wait, swimming
in the billabong, sleeping outside. Brilliant color and bold patterns fill each
page to the final, joyful spread of "Wonderful cool wet rain."

Bill Peet: An Autobiography

PICTURE BOOK BIOGRAPHY

AUTHOR/ILLUSTRATOR: Bill E. Peet
HC/PB: Houghton Mifflin
THEMES: biography; artists; art; movies; cartoons; careers; authors; jobs;
   writing

The story of a man who had two great careers—one as a Disney animator on
some of the greatest cartoons of all time, the other as the beloved author of
dozens of books for children, including *Chester, the Worldly Pig; Big Bad
Bruce;* and *Eli.* This is a great book to read if you want to know more about
how artists create, or if you just like Peet's books.

Birdie's Lighthouse

PICTURE BOOK

AUTHOR: Deborah Hopkinson • ILLUSTRATOR: Kimberly Bulcken Root
PB: Aladdin
THEMES: lighthouses; diaries; strong girls; Maine; courage; sea; family;
   fathers and daughters

It is 1855 and Birdie and her family live on an island off the coast of Maine
where her father works as the lighthouse keeper. When her father is taken ill
and a brutal northeaster hits, it is up to brave Birdie to save the day. Through
a diary format, we hear Birdie's words as she describes the joys and sorrows
of her life and we experience her thrills and doubts right along with her. A
wonderful portrait of a remarkable young girl.

Bodies From the Bog

NONFICTION

AUTHOR: James Deem • ILLUSTRATOR: Various (photographs)
HC/PB: Houghton Mifflin
THEMES: mummies; human body; history; prehistory; anthropology;
   science

Great information and gruesome pictures about some well-preserved unfortunates who have provided us with an excellent look at our long-ago ancestors.

The Body Atlas

REFERENCE

AUTHOR: Steve Parker • ILLUSTRATOR: Giuliano Fornari
HC: DK Publishing
THEMES: human body; science; nature; health

Do you know the correct name for your funny bone? Or why you yawn? Here's a good-size book that maps the human body inside and out. Detailed illustrations examine the workings of every muscle and organ.

The Borrowers

FICTION-FANTASY

AUTHOR: Mary Norton • ILLUSTRATOR: Beth and Joe Krush
HC/PB: Harcourt Brace
THEMES: little folk; family; adventure; England; secrets; friendship; escape

The Clock family has lived quite happily for years under the floor of an old English country home, "borrowing" what few things they need from the larger "human beans" residing above. Everything is very British and proper. Things get a bit knotty when young Arrietty befriends a human boy and the Borrowers' secret existence is discovered. If you have ever wanted an explanation for why things mysteriously disappear in your home, read this book (and its sequels: *The Borrowers Afield, The Borrowers Aloft, The Borrowers Afloat, Poor Stainless,* and *The Borrowers Avenged*).

Brother Eagle, Sister Sky: A Message From Chief Seattle

PICTURE BOOK

AUTHOR: Chief Seattle • ILLUSTRATOR: Susan Jeffers
PB: Puffin
THEMES: Native American; responsibility; nature; environment

"Reading to children when they are young paves the way for communication and conversation with them when they are teenagers."
—*Susan Jeffers, illustrator of* Brother Eagle, Sister Sky

"How can you buy the sky? How can you own the rain and the wind?" These words, attributed to Squamish Chief Seattle over one hundred years ago, express his respect for the earth. Jeffers has matched the beauty of words with stunning, luminous paintings and leaves readers with the final message, "Preserve the land and the air and the rivers for your children's children and love it as we have loved it." An extraordinary combination.

Brundibar

PICTURE BOOK

AUTHOR: Tony Kushner • ILLUSTRATOR: Maurice Sendak
HC: Michael di Capua Books
THEMES: opera; poverty; bullies; brothers and sisters; illness

When their mother wakes up ill one morning, small Pepicek and his even smaller sister, Aninku, hurry into town for milk to make her better. The children have no money, so they try to earn some by singing, until the wicked, bullying hurdy-gurdy grinder, Brundibar, puts a stop to it. Fortunately, "the wicked never win," so with the help of three animals and three hundred children, they sing for their money, buy the milk, defeat the bully, and return home to help their mother.

Based on a Czech children's opera that was performed fifty-five times by the children of the Nazi concentration camp, Terezin, Pulitzer Prize–winner Kushner's text is a joy to read aloud. Sendak's art makes a splendid accompaniment.

Bunnicula

FICTION-MYSTERY

AUTHORS: Deborah and James Howe • ILLUSTRATOR: Alan Daniel
HC: Atheneum • PB: Aladdin
THEMES: rabbits; dogs; cats; vampires; mystery; family; vegetables; pets; humor

> More cat, dog, and rabbit mysteries can be found in *The Celery Stalks at Midnight*, *Nighty-Nightmare*, *Howliday Inn*, and *Return to Howliday Inn.*

A funny book about a vampire bunny! Narrated by Harold, the well-meaning and slightly put-upon dog of the Monroe family, it recounts the introduction of a new member to the household—the mysterious white rabbit named Bunnicula. This is one of those perfect books for the age when a sense of humor and the ability to read longer books both emerge, hungry for a great adventure. A series of sequels follows, guaranteeing that your child will have more fun with Bunnicula and the gang after the last chapter of this book, which they no doubt will clamor for. Don't say we didn't warn you.

Casey Jones's Fireman: The Story of Sim Webb

PICTURE BOOK

AUTHOR: Nancy Farmer • ILLUSTRATOR: James Bernardin
HC: Phyllis Fogelman Books
THEMES: trains; folklore; disaster; African American

An exciting blend of history and imagination. Here, readers see the legendary train engineer Casey Jones through the eyes of his fireman, Sim

Webb. A terrific portrayal of a little-known character from African American history and folklore, told in breathtaking, adventuresome style with vibrant art by James Bernardin. A great train book.

The Castle in the Attic

FICTION-FANTASY

AUTHOR: Elizabeth Winthrop
HC: Holiday House • PB: Dell
THEMES: castles; magic; knights; England; mystery

A magical adventure story in which a lonely boy learns the secret of the mysterious model of a castle. Filled with toys come to life, knights, and wizards, this castle transports the reader along with William on a fantastic quest of derring do. Look for the sequel, *The Battle for the Castle*.

Catwings

FICTION-FANTASY

AUTHOR: Ursula LeGuin • ILLUSTRATOR: S. D. Schindler
HC/PB: Orchard
THEMES: fantasy; cats; flying

The sequels are *Catwings Return*, *Wonderful Alexander and the Catwings*, and *Jane on Her Own*.

An imaginative piece of writing that is sure to appeal to cat lovers as well as those who are ready to begin reading fantasy. Short in length but rich in character and detail, this is an excellent book to use as a first longer chapter book. It also reads aloud beautifully.

The Cello of Mr. O

PICTURE BOOK

AUTHOR: Jane Cutler • ILLUSTRATOR: Greg Couch
HC: Dutton
THEMES: war; music; courage; pride; musical instruments

Cutler doesn't say where this story takes place, but she focuses on a spot in the center of a war-torn city where the food truck comes in each week to feed the neighborhood. Here an elderly musician shows readers that music and courage create its own sustenance when the truck no longer comes. A powerful and moving tribute to human dignity in the midst of the tragedy of war.

Charlie and the Chocolate Factory

FICTION-FANTASY

AUTHOR: Roald Dahl • ILLUSTRATOR: Quentin Blake
HC: Knopf • PB: Puffin
THEMES: fantasy; contests; food; grandfathers and grandsons; candy;
    chocolate; comeuppance; misbehaving

Charlie Bucket and his grandfather take the journey of their lifetimes through the gates of Willy Wonka's famous chocolate factory. Four other children—a glutton for anything he can put in his stomach, a television fanatic, a spoiled brat, and a gum-loving girl who chews herself blueberry blue—join them. They travel along rivers of chocolate to a world where anything sweet is possible, unless you are not so sweet and end up as a bad nut or with Everlasting Gobstoppers or Fizzy Lifting Drinks. In typical Dahl fashion, young readers can rejoice in the rotten eggs getting their comeuppance while honest, brave, kind, good eggs like Charlie have the time of their lives. The sequel, *Charlie and the Great Glass Elevator*, picks up right where this leaves off and is almost as good.

★ Charlotte's Web   FICTION

AUTHOR: E. B. White • ILLUSTRATOR: Garth Williams
HC/PB: HarperCollins
THEMES: spiders; death; farms; courage; love; friendship; miracles; family; animals; life cycle; wisdom; change; pigs; fairs; self-respect

We agree with read-aloud advocate Jim Trelease when he recommends this book to be read aloud for your child's first long chapter book. Wilbur, Fern, Templeton, and the rest have been delighting children for generations, but it is Charlotte herself who provides the book with its soul. Many children first encounter the cycle of life through this story, and its depiction of birth, growth, change, death, loss, and renewal has the power to move children and adults alike. Charlotte's death is without question a monumentally sad event in the world of children's books, but such is the power of White's prose that it is how she lived that we remember. There may be no finer book on friendship ever written.

Chocolate Fever   FICTION

AUTHOR: Robert Kimmel Smith • ILLUSTRATOR: Gioia Fiammenghi
PB: Dell
THEMES: chocolate; obsession; adventure; change; family; illness; doctors

Henry Green loves chocolate. Nothing gets past his mouth without some form of chocolate on it or in it. When his obsession with his favorite food causes him to break out in little brown spots, he is diagnosed with Chocolate Fever. A funny look at what happens when we get too much of a good thing.

A Chapter a Day

Reading a chapter a day is a wonderful way to help children increase their ability to listen and visualize. When the time comes for that first book to be read in more than one sitting, start with *Charlotte's Web*. It's well written, with characters you care about from the second you meet them, and the chapters are not long. After that, we can make some suggestions, but ultimately you'll have to find your own way. All children are individuals with their own set of readiness and tastes. Remember, just a chapter or two at a time, building up listening endurance. Try these:

The Wonderful Wizard of Oz (Baum)
The Cricket in Times Square (Selden)
My Father's Dragon (Gannett)
Misty of Chincoteague (Henry)
Freddy the Detective (Brooks)
The Borrowers (Norton)
The Railway Children (Nesbit)
Babe, the Gallant Pig (King Smith)
A Bear Called Paddington (Bond)
Mr. Popper's Penguins (Atwater)
The Chronicles of Narnia (Lewis)

Story and folklore collections give you an opportunity to sample a wide range of styles and types of stories. They offer a chance to learn about family tastes and naturally break up reading into manageable pieces. These are some of our favorites:

The People Could Fly (Hamilton)
Short and Shivery (San Souci)
Cut from the Same Cloth (San Souci)
Every Living Thing (Rylant)
From Sea to Shining Sea (Cohn, ed.)
The Story Library series (Various)
With a Whoop and a Holler (Van Laan)
The Random House Book of Sports Stories (Schulman)

The Chocolate Touch

FICTION

AUTHOR: Patrick Skene Catling • ILLUSTRATOR: Margot Apple
PB: Dell
THEMES: chocolate; greed; mothers; folktale variations

". . . he didn't see the change right away. Then his lips began to feel sticky. He opened his eyes. His mother had turned into a lifeless statue of chocolate!" John Midas loves chocolate. He also loves his mother. Due to his greed and his unfortunate misuse of a strange old coin, everything he touches becomes the thing he most desires.

The Christmas Miracle of Jonathan Toomey

PICTURE BOOK

AUTHOR: Susan Wojciechowski • ILLUSTRATOR: P. J. Lynch
HC: Candlewick
THEMES: redemption; solitude; Christmas; loss; family; artists; woodworking;
    grief; single parents; creativity; loneliness

They call him Mr. Gloomy. Woodcarver Jonathan Toomey is a sour, bitter man living a life of solitude and still mourning the loss of his wife and child. How a widow and her son help him rejoin the human race is told in a heart-tugging style, with warm and beautiful illustrations, all combining to make a holiday classic.

The Christmas Menorahs: How a Town Fought Hate

PICTURE BOOK
NONFICTION

AUTHOR: Janice Cohn • ILLUSTRATOR: Bill Farnsworth
HC/PB: Albert Whitman
THEMES: Hanukkah; bullies; courage; taking action; Montana; prejudice

When a brick is thrown through the window of his home because it has a menorah in it, the entire town rallies behind Isaac Schnitzer's family and puts menorahs in their windows. Based on events that happened in Billings, Montana, in 1993, this story is somewhat preachy but very useful in showing how bigotry and hate can be fought in a nonviolent fashion.

The Chronicles of Narnia

FICTION-FANTASY

AUTHOR: C. S. Lewis
HC/PB: HarperCollins
THEMES: courage; siblings; friendship; redemption; sacrifice; adventure;
    fantasy; good vs. evil

One of the most beloved children's series of all time, and an excellent introduction to more sophisticated fantasy storytelling. Start reading these aloud to your five- or six-year-old and let the magic take effect. These are very well written, both in terms of the plotting and the characters—you believe in these children. You even believe in the talking lion, Aslan, as noble and majestic a character as ever written. There is a strong element of Christianity in the telling, and the whole thing can be viewed as an allegory, but it doesn't have to be—children usually don't see the parallels—and it is the power of Lewis's storytelling that compels, not the message.

In recent years there has been some controversy as to the proper order in which to read the Narnia books. Indeed, their publisher renumbered the series, driving purists to distraction. The reasoning behind this was to put the stories in order of Narnia chronology. Though this makes sense, we feel that *The Lion, the Witch & the Wardrobe* is such a perfect introduction to Lewis's world and the children that it should be read first, followed by *The Magician's Nephew, Prince Caspian, The Voyage of the Dawn Treader, The Silver Chair, The Horse and His Boy*, and *The Last Battle*.

Cinder Edna   PICTURE BOOK

AUTHOR: Ellen Jackson • ILLUSTRATOR: Kevin O'Malley
HC: Lothrop • PB: Mulberry
THEMES: fairy tales; individuality; jobs; folktale variation; strong girls;
    stepfamilies

Cinder Edna is Cinderella's next-door neighbor. Each one has a wicked stepmother and wicked stepsisters. But while Cinderella sits among the cinders thinking about all her troubles, Cinder Edna is learning a thing or two from doing all that housework—such as how to get spots off everything from rugs to ladybugs. On the night of the ball, Cinder Edna puts on a practical dress and penny loafers and hops on a bus. At the ball she meets the prince's brother who "runs the recycling plant and a home for orphaned kittens." It's a fun contrast, and the young reader is left with no doubt as to who lives happily ever after.

The Cod's Tale   PICTURE BOOK NONFICTION

AUTHOR: Mark Kurlansky • ILLUSTRATOR: S. D. Schindler
HC: Putnam
THEMES: history; fish; fishing; sea

Adapted from his best-selling book for adults, *Cod: A Biography of the Fish That Changed the World*, Kurlansky has, with illustrator Schindler, created a fascinating look at an influential and important fish. Much of the economy of the people of the North Atlantic depended on the cod, and this look at a great resource squandered is notable for the visual adaptation Schindler gives to Kurlansky's work, making this a great book for young readers.

Come Look with Me: Enjoying Art with Children

PICTURE BOOK NONFICTION

AUTHOR: Gladys Blizzard • ILLUSTRATOR: Various (paintings)
HC: Thomasson-Grant
THEMES: art; paintings; museums

The first of a terrific series of books that adults can use to help bring an appreciation of art to young children. Mixing open-to-interpretation questions with just enough facts, these books focus on seeing as opposed to knowing, and offer a welcoming entry into museums. Other titles in the Come Look with Me series include *Animals in Art, World of Play,* and *Exploring Landscape Art with Children.*

Cowboy Country

PICTURE BOOK

AUTHOR: Ann Herbert Scott • ILLUSTRATOR: Ted Lewin
PB: Clarion
THEMES: cowboys; grandfathers; horses; ranches; camping; jobs; U.S.A., the West

A grandfather shows his grandson the ropes in this realistic portrayal of cowboy life. Perfect for horse, western, and cowboy lovers.

The Cricket in Times Square

FICTION

AUTHOR: George Selden • ILLUSTRATOR: Garth Williams
HC: Farrar, Straus & Giroux • PB: Dell
THEMES: cats; mice; crickets; New York; cities; family; friendship

Selden's beloved characters make subsequent appearances in *Harry Cat's Pet Puppy, Tucker's Countryside, Harry Kitten and Tucker Mouse,* and several other books.

A streetwise, motormouth mouse named Tucker, his sidekick, a cat named Harry, a kindly boy named Mario Bellini, and a country cricket named Chester make up an unlikely quartet of friends in this loving look at the city of New York in the late 1950s. Mario's parents run a newsstand, though not very successfully, and in between their jaunts uptown and down the four pals manage to find a way to finally bring Mama and Papa Bellini the success they have longed for.

★ Cut from the Same Cloth

FOLKLORE COLLECTION

AUTHOR: Robert San Souci • ILLUSTRATOR: Jerry Pinkney
HC: Philomel • PB: Puffin
THEMES: folklore; strong women; tall tales; U.S. history; heroes

Ask anyone to list some tall tales characters and see what names come up. All men, right? Well, as Jane Yolen wrote in her introduction to this collection of legends and tales about American women, "They have been here all along, these American women of wonder, women of power . . . They have shot game and given birth, cut logs for the fire, sewn the shrouds for their neighbors, hoed and hewed and harvested. But silently." San Souci's collection of stories from every region in the country brings back those voices.

D'Aulaire's Book of Greek Myths

FOLKLORE COLLECTION

AUTHORS/ILLUSTRATORS: Ingri and Edgar Parin D'Aulaire
HC: Doubleday • PB: Dell
THEMES: Greek mythology; heroes; ancient history; folklore; ancient Greece

Arguably the best single-volume look at Greek mythology for kids. The D'Aulaires cover every major character and many of the minor ones in a readable and engaging style that has set the standard for mythology writing since the 1940s. If you need only one book on the subject, this is it.

★ Dear Mr. Henshaw

FICTION

AUTHOR: Beverly Cleary • ILLUSTRATOR: Paul O. Zelinsky
HC: Morrow • PB: Avon
THEMES: writing; mail; authors; gentle boys; trucks; loneliness; single parents

Moving and gently written, this is the bittersweet story of Leigh Botts, a lonely boy who misses his absent father and reaches out through letters to a writer of children's books. Sensitively exploring Leigh's heartache, Cleary has created one of her most memorable characters in a departure from her Henry, Beezus, and Ramona books, and won the Newbery Award in the process.

Dear Rebecca, Winter Is Here

PICTURE BOOK

AUTHOR: Jean Craighead George • ILLUSTRATOR: Loretta Krupinski
HC/PB: HarperCollins
THEMES: solstice; mail; grandmothers; writing; winter

A grandmother writes to her granddaughter Rebecca on December 21, our shortest day of the year. "'Winter is here,' we say. It is here, but you can't touch it or serve it snacks. You can't read it a book or make it do anything.

But it makes us do all sorts of things. I turn on my lights. You put on your mittens. The birds fly to the sunny underside of the Earth." George has captured the winter solstice, and in her notes she describes the four seasons in relation to the rotation of the earth around the sun.

The Dinosaurs of Waterhouse Hawkins
PICTURE BOOK

AUTHOR: Barbara Kerley • ILLUSTRATOR: Brian Selznick
HC: Scholastic
THEMES: dinosaurs; artists; courage; loss; art; science

Victorian artist Waterhouse Hawkins spent thirty years building the first life-size models of dinosaurs, first in England and then in New York. His enormous figures are surprisingly close to our current ideas of what dinosaurs looked like. Those who like to build models, have a fascination for dinosaurs, enjoy careful research, like reading about trailblazers, or simply enjoy an intriguing true story will find something for themselves in this oversized, beautifully illustrated book.

Dippers
PICTURE BOOK

AUTHOR: Barbara Nichol • ILLUSTRATOR: Barry Moser
HC/PB: Tundra
THEMES: Canada; illness; mystery; mothers and daughters; fantasy;
community

This is a strangely inviting tale, perfect for reading aloud. It tells of the time, long ago, when the dippers came to town, large flying animals—with leathery wings and big eyes—that resemble dachshunds. No one knows where they came from. Some people are bothered by them, and others aren't. With an air of mystery and in a tone that serves hushed remembrance, Nichol has crafted a tale that is remarkable as much for what it leaves out as for what it contains. Moser's illustrations are so good we can't imagine them done by another artist.

The Doll People is the latest addition to a classic genre: the "dolls come to life" books. It is the decidedly modern sensibilities of the authors, and especially illustrator Selznick, that make this book and its sequel, *The Meanest Doll in the World,* such delights to read.

The Doll People
FICTION

AUTHORS: Ann M. Martin and Laura Godwin •
ILLUSTRATOR: Brian Selznick
HC: Hyperion
THEMES: dolls; comparisons; family; change

Annabelle Doll has been eight years old for over one hundred years. She can count on what will happen week after week in the confines of her dollhouse with her porcelain family. Then one day the Funcrafts, a modern plastic doll family, move in. The authors have created a story with adventure, mystery, and a touch of whimsy, and Selznick has added his artistic boost of humor. Read this aloud to the younger crowd.

The Dragon New Year: A Chinese Legend PICTURE BOOK
AUTHOR: David Bouchard • ILLUSTRATOR: Zhong-Yang Huang
HC: Peachtree
THEMES: Chinese New Year; Chinese American; folklore; history, medieval times; dragons; grandmothers and grandsons; fear, general

A loving grandmother uses a legend adapted from Chinese history and folklore to comfort a small child frightened by the noise and bright lights of the Dragon Dance. Exquisite paintings make this a lovely book to share with groups during the traditional Chinese New Year celebration.

Draw 50 Series ACTIVITY
AUTHOR/ILLUSTRATOR: Lee J. Ames
PB: Doubleday
THEMES: art; drawing

Everything the budding artist wants to draw is covered in one of these books. Simple and straightforward, with tips to help the absolute beginner as well as those more comfortable holding a pencil, titles include *Draw 50 Cats, Draw 50 People, Draw 50 Athletes, Draw 50 Creepy Crawlies, Draw 50 Famous Cartoons*, and *Draw 50 Dinosaurs and Other Prehistoric Animals.*

A Drop of Water: A Book of Science and Wonder PICTURE BOOK
AUTHOR/ILLUSTRATOR: Walter Wick (photographs)
HC: Scholastic
THEMES: water; photographs, magnification; science experiments

These photos are so clear you feel you can lap water off the page. Starting with a clear drop, Wick photographs water magnified in its many states—steam, frost, ice, dew, a rainbow—each explained in simple text. An afterword offers tips on experiments children can try using simple objects.

The Easter Egg Farm PICTURE BOOK
AUTHOR/ILLUSTRATOR: Mary Jane Auch
HC/PB: Holiday House
THEMES: Easter; eggs; art; creativity; farm; chickens

Auch's pictures of her hilarious hens make you laugh before you read their stories. Here a hen lays wildly patterned eggs, ready to add to the fanciest Easter basket. Read this before egg decorating, for inspiration and a good laugh. Auch's other talented hens are found in *Peeping Beauty, Hen Lake,* and *Eggs Mark the Spot.*

Eloise
PICTURE BOOK

AUTHOR: Kay Thompson • ILLUSTRATOR: Hilary Knight
HC: Simon & Schuster
THEMES: hotels; mischief; New York; strong girls; humor

The sensibilities and humor are decidedly adult, but two generations of children have grown up to the adventures of the little girl who lives at the Plaza Hotel, and the next will surely follow. What makes Eloise work is her sheer, rampant self-absorption—the world exists for her and her alone. This child-centered view is especially funny when taken to the extreme of having a little girl terrorize the staff and guests of New York's finest hotel. Thompson's language is affected and starchy, and Knight's illustrations are old-fashioned and only in two colors, but these are part of the charm, so enjoy! There are sequels and merchandise for those who can't get enough, but for us the original can't be beat.

Emily
PICTURE BOOK

AUTHOR: Michael Bedard • ILLUSTRATOR: Barbara Cooney
HC: Doubleday • PB: Dragonfly
THEMES: individuality; shyness; writing; authors

Elegant writing combined with Cooney's usual fine paintings make this a treasure for anyone interested in the story of this reclusive writer. An imagined encounter between a young girl and poet Emily Dickinson is rendered with sensitivity and a feel for the period.

The Enormous Egg
FICTION

AUTHOR: Oliver Butterworth • ILLUSTRATOR: Louis Darling
HC/PB: Little Brown
THEMES: dinosaurs; farms; love; pets; responsibility; surprises; comparisons;
    science; scientists; eggs

A chicken lays an egg that hatches a triceratops, and a young boy struggles to balance his pet's needs and the media circus that ensues. Young Nate does the best he can, but it isn't every day a real dinosaur makes the papers. With the help of a kindly scientist it all turns out okay in the end, but along the way this fantasy moves from rural New England to Washington, D.C., and the adventures that follow are the sort you might expect when an extinct species makes a sudden reappearance. Folksy and full of fun, and Louis Darling's illustrations are, well, darling.

Erika's Story   PICTURE BOOK

AUTHOR: Ruth Vander Zee • ILLUSTRATOR: Roberto Innocenti
HC: Creative Editions
THEMES: Jews; Holocaust; courage; mothers and daughters; adoption;
　　　survival; history, World War II

She was born sometime in 1944. She does not know her birthday, her birth name, or anything else about the first months of her life before her mother threw her from a train headed for a Nazi death camp. With few words and realistic, breath-catching art, this is the story of Erika, who was tossed "to life."

The First Strawberries: A Cherokee Story   PICTURE BOOK

AUTHOR: Joseph Bruchac • ILLUSTRATOR: Ann Vojtech
HC: Dial • PB: Puffin
THEMES: Native American; disagreement; anger; strawberries; problem
　　　solving; sun

A quarrel between a man and his wife is resolved with the knowledge that "friendship and respect are as sweet as the taste of ripe, red berries." This Cherokee story shows that even after people argue they can still find peace and love with each other. There's a bonus: discover how strawberries first came into this world.

Follow the Dream   PICTURE BOOK

AUTHOR/ILLUSTRATOR: Peter Sis
HC: Knopf
THEMES: Columbus; history: Age of exploration; Native American;
　　　trailblazing; imagination

It's not possible to look quickly through a Peter Sis book; there's too much to discover. And this fifteenth century voyage with Christopher Columbus is no exception. Illustrations show details of the explorer's life as well as the imaginative speculations people had on what he would find when he ventured outside of their world. The story on its own is fascinating. Words and art combined, Sis has created a historical treasure.

Forging Freedom: A True Story of Heroism During the Holocaust

PICTURE BOOK BIOGRAPHY

AUTHOR/ILLUSTRATOR: Hudson Talbott

HC: Putnam

THEMES: heroes; Dutch; escape; history, World War II; bullies: rescue; refugees; Holocaust

Jaap Penratt is a hero. He didn't understand the German's hatred for Jews during the Nazi occupation, but he knew he had to do something for his Jewish neighbors in his hometown of Amsterdam. He began by forging their ID cards. When that wasn't enough, he designed a plan to smuggle hundreds over the border to freedom. The details in Talbott's breathtaking pictures are too many to catch in one reading. We recommend you come back to it with time to peruse.

 Hudson Talbott has been a neighbor of Penratt's for years. They've shared time together socially as well as the occasional chats that take place among neighbors. But it wasn't until Talbott heard an interview on public radio that he discovered that Penratt was a modern-day hero. Here's an opportunity to point out to your child that heroes come in many forms.

The Forgotten Door

FICTION–SCIENCE FICTION

AUTHOR: Alexander Key

PB: Scholastic

THEMES: science fiction; communication; gifted child; home; fitting in

 One of the most memorable books from my childhood. I spent sixty-five cents of my own money and ordered this from the school book club because the description sounded so good. It more than lived up to my expectations, and I reread it many times over the next few years. Still in print, this novel about a boy from another world trying to get home while coping with life on Earth can be a doorway to science fiction for the young reader.

Alphabet Books: Math & Science

In the companion book, *Q Is for Quark*, science fans get a chance to have similar fun. Other math and science alphabet books include *26 Letters & 99 Cents*, *The Ocean Alphabet Book*, *The Dinosaur Alphabet Book*, and *The Extinct Alphabet Book*.

G is for Googol: A Math Alphabet Book

NONFICTION

AUTHOR: David Schwartz • ILLUSTRATOR: Marissa Moss

HC: Tricycle Press

THEMES: math; dictionary; alphabet

B is for Binary, *F* is for Fibonacci, *G* is for Googol . . . for mathematicians or math resisters, this over-sized dictionary offers a different mathematical word or idea for each letter of the alphabet. Every letter represents several paragraphs of discussion accompanied by fun watercolor drawings by Marissa Moss. What is a rhombicosidodecahedron? Find out here in this book that entertains as it teaches.

Getting to Know the World's Great Artists Series
PICTURE BOOK BIOGRAPHY
AUTHOR/ILLUSTRATOR: Mike Venezia
HC/PB: Children's Press
THEMES: art; paintings; artists; sculpture

A straightforward, low-priced introduction to some of the most famous painters, their lives and work. Artists include Paul Klee, Botticelli, Rembrandt, Mary Cassatt, Edward Hopper, Diego Rivera, and Monet.

The Ghost Dance
PICTURE BOOK
AUTHOR: Alice McLerran • ILLUSTRATOR: Paul Morin
HC/PB: Clarion
THEMES: peace; Native American; war; dance; courage

Astounding art, fusing collage and paintings, and spare, evocative writing make this an important addition to the bookshelf. The hopeful message will give inspiration to those involved in the endless dance for peace.

The Girl Who Loved Wild Horses
PICTURE BOOK
AUTHOR/ILLUSTRATOR: Paul Goble
HC: Simon & Schuster • PB: Aladdin
THEMES: horses; Native American; flowers; insects; animals; birds

Goble's story tells of a young Indian girl who so loves the wild horses that graze near her village, she eventually becomes one. Caldecott Award illustrations boast full, double-page spreads of Goble's signature stylized art that reveal his respect for Native American culture. Other Goble books in the same tradition include *Buffalo Woman* and *Star Boy*.

Girls to the Rescue
ANTHOLOGY
EDITOR: Bruce Lansky
PB: Meadowbrook
THEMES: strong girls; folklore; gender roles; folktale variations; comparisons

A collection we can all use—fairy tales, all original, in which the girls do all the saving and demonstrate terrific moments of gallantry usually denied them in classic fairy tales. Want more? Look for Volumes 2, 3, 4, and 5, as well as a one-volume "Best of" edition.

Grandmother Bryant's Pocket

PICTURE BOOK

AUTHOR: Jacqueline Briggs Martin • ILLUSTRATOR: Petra Mathers
HC/PB: Houghton Mifflin
THEMES: loss; grandparents; herbs; wisdom; patience; courage; colonial
America; U.S.A., New England; yearning; healing

A small book that holds a lot of wisdom. During colonial times, young Sarah is sent from her Maine home to get away from the memories of a barn fire and goes to live with her grandparents. The remedies of herbs and time work their magic, ministered by Grandmother Bryant, Shoe Peg (her grandfather), and a one-eyed cat. A simple and lovely look at grief and healing.

For another alphabet book with a similar concept, see *The Z Was Zapped* (page 216).

The Graphic Alphabet

PICTURE BOOK

AUTHOR/ILLUSTRATOR: David Pelletier
HC: Orchard
THEMES: alphabet; language; point of view

Each letter takes on a graphic story of its own in this visual alphabet. The top of the *A* falls off in an avalanche. *B* bounces across the page. *C* circles in motion. *D* turns down to the devil. A turn of the page presents a separate work of art where vivid colors on black squares create an alphabet for those who know their letters.

The Great Kapok Tree

PICTURE BOOK

AUTHOR/ILLUSTRATOR: Lynne Cherry
HC/PB: Harcourt Brace
THEMES: rain forest; Brazil; animals, endangered; environment; conscience;
taking action; trees

Brilliantly colored paintings initially draw readers to this book, but it's the ecological message that maintains its popularity. Many creatures of the Brazilian rain forest try to persuade an ax-wielding man not to cut down their home. End papers include a map of the tropical rain forests of the world.

The Great Piratical Rumbustification

FICTION

AUTHOR: Margaret Mahy • ILLUSTRATOR: Quentin Blake
PB: Godine
THEMES: pirates; parties; librarians; change; reading

This story and its companion, "The Librarian and the Robbers," form a pair of reading delights in this slim volume, but be assured, there is plenty here to entrance the reader. Mahy's devil-may-care prose and vocabulary may challenge beginning readers, so we suggest these be read aloud. You will enjoy the tale of a pirate party to end all parties and then the story of a librarian who is kidnapped but winds up teaching her captors the love of reading.

Eager readers tend to devour his books, as reading one just makes you want to read more. To the reader's delight, there are clever connections between the books, with *Magic by the Lake* being a sequel to *Half Magic*, and Jane and company making a guest appearance in the library-book-jumping antics of *Seven Day Magic*. Katherine and Martha's children (Roger, Ann, Jack, and Eliza) take center stage in the Ivanhoe-inspired adventures of *The Knight's Castle* and its sequel, *The Time Garden*. Kip, Gordy, James, Laura, Lydia, and Deborah are introduced in *Magic or Not?* and their adventures continue in *The Well-Wishers*.

★ Half Magic

FICTION-FANTASY

AUTHOR: Edward Eager • ILLUSTRATOR: N. M. Bodecker
HC/PB: Harcourt Brace
THEMES: magic; family; reading; responsibility; fantasy; adventure; books; single parents

Jane, Mark, Katherine, and Martha have their lives turned upside down by a magic coin that grants exactly half of what its holder wishes. The first of seven marvelous adventures in the realm of magic by Eager, each featuring literate and clever children who must learn to tame the magic in their possession. Though they are old-fashioned—they were written in the 1950s but have the feel of classic children's fantasy—they hold up very well and make delightful read-alouds.

 Me again. "Free, free, free. Libraries are free!" Get your library card today.

Heartland

PICTURE BOOK

AUTHOR: Diane Siebert • ILLUSTRATOR: Wendell Minor
HC/PB: HarperCollins
THEMES: poem; U.S.A., the prairie

Glorious, epic, demands-to-be-read-aloud poetry highlights each of Siebert's books, some of them odes to distinctive geographic regions of the USA (*Heartland, Sierra, Mississippi,* and *Mojave*), and others, songs of transportation (*Truck Song, Plane Song, Motorcycle Song,* and *Train Song*). Her poetry, coupled with fine illustrations for each book, offers a beautiful introduction to both the grandeur of her subjects and the lyrical power of poetry.

Harry Potter and the Sorcerer's Stone

FANTASY FICTION
AUTHOR: J. K. Rowling
HC/PB: Scholastic
THEMES: magic; wizards; school; friendship; orphans; good vs. evil; sports; boarding
school; England

When the first edition of our book was published in 1998, we traveled the country for several weeks making media appearances. Without exception, every reporter asked us what our favorite books were from the current crop of new titles. We are fortunate that publishers send us advance copies of books to review, so we had read and loved a first novel that was being published with considerable fanfare at the exact time we were appearing on television across the country. *Harry Potter and the Sorcerer's Stone* was just showing up in book-stores, so when we said that it was the best book of 1998 and the most child-friendly novel we had read in a long time, this was news to most folks. People still remind us today that they first heard about Harry from us. Though we could not have anticipated the immense success the book would become (who could?), we knew the book was great and told every-one who asked. It did wonders for our credibility.

All the hype, media madness, merchandise, and movies cannot dull our intense love for the first book and our delight in the subsequent volumes, nor our eagerness to see how Rowling finishes her seven-book saga. However, the phenomenon that Harry Potter has become needs to be addressed. What we have learned from its success reinforces some of our deep-est held beliefs:

Length is only a problem if the book is dull. Our favorite quote, from a nine-year-old cus-tomer at Hicklebee's, in response to his parents' concern that one of the books is over seven hundred pages long, is: *"Cool! That means I won't get to the end as fast."*
Vocabulary need not be a barrier if the words are used creatively in context. The reader will figure it out. J. K. Rowling wrote the book she wanted to read and respected her readers enough not to condescend to them. If only all the writers who have tried to copy her success would remember that.
Nothing can beat word-of-mouth as the best way to market a book. Scholastic, Rowl-ing's publisher, knew it had a potential hit on its hands and created a marketing campaign that was aggressive for a first-time author. However, no amount of advertising could com-pare to the buzz about the book that spread across the country like wildfire in the autumn of 1998 and winter of 1999. People were reading the book to their children and talking about it to their friends; booksellers were hand-selling it to their customers; and librarians were book-talking it in schools and public libraries. More important, children, thousands of them, were talking about it on the playground and in the classroom. That is the kind of promotion that you cannot buy, force, or create—it can only happen when the book is good enough.

Reading aloud cannot be beat as a family activity. Harry created a media awareness of reading and children's books that got some families to read aloud to their children, and for that, more than anything, we are grateful.

 In the midst of all the Harry Potter chaos, one morning when I arrived at Hicklebee's, I found an origami owl stuck in the front door. Written on it was "Thanks for all you do." There was no signature, but it felt to us as if the thrill of a family's reading together—as a result of Harry Potter—was coming back to us.

 May I just put in a plug here for the extraordinarily well done audio versions of the Harry books, read by Jim Dale? I love books on tape, and these are among my favorites.

Of course, no good deed goes unpunished, and as soon as something becomes too successful there are legions waiting to tear it down, so Harry has his share of detractors. From those whose religious beliefs made them wary of the magic elements of the book, to some children's literature types who were incensed that Harry wasn't a good enough book to warrant all the attention, the Internet was filled with people discussing the pros and cons of the book. Some went so far as to claim that Harry's popularity was obscuring better-written works, ignoring completely that a rising tide floats all boats and that the media attention bestowed upon Harry spilled onto children's books as a whole. For the most part, mass media gives little time to children and less to children's literature, but there were a few months when TV, magazines, and newspapers actually paid attention to issues concerning children's books and reading, and we found that encouraging. That is, until the media got tired of promoting the good that Harry represented and focused almost solely on the detractors.

Unfortunately, once something attains the level of cultural phenomenon, we tend to forget the good aspects of it that got it there in the first place. We'd like to take this opportunity to remind our readers that the books are good—really good—and that Rowling is doing a terrific job of maintaining the promise of that first book. Yes, they get longer and more intense as they go, but Harry also gets older, and that isn't done too often in children's series, so there isn't a lot of precedent. We have always maintained that the first book reads aloud best to eight-year-olds and up, and that you should add a year for each additional title. We have heard of parents reading the entire series to their five-year-olds (yikes!). We do not recommend it.

Above all, the Harry Potter books have proven that, given the right set of circumstances, reading can be perceived by the general public as central to our cultural life. Thanks, Harry. You remind us that it's cool to be a reader.

SEQUELS: *Harry Potter and the Chamber of Secrets*; *Harry Potter and the Prisoner of Azkaban*; *Harry Potter and the Goblet of Fire*; **and** *Harry Potter and the Order of the Phoenix*.

Henry Huggins

FICTION

AUTHOR: Beverly Cleary
HC: Morrow • PB: Avon
THEMES: friendship; dogs; family; neighbors; humor

The cycle of books featuring Henry, his dog, Ribsy, his sometime friend/sometime nemesis, Beezus, and her little sister, Ramona, begins with this book. All the adventures of the children who live on Klikitat Street have stood the test of time and prove that Cleary is a writer who understands universal truths. As long as there is a thing called childhood, these books will remain popular for boys and girls who like a good laugh, a gentle reminder that we are all human and can make mistakes, and characters that seem like your best friends.

Henry and the gang's adventures continue in *Henry and Beezus, Henry and Ribsy, Henry and the Clubhouse, Henry and the Paper Route,* and *Ribsy.* Ramona takes off on her own in other titles. See *Ramona the Pest.*

★ Hey World, Here I Am!

POETRY COLLECTION

AUTHOR: Jean Little • ILLUSTRATOR: Sue Truesdell
PB: HarperCollins
THEMES: writing; family; friendship; self-respect; school

When I get up in front of a large group of people, sometimes I reach into my "insurance" bag for quotable treasures from books to help me through the first few minutes of shaky quivers. Jean Little's Hey World, Here I Am! *is one of my all-time favorites. She gets to the heart of things with humor and candid insights of a girl named Kate Bloomfield. I can go to any page and find a poem or a vignette that opens my audience to me with a shared experience. But I can't quote an example here. From* Today *and* About Notebooks *to* After English Class *and* Louisa Louisa, *I can't bear to quote just a part—the whole is required. So, find this gem, fall into a cozy chair, and read all or part before handing it over to your child to savor.*

Hip Cat

PICTURE BOOK

AUTHOR: Jonathan London • ILLUSTRATOR: Woodleigh Hubbard
HC/PB: Chronicle
THEMES: jazz; rhythm; music; individuality

Jazzy and very cool, this is a fabulous read-aloud picture book. Caution: the complex rhythms mimic those of an improvisational jazz performance. Read it through a few times to get comfortable with them and, like the hip cat daddy-o title character, you'll be the toast of the town with this delightful ode to individuality and music.

Homer Price

AUTHOR/ILLUSTRATOR: Robert McCloskey

HC: Viking • PB: Puffin

THEMES: towns; humor; community; neighbors; relatives; restaurants;
U.S.A., the Midwest; contests; heroes

Life in a midwestern small town never sounded as good as when McCloskey describes it in this book and the sequel, *Centerburg Tales*. Homer is a good-old, all-around American boy, and you come to know him, his family, and the whole town of Centerburg mighty fine in these six stories about doughnuts, missing jewelry, progress, small-town politics, the Pied Piper, history pageants, and more doughnuts.

How a Book Is Made

AUTHOR/ILLUSTRATOR: Aliki

HC/PB: HarperCollins

THEMES: books; authors; illustrators; color; creativity; writing; patience;
reading

With thoroughness, Aliki shows how the author gets the idea, the idea gets written down, the publisher decides to publish, and the book gets made as well as sold, allowing the reader to follow the process every step of the way. The information is conveyed in a two-level method, with the main story in larger type and the more detailed nuts and bolts in smaller type, but what nuts and bolts they are! You can learn all you want to know about the mechanics of publishing a book here, making this an excellent book to use with writers, young and old.

How Ben Franklin Stole the Lightning

AUTHOR/ILLUSTRATOR: Rosalyn Schanzer

HC: HarperCollins

THEMES: inventors; scientists; lightning; electricity; science; problem solving;
U.S. history, Colonial America

Ben Franklin was an author, athlete, musician, printer, cartoonist, shopkeeper, soldier, politician, weather forecaster, and world traveler. He helped to write the Declaration of Independence and the Constitution of the United States. Each playful picture shows Franklin solving, performing, discovering, or inventing things he is famous for as well as some that may surprise you. Read this to young scientists as well as to the child who is overwhelmed when asked to accomplish more than one task.

The Hunter: A Chinese Folktale

PICTURE BOOK

AUTHOR: Mary Casanova • ILLUSTRATOR: Ed Young
HC: Atheneum
THEMES: hunting; hunger; drought; snakes; hunter; floods; folktales;
China; choices

The people in his Chinese village are suffering from a drought, and even
though Hai Li Bu is a good hunter, he cannot find enough food to keep them
from starving. One day he makes a pact with the Dragon King of the Sea that
he will learn the language of animals and never reveal this secret to anyone.
What he doesn't know then is that this agreement will force him to choose
between the life of the villagers and his own. Caldecott medalist Ed Young's
ink and color washes will make you pick up this treasure to begin with; the
tale will ensure that you read it again.

I Spy Two Eyes: Numbers in Art

PICTURE BOOK NONFICTION

AUTHOR: Lucy Micklethwait • ILLUSTRATOR: Various
HC: Greenwillow • PB: Mulberry
THEMES: counting; numbers; art; artists; paintings

A counting book featuring twenty works of art, ranging from the fifteenth
century to the present. Each page challenges a child to find the correct number of images by becoming familiar with the famous paintings. Also in this
series: *I Spy: An Alphabet in Art.*

I Want to Be a Veterinarian

PICTURE BOOK NONFICTION

> Others in the series: *I Want to Be an Astronaut, . . . a Fashion Designer, . . . a Chef, . . . an Environmentalist, . . . a Dancer;* and *. . . an Engineer.*

AUTHORS: Stephanie Maze and Catherine O'Neil Grace •
ILLUSTRATOR: Various (photographs)
HC: Harcourt Brace
THEMES: jobs; veterinarians; animals

There are private practices, house calls, farm calls,
zoo calls, and jungle calls. This overview of what it takes to be veterinarian
doesn't simply whet young appetites; it lists sources of information and suggests that if you have the qualities it takes to be a vet, "go for it."

I, Houdini

FICTION

AUTHOR: Lynne Reid Banks
PB: Yearling
THEMES: hamsters; escape; family; self-respect; confidence

"I am Houdini. No, no, no. Not that one—of course not. He's dead long ago. Besides, he was a human being and I am a hamster. But let me assure you that as my namesake was no ordinary man, I am no ordinary animal." That is the voice of Houdini, a boastful hamster who tells his story. Anyone who has had a hamster will understand that they come with escape claws that allow them to dig in and out of most anywhere. Young readers will want to dig into this story for a glimpse of what goes on in their furry little minds.

If the World Were a Village   PICTURE BOOK NONFICTION
AUTHOR: David J. Smith • ILLUSTRATOR: Shelagh Armstrong
HC: Kids Can Press
THEMES: math; geography; diversity; religion; community; language

It's hard to picture over six billion people on the planet and compare their similarities and differences. It would be a lot easier if we could pretend that the whole world is a village of just one hundred people. This is exactly what Smith has done. In his village we discover that twenty-two people speak a Chinese dialect, twenty-four have TVs, and five of them are from the United States. The facts are fascinating and promise surprises.

If You're Not from the Prairie   PICTURE BOOK
AUTHOR: David Bouchard • ILLUSTRATOR: Henry Ripplinger
HC: Atheneum • PB: Aladdin
THEMES: U.S.A., the prairie; writing; rhythm; repetition

Through poetry, the sun, the wind, the sky, and the flatness of the plain are remembered in this visually stunning book about contemporary life on the prairie. The rhythm and repetition of the language invites young writers to reflect similarly on their own memory of a familiar place.

If You're Not Here, Please Raise Your Hand   POETRY COLLECTION
AUTHOR: Kalli Dakos • ILLUSTRATOR: G. Brian Karas
HC: Simon & Schuster • PB: Aladdin
THEMES: school; self-respect; friendship; teachers; point of view

Funny and thought-provoking, Dakos writes with sensitivity about what students and teachers experience and feel.

If Your Name Was Changed at Ellis Island   PICTURE BOOK NONFICTION
AUTHOR: Ellen Levine • ILLUSTRATOR: Wayne Parmenter
PB: Scholastic
THEMES: immigration; Ellis Island; courage; change; names

If you and your child are discussing immigrants, take a look at this. It answers questions children might ask about people arriving on Ellis Island. "What happened if you were sick?" "Where would you sleep?"

James and the Giant Peach
FICTION-FANTASY

AUTHOR: Roald Dahl
HC: Knopf • PB: Puffin
THEMES: fantasy; peaches; aunts; family; grasshoppers; worms; spiders; ladybugs; centipedes; New York; courage; survival

When James Henry Trotter was about four years old, his ". . . mother and father went to London to do some shopping, and there a terrible thing happened. Both of them suddenly got eaten up (in full daylight, mind you, and on a crowded street) by an enormous angry rhinoceros which had escaped from the London Zoo." Poor James has to go live with his horrible Aunt Sponge and Aunt Spiker. It wasn't until the little man with the glowing bag came and the peach grew and James found that a centipede, earthworm, spider, ladybug, grasshopper, and glowworm could become his family that life took a turn for the best.

Keepers of the Earth: Native American Stories and Environmental Activities for Children
FOLKLORE COLLECTION

AUTHOR: M. Caduto and J. Bruchac • ILLUSTRATORS: J. K. Fadden and C. Wood
HC/PB: Fulcrum
THEMES: Native American; environment; animals; plants; crafts; nature

Keepers of the Earth is the first of an incredible trilogy packed full of Native American stories, information, and projects to help children appreciate and conserve our natural world. Other titles include *Keepers of the Animals* and *Keepers of Life: Discovering Plants Through Native American Stories and Earth Activities for Children.*

The Kid in the Red Jacket
FICTION

AUTHOR: Barbara Park
HC/PB: Knopf
THEMES: moving; self-respect; friendship; humor; school; change; neighbors; community

Howard thinks moving from Arizona to Massachusetts is rotten. When he gets there all the kids in his new town act as though he's invisible—except for a six-year-old neighbor girl who he can tell right away is weird. For anyone who's felt out of place, here's a big dose of humor with some understanding mixed in.

Kidding Around Washington, D.C.

NONFICTION

AUTHOR: Debbie Levy
PB: John Muir Publications
THEMES: travel; Washington, D.C.

This series is so cool we can't think why someone didn't think of it earlier. Aimed at eight- to twelve-year-olds, but useful when read to their younger siblings, these travel guides address their interests and needs and make the prospect of family travel inclusive. Most guidebooks give lip service to kid concerns, but these speak directly to them. Buy one for your kids before going on a trip—they'll thank you. Cities include Atlanta, Boston, New York, Paris, Santa Fe, and San Francisco, among others.

King Arthur: The Sword in the Stone

PICTURE BOOK

AUTHOR/ILLUSTRATOR: Hudson Talbott
HC: Morrow
THEMES: King Arthur; adventure; England; folklore; heroes; knights; love

If you are going to do a picture book of King Arthur, there should be bigger-than-life hear-the-horses-gallop scenes, and Talbott knows how to do them. He even adds an occasional see-the-dragon-breathe-fire scene. Exquisitely rendered paintings are guaranteed in a Talbott book, but it should be mentioned that his skill as a reteller makes this more than a coffee-table book.

When the time comes to introduce your children to Camelot, Talbott offers the perfect opportunity. Longer than traditional picture books, yet not epic in length as most versions for older readers, these beautiful, illustrated storybooks make excellent read-alouds. Look for the sequels *Excalibur, King Arthur and the Round Table*, and *Lancelot*.

King of the Wind

FICTION

AUTHOR: Marguerite Henry • ILLUSTRATOR: Dennis Wesley
PB: Aladdin
THEMES: adventure; Mideast; racing; horses

If you have a horse lover on your hands, introduce her to this classic Newbery Award–winning novel about a champion racehorse by the author of *Misty of Chincoteague*.

The Kingfisher Book of the Ancient World

REFERENCE

AUTHOR: Hazel Mary Martell
HC: Kingfisher
THEMES: history, ancient history; ancient Egypt; ancient Greece; ancient Rome

The best book of its kind for kids, full of maps, charts, interesting text, and all the information you could ever want about every region of the world and the cultures that existed there long ago.

Kingfisher Science Encyclopedia

REFERENCE

EDITOR: Charles Taylor
HC: Kingfisher
THEMES: science

A solid, one-volume, all-purpose science reference book. The organization and design are very appealing and we could find what we were looking for easily.

The Last Princess: The Story of Princess Ka'iulani of Hawai'i

PICTURE BOOK BIOGRAPHY

AUTHOR: Fay Stanley • ILLUSTRATOR: Diane Stanley
HC: HarperCollins
THEMES: Hawaii; princesses; biography; islands; cultural diversity; courage; taking action

Diane Stanley's vibrant paintings are a perfect match for her mother Fay's biography of Hawaii's Princess Ka'iulani.

Leagues Apart: The Men and Times of the Negro Baseball Leagues

PICTURE BOOK NONFICTION

AUTHOR: Lawrence Ritter • ILLUSTRATOR: Richard Merkin
HC: Morrow • PB: Mulberry
THEMES: baseball; African American; prejudice; determination

Before the 1950s, racist rules prevented black athletes from playing in the major leagues, regardless of their skills. In this story of the Negro Leagues, where players like Hank Aaron and Willie Mays got their starts, Lawrence Ritter blends history with brief biographies and reminds his readers not to glamorize the Negro league experience. "These talented men were not in the Negro Leagues by choice. They were there because of high walls erected in the name of segregation and maintained by racism."

The Legend of Mexicatl

PICTURE BOOK

AUTHOR: Jo Harper • ILLUSTRATOR: Robert Casilla
HC/PB: Turtle Books
THEMES: Mexico; wisdom; leadership; faith; desert; legends

"Some day, a man of wisdom and courage will rise up among us and take us from this desert." These words from Mexicatl's mother had been passed down through the generations. Little did he suspect that the Great Spirit would choose him to lead his people to a better land. This is the story of how the people chose to be called Mexicans.

The Librarian Who Measured the Earth

PICTURE BOOK BIOGRAPHY

AUTHOR: Kathryn Lasky • ILLUSTRATOR: Kevin Hawkes
HC: Little Brown
THEMES: math; language; biography; ancient Greece; geography;
Eratosthenes; punctuation; librarians

Over two thousand years ago a very smart baby was born. His name was Eratosthenes. In his lifetime he asked a lot of questions, and he wrote the first geography book . . . invented punctuation and grammar . . . made the first map of the world . . . used a grapefruit to measure the earth (and was only about two hundred miles off by today's standards). A fascinating illustrated biography!

AUTHOR SPOTLIGHT ON
KATHRYN LASKY

Kathryn Lasky's ability to write fiction and nonfiction for all ages puts her in a very select group of authors who continually amaze us. We're not talking about the kinds of writers who are known primarily for one genre of book and then dabble in another. Lasky can and does write fiction, both contemporary and historical, with the same level of assurance and quality that she does nonfiction or picture books.

Because of her storytelling gift, Lasky writes nonfiction in a thoroughly engaging style, resulting in books that are informative and entertaining. She is one of the few writers to receive a Newbery Honor for a nonfiction work *Sugaring Time*, an account of the Vermont tradition of gathering maple sap to make maple syrup. A writer of a wide range of interests,

Lasky happens to be married to gifted photographer Christopher G. Knight. They have collaborated on a variety of remarkable photo essays, including *Days of the Dead; Monarchs* (about butterflies); *The Most Beautiful Roof in the World* (the rain forest); *Interrupted Journey: Saving Endangered Sea Turtles; Shadows in the Dawn: The Lemurs of Madagascar;* and *Searching for Laura Ingalls: A Reader's Journey*, which we recommend as a supplement to any child's enjoyment of the *Little House on the Prairie* books.

Venturing into the realm of picture-book biography, Lasky has written some of the finest examples of the form: *The Librarian Who Measured the Earth; Brilliant Streak: The Making of Mark Twain; Vision of Beauty: Sarah Breedlove Walker;* and *A Voice of Her Own: The Story of Phyllis Wheatly, Slave Poet.*

Her picture books are a diverse lot, ranging from her somber, original Native American tale *Cloud Eyes* (illustrated by Barry Moser) to her speculations on the origins of early cave painting, *First Painter* (illustrated by Rocco Baviera), to her inspiring account of a seventy-five-year-old woman's learning to swim, *Sea Swan* (illustrated by Catherine Stock). A marvelous sense of place and time enhances most of her work, none more so than *Marven of the Great North Woods* (illustrated by Kevin Hawkes), based on her father's childhood adventure in a logging camp. Her love of Boston flavors both the warmly engaging *I Have an Aunt on Marlborough Street* (illustrated by Susan Guevara) and the historically accurate and often absurdly humorous retelling of the founding of the Audubon Society, *She's Wearing a Dead Bird on Her Head!* (illustrated by David Catrow). For younger readers, her delightful story of the trials and tribulations of the cafeteria, *Lunch Bunnies* (illustrated by Marilyn Hafner) and its sequels will give confidence and more than a few giggles, and those in search of a suitable first scary story need look no farther than Lasky's wacky *Porkenstein* (illustrated by David Jarvis).

In the area of fiction, Lasky has struck gold with her *Starbuck Family Adventures*, three exciting novels about two pairs of telepathic twins and the mysteries they solve. These are examples of the very best formula fiction; bridging the gap between science fiction and mystery, they are perfect books to give to adventure-hungry fourth- and fifth-graders. The individual titles are *A Voice in the Wind, Double Trouble Squared,* and *Shadows in the Water.*

Lasky has distinguished herself as one of the premier writers of historical fiction for young people, ranging from her first novel, *Night Journey* (illustrated by Trina Schart Hyman), a gripping story of escape and emigration from czarist Russia, to her chronicles of American history, *Beyond the Burning Time* (about the Salem witch trials), *True North: A Novel of the Underground Railroad,* and her outstanding contributions to the Dear America series.

In all of her writing, Lasky's respect for the reader shines. She knows that if she can write about something she finds interesting and tell a good story, she has done her job. No matter what the subject or format, Lasky never lets the reader down—her name on a book is a sign of quality and a promise from a storyteller that a treasure lies waiting within.

Linnea in Monet's Garden   PICTURE BOOK NONFICTION

AUTHOR: Christina Bjork • ILLUSTRATOR: Lena Anderson
HC: R & S Books
THEMES: Monet; art; Paris; plants; flowers; travel; artists; painting; gardens

Begin with Anderson's watercolor illustrations of a young traveler curious about Monet's waterlilies. Add photographs of his garden along with reproductions of his paintings, and you have the story of Linnea, a delightful character who offers a colorful lesson in art history.

The Little House on the Prairie   FICTION

AUTHOR: Laura Ingalls Wilder • ILLUSTRATOR: Garth Williams
HC/PB: HarperCollins
THEMES: community; relatives; courage; change;
U.S. history, frontier life; U.S. history, Westward
movement; U.S.A., the prairie; family

> Others in the series: *Farmer Boy, On the Banks of Plum Creek, By the Shores of Silver Lake, The Long Winter, Little Town on the Prairie, These Happy Golden Years, The First Four Years.*

TV promoted *The Little House on the Prairie,* making it the most familiar and most often requested of the books by Laura Ingalls Wilder. Published in 1932, *Little House in the Big Woods* was the first of nine books about Laura Ingalls and her family. Lest you think, however, that TV is the only reason these have stood the test of time, we want to assure you that there may be no finer depiction of American prairie life in all of fiction. Beginning in a log house in Wisconsin when Laura was a young girl, the series takes the family west by covered wagon and ends with grown-up Laura marrying, moving with her husband into their own homestead, and giving birth to their daughter.

Little Ships: The Heroic Rescue at Dunkirk in World War II   PICTURE BOOK

AUTHOR: Louise Borden • ILLUSTRATOR: Michael Foreman
HC: McElderry • PB: Aladdin
THEMES: history, World War II; boats; strong girls; courage; community; England; rescue

Gripping stuff—the kind of storytelling that makes history come alive. The amazing story of the evacuation at Dunkirk is told through the eyes of a young girl, a passenger on her father's boat. Her narration makes this moment of epic bravery into a personal event, thereby reminding us that great moments in history happened to real people, not just names in a book.

★ Lives of the Musicians: Good Times, Bad Times (and What the Neighbors Thought)

BIOGRAPHY COLLECTION

AUTHOR: Kathleen Krull • ILLUSTRATOR: Kathryn Hewitt
HC/PB: Harcourt Brace
THEMES: biography; music; humor; creativity; cultural diversity

Artists, athletes, presidents, writers, and extraordinary women get the same treatment in Krull and Hewitt's other books in the *Lives of the . . .* series.

Personal stories of twenty musicians from Vivaldi to Woody Guthrie. What a way to take children into the past! Give them details, individual quirks, the behind-the-scenes nitty gritty. Beethoven "couldn't be bothered with clean or stylish clothes. When his clothes became too dirty and disgusting, his friends took them away during the night and brought new ones. Beethoven never noticed." Describes the good times and bad times through the life stories of diverse musical figures.

Love, Ruby Lavender

FICTION

AUTHOR: Deborah Wiles
HC/PB: Harcourt Brace
THEMES: grandmothers; loss; grief; chickens; U.S.A., the South; family

Here is a wonderful, humorous debut novel with warm southern characters ("good friendly folks and a few old soreheads"), a small close-knit community (Hallelulia, Mississippi, population: four hundred), and a strong heroine. Miss Eula, everyone's perfect grandmother, is taking time away from home and her beloved granddaughter, Ruby Lavender, to recover from the loss of her husband. Dealing gently with issues of grief and shame, and featuring wildly funny characters and a knack for the southern turn of phrase ("Good garden of peas!" has become one of our favorite exclamations), Ruby and company will affirm your faith in human nature and reminds you that, as Miss Eula puts it, "Life does go on."

Ma Dear's Aprons

PICTURE BOOK

AUTHOR: Patricia McKissack • ILLUSTRATOR: Floyd Cooper
HC: Atheneum • PB: Aladdin
THEMES: mothers and sons; African American; jobs; family; love; single
        parents; U.S. history, Reconstruction; strong women

A collaboration between a master storyteller and an illustrator who are both at the height of their powers. Ma Dear has an apron for each day of the week, signaling that day's particular chore—taking in wash, cleaning the house, baking pies. Told by her young son, this picture of life in the South during Reconstruction is so loving you can feel Ma Dear's hugs.

Make a Wish, Molly   FICTION

AUTHOR: Barbara Cohen • ILLUSTRATOR: Jan Naimo Jones
PB: Dell
THEMES: traditions; celebrations; Passover; cultural diversity; immigration; friendship; Jews; birthdays; birthday parties

Molly, a recent immigrant, has to find a balance between her own background and the tradition of her new friends. Birthday celebrations, Passover, religious tolerance, and the meaning of friendship are all touched on here in this companion to Cohen's *Molly's Pilgrim*.

Matilda   FICTION-FANTASY

AUTHOR: Roald Dahl • ILLUSTRATOR: Quentin Blake
HC: Viking • PB: Puffin
THEMES: school; self-respect; teachers; family; strong girls; gifted children; playing tricks; comeuppance; cruelty

Children love this hilariously funny novel about a girl with special powers who gets back at her parents for treating her as though she were "scabs and bunions." And when the mean headmistress, Miss Trunchbull, picks on Matilda's favorite teacher, she gets her back in major proportions. As usual Dahl offers up a treat for young readers, who wish they could be Matilda—if only for one day—experiencing their own get-backs through practical jokes and concentrated energy.

Max Makes a Million   PICTURE BOOK

AUTHOR/ILLUSTRATOR: Maira Kalman
HC: Viking
THEMES: jobs; family; yearnings; art; creativity; friendship; zany; writing; poets

Max the poet, the dreamer, the dog, makes his memorable debut. Full of zany characters, richly odd art, fabulous language, and jokes galore, this is at heart a story about growing up and leaving home. It's about the two things every child needs: roots and wings. You will cheer as you watch Max soar on his wings. Max goes on to other adventures in other books, but none grab us the way this one does.

Minty: A Story of Young Harriet Tubman
PICTURE BOOK BIOGRAPHY

AUTHOR: Alan Schroeder • ILLUSTRATOR: Jerry Pinkney

HC: Dial • PB: Puffin

THEMES: Harriet Tubman; biography; slavery; Underground Railroad;
African American; courage; escape

When Harriet Tubman was a child, her father taught her how to find the North Star to mark her way and how to read trees. She learned how to skin a squirrel, to fish with only a string and a nail, to do birdcalls, and to run barefoot through the woods without making a sound. This is the story of a strong-willed child who escaped from slavery and someday would help hundreds of others to do the same.

Misoso: Once Upon a Time Tales from Africa
FOLKLORE COLLECTION

AUTHOR: Verna Aardema • ILLUSTRATOR: Reynold Ruffins

HC: Knopf

THEMES: Africa; fables; folklore; traditions; history; African culture

These African fables are great fun to read on your own or aloud to someone who can use a good story. Glossaries and interesting notes about African history and traditions are included with each tale.

Mistakes That Worked
NONFICTION

AUTHOR: Charlotte Foltz Jones • ILLUSTRATOR: John O'Brien

HC/PB: Doubleday

THEMES: inventions; creativity; biography; mistakes; history

A treasure trove of interesting facts and behind-the-scenes information about lots of things we use every day, all of them created unintentionally. Clever line drawings add a touch of humor, enticing nonreaders as well as fact buffs. *Accidents May Happen* is a companion book.

Misty of Chincoteague
FICTION

AUTHOR: Marguerite Henry • ILLUSTRATOR: Wesley Dennis

PB: Aladdin

THEMES: horses; Virginia; captivity; family

Misty appears again in *Stormy, Misty's Foal.* Other terrific books by Henry include the Newbery-winning *King of the Wind, Brighty of the Grand Canyon,* and *Born to Trot.*

For years, the best books about horses came from Marguerite Henry. Though based on real animals, her books are fiction, and her storytelling skills make these engaging reads that children have loved for generations. Misty tells the story of the wild ponies of Assateague Island, Virginia, and the annual pony roundup when the horses are driven across an inlet to captivity.

Molly's Pilgrim
FICTION

AUTHOR: Barbara Cohen • ILLUSTRATOR: Michael J. Deraney
HC/PB: Morrow
THEMES: immigration; Russia; traditions; cultural diversity; teasing; fitting in; Thanksgiving; celebrations; school; Pilgrims; Jews

Molly wants to go back home to Russia where she fit in, or even to New York, where there are other Jewish kids. In Winter Hill she looks and sounds different from everyone else in her third-grade class. This tender tale of a modern day Pilgrim confronts the feelings of children who are teased by their classmates because of their differences. For more about Molly, see *Make a Wish, Molly* (page 302).

Money, Money, Money: The Meaning of the Art and Symbols on United States Paper Currency
PICTURE BOOK NONFICTION

AUTHOR/ILLUSTRATOR: Nancy Winslow Parker
HC: HarperCollins
THEMES: money; government; U.S. history; symbols

Loot. Greenbacks. Scratch. Clams. Moolah. Do you know which bills don't have pictures of presidents? How many $100,000 bills are in circulation? What techniques have been invented to stop counterfeiters? Entertaining and informative, this book provides everything you'll need to know about the history of United States paper money.

Mr. Lincoln's Way
PICTURE BOOK

AUTHOR/ILLUSTRATOR: Patricia Polacco
HC: Philomel
THEMES: school; cultural diversity; prejudice; bullies; birds; patience

The kids in Mr. Lincoln's school think he is the "coolest principal in the whole world," except for Eugene Esterhause, who hates everyone who's different from him. He pushes kids and calls them names. When Mr. Lincoln discovers that "Mean Gene" likes birds, he uses them to help him overcome his intolerance. Polacco has again created a story in a multicultural setting where understanding and patience can create change in difficult situations.

Mr. Popper's Penguins

FICTION

AUTHORS: Richard and Florence Atwater
HC/PB: Little Brown
THEMES: penguins; skating; U.S. history, the 1920s; gifts; resourcefulness;
    problem solving

An unexpected gift of penguins from the explorer Admiral Peary results in a houseful of waddling, fish-eating pets. A classic that produces much hilarity in the scenes of a houseful of penguins and the poor, at-wits'-end Popper family. Becoming entertainers seems to be the best solution, and a family of skating, trick-performing penguins is what they become. Delightful.

Mrs. Piggle-Wiggle

FICTION

AUTHOR: Betty MacDonald • ILLUSTRATOR: Hilary Knight
HC/PB: HarperCollins
THEMES: humor; manners; problem solving

Mrs. Piggle-Wiggle's wisdom knows no bounds. Every single child with a problem has been sent to her by parents at their wit's end and she has cured them all of their ailments, be they lying, stealing, not taking a bath, or being a crybaby. These clever books, four in all, are a bit dated, but their heart is still intact—children love Mrs. Piggle-Wiggle, then and now.

My Brother Martin: A Sister Remembers
Growing Up with the Rev. Dr. Martin

PICTURE BOOK BIOGRAPHY

AUTHOR: Christine King Farris • ILLUSTRATOR: Chris Soentpiet
HC: Simon & Schuster
THEMES: Martin Luther King Jr.; brothers and sisters; African American;
    Civil Rights; family

The childhood of one of our greatest leaders is described with humor and warmth by his sister, who shared it with him. Farris offers firsthand accounts of events that inspired King's sense of activism, including the moment he pledged "... to turn this world upside down." Soentpiet's luminous watercolors work in perfect harmony with Farris's words.

Olympia: Warrior Athletes of
Ancient Greece

PICTURE BOOK NONFICTION

AUTHOR: David Kennett • ILLUSTRATOR: Dyan Blacklock
HC: Walker
THEMES: comic-book style; Ancient Greece; Olympics; sports

Illustrated in a graphic novel style, this is the best look at the original Olympics we've seen. There is not a lot of text, but the artwork is sophisticated and carries the lion's share of the narrative, making this an excellent book for older nonreaders.

On Beyond a Million: An Amazing Math Journey

PICTURE BOOK NONFICTION

AUTHOR: David M. Schwartz • ILLUSTRATOR: Paul Meisel
HC: Bantam Doubleday Dell • PB: Dragonfly
THEMES: math; numbers; counting; measurement; concepts; comparisons

The concept of really big numbers gets a workout in Schwartz's episodic style, peppered with lots of facts and trivia. This is the book that will teach children that infinity is not a number—which is just one of its many uses.

Only Opal: The Diary of a Young Girl

PICTURE BOOK BIOGRAPHY

AUTHORS: Opal Whiteley and Jane Boulton • ILLUSTRATOR: Barbara Cooney
PB: Paperstar
THEMES: U.S. history, early 20th century; death; solitude; nature; Oregon;
pioneers; biography; diaries; U.S. history, frontier life

Opal Whiteley describes her love of nature and her life following her parents' death at the turn of the century. In this adaptation of her writings the language is rich, and the story brings the reader back to a time when a child's day was filled with work, hope, and time to appreciate the quiet of the plants, animals, birds, and space. "When I feel sad inside I talk things over with my tree. I call him Michael Raphael. It is such a comfort to nestle up to Michael Raphael. He is a grand tree. He has an understanding soul." It is a good thing for children to be exposed to all kinds of writing and art. This gem provides fine examples of both.

Owls in the Family

FICTION

AUTHOR: Farley Mowat • ILLUSTRATOR: Robert Frankenberg
PB: Dell
THEMES: owls; family; pets; humor; Canada

A youthful reminiscence from one of North America's great nature writers. Billy, Bruce, and Mutt, the stars of Mowat's earlier book *The Dog Who Wouldn't Be*, return, adding Wol and Weeps, a pair of owls, to the family menagerie, driving Mutt crazy and creating several hilarious adventures. Our favorite is the scene in which Wol interrupts family dinner by showing off his latest kill—a dead skunk!

Pablo Remembers: The Fiesta of the Day of the Dead

PICTURE BOOK NONFICTION

AUTHOR/ILLUSTRATOR: George Ancona (photographs)

HC: Lothrop

THEMES: Day of the Dead; Mexico; ancestors; family; community; rituals; traditions

Ancona's other photo essays about native American and Mexican life include *The Pinata Maker*, *Fiesta USA*, and *Pow Wow*.

On October 30, Mexican people everywhere prepare for The Day of the Dead. Ancona describes the elaborate preparations through the eyes of a young Mexican boy and his family. Colorful photographs capture details of this celebration honoring the spirits of the dead. Here is a book that presents with care a holiday observed by many Mexican American families.

Paddle-to-the-Sea

PICTURE BOOK

AUTHOR/ILLUSTRATOR: Holling Clancy Holling

HC: Houghton Mifflin • PB: Sandpiper

THEMES: sea; boats; maps; journeys; adventure; geography; Canada; Native American

In Canada an Indian boy carves a foot-long canoe. "I made you, Paddle Person, because I had a dream. . . . You will go with the water and you will have adventures that I would like to have. But I cannot go with you, because I have to help my father with the traps." First published in 1941, this mapped adventure continues to enthrall readers, who float, dive, and wash along on a canoe journey from Lake Superior all the way to the Atlantic Ocean.

Peacebound Trains

FICTION

AUTHOR: Haemi Balgassi • ILLUSTRATOR: Chris Soentpiet

HC/PB: Clarion

THEMES: Korea; war; family; separation; hardship; immigration; trains; peace; memories

A look at the devasting effects war has on families. This war is the Korean conflict, and this family is author Balgassi's mother's. Told in a straightforward style and with luminous art by Soentpiet, this tale of wartime separation will linger in the memory and the heart.

AUTHOR SPOTLIGHT ON
VIRGINIA HAMILTON

Virginia Hamilton was a gifted writer—a storyteller with the heart and skill of a poet. Whether writing novels of fantasy or gritty reality, picture books or biographies, she wove words together with such mastery that the reader is often stunned by the imagery. A demanding writer who believed strongly in the bond of language between herself and her audience, she often experimented with style and form in her quest to portray the African American experience and to best serve the tale she sought to tell.

Though skilled at writing the picture book (*Jagarundi, The Bells of Christmas*, and *The Girl Who Spun Gold* are but a few of her successes in this arena), it is as a novelist that she made her mark, winning a Newbery Award for *M.C. Higgins the Great* in 1975, as well as three Newbery Honors. Her books *Zeely, Arrilla Sun Down, The House of Dies Drear*, and especially *The Planet of Junior Brown* established her as one of the great novelists for young adults. These are not "easy" books—they cannot be read frivolously or readily forgotten, and young readers may require some assistance from adults to help them to fully appreciate these books' richness.

Hamilton's mastery of language makes her novels a pleasure to read aloud, but the feeling of the spoken word is even more prevalent in Hamilton's collections of stories and folklore. In books like *The Dark Way: Stories From the Spirit World; Her Stories; When Birds Could Talk and Bats Could Sing; The Adventures of Bruh Sparrow, Sis Wren and Their Friends; In The Beginning: Creation Stories From Around the World; Bruh Rabbit and the Tar Baby Girl*; and the multiple-prizewinning *The People Could Fly*, the retellings are so good, the writing so sure, and the feel of the time, place, and culture so inviting that one need only speak the words as they are written to bring the stories to life—Hamilton has done the work for us. Even when she did not write in a dialect, the care with which she chose her words and her judicious use of rhythm create a feel of another place when read out loud.

In her historical fiction (*Willie Bea and the Time When the Martians Landed*), science fiction (*Justice and Her Brothers, Dustland*, and *The Gathering*), biography (*Anthony Burns: The Defeat and Triumph of a Fugitive Slave*), or her other novels, which defy easy categorization (*Sweet Whispers, Brother Rush*, and *Plain City*), Hamilton delivered a brilliant reading experience and held the lamp of her considerable talent up to illuminate the life of the African American child for over thirty years. We are bereft at the loss of her inspiring talent.

★ The People Could Fly

FOLKLORE COLLECTION

AUTHOR: Virginia Hamilton • ILLUSTRATORS: Leo and Diane Dillon
HC/PB: Knopf
THEMES: folklore; African American; storytelling

An outstanding collection of African American folklore, all on the subject of freedom, and with perfect illustrations by the Dillons. Hamilton's gift for adapting oral-tradition stories into written form is unsurpassed, and the inclusion of the voices of her ancestors to amplify the truth of the folktales is a brilliant touch. There is a CD version of the tales that accompanies many hardcover editions—the narration is by James Earl Jones, and it is a fitting complement to the beauty of the book.

Ramona the Pest

FICTION

AUTHOR: Beverly Cleary • ILLUSTRATOR: Louis Darling
HC: Morrow • PB: Avon
THEMES: sisters; humor; family; neighbors; school;
    friendship; mistakes

> All Cleary's books read aloud well, and we suggest starting off with *Ramona the Pest* and working your way through the others, which include *Ramona the Brave, Beezus and Ramona, Ramona and Her Father, Ramona and Her Mother,* and *Ramona's World.*

Ramona, who started off as a supporting character in Beverly Cleary's *Henry Huggins* books, quickly asserted her irrepressible self and became the subject of a bunch of novels of her own. A child nearly everyone can identify with, Ramona is one of the most beloved characters in children's books. Her mistakes, her schemes and ideas, and most of all, her hilarious adventures have endeared her to millions of children.

★ Rapunzel

PICTURE BOOK

AUTHOR/ILLUSTRATOR: Paul O. Zelinsky
HC: Dutton • PB: Puffin
THEMES: folklore; captivity; love; magic; solitude; hair; separation; mothers
    and daughters; change; coming of age

A beautifully crafted retelling that features museum-quality art, all from the hands of one of our most gifted author/illustrators. His sensitive retelling stresses different aspects of the story than you may have grown up with, and his paintings give tremendous weight to his themes, each surpassing the previous in its beauty and depth of feeling. A stunning piece of work.

★ Rattlesnake Dance: True Tales, Mysteries, and Rattlesnake Ceremonies

PICTURE BOOK NONFICTION

AUTHOR/ILLUSTRATOR: Jennifer Owings Dewey

PB: Boyds Mills

THEMES: Native American; nature; snakes; biography; folklore

By the second sentence we were hooked. "...I felt the strike. There was stunning pain from the instant the twin fangs pierced the soft, fleshy side of my hand." Dewey is a pro at fusing interesting scientific facts with her own experiences. When she was nine, a rattlesnake bit her. A year later she observed Hopi snake dancers, and as an adult saw a "rattlesnake dance" between two male rattlers. Each account of her experiences includes detailed drawings and "fact boxes" featuring information about the snakes. Just about any curiosity you have about rattlers will be answered here, including where in the United States you can find them.

The Real McCoy: The Life of an African-American Inventor

PICTURE BOOK BIOGRAPHY

AUTHOR: Wendy Towle • ILLUSTRATOR: Wil Clay

PB: Scholastic

THEMES: biography; African American; trains; jobs; inventions; prejudice; courage; determination

Read about Elijah McCoy, honored in this biography for his inventions, including a lubricating cup that made his job on the railroad more efficient. Others tried to copy his designs, but engineers asked for *The Real McCoy*.

Red Hot Hightops

FICTION

AUTHOR: Matt Christopher

PB: Little Brown

THEMES: sports

The premier writer of sports fiction for children, Christopher is there for kids when they go through the phase of reading only books with games in them. His comforting style, stressing character and the rules of the game, will attract reluctant readers of a wide range of ages. Though he wrote mostly of baseball in his earlier novels, his later work included a variety of sports that reflect the interests of today's children.

 When my son, Anthony, was eight, he went through quite a Matt Christopher phase. Here are his favorites: *Baseball Flyhawk, The Basket Counts, The Comeback Challenge, Ice*

Magic, The Year Mom Won the Pennant, The Hockey Machine, and biographies of Steve Young, Emmet Smith, and Ken Griffey Jr.

Riding Freedom

HISTORICAL FICTION

AUTHOR: Pam Muñoz Ryan
HC/PB: Scholastic
THEMES: strong women; horses; gender roles; secrets

One-eyed Charley Parkhurst, a stagecoach driver, lived her life as a man and became the first woman to vote in the state of California. This excellent piece of historical fiction is a winner of the California Young Reader Medal and a fascinating account of a life many cannot imagine living. Charlie really did.

Rome Antics

PICTURE BOOK

AUTHOR/ILLUSTRATOR: David Macaulay
HC: Houghton Mifflin
THEMES: Rome; Italy; birds; journeys; cities; architecture

> Other highly recommended titles by Macaulay include *Mill, Unbuilding, Castle, Underground, Pyramid, City, Cathedral,* and *Ship.*

A bird's-eye view takes on full meaning in this swooping, tumbling, soaring view of Rome's famous architectural wonders. The Coliseum, Pantheon, palazzos, and arches are seen from the perspective of a pigeon delivering a note. Future architects and travelers will find hours of details from the Arch of Constantine to the walls of the Palazzo Spada. And the pigeon's message? It will leave you smiling.

Round Buildings, Square Buildings, and Buildings That Wiggle Like a Fish

PICTURE BOOK NONFICTION

AUTHOR/ILLUSTRATOR: Philip M. Isaacson
HC: Knopf
THEMES: architecture; buildings; dwellings; way things work

From temples to shacks to airline terminals, readers get a close-up look at all kinds of structures. Full-color photographs and poetic text make the discussion of architectural materials and elements anything but boring. Don't limit this book to future architects. Choose it for anyone interested in design and how things work.

Sadako and the Thousand Paper Cranes   FICTION

AUTHOR: Eleanor Coerr • ILLUSTRATOR: Ronald Himler
HC: Putnam • PB: Puffin
THEMES: Japan; courage; illness; death; family; peace;
    friendship; origami; war

You'd think a picture-book version of *Sadako and the Thousand Paper Cranes* might lose some of its potency, but the story is just as affecting in *Sadako*, which features art by Ed Young. The powerful art makes a strong impression, though, and we recommend that you read it first before deciding to share it with a child under seven.

A heartbreaking tale that serves to remind us of the personal cost of war. Stricken with leukemia as a result of the bombing of Hiroshima, brave Sadako vows to fold one thousand paper cranes so that the gods will make her well. When she dies, her classmates fold the remaining 356. A statue of Sadako stands in Hiroshima Peace Park, a testament to her courage and the wish for peace.

Safari Journal: The Adventures in Africa of Carey Monroe   PICTURE BOOK

AUTHOR/ILLUSTRATOR: Hudson Talbott
HC: Harcourt Brace
THEMES: Africa; Masai; adventure; journals; safaris; Swahili; animals;
    endangered

World traveler Talbott has used his experience among Kenya's Masai as the basis for an exciting adventure. Using the same journal device as he did in *Amazon Diary* (out of print, but find a copy for your young adventurers), Talbott's integration of the visuals with the text once again results in a superbly readable story, giving the reader a you-are-there experience. This time, a twelve-year-old boy takes a reluctant trip to Kenya, but winds up on a safari with thrilling results. This daringly different blend of fiction and fact gives readers knowledge about wildlife, the dangers they face, and the steps that are being taken to ensure their preservation. Inspiring and exciting, this book is bound to captivate an eight- to eleven-year-old adventurer.

Saint Francis   PICTURE BOOK BIOGRAPHY

AUTHOR/ILLUSTRATOR: Brian Wildsmith
HC: Eerdmans
THEMES: saints; peace; Catholicism; biography; animals; Italy; Christianity;
    religion

A gloriously illustrated and deeply religious account of the life of Saint Francis of Assisi, the founder of the Franciscan Order of friars.

Scary Stories to Tell in the Dark: Collected from American Folklore

FOLKLORE COLLECTION

AUTHOR: Alvin Schwartz • ILLUSTRATOR: Stephen Gammell
HC/PB: HarperCollins
THEMES: horror; scary stories; folklore

A terrific collection of read-aloud, scream-aloud and shriek-aloud tales, mostly short and creepy. Schwartz collected various versions of well-known and obscure tales from all over the United States. Accompanied by Gammell's eerie and disturbing line drawings, these make for some pretty ghoulish reading. They work like a charm at campfires, sleepovers, or any time you want to put a little fright into the occasion.

> There are two sequels: *More Scary Stories to Tell in the Dark* and *Scary Stories Three*.

The Secret Garden

FICTION

AUTHOR: Frances Hodgson Burnett • ILLUSTRATOR: Tasha Tudor
HC/PB: HarperCollins
THEMES: gardens; illness; secrets; magic; birds; orphans; uncles; England; strong girls; imagination; friendship; faith

First published in 1911, this classic novel continues to bolster home, school, library, and bookstore shelves. It's got the right elements to tug on heart-strings: Mary Lennox, recently orphaned, bedridden Colin Craven, and Dickon, who can make anything grow and understands the language of nature. Rich with imagination, friendship, and faith. Read it aloud or relish it quietly alone.

See You Around, Sam

FICTION

AUTHOR: Lois Lowry
HC: Houghton Mifflin • PB: Dell
THEMES: family; running away; Halloween; neighbors; community

A very funny book about running away from home. It's part of the *Anastasia Krupnik* series, but a standout that merits special mention. Sam is feeling unappreciated and decides to head out to Sleetmute, Alaska, where he can lie around in a pile with walruses, all because his mother will not let him wear his plastic vampire fangs in the house. Sam is never funnier than in this story, but he never becomes an object of ridicule. He takes his running away seriously, and everyone—family, friends, and neighbors alike—respect that in him, even as they undermine his plans. Look for Sam's further adventures in *Zooman Sam*.

I am so glad that Lowry invented Sam to replace Anastasia as the star of this terrific sequence of books for middle grades. I actually like Sam best, but don't tell anybody.

The Serpent Slayer and Other Stories of Strong Women
FOLKLORE COLLECTION

AUTHOR: Katrin Tchana • ILLUSTRATOR: Trina Schart Hyman
HC: Little Brown
THEMES: fairy tales; strong women; strong girls; courage; cleverness; adventure

Conquering dragons! Outwitting robbers! This collection of fairy tales from all over the world is about brave and clever women who work their way out of difficult situations. Schart Hyman's bold, full-color paintings fill the pages of this over-sized storybook. We especially like her eyeless serpent and horrifying ogre.

The Shrinking of Treehorn
FICTION

AUTHOR: Florence Parry Heide • ILLUSTRATOR: Edward Gorey
HC/PB: Holiday House
THEMES: family; humor; point of view; change

Dry and unsettling, this hilarious story introduces a small boy who is shrinking, and no one seems to notice except the reader and him. Heide and Gorey work in tandem to produce a look at how the adult world ignores children that is not found in other books—except the sequels, *Treehorn's Treasure* and *Treehorn's Wish*.

Sideways Stories from Wayside School
FICTION

AUTHOR: Louis Sachar • ILLUSTRATOR: Julie Brinckloe
HC: Morrow • PB: Avon
THEMES: humor; school; friendship; teachers; zany

Laugh-out-loud funny tales about the craziest school in fiction. A novel-length collection of stories, it's one of the surest books to turn on a reluctant reader that we have found. More Wayside stories can be found in *Wayside School Is Falling Down* and *Wayside School Gets a Little Stranger*.

The Silk Route: 7,000 Miles of History

PICTURE BOOK NONFICTION

AUTHOR: John Major • ILLUSTRATOR: Stephen Fieser
PB: HarperCollins
THEMES: China; Mideast; history; silk; journeys; trade; maps; ancient history

Trace the early journey of the silk trade and learn some history about the stops on the way. Beginning in the capital city of China's Chang'an, this voyage takes readers seven thousand miles to the marketplace in Byzantium. A map of the route is included along with "A Closer Look"—more details for the curious.

A Small Tall Tale from the Far Far North

PICTURE BOOK

AUTHOR/ILLUSTRATOR: Peter Sis
HC/PB: Farrar Straus
THEMES: Arctic; journeys; folklore; maps; trailblazing; Inuit; tall tale

One hundred years ago folk hero Jan Welzi rode off in a horse-drawn cart, traded the cart for a sled pulled by reindeer, and was gone for thirty years. This is his story. Sis's detailed paintings include maps, storyboards, panoramas, and even an Inuit myth told in pictographs. A perfect book for sharing, but each child will want time to quietly absorb these details.

★ So You Want to Be President?

PICTURE BOOK NONFICTION

AUTHOR: Judith St. George • ILLUSTRATOR: David Small
HC: Philomel
THEMES: U.S. presidents; U.S. history; biography; comparisons

> St. George and Small apply their prize-winning format to creativity in their follow-up, *So You Want to Be an Inventor?*

Presidents have come in almost every variety: There have been generals like George Washington and actors like Ronald Reagan; they have been tall and short, serious and filled with humor. David Small's wildly funny pictures—which earned him a Caldecott Medal—will keep young readers in stitches as they learn about the idiosyncrasies of our nation's leaders.

The Spider and the Fly

PICTURE BOOK

AUTHOR: Mary Howitt • ILLUSTRATOR: Tony DiTerlizzi
HC: Simon & Schuster
THEMES: poem; spiders; flies; hunting; danger

" 'Will you walk into my parlor?' said the Spider to the Fly . . ." It's not a good idea to fall for a stranger's line. Parents have been warning their youngsters about this long before pre-Victorian times, when this poem was first written. DiTerlizzi's black-and-white art is reminiscent of an old horror film. The fly is so sweet and innocent and the spider such an evil predator that melodramatic humor is prevalent throughout.

 I read the note to "Dearest Readers" from the spider at the end. It was great fun . . . until the last paragraph when the spider warns, "Dear sweet friend, be advised that spiders are not the only hunters and bugs are not the only victims. Take what has transpired . . . to heart, or you might well find yourself trapped in some schemer's web!" Now, that is not funny!

★ Starry Messenger: Galileo Galilei   PICTURE BOOK BIOGRAPHY
AUTHOR/ILLUSTRATOR: Peter Sis
HC: Farrar, Straus & Giroux

THEMES: Galileo; astronomy; biography; math; Italy;
scientists; science; telescopes; stars

Another brilliant picture book biography, *The Tree of Life*, is Sis's remarkable story of Charles Darwin. Detailed pictures, charts, maps and diary pages create an inside look at the life of the nineteenth-century naturalist, geologist, and thinker.

This view of the life of Galileo Galilei works at several levels. The first time through you might consider turning the pages just for the purpose of admiring each detail of art. Next, read the simple text at the bottom of each page for the story of this extraordinary man. And then for a grand finale, look for the handwritten details of history along with Galileo's own words, written more than three hundred years ago. The whole family can find pleasure here, individually or as a group.

★ Stone Fox   FICTION
AUTHOR: John Reynolds Gardiner • ILLUSTRATOR: Marcia Sewall
HC/PB: HarperCollins
THEMES: dogs; grandfathers; Native American; farms; courage; pets;
competition; determination; kindness

Heart-tugging, inspiring, eighty-one pages long, *Stone Fox* takes the breath away. We recommend reading it aloud or as a jewel to be taken off for the pleasure of enjoying alone. Little Willy's struggle to save his family's farm from the tax collector and Stone Fox's need to buy back land for his Shoshone people make them both determined to win prize money in a sled race. The ending will stay with you. It will warm your heart.

 Break your heart is more like it. Get that hankie ready.

The Story of Money

PICTURE BOOK NONFICTION

AUTHOR: Betsy Maestro • ILLUSTRATOR: Giulio Maestro
HC/PB: Clarion
THEMES: money; history; ancient history

Here's the most thorough book we have seen on the subject of money. Beginning in prehistoric times, it traces the use of money through five thousand years to now.

Stringbean's Trip to the Shining Sea

PICTURE BOOK

AUTHOR: Vera B. Williams • ILLUSTRATOR: Vera B. and Jennifer Williams
HC: Greenwillow • PB: Mulberry
THEMES: mail; travel; U.S.A., the West; writing; brothers; family

Stringbean and his brother take a trip west one summer in a truck with a little house built on the back. They tell their story through postcards and snapshots sent home. "We went to see the oldest living things in the whole world. They are trees called Bristlecone Pine trees. They are much older than you, Grandpa. One of them might need 4900 candles." Young readers will laugh, learn about things on the way, and perhaps discover a new interest in writing.

 This is more than a look at a cross-country trip. Stringbean and his much older brother are virtual strangers at the beginning and have much to learn about each other. How wonderful for them that Vera Williams gave them this opportunity.

Stuart Little

FICTION-FANTASY

AUTHOR: E. B. White • ILLUSTRATOR: Garth Williams
HC/PB: HarperCollins
THEMES: mice; adventure; birds; searches; family

Stuart Little is a properly dressed mouse who lives in New York City with his human family. He enjoys adventures. But when his best friend, Margalo, disappears from her nest, he sets out to find her and ends up having the biggest adventure of his life.

 Ewww! I was completely creeped out by this book as a child. I simply could not accept a mouse being born to a human. Garth Williams's wonderful illustrations somehow only made it worse. Clearly, I'm not alone in this, because in the movie they had the good sense to make Stuart adopted.

 It made perfect sense to me.

Sweet Clara and the Freedom Quilt

PICTURE BOOK

AUTHOR: Deborah Hopkinson • ILLUSTRATOR: James Ransome
HC/PB: Knopf
THEMES: slavery; courage; African American; quilts; gifted children;
cleverness; maps; escape; freedom; navigation; Underground Railroad

A clever young slave creates a quilt with a map stitched into it to guide herself and others to freedom. A powerful blend of prose and art, matched by the sequel, *Under the Quilt of Night*.

★ Sweet Words So Brave: The Story of African American Literature

PICTURE BOOK NONFICTION

AUTHORS: Barbara K. Curry and James Michael Brodie • ILLUSTRATOR: Jerry Butler
HC: Zino Press
THEMES: African American; authors; U.S. history;
grandfathers and granddaughters; writing; slavery

Illustrator Jerry Butler has written a companion book, *A Drawing in the Sand: A Story of African American Art.*

From Phillis Wheatley, the first published African American poet, to Toni Morrison, the first African American to win the Nobel Prize for literature, a man tells this compelling chronicle of black American writers to his granddaughter. "Come sit by me, child, I have stories to tell about folks from places like Nigeria and Senegal. They were orators turned into writers, brave all in all." Pay attention to this powerful work with bold oil paintings and inspiring quotes, which tells the history of the story makers whose words have created the rich work that make up African American literature.

The Tales of Uncle Remus

FOLKLORE COLLECTION

AUTHOR: Julius Lester
HC: Dutton • PB: Puffin
THEMES: folklore; African American; trickster tales; humor

Forty-eight side-splitting tales of one wily rabbit who out tricks (or tries to) just about every big and little critter around, including Brer Bear and Mr. Man. Lester adds just enough dialect to stay in touch with the original stories and keeps the fun in these tales of Brer Rabbit and his friends—and enemies. Look for *Uncle Remus: The Complete Tales* for all the stories collected in one volume.

Talking Walls
PICTURE BOOK NONFICTION

AUTHOR: Margy Burns Knight • ILLUSTRATOR: Anne Sibley O'Brien
HC/PB: Tilbury House
THEMES: walls, cultural diversity; social studies; China; Australia; Egypt;
Africa; Peru; New Mexico; Mexico; Quebec; Washington, D.C.; France;
Jerusalem; religion; India; Germany

Before I built a wall I'd ask to know What I was walling in or walling
out . . . —Robert Frost.

Differences and similarities of cultures throughout the world are viewed
from the perspective of the walls they have built. From the Great Wall of
China to the Berlin Wall, a fascinating tour.

The Ten Mile Day and the Building
of the Transcontinental Railroad
PICTURE BOOK NONFICTION

AUTHOR/ILLUSTRATOR: Mary Ann Fraser
PB: Henry Holt
THEMES: U.S. history, Westward movement; railroad; Chinese American;
Irish American; Chinese culture; Irish culture; jobs; competition; change

One amazing day the East and West were linked for train travel in an event in
which hundreds of Chinese and Irish workers raced to lay ten miles of track
on the Transcontinental Railroad. This is their story.

The Three Questions: Based on a Story By Leo Tolstoy   PICTURE BOOK

AUTHOR/ILLUSTRATOR: Jon J. Muth
HC: Scholastic
THEMES: wisdom; kindness; behavior; animals

Nikolai wants to be a good person so he asks his animal friends to help
him answer three questions: "When is the best time to do things? Who is
the most important one? What is the right thing to do?" Leo, a wise old
turtle, lets him discover for himself that the one important time is now, the
most important one is the one you are with, and the most important thing
is to do good for the one who is standing at your side. Soft watercolors
complement the hushed, contemplative tone of the words. An author's
note at the back explains that Tolstoy's original story is about a czar who is
looking for answers to "the three questions." This tale is bound to start a
discussion.

Through My Eyes

PICTURE BOOK BIOGRAPHY

AUTHOR: Ruby Bridges

HC: Scholastic

THEMES: prejudice; courage; U.S. history, the 60s; civil rights

In November 1960, America watched six-year-old Ruby Bridges, surrounded by U.S. marshals, walk through a crowd of threatening segregationists into her school. Relying on her childhood memories, Bridges tells her story of that day and of events in her life that lead up to the present. Dramatic photographs and quotations from adults who observed her add detail and perspective to this moving story of innocence and courage.

The Time Warp Trio

FICTION

AUTHOR: Jon Scieszka • ILLUSTRATOR: Lane Smith

HC: Viking • PB: Puffin

THEMES: time travel; adventure; humor

This is great series to give to reluctant readers, as it is action packed and lots of fun. A rollicking set of adventures through time and space, full of laughs. The series starts with *The Good, the Bad, and the Goofy*, and there are lots of sequels, including *Your Mother Was a Neanderthal; Knights of the Kitchen Table; The Not-So-Jolly Roger; Viking It and Liking It; Hey Kid, Want to Buy a Bridge;* and *2095*.

Tomas and the Library Lady

PICTURE BOOK BIOGRAPHY

AUTHOR: Pat Mora • ILLUSTRATOR: Raul Colon

HC: Knopf • PB: Dragonfly

THEMES: reading; migrant farmworkers; grandfathers; Hispanic; storytelling; libraries; librarians

The best book we have seen about the wonderful way librarians can change lives. Tomas's grandfather is a storyteller, and no matter where they are in their yearly migration between Texas and Iowa, the family gathers around the fire each evening after their work in the fields is done and is treated to the gift of a story. Tomas knows them all by heart and hungers for more, so his grandfather tells him about the stories to be found in the library. Tomas's tenuous approach to this strange and wonderful place is perfectly met by a kind, patient, and generous librarian, who helps him find the world of stories he longs for. This would be a good enough tale, but the reader finds out that it really happened—Tomas grew up to become the first minority chancellor of the University of California. This is a beautiful, inspiring testament to the power of story, both told and written, and a vision of the rewards of education that will reach across cultures.

 "Free, free, free. Libraries are free!" I tell you the library is a wonderful place. I'll see you there.

★ The True Story of the Three Little Pigs
PICTURE BOOK

AUTHOR: Jon Scieszka • ILLUSTRATOR: Lane Smith
HC: Viking • PB: Puffin
THEMES: wolves; pigs; humor; folktale variations; zany

Jon Scieszka and Lane Smith make us laugh. This twisted tale will get you laughing, too. If you think you know the story of the Three Little Pigs, A. Wolf will set you straight. ". . . I'll let you in on a little secret. Nobody knows the real story, because nobody has ever heard my side of the story." It's outrageous, and this author and illustrator's perfectly matched words and art result in a picture book third-graders will love, if their older siblings are willing to share.

Uncle Jed's Barbershop
PICTURE BOOK

AUTHOR: Margaree Mitchell • ILLUSTRATOR: James Ransome
PB: Aladdin
THEMES: family; determination; African American; pride; jobs; community;
    self-respect; patience

Uncle Jed has a goal: to own his own barbershop. Even when times get hard, he never loses sight of his vision. This picture-book tale is a testament to determination, pride, and a person's need to have something he can call his own.

Until I Met Dudley: How Everyday Things Really Work
PICTURE BOOK NONFICTION

AUTHOR: Roger McGough • ILLUSTRATOR: Chris Riddell
HC: Walker
THEMES: imagination; science; comparisons; the way things work; humor

This book is packed with solid information about how common household items really work, but its real treasure is the imaginative explanations that the children concoct before being told the truth. This is a delightful combination of fact and fancy and will appeal to both realists and dreamers.

The Velveteen Rabbit

AUTHOR: Margery Williams • ILLUSTRATOR: William Nicholson
HC: Doubleday • PB: Avon
THEMES: toys; rabbits; love; illness; magic; fairies; Christmas; change

One day the velveteen rabbit asked the skin horse, "What is real?" "When a child loves you for a long, long time, not just to play with, but REALLY loves you, then you become Real," said the skin horse. ". . . by the time you are Real, most of your hair has been loved off, and your eyes drop out and you get loose in the joints and very shabby. But these things don't matter at all, because once you are Real you can't be ugly, except to people who don't understand." From its first waiting moment in the Christmas stocking, to its final release by the nursery magic Fairy, the velveteen rabbit's enchanting tale leaves young readers and listeners taking a new look at their own favorite toys.

The Village that Vanished

AUTHOR: Ann Grifalconi • ILLUSTRATOR: Kadir Nelson
HC: Dial
THEMES: Africa; slavery; community; courage

". . . Gather round, my people, gather round! And hear the voices of your ancestors in this tale of courage and of sacrifice." So begins the story of Abikanile and her mother, who rescue the people of their small village, hidden deep in the African forest. When slavers ride in on horseback with their long guns to capture the unarmed farmers and to shackle their children, they find only an old woman shelling pea beans. Discouraged, they leave and never return. The art is breathtaking and the story passed down through generations is unforgettable.

Volcano: The Eruption & Healing of Mount St. Helens

AUTHOR: Patricia Lauber • ILLUSTRATOR: Photographs
HC: Simon & Schuster • PB: Aladdin
THEMES: nature; volcanoes; science

Lauber is an author who can be counted on to bring an interesting perspective to nonfiction. Always informative in an accessible style, she is a good author to turn to for book reports and research for third- to seventh-graders. This is one of the best books about volcanoes we know.

The War with Grandpa

FICTION

AUTHOR: Robert Kimmel Smith
PB: Dell
THEMES: grandfathers and grandsons; home; solitude;
    sharing; conflict; problem solving; anger; war; lessons

For other looks at grandparent-grandchild conflict, see *Sun and Spoon* by Kevin Henkes and *Luka's Quilt* by Georgia Guback.

War is serious stuff, not a game. Peter learns this when he decides to wage war on his grandfather to get his room back. A widower, Grandpa has moved into the house and takes Peter's room because it does not require climbing stairs to get to. Peter gets angry and Grandpa decides to teach him a lesson. This is a sensitive and thought-provoking novel.

The Weaving of a Dream

PICTURE BOOK

AUTHOR/ILLUSTRATOR: Marilee Heyer
HC: Viking • PB: Puffin
THEMES: China; folklore; weaving; fantasy; magic; fairies; greed; envy;
    mothers and sons

A skillful retelling of a Chinese folktale, accompanied by breathtaking art. The story of a weaver whose tapestries come to life could find no better vessel than Heyer's vivid paintings.

★ Weslandia

PICTURE BOOK

AUTHOR: Paul Fleischman • ILLUSTRATOR: Kevin Hawkes
HC/PB: Candlewick
THEMES: ancient history; community; fitting in; gifted child; cleverness;
    resourcefulness; creativity

Every nonconformist kid who is too smart for his own good can take comfort in the ultimate triumph of Wesley as he builds his own civilization and confidently uses it as a tool for gaining acceptance. The sheer cleverness of this young boy (and Fleischman's tale) is awe-inspiring, and the art elevates the story at every turn. It's a thought-provoking read-aloud and as a bonus can be used to supplement the teaching of ancient cultures.

 This is one of those gems that teach young readers to value the child who moves to the beat of his own drum, without the lecture that usually accompanies the lesson.

Where the Sidewalk Ends: Poems and Drawings

POETRY COLLECTIONS

AUTHOR/ILLUSTRATOR: Shel Silverstein

HC: HarperCollins

THEMES: variety; humor; rhyme

At his best, there is no better than Silverstein at grasping the essential qualities of humor, irreverence, and subversion in childhood. He understands how much of their lives children spend at the mercy of adults, who have simply forgotten what being a kid is all about, and he's not afraid to reveal things that adults think should be kept secret. His poems and drawings have become classics, and are mentioned as favorites by children everywhere, even if they say they don't like poetry. His later collections, *The Light in the Attic* and *Falling Up*, offer more of the same, but for our money, this is the book we cannot live without.

The Whipping Boy

FICTION

AUTHOR: Sid Fleischman • ILLUSTRATOR: Peter Sis

HC: Greenwillow • PB: Troll

THEMES: mischief; responsibility; literacy; adventure; kidnapping; princes; comparisons; villains

Nasty Prince Brat gets away with all sorts of horrid behavior. Whenever he is to be punished, he has his whipping boy brought in to be his surrogate. When they switch places for real, each learns something about the life of the other. They reunite at story's end as friends, but not until after a whole lot of adventures. Fast paced and entertaining, this Newbery Medal winner is one of the most reader-friendly books ever to win that award.

White Dynamite and Curly Kidd

PICTURE BOOK

AUTHORS: Bill Martin Jr. and John Archambault • ILLUSTRATOR: Ted Rand

HC/PB: Henry Holt

THEMES: cowboys; fathers and daughters; courage; yearnings; rhythm

The combination of Bill Martin Jr. and John Archambault has produced some clever, complex read-alouds, and this is one of their best. Young Lucky's dad is a bull rider called Curly Kid. As they help prepare Curly for a ride on White Dynamite, Lucky keeps up a nervous one-sided conversation about the bull, other rodeo riders, and Lucky's desire to be a bull rider some-day, occasionally punctuated by a one-syllable response from Curly. Using rhythm and a sure knack for the spoken word, the authors have created a dialogue that reveals volumes about the characters and tells a compelling story, but still offers a surprise on the last page—Lucky is a girl.

Another collaboration from this talented pair, also featuring the luminous art of Ted Rand, is *Knots on a Counting Rope,* which shares many of the pleasures and themes of *White Dynamite*—a dialogue between a child and an adult, a child yearning for something beyond expectations, and a surprise ending.

White Socks Only   PICTURE BOOK

AUTHOR: Evelyn Coleman • ILLUSTRATOR: Tyrone Geter
HC/PB: Albert Whitman
THEMES: African American; prejudice; magic; bullies; misunderstanding;
    comeuppance; civil rights

Grandma tells of when she was a little girl and wanted to see if it was really possible to fry an egg on the sidewalk on the hottest day of the year. But the sidewalk was in town, and one can get mighty thirsty watching an egg fry in the noonday sun. This was the South, years ago, when water fountains were labled "Whites Only." This uplifting story tells of how a young girl's honest mistake (she thought the word "whites" referred to her socks) inspired blacks to give bigotry its comeuppance, with the help of a little magic from the Chicken Man.

Who Belongs Here? An American Story   PICTURE BOOK NONFICTION

AUTHOR: Margy Burns Knight • ILLUSTRATOR: Anne Sibley O'Brien
HC/PB: Tilbury House
THEMES: comparisons; prejudice; refugees; Cambodia; cultural diversity;
    immigration

Knight and O'Brien have designed a book with three voices. The first belongs to a boy from Cambodia who is making his home in the United States. The second is the narrator's, who gives anecdotes relating experiences of other refugees and their contributions to American culture, and the third is the voice that asks questions like "What if everyone who lives in the U.S. but whose ancestors came from another country was forced to return to his or her homeland?" "Who would be left?" This is a natural for encouraging children to talk about their feelings of intolerance.

William Shakespeare & the Globe   PICTURE BOOK NONFICTION

AUTHOR/ILLUSTRATOR: Aliki
HC/PB: HarperCollins
THEMES: Shakespeare; England; history, the Renaissance; theater; poets;
    biography; writers; playwrights

Engaging text, detailed illustrations with informative captions, and a logically organized design provide a fine introduction to both bard and theater. Aliki shows us the life and times of Shakespeare as well as the story of actor Sam Wanamaker, the driving force behind the modern rebuilding of the Globe Theatre.

★ Wingwalker

FICTION

AUTHOR: Rosemary Wells • ILLUSTRATOR: Brian Selznick
HC: Hyperion
THEMES: fairs; fathers and sons; flying; fear; U.S. history, the Depression;
    jobs; community; courage; U.S.A., the Dust Bowl; family; friends;
    change; comparisons

In the 1930s the Dust Bowl came, and with it families fell into poverty and their dreams turned to dust. Reuben was a carefree second-grader living with his parents in rural Oklahoma when his father lost his job and took on another as an airplane wing walker with a Minnesota traveling carnival. Reuben found himself "on the road" with his parents, a tattooed lady, and a fire-eater. Wells—whose writing shines—shows us a family and community that are kind, courageous, and resilient. Selznick's soft, muted paintings are reminiscent of the sepia photographs of the thirties.

 This incredible story is about community and resilience and mustering up nerve to go farther than you ever thought you could. For a child who has to go through change, or has a fear of someone who appears different, it's powerfully good.

The Wolves in the Walls

PICTURE BOOK

AUTHOR: Neil Gaiman • ILLUSTRATOR: Dave McKean
HC: HarperCollins
THEMES: girls, strong; wolves; pigs; houses; problem solving; perseverance;
    imagination; scary stories

Lucy knows there are wolves in the walls of her house. After all, she can hear them at night, "plotting their wolfish plots, hatching their wolfish schemes." The scary thing is, no one believes her until its too late. Gaiman's text is chilling and strange and McKean's art makes you want to pull back with each turn of the page the way you did when you were a child and knew that a monster was about to jump out of the closet. Well known in the world of comics and graphic novels, these masters of the creepy have created a superb illustrated story for older kids. We think nine- to-eleven-year-olds will love this!

 I agree it is CREEPY, but I did end up laughing by the end. After the first few pages I found myself stunned by the perfect harmony between this writer and artist. Brilliant!

The Wonderful Wizard of Oz

FICTION-FANTASY

AUTHOR: L. Frank Baum • ILLUSTRATOR: W. W. Denslow

HC: Morrow

THEMES: home; magic; wizards; adventure; witches; friendship; courage; fantasy; self-respect; journeys; strong girl

One of the great American works of fiction. If you have only seen the movie, you don't know half of it! This lovingly produced facsimile of the original edition makes the perfect gift for any child. There are many subsequent books about Oz, Dorothy, and the gang, and they vary in quality. Many people go on to read as many of them as they can find. But don't let a child grow up without at least one trip to Oz.

Cinderella

Other evidence that Cinderella can be found around the world shows up in *Korean Cinderella*, *Egyptian Cinderella*, *The Irish Cinderlad* (Climo), *Sootface* (Ojibwa—San Souci), *The Talking Eggs* (Creole—San Souci), and *The Brocaded Slipper and Other Vietnamese Tales* (Vuong). Other variations with a more modern slant include *Cinder Edna* (Jackson), *Fanny's Dream* (Buehner), *Cinderella's Rat* (Meddaugh), *If the Shoe Fits* (Whipple), and *On Stage Backstage at the Night Owl Theater* (Hayes).

Yeh-Shen: A Cinderella Story from China

PICTURE BOOK

RETOLD BY: Ai-Ling Louie • ILLUSTRATOR: Ed Young

HC: Philomel • PB: Paperstar

THEMES: China; stepfamilies; kings; folktale variation; jobs; festivals

Most of us are familiar with the European fairy tale of Cinderella. As a matter of fact, we've even categorized Yeh-Shen as a "folktale variation." But, surprisingly, this version was found in one of the ancient Chinese manuscripts written during the T'ang dynasty. That would make it at least one thousand years older than the earliest known Western version of the story. That's an interesting bit of information, but the reason to choose this is not its history, it's because of the beauty of Young's radiant pastel and watercolor paintings and because it's a story well told.

Poetry

Poetry is one of the most plentiful genres of books for young readers, with styles ranging from simple rhyme, to haiku, to epic verse, and offering numerous opportunities for illustrators to show their best efforts. Whether in a picture-book format or a collection of verse, poems are a fundamental part of the reading experience.

SOME FAVORITE ANTHOLOGIES:

Talking Like the Rain: A Read-to-Me Book of Poems
EDITORS: X. J. and Dorothy Kennedy • ILLUSTRATOR: Jane Dyer

The Invisible Ladder: An Anthology of Contemporary Poems for Young Readers
EDITOR: Liz Rosenberg
    Accompanied by memories and photos of their childhood, this is an eclectic mix from forty American poets that reaches across the chasm of age and becomes a bridge to the appreciation of poetry for middle-graders and teens.

Classic Poems to Read Aloud
EDITOR: James Berry
    A wonderful volume of poetry, all classics, and all begging to be read aloud.

Walking the Bridge of Your Nose
EDITOR: Michael Rosen • ILLUSTRATOR: Chloe Cheese
    Wordplay abounds in this collection, a veritable treasure trove of puns, rhymes, tongue twisters, and other types of witty uses of language.

Never Take a Pig to Lunch: And Other Poems About the Fun of Eating
EDITOR/ILLUSTRATOR: Nadine Bernard Westcott
    Fun food poems for the lower elementary set.

Soul Looks Back in Wonder
EDITOR/ILLUSTRATOR: Tom Feelings
    There are two good reasons to consider this gem for your library: the powerful poems by African American writers and Tom Feelings's extraordinary illustrations.

Winter Poems
AUTHOR: Barbara Rogasky • ILLUSTRATION: Trina Schart Hyman
    A winter collection notable for its focus on the season and not its holidays.

SOME OF OUR FAVORITE COLLECTIONS:

The Best of Michael Rosen
AUTHOR: Michael Rosen • ILLUSTRATOR: Quentin Blake

Polkabats and Octopus Slacks
AUTHOR/ILLUSTRATOR: Calef Brown
   Zany, off-the-wall poems and equally odd drawings. Irresistible!

A Child's Garden of Verses
AUTHOR: Robert Louis Stevenson
   There are several illustrated versions of this indispensable classic. We like the art by Tasha Tudor and Jessie Willcox Smith best.

Hailstones and Halibut Bones
AUTHOR: Mary O'Neill • ILLUSTRATOR: John Wallner
   With vibrant poems about color that leap off the page, this masterpiece of descriptive writing will encourage artists and writers to reach for new heights.

Honey, I Love and Other Love Poems
AUTHOR: Eloise Greenfield • ILLUSTRATORS: Leo and Diane Dillon

Sweet Corn: Poems
AUTHOR/ILLUSTRATOR: James Stevenson
   Short poems. Simple, affecting, and to the point. A treasure. Look for the companion books *Candy Corn*, *Corn-Fed*, and *Corn Chowder*.

Sad Underwear and Other Complications
AUTHOR: Judith Viorst • ILLUSTRATOR: Richard Hull
   Viorst's humorous poems, written from a child's point of view, are intertwined with truths, traumas, and possibilities. Look for *If I Were in Charge of the World . . . and Other Worries* for more Viorst poetry.

OUR FAVORITE POETS AND THEIR BOOKS:

Paul B. Janeczko
   He publishes three kinds of poetry books: collections of his own work (*A Poke in the Illustrator: A Collection of Concrete Poems*), anthologies of carefully selected gems (*I Feel a Little Jumpy Around You: A Book of Her Poems & His Poems Collected in Pairs*, coauthored with Naomi Shihab Nye), and selections like *Poetry From A To Z: A Guide for Young Writers* and *Seeing the Blue Between: Advice and Inspirations for Young Poets*, which offer insights and encouragement to young writers.

Marilyn Singer
   This outstanding writer creates vibrant collections that reflect on our relationship with the natural world. Our favorites are *Footprints on the Roof: Poems About the Earth; How to Cross a Pond: Poems About Water;* and *The Company of Crows*.

Alice Schertle
   Schertle's poetry uses language with maximum assurance, wresting potent imagery from the most mundane subjects. Among our favorites of her picture books are *A Lucky Thing; How*

Now, Brown Cow; Keepers; and Advice for a Frog, all of which are sadly out of print as of this writing. Look for them in your library.

Janet Wong

A Suitcase of Seaweed and Other Poems offers humorous and touching poems divided into three sections: Korean, Chinese, and American, reflecting the cultures that make up writer Janet Wong's own family. For more of Wong's poems, look for Night Garden: Poems from the World of Dreams; Behind the Wheel: Driving Poems; The Rainbow Hand: Poems About Mothers and Children; Knock on Wood: Poems About Superstitions; and Good Luck Gold and Other Poems.

Douglas Florian

Florian takes a theme and runs with it in every one of his marvelous picture books of brief, quirky poems. Look for Insectlopedia; Laugh-eteria; Monster Motel; Mammalabilia; Beast Feast; and Bow Wow Meow Meow: It's Rhyming Cats and Dogs.

Naomi Shihab Nye

An outstanding poet whose work as an editor and writer is often aimed at teens and adults, Nye has produced several collections that will bring a culturally diverse perspective to any mix of poetry for children: This Same Sky: A Collection of Poems from Around the World; Salting the Ocean: 100 Poems by Young Poets; and Is This Forever, or What: Poems and Paintings from Texas.

Jack Prelutsky

Jack Prelutsky's poems often stretch a child's vocabulary. He is the acknowledged master of verse for children, one whose strength as a poet is matched by his genius as an anthologizer. Working with gifted illustrator Peter Sis, he has created unsurpassed picture books of imaginative verse (The Dragons Are Singing Tonight, Monday's Troll, and Scranimals).

No poetry bookshelf is complete without Prelutsky's anthologies and collections, and there are many to look for: For Laughing Out Loud, The Beauty of the Beast, For Laughing Out Louder, It's Raining Pigs & Noodles, Something Big Has Been Here, New Kid on the Block, Read-Aloud Rhymes for the Very Young, A Pizza the Size of the Sun, Ride a Purple Pelican, and Beneath a Blue Umbrella.

Even if your poetry shelf is packed, make room for The Random House Book of Poetry for Children. The upbeat match of Arnold Lobel's illustrations with Prelutsky's selections offers a choice collection for any child.

If you spend enough time talking to children about poetry, they will want to try their hand at writing some. In addition to Paul Janeczko's books, above, we really like Avis Harley's Fly With Poetry and Leap Into Poetry, two alphabet books that allow young poets to compare various forms, meters, rhymes, and arrangements.

PART FOUR

Books for Children in Middle Elementary Grades

Listening/Interest Level: Middle Elementary (M)/ Reading Level: Middle Elementary (M)

These are the longer works, fiction and nonfiction, that make for excellent reading experiences for our M readers. The topics and concerns are complex and multivaried, with interests ranging from Greek mythology to science, and the themes in fiction ask for a reader to ponder and make choices about characters and situations.

Abel's Island   FICTION
AUTHOR/ILLUSTRATOR: William Steig
HC/PB: Farrar, Straus & Giroux
THEMES: mice; survival; determination; floods; home; problem solving;
    islands; yearning; love

A pampered mouse learns the techniques of survival when he is swept away from home and loved ones by a flood. He lands on an island, and his determined attempts to get home and return his wife's scarf are consistently thwarted. He finds he is one tough little mouse, and as he spends a year on his island foraging for food and eluding predators, he realizes how good his life was. His ultimate reunion with his wife is heartening, and Steig's humorous touches help make this Newbery Honor book a satisfying read.

Action Jackson   PICTURE BOOK BIOGRAPHY
AUTHORS: Jan Greenberg and Sandra Jordan • ILLUSTRATOR: Robert Andrew
    Parker
HC: Roaring Brook Press
THEMES: art; painting; artists

Readers are not only introduced to Pollock's stunning original work but also get a look behind the scenes of the creation and reception of one of his paintings. Excellent notes follow the story, including photos and a bibliography. Parker's watercolors do not attempt to compete with Pollock's groundbreaking paintings, but serve the story well, allowing a great contrast between styles.

Alice's Adventures in Wonderland   FICTION-FANTASY

AUTHOR: Lewis Carroll • ILLUSTRATOR: John Tenniel
HC: Morrow
THEMES: fantasy; zany; journeys; magic; strong girls; adventure

One of the great classics of childhood, though we feel it is better introduced in later years rather than earlier. Dense and hard to follow in spots, the book is a far different thing from the many Disneyesque versions that have been made of it on TV and film, so be warned that it may not enchant your five-year-old the way the cartoon does. But when you have an inquisitive nine-year-old on your hands, one who thinks she is getting too smart for "baby" books, that is the time to surprise her with Carroll's masterpiece. Do not neglect to follow up with the sequel, *Through the Looking Glass*. You'll be surprised at how much you think is in *Alice* actually comes from the later book.

Amelia's Notebook   PICTURE BOOK

AUTHOR/ILLUSTRATOR: Marissa Moss
PB: Pleasant Company
THEMES: school; friendship; moving; diaries; humor

There are many sequels, including *Amelia Writes Again*, *My Notebook (With Help from Amelia)*, *Amelia Works It Out*, and *Amelia's School Survival Guide.*

Amelia's Notebook looks as if it's written on a regular composition book. It is filled with writings and drawings and thoughts and ideas—all belonging to nine-year-old Amelia, who has just moved to a new house. As Amelia adjusts to her new school she gripes about cafeteria food, misses her best friend, makes new friends, and experiences a lot of the feelings shared by other nine-year-olds, who will read every detail.

Anne of Green Gables   FICTION

AUTHOR: L. M. Montgomery
PB: Bantam
THEMES: orphans; family; strong girls; community; neighbors; Canada; adoption; farms

Matthew and Marilla Cuthbert had requested a boy orphan to be sent to help them work on their farm, not a spunky, talkative redheaded girl. But Anne wins their hearts at Green Gables farm, and by the time she pleads, "Oh, please, Miss Cuthbert, won't you tell me if you are going to send me away or not? I've tried to be patient all the morning, but I really feel that I cannot bear not knowing any longer," Anne has found a new home.

Are You There God? It's Me, Margaret   FICTION

AUTHOR: Judy Blume
HC: Atheneum • PB: Dell
THEMES: coming of age; humor; secrets; family

Funny, irreverent, and as pertinent to kids' lives as she was twenty years ago, Blume remains a powerful force in books for children. Her status as one of the most banned authors in America seems not to be fading, and it is her no-holds-barred style that both delights children and irritates censors. Whether writing about families, school, friendship, or secrets, Blume knows how kids of all ages feel and isn't afraid to let them know she is on their side. Our favorites of her books besides this one include *Blubber; Here's to You, Rachel Robinson; Otherwise Known as Sheila the Great; Tales of a Fourth Grade Nothing;* and *Superfudge.*

Around the World in a Hundred Years   PICTURE BOOK NONFICTION

AUTHOR: Jean Fritz • ILLUSTRATOR: Anthony Bacon Venti
HC: Putnam • PB: Paperstar
THEMES: history, 16th century; geography; courage; trailblazing; maps; journeys

From Henry the Navigator to Magellan, Fritz follows the achievements of ten men who traveled to India, Africa, the Americas, and eventually around the world. Each chapter begins with a map of an explorer's voyage. Straightforward text and humor make up the stories that bring these historical characters to life.

★ Baby   FICTION

AUTHOR: Patricia MacLachlan
HC: Delacorte • PB: Dell
THEMES: adoption; loss; grief; babies; choices; homelessness; family

Twelve-year-old Larkin returns home one day to discover a baby sitting in a basket in the driveway of her family's house. The only clue to how the baby got there is a note from the child's mother saying, "This is Sophie. She is almost a year old and she is good. I cannot take care of her now, but I know she will be safe with you . . . I will come back for her one day." Larkin and her family care for the baby, knowing that it is temporary, yet allowing Sophie to fill a void that the author takes her time in revealing. The brilliance of MacLachlan's writing lies in her ability to convey the silence of people who have no words for what they are feeling. This is a powerful book about loss and redemption, and though it is well within the ability of a ten-year-old to read and appreciate, we like to give this book to adults as an example of the kind of astonishing writing they miss by neglecting to read children's books.

The Bad Beginning (A Series of Unfortunate Events, Book 1) FICTION

AUTHOR: Lemony Snicket • ILLUSTRATOR: Brett Helquist
HC: HarperCollins
THEMES: orphans; adventure; siblings; humor; mishaps

Like an Edward Gorey drawing come to life, or a parody of every dreadful Victorian orphan novel you've never read, this first in a series of thirteen (of course!) is one of the funniest books for children ever written—if you find treachery, disaster, and peril funny. We do, especially when served up in Mr. Snicket's knowing and wry style. Apparently, so do hundreds of thousands of children who have taken this series to their wretched little hearts and devoured them whole, clamoring for more misadventures of the wildly unlucky but resilient Baudelaire orphans. Though there is a sameness to subsequent volumes in the series—a requirement of successful series fiction—we think the books grow funnier the gloomier things get for the children and the more mischievous the storytelling becomes.

Clever readers have already ascertained that the identities of the narrator and the mysterious Beatrice, to whom each volume is dedicated, are becoming increasingly important, not to mention the story-behind-the-story concerning Lemony Snicket's true identity. All is being revealed slowly and surely, and a true master is leading those of us who love the series down a garden path. It is a delight to be enthralled by such a plan.

 I realize that these books are not to everyone's taste, but when I think about it, I don't usually care much for books that are.

Lemony Snicket's lament found on the back cover is irresistibly enticing: "It is my sad duty to write down these unpleasant tales. There's nothing stopping you from putting this book down at once and reading something happy if you prefer that sort of thing."

The Ballad of Lucy Whipple

FICTION

AUTHOR: Karen Cushman
HC: Clarion • PB: HarperCollins
THEMES: survival; U.S. history, Westward movement; courage; California;
U.S. history, gold rush, pioneers; strong girls

Karen Cushman's first book, *Catherine Called Birdy*, won a Newbery Honor award. Her second, *The Midwife's Apprentice*, won the Newbery Medal. This, her third, will not disappoint. Lucy Whipple, jaw set, shoulders back, fights for her place out west where "There is no school and no lending library, no bank, no church, no meetinghouse, no newspaper, no shopping, no parties or picnics, no eggs, no milk." You are bound to laugh, but will also gain a clear sense of what life was like for the early settlers.

★ The Barn

FICTION

AUTHOR: Avi
HC: Orchard • PB: Avon
THEMES: gentle boys; illness; family; choices; siblings; communication; U.S.
history, frontier life; farms; fate; handicaps; fathers and sons; taking
action; responsibility; gifted child; wisdom; barns

An outstanding novel that will speak to anyone who has ever had to deal with an ill parent. In 1850s Oregon a ten-year-old boy is called home from school to help his older brother and sister out when their father has a stroke. The bright boy is able to communicate with his father despite his infirmity and enters into a power struggle with his siblings over the fate of the family farm. With writing that sings from the page, this is a novel to read, weep over, and treasure.

Baseball in April and Other Stories

SHORT STORY COLLECTION

AUTHOR: Gary Soto
HC/PB: Harcourt Brace
THEMES: family; friends; success; challenges; Spanish words; love; Latinos;
neighborhood; failure; honesty

Soto steps into the minds of Latino youth struggling with the successes and failures of growing up in California's Central Valley. These short stories, peppered with Spanish words and idioms, will hit a familiar chord in many young readers working their way to adulthood. There is a sequel: *Local News*.

Bat 6

FICTION

AUTHOR: Virginia Euwer Wolff
HC/PB: Scholastic
THEMES: baseball; Japanese internment; prejudice

With great skill and style, Wolff introduces us to twenty-one narrators, each a member of a girl's softball team in a small Oregon town in 1949. The effects of blind racism are examined and the multiple points of view give us many more sides of a story than we usually get in fiction.

The Bear's House

FICTION

AUTHOR: Marilyn Sachs
PB: Puffin
THEMES: imagination; dolls; school; family; poverty; bullies; mental illness

Fran Ellen will break your heart as she struggles to stay on top in a world of bullies, poverty, and a mentally ill mom. Her imagination provides solace when she finds a family she can live with in a classroom dollhouse. A sensitizing story for readers, who will identify Fran as a child whose family does not fit in with society's "norm." For more of this amazing young girl, read *Fran Ellen's House*.

Belle Prater's Boy

FICTION

AUTHOR: Ruth White
HC: Farrar, Straus & Giroux • PB: Dell
THEMES: U.S.A., Appalachia; mothers; friendship; family; cousins; loss; self-
    respect; death; mystery

"Around 5:00 a.m. on a warm Sunday morning in October 1953, my Aunt Belle left her bed and vanished from the face of the earth." The story begins with this fact. Twelve-year-old Gypsy wants to know exactly what happened. Becoming best friends with her cousin Woodrow, Aunt Belle's son, brings her closer to the truth. Readers see how differently people respond to loss. They also get a glimpse into life in a small Appalachian town through characters that are poignant, funny, sad, and inspiring in this incredibly worthwhile book.

Ben and Me

FICTION

AUTHOR/ILLUSTRATOR: Robert Lawson
HC/PB: Little Brown
THEMES: U.S. history, American Revolution; mice; kites; U.S. history, colonial
    times; electricity; friendship; lightning; storms; inventions; trailblazing

The classic story of Ben Franklin, as told by a mouse who was there for all the history. He now steps forward to let the world know of his important role in Ben's achievements. This is a whimsical look at history and a good way to interest kids in it. Also see *Mr. Revere and I*.

The Birchbark House
FICTION

AUTHOR: Louise Erdrich
HC/PB: Hyperion
THEMES: Native American; family; community; girls, strong; coming of age;
U.S. History, 19th Century; U.S.A., the Midwest

In the first of a cycle of novels partly based on her own family history, Erdrich offers a compelling and original saga told from the point of view of a young Ojibwa girl on an island in Lake Superior in 1847. The comparisons to Laura Ingalls Wilder cannot be overlooked, not only in the portrayal of a loving Native American family in contrast to the portrayal of Indians and white families in the *Little House* books, but for the use of Erdrich's own pencil illustrations, reminiscent of Garth Williams's in their softness and power.

What a pleasure it is to read this novel and love it not only for its accessible portrayal of a people told by one of their own, but because it is a great story, with a completely believable heroine who can compare favorably to anyone from E. B. White's Fern to Laura herself in the pantheon of American children's literature.

★ Black Ships Before Troy
FICTION

AUTHOR: Rosemary Sutcliff • ILLUSTRATOR: Alan Lee
HC: Delacorte
THEMES: folklore; ancient history; ancient Greece; Greek mythology; the
Iliad; war; adventure; heroes

Sutcliff and Lee's *The Wanderings of Odysseus* is a retelling of the *Odyssey* that holds to the same high standards as their earlier book.

A brilliant retelling of the *Iliad* by the late Sutcliff, with remarkable illustrations by Alan Lee. Open this book to any page to test the writing. Written squarely on the sixth-grade reading level, it is addictive reading for anyone even remotely interested in Greek mythology. Recommend it to readers looking for adventure. It stretches vocabulary, and the powerful illustrations help to move even the wary reader forward.

Blitzcat
FICTION

AUTHOR: Robert Westall
PB: Scholastic
THEMES: England; cats; history, World War II; war; courage

Westall has taken day-to-day events in World War II England, added a cat's journey, and given his readers a glimpse into the lives of several people experiencing war firsthand. Good historical fiction goes a long way to making young readers interested in history, and this is a prime example.

Blubber
FICTION

AUTHOR: Judy Blume

PB: Dell

THEMES: overweight; bullies; school; friendship; teasing; cruelty

A brilliant book about how rotten kids can be to each other. See *Are You There God? It's Me, Margaret*.

Blue Skin of the Sea
FICTION

AUTHOR: Graham Salisbury

HC: Delacorte • PB: Dell

THEMES: Hawaii; fishing; coming of age; courage; friendship; sea; school; sharks; storms; fear of water; love

In this remarkable debut novel of stand-alone but interconnected short stories, we watch Sonny Mendoza grow up on the Big Island of Hawaii in the fifties and sixties. His journey from childhood through adolescence is marked by encounters with sharks, hurricanes, friendships, and his coming to terms with his fear of the sea, something quite uncommon on an island. Salisbury's portrait of island life makes it seem both exotic and familiar, and this novel will appeal to a wide range of readers.

The Boggart
FICTION-FANTASY

AUTHOR: Susan Cooper

HC: McElderry • PB: Aladdin

THEMES: Scotland; castles; fantasy; trickster tales; magic; ghosts; gifted child; Canada; computers

It's one thing for Emily and Jess Volnik's family to inherit a crumbly old castle in Scotland, but when an invisible, shape-changing, prank-playing spirit comes with it, it's another thing altogether. This is the stuff of which classics are made: mystery, magic, mischief, and an irresistible sprite that will have readers clamoring for more. For additional adventures, check out *The Boggart and the Monster*.

A Book of Artrageous Projects

NOVELTY

AUTHOR: Editors of Klutz Press

HC: Klutz Press

THEMES: art; creativity

Created in conjunction with the Metropolitan Museum of Art in New York, this is one of the best books those wizards at Klutz have produced. You can't keep from running your fingers over the various pages, itching to start on one of the many projects inside. All the supplies necessary to unleash the artist within the most noncreative person accompany the text, and before long, you'll be reading, weaving, painting, pounding, poking, soaking, rubbing, and stickering yourself into a frenzy. Highly contagious fun.

★ The Bridge to Terabithia

FICTION

AUTHOR: Katherine Paterson

HC/PB: HarperCollins

THEMES: death; gifted child; loss; grief; friendship; fitting in

Of Paterson's two Newbery winners, this story of two outsider children and their magical, life-affirming relationship may be her most popular. This is a moving book that reads rather easily considering the toughness of the subject matter: the devastating and sudden loss of a dear friend. Terabithia lives inside people for years after reading about it. Do not miss the chance to discover its beauty for you and your family.

Bud, Not Buddy

FICTION

AUTHOR: Christopher Paul Curtis

HC: Delacorte • PB: Dell

THEMES: fathers and sons; music; musicians; jazz; searches; family; U. S. History, the 1920s; African American

Winner of the Newbery Medal, this is a funny, poignant, and fantastic novel about searching for family during the Jazz Age. Bud Caldwell is on the run, in search of the man he believes to be his father. He doesn't have much to go on, just a flyer showing a jazz musician, but he's not going back to the abusive life of an orphan in foster homes. Guided by his instincts and his "Rules and Things for Having a Funner Life and Making a Better Liar Out of Yourself," Bud encounters wild adventures, a little danger, and his first kiss— "busting slob," he calls it. Curtis perfectly balances humor and poignancy, and gets the time, place, and emotions just right in this outstanding book. Great for reading aloud.

AUTHOR SPOTLIGHT ON
KATHERINE PATERSON

We do not toss around words like *moral* lightly, either in the sense of the message many folks want to find at the end of a story, or in the sense of righteous, upstanding, or virtuous. However, the work of Katherine Paterson inspires us to reach for the term *moral* in all its forms. There is simply no better writer for children who grapples with the issues of morality than she.

And grapple she does, like Jacob and the Angel, with the possibility of redemption for her characters, many of whom are dealt some of life's most difficult blows. In every Paterson book, from her earliest trilogy of novels set in Feudal Japan (*The Sign of the Chrysanthemum; The Master Puppeteer; Of Nightingale's That Weep*), through her picture books (*The King's Equal; The Angel and the Donkey; The Tale of the Mandarin Ducks; Celia and the Sweet, Sweet Water*), and contemporary novels (*Come Sing, Jimmy Jo; Park's Quest; Preacher's Boy; Flip-Flop Girl; The Field of the Dogs*), her characters are offered a chance at salvation. Not Christian salvation, specifically—though her beliefs inform much of her work (she is a minister's wife and former missionary); she is not a writer who preaches. Often the salvation to be had comes down to a hard choice, and sometimes her characters do not take what is offered them. But in every shining sentence of Paterson's work exists the understanding that if children can rise above themselves, their families, and their adversity to attain a kind of grace, so can we all. We are frequently moved to tears by her books.

We would venture to say that the Newbery-winning *A Bridge to Terabithia* is the most beloved of all Paterson's work, and Jess and Leslie's adventures have no doubt inspired thousands of other children to create kingdoms of their own, as well as offered many children their first taste of the desolation of loss. We are also fond of *Jacob Have I Loved*, Paterson's other Newbery winner, with its superb portrayal of sibling rivalry. Louise is a hard girl to like, and her story may strike a little close to home to some feuding sisters, but there is no arguing with the power of Paterson's retelling of the story of Jacob and Esau, nor her insight into family dynamics.

Paterson champions "difficult" kids in her books, and understands how important family is to them. In *The Great Gilly Hopkins* we are introduced to an eleven-year-old in the foster care system, one of the most deliberately unlikable main characters in all of children's books, but Paterson reveals the heart yearning for family that lies under Gilly's tough veneer and we are won over in the end. A similar yearning can be found in Angel Morgan, who tries to keep her family together in *The Same Stuff as Stars*, though this book is no "Gilly Revisited," but rather a powerful and moving look at children managing to survive in the underbelly of our society.

Paterson's ability to handle more difficult themes for young readers is greatly aided by the warmth and humor she brings to her storytelling. They are particularly evident in her early readers. Her Marvin books (*Marvin's Best Christmas Present Ever, The Smallest Cow in the World*, and *Marvin One Too Many*) are among the very best in the field, never sacrificing character or story despite the restricted vocabulary.

Her Christmas short story collections (*Angels and Other Strangers* and *A Midnight Clear*) make wonderful read-alouds. Her novels of nineteenth-century Vermont (*Lyddie* and *Jip: His Story*) are among the best historical novels written for children, and her thoughtful nonfiction about God (*Who Am I?*) offers children more excellence from which to choose. Her insight into her chosen field makes *The Invisible Child: On Reading and Writing Books for Children* a must-read for adults interested in children's books.

Whenever we finish a book by Paterson we are filled with feelings of uplift, goodness, and gratitude for the rich possibility of the human spirit.

Katherine Paterson makes me believe in the possibility of God.

★ Bull Run

FICTION

AUTHOR: Paul Fleischman

HC/PB: HarperCollins

THEMES: fighting; point of view; comparisons; diversity; U.S. history, Civil War

Step back in time for a look at characters, Northern and Southern, who were affected by the Battle of Bull Run. It's impossible to read this account of war without thinking about the perspectives of both sides. As a bonus, this makes for great reader's theater.

 If there had been books like this available when I was a young student, I'm sure I would have been more interested in history.

But That's Another Story: Favorite Authors Introduce Popular Genres

SHORT STORY ANTHOLOGY

EDITOR: Sandy Asher

PB: Walker

THEMES: reading; writing; authors

If you have a reader who is a slave to one genre, use this book as an introduction to the different categories of fiction available to him. Thirteen writers have contributed an original short story to this collection and each is interviewed by editor Asher, to give the reader a tantalizing glimpse at what is going on in other sections of the bookstore. In addition, this is a valuable book to use with young writers, who fall prey to many of the sameness traps as young readers.

By the Great Horn Spoon

AUTHOR: Sid Fleischman • ILLUSTRATOR: Eric Von Schmidt

HC/PB: Little Brown

THEMES: U.S. history, Westward movement; U.S. history, the Gold Rush;
   California; humor; hiding; adventure

Eureka! The California Gold Rush has begun, and young Jack Flagg has set out from Boston with his trusty sidekick, Praiseworthy, to seek his fortune. Young readers will have a rip-roaring time with this adventurous duo.

Cat Running

FICTION

AUTHOR: Zilpha Keatley Snyder

HC: Delacorte • PB: Dell

THEMES: racing; poverty; homelessness; track and field; California;
   competition; prejudice; strong girls; U.S. history, the Depression;
   U.S.A., Dust Bowl

Set in central California during the Great Depression, this novel nonetheless deals with many of today's issues: poverty, homelessness, and prejudice. A fast-paced adventure about a strong-willed runner who is the best in her town and a new competitor who doesn't even bother to put shoes on his feet, it will keep the pages turning.

> "One of the first books I read for pure pleasure was *Hawaii*. It took me to a place I had never been and introduced me to people I'd never met . . . in a time I could never visit. At times I was shocked. At times I was delighted. When I finished that book I couldn't wait to pick up another one . . . to make another journey far from my Indiana farm."
> —*Jim Davis, creator of* Garfield

★ Catherine, Called Birdy

FICTION

AUTHOR: Karen Cushman

HC: Clarion • PB: HarperCollins

THEMES: diaries; history; medieval times; family; strong
   girls; independence

"The stars and my family align to make my life black and miserable. My mother seeks to make me a fine lady—dumb, docile, and accomplished—so I must take lady-lessons and keep my mouth closed . . . My father, the toad, conspires to sell me like cheese to some lack-wit seeking a wife." Medieval life, as recounted in the diary of feisty, independent Birdy is funny, horrifying, and fascinating. Cushman's writing transports the reader from the present world to the world of 1290 into a life so real it's hard not to scratch for fleas with the turn of a page. When this story ends, turn to *The Midwife's Apprentice*, another fabulous piece of historical fiction from Cushman—and winner of the Newbery Medal.

The Cay

FICTION

AUTHOR: Theodore Taylor

HC: Random House • PB: Dell

THEMES: blindness; courage; rescue; adventure; cultural diversity; prejudice; Caribbean; loss; friendship; history, World War II; survival; elderly and children

A racist boy depends upon an old black man in the aftermath of the sinking of a freighter in the Caribbean during World War II. This is a survival story, an adventure tale, and a plea for racial tolerance all rolled into one, and it reads beautifully. No wonder it has been on school reading lists for years— children respond well to this story and have been clamoring for over thirty years for a sequel. Taylor ultimately fashioned a different sort of follow-up book, *Timothy of the Cay*, which is both the story of what happened before the events of the first book and after. Read together or separately, the two books offer an unforgettable portrayal of friendship.

Charlie Pippin

FICTION

AUTHOR: Candy Dawson Boyd

PB: Puffin

THEMES: monuments; fathers and daughters; African American; peace; strong girls; death; Vietnam Veteran's Memorial; U.S. history, Vietnam War

Charlie Pippin's dad is acting crankier than usual and won't talk about what's bothering him. When eleven-year-old Charlie decides to figure things out for herself, her curiosity leads her to the Vietnam Memorial and to his past. Boyd handles this war veteran's problems with sensitivity while showing that an understanding heart can begin to heal deep scars.

Chasing Redbird

FICTION

AUTHOR: Sharon Creech

HC/PB: HarperCollins

THEMES: coming of age; friendship; grief; death; siblings; farms; trailblazing; camping; guilt; family life; strong girls

For another journey of self-discovery, read Creech's The *Wanderer*, where thirteen-year-old Sophie joins five other members of her "family" as a crew member on a boat, sailing across the Atlantic toward her grandfather.

When thirteen-year-old Zinny discovers an overgrown trail that begins on her family farm, she decides to clear it to have time on her own away from her family, where she can think. Her aunt has died. Her uncle is acting strange. And she can't get her cousin Rose out of her mind—Rose, who died of the whooping cough she got from Zinny. Thirteen is not an easy age, especially when grief, guilt, and a boy named Jake complicate it. Creech shows her readers, with a touch of mystery, how one girl clears her problems along with a trail through the "whole wide-open countryside."

Child of the Owl

FICTION

AUTHOR: Laurence Yep

PB: HarperTrophy

THEMES: family; ancestors; folklore; Chinese; Chinese American; fitting in;
U.S. history, the 1960s; grandmothers and granddaughters; California;
San Francisco; Chinatown

A third-generation Chinese American girl learns of her heritage and the mystical connection to an owl charm when she goes to live with her grandmother in San Francisco's Chinatown of the 1960s. Yep's portrayal of a Chinese family adapting to life in America stretches across many novels (collectively, they are known as *The Golden Mountain Chronicles*), moving back and forth through history and providing an extraordinary account of time, place, and culture.

Children of the Dust Bowl: The True Story of the School at Weedpatch Camp

NONFICTION

AUTHOR: Jerry Stanley • ILLUSTRATOR: Photographs

PB: Crown

THEMES: U.S.A., the Dust Bowl; U.S. history, the Depression; homelessness;
survival; getting along; prejudice

This is the true story of the children of migrant workers from Oklahoma who helped to build a school at a farm labor camp in California. A useful piece of nonfiction to have on hand when discussing Steinbeck's *The Grapes of Wrath*, as Steinbeck's personal interest in the school is detailed in Stanley's fine account of this important achievement.

Christmas in the Big House, Christmas in the Quarters

NONFICTION

AUTHORS: Patricia C. and Frederick McKissack • ILLUSTRATOR: John Thompson

HC/PB: Scholastic

THEMES: slavery; U.S. history, pre–Civil War; Christmas; family; prejudice;
comparisons; cultural diversity; traditions; jobs; community

It's 1859 in Virginia, and slaveholders and slaves ready themselves for the holidays. The McKissacks compare the two dwellings and contrast the lifestyles within. Songs, recipes, and poems merge with the text to offer an inside look at how it was.

SPOTLIGHT ON
LAURENCE YEP

Lawrence Yep writes for the outsider in every child. Growing up as a non-Chinese-speaking Chinese American in a black neighborhood in San Francisco, and attending school in China-town, Yep had a great deal of trouble fitting in. As a response to his feelings of alienation, he began to write science fiction and was first published while still in high school. In his own words, "When I wrote . . . I could reach into the box of rags that was my soul and begin stitching them together . . ."

Laurence Yep knows what it feels like to try and fit in, and it shows in his novels. As he began to discover and claim his cultural identity through writing, setting his stories in and around Chinese as well as Chinese American locales, he explored themes of tolerance and the use of the imagination as a survival mechanism of childhood; the result has been insightful novels that transcend culture and speak to all children. Any child can identify with his sensitivity to growing up feeling out of synch, but it is the burgeoning adolescent who will find his works like *Child of the Owl, Dragonwings* (a Newbery Honor book), and *Dragon's Gate* (also a Newbery Honor book) most compelling.

Yep has written books in successful series, with his *The Journal of Wong Ming-Chung: A Chinese Miner, California, 1852* being a standout of the *My Name Is America* books and his *Spring Pearl: The Last Flower*, one of the first titles in the *Girls of Many Lands* series.

Yep's retellings of myths and legends of old China show how stories hop continents and settle, grow, and change with each generation while maintaining their essential core. *The Rainbow People, Tongues of Jade*, and the picture book *The Man Who Tricked a Ghost* all demonstrate Yep's ability to capture a classic tale and make it new and fresh in the telling.

Yep's sequence of fantasy novels about the dragon princess Shimmer and her quest to regain her lost kingdom ranks as one of the best of the genre. *Dragon of the Lost Sea, Dragon Steel, Dragon Cauldron*, and *Dragon War* make up this quartet.

As an editor, Yep has overseen the publication of *American Dragon: Twenty-five Asian American Voices*, an outstanding anthology. In collaboration with artists Kam Mak and the team of Jean and Mou-Sien Tseng, he has created beautiful picture books, among them *The Dragon Prince, The City of Dragons*, and *The Boy Who Swallowed Snakes*. His fictional retelling of the events surrounding the dropping of the first atomic bomb makes for compelling reading in *Hiroshima: A Novella*, and his memoir *The Lost Garden* gives tremendous insight into the making of a writer.

Yep's prodigious output never diminishes the high quality of his work. Whatever he chooses to write about, he has established himself as a voice with which to be reckoned, and we count him among the authors whose work never ceases to thrill us.

The City of Gold and Lead

SCIENCE FICTION

AUTHOR: John Christopher
PB: Aladdin
THEMES: gifted child; courage; invasion; good vs. evil; science fiction

First in a classic trilogy that has served as an introduction to science fiction for generations of children. If your child likes *Animorphs*, make sure he knows about these. Other titles are *The Pool of Fire* and *The White Mountains*.

Coraline

FICTION

AUTHOR: Neil Gaiman • ILLUSTRATOR: Dave McKean
HC: HarperCollins
THEMES: courage; mothers and daughters; fear; girls, strong

This story gave us the creeps. No wonder. It takes place in an old house with a mysterious door off the drawing room, strange shadows, a detached hand, and parents who aren't who they seem to be. Coraline is a clever, daring character that, in spite of her terror, does what's necessary to save her parents from the clutches of evil. This will make an excellent story to read aloud to any child ready for a good shiver. Though not violent or morbid, it is not for the faint of heart—we're not confident about the security of the evil hand's ultimate place of confinement, and that could cause bad dreams. Ultimately, what we remember is the resilience and determination of Coraline, a gritty young heroine who saves the day, joining the ranks of legendary children's favorites. There is an excellent audio version of this tale, read by the author.

The Dark-Thirty: Southern Tales of the Supernatural

FOLKLORE COLLECTION

AUTHOR: Patricia McKissack • ILLUSTRATOR: Brian Pinkney
PB: Yearling
THEMES: African American; U.S.A., the South; horror; folklore; storytelling; scary stories; spooky stories

An outstanding collection of stories that range from disturbing to spooky to downright terrifying. Excellent to have on hand when kids start gravitating toward scarier tales, as it not only will feed their need to be frightened but also will help highlight how scary stories are a part of all our cultures.

★ Dave at Night

FICTION

AUTHOR: Gail Carson Levine
HC/PB: HarperCollins
THEMES: orphans; U.S. history, the 1920s; Jews; Harlem; community;
     adventure; elderly and children; yiddish

Newbery Honor–winner Gail Carson Levine (*Ella Enchanted*) has written a book that is so rich you will want to savor every moment. It's a great orphan book (and everyone loves a plucky, heroic orphan), a fabulous book for boys (with adventure, escape, cruelty, and triumph, and raunchy boy talk of the 1920s), a vivid portrayal of Yiddish life, and a look through the eyes of a child at one of the most fertile periods in American culture—the Harlem Renaissance.

The Daydreamer

FICTION-FANTASY

AUTHOR: Ian McEwan • ILLUSTRATOR: Anthony Browne
PB: Doubleday
THEMES: imagination; point of view; dreams; fantasy; individuality;
     daydreams

This is a book about a special child—the kind who tends to stare out the window instead of paying attention in class. He may have trouble keeping focused on the matter at hand because his imagined life is far more interesting than anything else going on. This kind of kid has a rich inner world that can sometimes get mixed up with reality, and this book shows his fantasies in all their glory. Terrific fantasy writing, sure to captivate the right kid.

Dear America Series

FICTION

AUTHOR: Various
HC: Scholastic
THEMES: U.S. history; diaries; strong girls

A series of fictional diaries by young women written at various times in America's history. With different writers there is bound to be varying quality to the volumes, but Kathryn Lasky's Pilgrim journal *Journey to the New World: The Diary of Remember Patience Whipple, Mayflower, 1620* is superb, exemplifying the goals of this laudable attempt to bring history to life, warts and all.

Other titles of note include *The Winter of the Red Snow* by Kristiana Gregory (about the American Revolution), *I Thought My Soul Would Rise and Fly* (about the experience of slavery), and *A Picture of Freedom* (about the Civil War), both by Patricia McKissack. Spinoff series include *The Royal Diaries*, each a fictionalized account of a princess or queen at a crucial point in her life, and *My Name Is America,* which features stories about boys and young men in the same fictionalized diary format.

Eating the Plates: The Pilgrim Book of Food and Manners
NONFICTION

AUTHOR: Lucille Recht Penner
PB: Aladdin
THEMES: U.S.A., New England; U.S. history, colonial America; eating; Thanksgiving; traditions; Pilgrims; food; manners

Fascinating and full of interesting details that will keep a kid reading long after she finds the fact she is looking for. This book describes the customs and food rituals of the Pilgrims.

The Egypt Game
FICTION

AUTHOR: Zilpha Keatley Snyder
HC: Atheneum • PB: Dell
THEMES: ancient Egypt; costumes; obsession; mystery; traditions; rituals; friendship; games; codes

Melanie, April, and their friends are really into ancient Egypt. They hold regular meetings to act out their love of Egyptian lore, immersing themselves in the culture, from hieroglyphics to the costumes of the era. When strange things start to happen, it is only logical to connect them with the Ceremonies of the Dead and the Oracles, and the children start to wonder if things have gotten out of hand. Here is a wonderful mystery to give to a child who is completely smitten with a culture, place, or time—not just Egypt.

> "Freedom now appeared, to disappear no more. It was heard in every sound, and seen in every thing. It was ever present to torment me with a sense of my wretched condition. I saw nothing without seeing it, I heard nothing without hearing it, and felt nothing without feeling it. It looked from every star, it smiled in every calm, breathed in every wind, and moved in every storm."
>
> —*Frederick Douglass*
> *(after he finally learned to read)*

Escape from Slavery: The Boyhood of Frederick Douglass in His Own Words
BIOGRAPHY

EDITOR/ILLUSTRATOR: Michael McCurdy • AUTHOR: Frederick Douglass
HC/PB: Knopf
THEMES: U.S. history, the Civil War; autobiography; slavery; African American; escape; freedom

This powerful account of Frederick Douglass's life—in his own words—is likely to move readers into learning more about this extraordinary man.

★ Esperanza Rising
FICTION

AUTHOR: Pamela Muñoz Ryan
HC/PB: Scholastic
THEMES: Mexico; California; migrant farmworkers; family; strong girls; work; survival; courage; community

Esperanza's life takes a turn when her father is killed on their ranch in Mexico. She has been accustomed to fancy clothes and a lovely home with servants. Suddenly she finds herself living in central California in a small one-room shack with another family, working along with migrant farmworkers. Esperanza learns about survival and the riches family and community hold in this moving, lyrical story. *Esperanza* means *hope,* and Ryan has made sure that this story, inspired by the life of her grandmother, lives up to its name.

The Fall (The Seventh Tower, Book 1)
FICTION

AUTHOR: Garth Nix
PB: Scholastic
THEMES: fantasy; adventure; castles; sun

Australian author Nix, known for his young adult fantasies *Shade's Children* and *Sabriel* has created an adventure set in a world where the only place that has sun is a castle of seven towers, and where people live on different levels, according to their place in life. Tal is a boy who must find a sunstone—which gives off light, warmth, and magic—in order to save his family. This series will hook young fantasy enthusiasts.

FEG: Ridiculous Poems for Intelligent Children
POETRY

AUTHOR: Robin Hirsch • ILLUSTRATOR: Ha
HC: Little Brown
THEMES: palindromes; puns; puzzles; haiku; spoonerisms; poetry; language; humor; wordplay; writing

Using a combination of fanciful graphic images and a mixture of viewpoints, this book bring alive the tools of writing poetry. At the top of each page you'll find a poem illustrating a certain style (alliteration, haiku, ono-matopoeia, palindrome, sonnet, spoonerism) and at the bottom descriptions, definitions, and strategies that encourage clever methods to express oneself in thoughtful and unself-conscious ways.

 Don't be deterred by the title. (I found it off-putting.) After the first few pages I could hardly put the book down. I howled in appreciation at the humor and cleverness, and learned a few things in the process.

Five Children and It
FICTION-FANTASY

AUTHOR: E. Nesbit
PB: Puffin
THEMES: magic; wishes; adventure; family; fairies; fantasy; siblings

A delightful and influential fantasy about the discovery of a Psammead, or sand fairy, by a quintet of siblings. Wishes abound, once the Psammead gets over having his sleep disturbed. The adventures of these very British children are a bit precious by today's standards, but every writer since who has written of children and magic owes a debt to Nesbit. Reading aloud will help smooth over some of the unfamiliar language and, after all, why should the children have all the fun?

The Folk Keeper
FICTION

AUTHOR: Franny Billingsley
HC: Atheneum • PB: Aladdin
THEMES: fantasy; courage; disguises; magic; folklore; change

Ooooh, is this a good one! Great sense of place and use of folklore; this story of a young girl who disguises herself as a boy in order to tend "the folk" is full of tense adventure. To tell too much would rob the story of its pleasures, but if you like transformation stories and good fantasy writing, this is one for you.

The Forestwife
FICTION

AUTHOR: Theresa Tomlinson
PB: Dell
THEMES: history; medieval life; Robin Hood; herbs; point of view; healing; strong girls; hunting

We know Robin Hood's story, but this tale gives us Marian's point of view along with a dose of medieval times. A hunter, a solver of mysteries, and a healer, Marian learns which herbs to use as a cure and which plants work best for making dyes. This is no passive Marian waiting around in the forest to be rescued.

The Four-Story Mistake
FICTION

AUTHOR: Elizabeth Enright
HC: Henry Holt • PB: Puffin
THEMES: family; dance; siblings

A charming series that has been a favorite of children for generations. The Melendy family is the stuff of classic children's writing—solid characters you care about, humorous and believable adventures, and a family that you wish were your own. The other titles are *The Saturdays, Then There Were Five,* and *Spiderweb for Two.*

The Fragile Flag
FICTION

AUTHOR: Jane Langton
HC/PB: HaperCollins
THEMES: courage; strong girls; peace; fables; worry; conscience; taking action

The Fragile Flag is part of The Hall Family Chronicles, a lovely sequence of novels mixing realism and fantasy, which also includes *The Diamond in the Window, The Swing in the Summerhouse, The Astonishing Stereoscope, The Fledgling,* and *The Time Bike.*

A lot has changed in the world since Jane Langton wrote this modern-day fable of one girl's vision of peace, but no matter how dated the story becomes, it will have value until the day when there are simply no more weapons of mass destruction. Fables set in contemporary times are hard to pull off—most of us like our fantasy set in the past or in an imaginary place—but Langton's Georgie is a true visionary as well as an authentic child. Read this aloud as a family or in a classroom and use it as a basis to discuss what can be done to work toward peace.

From Slave Ship to Freedom Road
PICTURE BOOK

AUTHOR: Julius Lester • ILLUSTRATOR: Rod Brown
HC: Dial
THEMES: African American; slavery; freedom

An important work on a difficult subject. Lester uses his powerful command of the language to help the reader understand the experience of being enslaved. He asks such questions as: "How would I feel if that happened to me?" "Would you risk going to jail to help someone you didn't know?" and "You are free, but are you?" Rod Brown's paintings are stunning. This book will inspire discussion.

From the Mixed-Up Files of Mrs. Basil E. Frankweiler

FICTION

AUTHOR/ILLUSTRATOR: E. L. Konigsburg

HC: Atheneum • PB: Aladdin

THEMES: New York; running away; museums; art; humor; mystery

The Metropolitan Museum of Art seems an unlikely choice for young runaways seeking refuge, but when Claudia and Jamie sneak away from home, that is exactly where they end up. And when a question arises over the authenticity of a piece of art, they find themselves in the midst of a suspense-filled adventure. Konigsburg's Newbery Medal–winning story is fine for reading aloud, but we also recommend this for young readers ready to get lost in a good book.

Get on Board: The Story of the Underground Railroad

NONFICTION

AUTHOR: Jim Haskins

PB: Scholastic

THEMES: slavery; escape; Underground Railroad; songs; courage

This gives details of some of the people who traveled the secret and risky route out of slavery. There's even a chapter of railroad songs that helped release emotions, as well as spread information.

A Girl from Yamhill

BIOGRAPHY

AUTHOR: Beverly Cleary

HC: Morrow • PB: Avon

THEMES: U.S. history, between the World Wars; Oregon; autobiography; authors

The early years of the life of the writer who grew up to create *Ramona the Pest* and *Henry Huggins,* told in a straightforward manner that minimizes none of the hardships. Excellent autobiographical writing that gives a sense of time and place as well as the events that shaped her life. A sequel, *My Own Two Feet,* covers her early adulthood.

Girls of Many Lands series

HISTORICAL FICTION

AUTHORS: Various

HC/PB: Pleasant Company

THEMES: strong girls; history

The latest entry in the crowded historical series market is from the people who gave us *The American Girl* books. Featuring well-crafted books by notable writers with more than a little knowledge of the cultures in question, this is an excellent addition to the bookshelves. Each book tells the tale of a girl during an interesting historical time for her particular culture, and features a finely tuned mix of history and fancy. Titles include *Cecile: Gates of Gold* by Mary Casanova (France in the early eighteenth century); *Neela: Victory Song* by Chitra Banerjee Divakaruni (India in the last days of British rule); *Spring Pearl: The Last Flower* by Laurence Yep (China during the Opium War of 1857); *Saba: Under the Hyena's Foot* by Jane Kurtz (Ethiopia in the nineteenth century); and *Minuk: Ashes in the Pathway* by Kirkpatrick Hill (Western Alaska in 1890, among the Yup'ik people).

Gladiator   NONFICTION
AUTHOR/ILLUSTRATOR: Richard Watkins
HC/PB: Houghton Mifflin
THEMES: ancient history; ancient Rome; athletes; sports; captivity; soldiers; fighting; slavery

An in-depth look at the life of the great Roman combatants, full of fascinating facts and enough gory details to intrigue the most bloodthirsty among us. Good example of how to get kids to read history by focusing on the less stuffy aspects. We guarantee that they will fight over this one.

The Graduation of Jake Moon   FICTION
AUTHOR: Barbara Park
HC: Atheneum • PB: Aladdin
THEMES: grandfathers; Alzheimer's disease; illness; caretakers

Jake is fourteen years old. He's always been close to his grandfather, Skelly. But now Skelly has Alzheimer's disease and Jake can no longer count on him. He has to help him fasten the Velcro on his sneakers and clean food off his face. It's embarrassing when his friends are over because he never knows how Skelly will act. Park has an ability to take a rough situation, add a dose of humor and compassion, and allow readers to understand the difficulties in dealing with a debilitating disease.

The Grapes of Math   PICTURE BOOK NONFICTION
AUTHOR: Greg Tang • ILLUSTRATOR: Harry Briggs
HC: Scholastic
THEMES: math; numbers; rhymes; puzzles

Tang tackles a look at math from a different angle. He doesn't rely on formulas and memorization. Instead, he shows how to add, subtract, and multiply by grouping, patterns, and a dose of creativity. Bright pictures and rhyming clues encourage readers to open their minds to new ways of finding mathematical solutions. At the back of the book they'll find a round up of the process and solutions. Here's an example of a picture-book perfect for the older set.

The Great Fire   NONFICTION

AUTHOR: Jim Murphy
HC/PB: Scholastic
THEMES: U.S. history, late 19th century; Chicago; fire; disaster

Dramatic details from people who were there during the 1871 Chicago fire combine with Murphy's riveting text to create a story that holds the attention of even the most skeptical about nonfiction. His *Blizzard: The Storm That Changed America* is equally good. Look for it, as well.

The Greek News   PICTURE BOOK NONFICTION

AUTHOR: Anton Powell • ILLUSTRATOR: Philip Steele
PB: Candlewick
THEMES: ancient Greece; ancient history; newspapers; Greek mythology

A smashing series that takes history and brings it vividly to life with a jolt of journalism. In newspaper layout, the crucial facts of the day are presented, tabloid-style, with headlines, sidebars, and plenty of illustrations. A sure-fire bet to entice nonreaders and delight history buffs. Also: *The Egyptian News, The Roman News,* and *The Aztec News.*

Grossology: The Science of Really Gross Things   NONFICTION

AUTHOR: Sylvia Branzei • ILLUSTRATOR: Jack Keely
PB: Price Stern & Sloan
THEMES: science experiments; humor, gross; science; nature

Everything you've never wanted to know about scabs, snot, vomit, and dandruff. A terrific way to bring otherwise reluctant kids to an understanding of science, if you have the stomach for it. Look for a sequel, *Grossology and You,* that goes into even more depth.

Growing Up It's a Girl Thing: Straight Talk About First Bras, First Periods, and Your Changing Body   PICTURE BOOK

AUTHOR: Mavis Jukes • ILLUSTRATOR: Debbie Tilley
PB: Knopf
THEMES: sex; sexuality; coming of age; health; change; puberty; girls

Straightforward and funny, Jukes answers questions girls have to think about, like buying bras, puberty, and sexuality.

 I wish I'd had this book when I was a preteen. There were fascinating, creative ideas going around back then. It would have been fun finding humor in the realities of growing up, not just in what we'd made up. If this had existed when they were younger, my daughters would have devoured it from front to back.

Guests   FICTION
AUTHOR: Michael Dorris
HC/PB: Hyperion
THEMES: Native American; Pilgrims; food; change; traditions; celebrations; strangers; prejudice; U.S. history, colonial America

A Native American boy is cautious about the visitors who are invited to join the Harvest Festival. "The guests will spoil everything, even my memory of other times. I wished they had never left wherever they came from before they came here. I wished they would return there again and forget the trail through the sea that they followed." Dorris's novel captures the feelings of a young boy who knows there must be change, in himself and in the world around him.

The Guinness Book of World Records   REFERENCE
AUTHOR: Norris McWhirter
HC: Guinness Media • PB: Bantam
THEMES: trivia; comparisons

Children who swear they hate reading can often be found looking at reference and nonfiction books that pique their interests. This is the king of all reference books, and a good, safe bet to give to that militant nonreader. Better yet, leave it in the bathroom and see if pages don't get turned down.

Harlem   PICTURE BOOK
AUTHOR: Walter Dean Myers • ILLUSTRATOR: Christopher Myers
HC: Scholastic
THEMES: Harlem; survival; African American; U.S. history, 20th century; community; poem; city life; New York

This is one of those books in which the words are so rich and the art is so powerful that you find yourself drawing it up to your chest and inhaling before going through it again. It's a history of Harlem in a poem that makes you feel the pulse of the past and of the present. "A journey on the A train that started on the banks of the Niger and has not ended."

AUTHOR SPOTLIGHT ON
WALTER DEAN MYERS

With an ear for urban dialogue and a range of interesting and eccentric characters, Walter Dean Myers has distinguished himself with his writing for middle-grade readers and young adults. Equally adept at handing serious and lighthearted topics, Myers instills much of his writing with a sense of humor and general optimism. His positive portrayals of children and teenagers grappling with the issues of urban life offer young readers hope, role models, and exceptional reading.

This is not to say that Myers shies away from the harder issues. He is respected as one of the premier writers for teens, though that is not the scope of our attention here. His middle-grade fiction ranges from depictions of the triumphs and hardships of three hundred years of African American history (*The Glory Field* and *The Righteous Revenge of Artemis Bonner*) to a powerful picture book for older readers about the experience of being a soldier in Vietnam, *Patrol*. But it is with warm, humorous, and authentic-feeling books such as *Hoops*; *The Mouse Rap*; *Fast Sam, Cool Clyde, and Stuff*; *A Handbook for Boys*; and *Motown and Didi* that Myers has carved a niche for himself, as no one writes better about the day-to-day concerns and lives of urban black kids.

Myers writes poetry and uses it to good advantage, whether accompanying his collection of antique photographs (*Brown Angels*), giving stylistic weight to his themes (*The Mouse Rap* cleverly uses his original rapping poetry at the beginning of each chapter), or creating stunning full-length odes to times and places crucial to our understanding of black history (*Harlem* and *Blues Journey* which have outstanding art by Myers's son, Christopher).

From time to time, Myers will write an original tale and offer it in picture-book form. *The Story of the Three Kingdoms* (illustrated by Ashley Bryan), *How Mr. Monkey Saw the Whole World* (illustrated by Synthia Saint James), and his dogs versus cats historical swashbuckler *Three Swords for Granada* are shining examples of Myers's rich storytelling gift.

In the world of nonfiction for young readers Myers has distinguished himself with books like *Now Is Your Time: The African American Struggle for Freedom*; *The Greatest: Muhammad Ali*; and *Malcolm X: By Any Means Necessary*, bringing to these works a novelist's gift for making subjects come to life and a factual narrative that reads like fiction.

We can think of no other writer who has provided more compulsively readable books, spanning styles and formats, about urban life for youth of all races with an uplifting and balanced view of childhood than Walter Dean Myers.

★ Harriet the Spy   FICTION

AUTHOR/ILLUSTRATOR: Louise Fitzhugh

HC/PB: HarperCollins

THEMES: school; friendship; family; writing; loss; secrets; revenge; lying; spying; truth; diaries

Even though she is the heroine of the book, Harriet is not particularly likable; she is flippant and often disrespectful, and is always writing down her ruthless observations about people in her notebook. She wants to be a writer, and her beloved nurse, Ole Golly, has raised her with wisdom from classic literature, encouraging her "to thine own self be true." Ole Golly leaves to get married, saying that eleven is too old to have a nurse, and Harriet's world changes drastically. When her notebook falls into the hands of her astonished classmates, their vengeful attitudes and deliberately mean actions confuse Harriet, causing her to act similarly toward them. Harriet's parents are too busy with their own lives to be of any use to her until the situation becomes too awful to ignore. How this all gets resolved, with hurt feelings soothed, friendships restored, parents coming to new understandings, and, most important, Harriet being true to herself while learning how to get along better in the world, makes for a once-in-a-lifetime reading experience. There is no one in all of fiction quite like Harriet M. Welsch.

★ Hatchet   FICTION

AUTHOR: Gary Paulsen
PB: Aladdin
THEMES: survival; airplanes; solitude; resourcefulness; divorce; courage

A perfect book about survival in the wilderness, featuring a boy named Brian whose heartbreak and resourcefulness you will remember for the rest of your life. Sequels include *The River; Brian's Winter;* and *Brian's Return;* as well as *Guts: The True Stories Behind Hatchet and the Brian Books.*

★ The Hobbit   FICTION-FANTASY

AUTHOR: J. R. R. Tolkien
HC: Houghton Mifflin • PB: Ballantine
THEMES: fantasy; adventure; courage; maps; community; fighting; good
versus evil; little folk

"In a hole in the ground there lived a hobbit. Not a nasty, dirty, wet hole, filled with the ends of worms and an oozy smell, nor yet a dry, bare, sandy hole with nothing in it to sit down on or to eat: it was a hobbit-hole, and that means comfort." Hobbits are tiny, sociable little people who like parties, feastings, and peace and quiet in their lives. They live in a land called The Shire, found between the River Brandywind and the Far Downs. This is a story about the Hobbits and about one Bilbo Baggins, who travels far from home and brings back the One Ring of Power along with adventure to the Hobbits' once peaceful world. *The Hobbit* is the prequel to Tolkien's trilogy,

The Lord of the Rings. Though this introduction to Tolkien's fantasy world is a perfect book to read aloud as a family when the children hit eight, the subsequent volumes take a leap in terms of sophistication and may be better left for discovery in the early teens. We have always felt that *The Hobbit* is a children's book and the other three are not, but you and your child will need to make that decision for your family.

AUTHOR SPOTLIGHT ON
GARY PAULSEN

Gary Paulsen has done as much as anyone to create an atmosphere of cool where reading is concerned. Adventure and humor are his trademarks, along with quiet novels that seem, on the surface, to have come from the pen of a different writer than the man who gave us *Harris and Me* and *Hatchet*.

Gary was a nonreader as a boy and a young man. He knows a lot about why boys do not read and uses his knowledge to fashion books that are irresistible to that kind of child. What makes his skill so impressive is that while he attracts the kids who are on the outside of the world of reading, he does not drive away the insiders. He is a great storyteller, and we all respond to that.

He has written lyrical picture books (*Worksong, Dogsong, Canoe Days*, and *The Tortilla Factory*) and nature-oriented nonfiction (*Father Water, Mother Woods; Guts: The True Stories Behind Hatchet and the Brian Books*; and *Puppies, Dogs and Blue Northers*), but he is primarily known as a novelist. His novels fall generally into three categories:

Adventure—Reknowned for having written *Hatchet*, which is one of the most widely read novels for young readers published in the last twenty years. Paulsen's fame stems from his skill as a master of the survival story. In addition to *Hatchet's* sequels (*The River, Brian's Winter*, and *Brian's Return*), we hope fans of those books will check out *The Voyage of the Frog, The Haymeadow*, and *The White Fox Chronicles* the next time they need a good adrenaline rush.

Humor—Laugh-out-loud, side-slapping, not-always-in-the-best-taste *funny!* There aren't enough writers who know how to make kids laugh. His novels *The Schernoff Discoveries, How Angel Peterson Got His Name*, and *Harris and Me* (one of the funniest books ever written!) are guaranteed winners and will delight young readers—especially (but not exclusively) boys.

Quieter novels—Neither sidesplitters nor thrilling page-turners, these are books that grapple with many aspects of the lives of young people and the world in which they live. They cannot all be grouped together by any criteria other than the fact that they examine deeply held moral issues with an open and questioning eye. Their topics cover a lot of ground, from slavery to religious fervor, gun issues to homelessness, all with characteristic sensitivity and plenty of room for the reader to make up his own mind. Our favorites of these include *The Cook Camp, The Monument, Dancing Car, Nightjohn, The Tent, Alida's Song, The Crossings*, and *The Winter Room*.

It's a tremendous and satisfying output from a writer who offers up a great storytelling adventure every time, regardless of how he may make you gasp, guffaw, or think.

★ Holes

FICTION

AUTHOR: Louis Sachar

HC: Farrar, Straus & Giroux • PB: Yearling

THEMES: prison; escape; treasure; adventure; fate; family; friendship; good
vs. evil; desert; boys, gentle

There is almost no need to recommend this book to young readers, as we
cannot think of a book (Harry Potter included) that more kids have told us
about than this fabulous Dickensian adventure, set in the most dreadful of
work camps in the middle of a dry Texas lake bed. If, by chance, you have not
yet encountered it, read it. Or, if your children haven't read it, here is the perfect book to read aloud as a family or to listen to on tape.

More than any other request I get, kids ask me if there are any other books like *Holes*. Often,
the ones asking are kids who don't usually like to read but pronounce it the best book ever.
Sadly, I have to admit that there aren't many books that will grab a reader and hold him the
way Sachar's masterpiece does, even his other books. I offer them *Wringer* or *Maniac Magee*
by Jerry Spinelli, or *House of the Scorpion* or *A Girl Named Disaster* by Nancy Farmer, great
books that almost hit the mark, but I am waiting for the perfect suggestion to come along.
We can only hope that Louis Sachar has another treat in store for us all.

Hoot

FICTION

AUTHOR: Carl Hiaasen

HC: Knopf

THEMES: environment; endangered species; homelessness; Florida; new
experiences; friends; bullies; owls; running away; mystery

Alligators, snakes with glittery tails, crooked politicians, bullies, slippery fish,
a runaway eco-avenger named Mullet Fingers, and some adorable burrow-
ing owls are all waiting for Roy Eberhardt when he moves to Coconut Cove.
Hiaasen's first book for the younger set has all the makings of a classic.

A House Called Awful End (The Eddie Dickens Trilogy)

FICTION

AUTHOR: Philip Ardagh • ILLUSTRATOR: David Roberts

HC: Henry Holt

THEMES: humor; aunts; uncles; orphans

"When Eddie Dickens was eleven years old, both his parents caught some
awful disease that made them turn yellow, go a bit crinkly around the edges,
and smell of old hot-water bottles." This is when Eddie is taken by his Mad
Uncle Jack and Mad Aunt Maud, and begins an adventure that includes

eccentric strolling actors, St. Horrid's Home for Grateful Orphans, and a carnival float shaped like a giant cow. If they like ridiculous, offer them this, as well as the sequels, *Dreadful Acts* and *Terrible Times*.

The House with a Clock in Its Walls

FICTION-MYSTERY

AUTHOR: John Bellairs
PB: Puffin
THEMES: horror; mystery; adventure

Well written, though they stick close to their "formula," Bellairs's suspense-filled and entertaining mystery thrillers are the perfect reads for children who are progressing fast beyond their own second- or third-grade reading levels but may not be emotionally ready for the more frightening horror novels the older kids are reading. In fact, these are so good that many of the fifth- and sixth-graders who read nothing else but adult horror become huge fans of Bellairs's work when introduced to him. There are many novels, and some of the best are *The Trolley to Yesterday, The Vengeance of the Witch-Finder,* and *The Ghost in the Mirror.*

I Am Lavina Cumming

FICTION

AUTHOR: Susan Lowell • ILLUSTRATOR: Paul Mirocha
PB: Milkweed Editions
THEMES: California; San Francisco; family; courage; strong girls;
    earthquakes; coming of age; U.S. history, early 20th century

Travel back in time and meet a young girl on a train ride away from home for the first time. Ten-year-old Lavina's mother has died and her father cannot raise her properly on their Arizona ranch, so she is on her way to California to live with an aunt she has never met. This coming-of-age novel, set at the time of the Great San Francisco Earthquake, is sure to turn young readers into fans of historical fiction.

I Am the Mummy Heb-Nefert

PICTURE BOOK

AUTHOR: Eve Bunting • ILLUSTRATOR: David Christiana
HC/PB: Harcourt Brace
THEMES: point of view; ancient history; rituals; death; memories; love;
    ancient Egypt; mummies; burial

This picture book is not for younger children, but it simply screams to be used for sixth grade. Narrated from the point of view of a mummy, this story brings Ancient Egypt alive in a most unusual and intriguing way. Master storyteller Bunting is mightily aided by the awesome power of David Christiana's art.

I Rode a Horse of Milk White Jade

FICTION

AUTHOR: Diane Lee Wilson

PB: HarperTrophy

THEMES: horses; handicaps; girls, strong; community; Asia; history, medieval times

A gripping read, a strong heroine, a historical novel with real power, a setting that is unique (Mongolia and the steppes of China during the reign of Kublai Khan), and a horse book, to boot. This is a good one.

The Illyrian Adventure

FICTION

AUTHOR: Lloyd Alexander

HC: Dutton • PB: Puffin

THEMES: adventure; strong girls; journeys; history, early 20th century

"Miss Vesper Holly has the digestive talents of a goat and the mind of a chess master. She is familiar with half a dozen languages and can swear fluently in all of them. She understands the use of a slide rule but prefers doing calculations in her head. She does not hesitate to risk life and limb—mine as well as her own. No doubt she has other qualities as yet undiscovered. I hope not." So begins the first in a series of adventures featuring a marvelously intrepid heroine (Miss Holly), as told by her harried guardian, Professor Brinton Garrett. Rollicking good fun, full of historical adventure à la Indiana Jones, these are for any reader who likes page turning at a fast clip. The other titles are *The El Dorado Adventure, The Drackenberg Adventure, The Sedera Adventure,* and *The Philadelphia Adventure.*

> "My first real, beloved, grown-up books were not the great classics many writers claim they devoured before they could digest solid food. They were the Claudia books, which sucked me into the joy of total immersion when I was going on fifteen. I'm not even ashamed. I have a feeling that if I reread this series now, I would still love Claudia, laugh myself sick, fall in love with David, and suffer a physical shock and sorrow when their son Bobby is run over and killed.
>
> The books you love when you're young build your bones. They become part of you and never, ever leave you. That's why it's so important for people in charge of children to realize that books fill our empty spaces, and that, in all of us, these spaces come in different shapes and sizes. It follows that people read what they need.
>
> —*Lynne Reid Banks, author of* **The Indian in the Cupboard**

★ The Indian in the Cupboard

FICTION-FANTASY

AUTHOR: Lynne Reid Banks • ILLUSTRATOR: Brock Cole

HC: Doubleday • PB: Avon

THEMES: Native American; little folk; magic; fantasy; adventure; friendship; toys; cowboys

Nine-year-old Omri's birthday present from his best friend is a secondhand, tiny plastic Indian. His brother's gift is an old medicine cupboard for which his mother provided a box of old keys. One is the perfect fit. At bedtime, Omri places the Indian in the cupboard, turns the lock, and sleepily closes his eyes. "Just as he was dropping off to sleep his eyes snapped open. He had thought he heard a little noise . . . but no. All was quiet. His eyes closed again." This gem is not simply a magical adventure. It stretches into territory that includes a young boy's sense of responsibility, moral dilemmas, and the ability to give life—and take it away. Read it aloud, or give it to a fourth- or fifth-grader to relish. We'd hate to have it lost on very young children, who could miss some important elements, never to return to experience its full pleasure. When the first volume has been devoured, readers will want to go on to others in the series, exciting adventures on their own: *The Return of the Indian, The Secret of the Indian,* and *The Mystery of the Cupboard.*

Island of the Blue Dolphins

FICTION

AUTHOR: Scott O'Dell • ILLUSTRATOR: Ted Lewin
HC: Houghton Mifflin • PB: Dell
THEMES: Native American; solitude; courage; strong girls;
   survival; loneliness; death; loss; coming of age; islands; Channel Islands

O'Dell's ability to tell powerful stories in the first person is evident in many of his fine books for young readers, including *Zia* (the sequel to *Island*), *Streams to the River, River to the Sea, Black Star, Bright Dawn, My Name Is Not Angelica* and *The Black Pearl.*

A masterpiece, and named by the Children's Literature Association as one of the ten best American children's books ever written. Based on an actual event, here is the unforgettable story of Karana, living alone on an island for eighteen years in the aftermath of the slaughter of her tribe. Her account of the loss of her brother is heartrending, her epic adventure of survival thrilling, and her record of solitude and its effect inspiring as the reader watches her mature and come into her own as a person. When she is rescued at the book's end, it is with some sadness that she leaves the island that she made her home.

The Janitor's Boy

FICTION

AUTHOR: Andrew Clements
HC: Simon & Schuster • PB: Aladdin
THEMES: school; community; fathers and sons

A poignant book about fathers and sons. Embarrassed by the fact that his father is the school janitor, a boy starts out causing trouble but comes to understand the special place his father holds in the school and town. Clements's popular novels (*Frindle, The School Story, The Landry News*) are remarkable for their ability to pinpoint the tensions between adults in power and smart kids who question them.

Jeremy Thatcher, Dragon Hatcher   FICTION-FANTASY
AUTHOR: Bruce Coville • ILLUSTRATOR: Gary A. Lippincott
HC: Harcourt Brace • PB: Aladdin
THEMES: dragons; magic; responsibility; choices; love; consequences

Mr. Elives's Magic Shop is not the kind of place you can find easily. Usually it finds you, and only when you need it. And then a magical item chooses you and the adventure begins. In later books Jennifer Murdley learns a lesson about the true meaning of beauty from a talking toad (*Jennifer Murdley's Toad*), and Charlie Eggleston suffers through the wisecracks and awful jokes of a talking skull (Yorick's, no less) on his way to an encounter with Truth herself (*The Skull of Truth*). But in this book, Jeremy Thatcher's destined item is a multicolored ball, an egg containing a tiny dragon that communicates with him telepathically. Raising a mischief-loving dragon named Tiamat isn't easy, and as she grows she teaches him more about love than he ever knew it was possible to know. Coville has a knack for mixing realism and fantasy, laughter and tears into a potion that makes for superb reading. This is our favorite of his books, and it fits solidly in the canon of dragon tales after Jackie French Koller's *Dragonling* books but before Jane Yolen's *Pit Dragon Trilogy*.

Joey Pigza Swallowed the Key   FICTION
AUTHOR: Jack Gantos
HC: Farrar, Straus & Giroux • PB: HarperCollins
THEMES: school; ADD; hyperactivity; getting along; solutions; mothers and
    sons; teachers; abuse

Joey Pigza has attention deficit disorder or, as he puts it, "At school they say I'm wired bad, or wired mad, or wired sad, or wired glad, depending on my mood and what teacher has ended up with me. But there is no doubt about it, I'm wired." Fast paced, poignant, and funny; readers follow Joey as he charges through each day while his teachers, school nurse, and mother search for a solution. Gantos's sequel, *Joey Pigza Loses Control*, was awarded a Newbery Honor in 2001. *What Would Joey Do?* completes the trilogy.

Journey

AUTHOR/ILLUSTRATOR: Patricia MacLachlan
HC: Delacorte • PB: Dell
THEMES: family; memories; abandonment; grandfathers and grandsons; farms; photographs; family history; cats; pets; memory

FICTION

Reeling from the sudden exit of his mother from his life, and clinging to the hope that she will someday return, young Journey searches for a way to cope with his anger and devastating sense of loss. How his remaining family members fill in the holes in both his memory and his heart and how Journey comes to realize the source of love that has always been there for him make this one of MacLachlan's most poignant works. Her spare, elegant writing is full of depth and feeling, and her ability to find light, humorous moments amid the sadness creates an atmosphere of warmth that envelops the reader. Love and a little time can heal most things, and Journey is blessed with both.

> "A book for two voices requires two readers. Reading it is a social, not a solitary, pastime. All through my years at home it was my parents' habit after dinner to retire to the living room to play a game or two, games my sisters and I often joined. As with geologic eras, those years could be divided into concentration and rummy, early cribbage, chess, double solitaire, late cribbage, and so on. For a time, my mother copied out the cryptogram from the *Saturday Review* and raced my father in decoding it. I'm sure that those thousands of evenings, that education in the pleasures of being with others, in the joys to be found in joint amusements impossible alone, led in large part to my two-voiced books. One hand can't produce a clap, or play a game of checkers. Two can. Synergy! The television, I might add, was in a different room and seldom seemed to be on. A family watching television together isn't engaged in a cooperative activity; they're each playing solitaire."
> —*Paul Fleischman, author of* Joyful Noise, *from his Newbery Medal acceptance speech*

★ Joyful Noise: Poems for Two Voices

POETRY COLLECTION

AUTHOR: Paul Fleischman • ILLUSTRATOR: Eric Beddows
HC/PB: HarperCollins
THEMES: sound; rhythm; insects; nature

Fleischman's poetic guide to the insect world—from "Book Lice" to "Whirligig Beetles" and "House Crickets"—offers more than a soaring, spinning, glimpse into bug behavior. It creates the opportunity to experience a "musical duet" performed by two readers simultaneously. And whether you are a listener or reader, you will be richer for participating.

Julie of the Wolves

FICTION

AUTHOR: Jean Craighead George
HC/PB: HarperCollins
THEMES: Inuit; San Francisco; friendship; Alaska; wilderness; courage; wolves; fathers; coming of age; adventure; strong girls

"Some slight gesture that meant nothing to her had apparently meant something to the wolf. His ears shot forward angrily and it seemed all was lost. She wanted to get up and run, but she gathered her courage and pranced closer to him." For Miyax, lost in the Alaskan wilderness with neither food nor direction, it was an act of survival. She had learned the ways of nature from her father, but things had changed. A compelling tale of courage with a deep respect for nature, this Newbery Medal winner is the perfect choice for an animal lover with a taste for adventure. The story continues in *Julie and Julie's Wolf Pack*.

King of Shadows

FICTION

AUTHOR: Susan Cooper
HC: McElderry • PB: Aladdin
THEMES: time travel; Shakespeare; fantasy; theater; actors and acting

A wonderful fantasy about a young actor who journeys back to the days of the original Globe Theatre and acts with the master himself. Those who enjoy theater will enjoy the acting scenes; those who enjoy a time travel novel will enjoy how Cooper makes all the parts work in this finely crafted tale by one of our best fantasy writers.

Lassie Come Home

FICTION

AUTHOR: Eric Knight
HC/PB: Henry Holt
THEMES: family; lost; dogs; courage; separation; pets; England; Scotland; love

The classic boy and a dog story and the basis for countless movies and television episodes, this is a story of rare courage and heart. The reason it has lasted and become a part of our pop culture is its timelessness. You'll love reading this aloud to your family.

Leonardo's Horse

PICTURE BOOK BIOGRAPHY

AUTHOR: Jean Fritz • ILLUSTRATOR: Hudson Talbott
HC: Putnam
THEMES: Leonardo da Vinci; Italy; history, the Renaissance; artists; dreams; obsession; horses

Fritz focuses here on the dream of one of the world's geniuses and the tale of its posthumous realization. The real treasure, though, is the art. Every aspect of the design of this book shows that Leonardo inspired Talbott to excel his best work, resulting in a most impressive looking volume, worthy of museums.

Let It Shine: Stories of Black Women Freedom Fighters

NONFICTION

AUTHOR: Andrea Davis Pinkney • ILLUSTRATOR: Stephen Alcorn
HC: Harcourt
THEMES: women, independent; courage; prejudice; leaders; civil rights;
African American U.S. history

Pinkney tells the stories of ten women who, through courage in the face of prejudice and oppression, paved the way for change in the lives of generations of women. From Sojourner Truth ("Ain't I a Woman?") to Shirley Chisholm ("Someday, somewhere, somehow, someone other than a white male could be President."), each entry begins with a quote. Alcorn's incredible paintings clearly show the strength of these women.

★ Lily's Crossing

FICTION

AUTHOR: Patricia Reilly Giff
HC: Delacorte • PB: Dell
THEMES: U.S. history, World War II; grandmothers, refugees; fathers and
daughters; taking action; courage; individuality; strong girls; friendship;
separation; lying

You will never forget Lily, a heroine who ranks with Ramona Quimby and Anne of Green Gables for sheer spunkiness, as she copes with the changes World War II has brought to her life. Chief among these is the absence of her beloved father and having to live with her grandmother in Far Rockaway, New York. Headstrong and given to flights of fancy that some people think are lies, Lily is a handful, but a more loving and sympathetic portrayal of such a child would be hard to imagine. A treasure.

Lincoln: A Photobiography

BIOGRAPHY

AUTHOR: Russell Freedman • ILLUSTRATOR: Photographs
HC/PB: Clarion
THEMES: Abraham Lincoln; biography; U.S. history, Civil War, speeches; U.S.
presidents

Photographs, direct quotes from Lincoln, and excerpts from his own speeches add to this fascinating Newbery Medal–winning photo biographical history of President Lincoln, including his boyhood, marriage, professional life, and the presidency. Freedman is known for other intriguing photo-essays, including *Franklin Delano Roosevelt* and *Eleanor Roosevelt*.

The Lost Years of Merlin

FICTION-FANTASY

AUTHOR: T. A. Barron
HC: Philomel • PB: Berkley
THEMES: King Arthur; fantasy; magic; journeys;
wizards; England; Wales; coming-of-age;
adventure; mystery; good vs. evil

When you finish this five-part epic (*The Seven Songs of Merlin* is the second, followed by *The Fires of Merlin*, *The Mirror of Merlin*, and *The Wings of Merlin*) you will have a different image of the great wizard in your head from the traditional old guy with a long beard. Barron has given us a more complete look at Merlin and his life than any previous writer for young readers.

"I sucked in my breath, then urged the hawk into another dive. We shot down toward the same open window as before. Wind tore at me, screaming in my ears." Action-filled images, loyal, brave, and wicked characters, and a young hero's quest for his identity make this page-turner an imaginative introduction to the boyhood of Merlin, the legendary enchanter.

Made in China: Ideas and Inventions from Ancient China

NONFICTION

AUTHOR: Suzanne Williams • ILLUSTRATOR: Andrea
Fong
HC: Pacific View Press
THEMES: trailblazing; China; ancient history; inventions; science
experiments; science; maps

"You can't hunt rhinoceros in China. But once you could." So begins a fascinating account of China from four thousand years ago to the 1500s. Don't limit this one to history projects. Any curious child will want to learn how the Chinese made salt, paper, calendars, compasses, even a seismograph to measure earthquakes. They recycled old tools, discovered natural gas, created Chinese medicine. With words and a mix of maps, photographs, and drawings, this will whet the appetite of future historians and scientists.

★ Maniac Magee

FICTION

AUTHOR: Jerry Spinelli
HC/PB: Little Brown
THEMES: cultural diversity; track and field; tall tales; individuality; diversity;
hopelessness; prejudice; friendship; fables; orphans

"They say Maniac Magee was born in a dump. They say his stomach was a cereal box and his heart a sofa spring. They say he kept an eight-inch cockroach on a leash and that rats stood guard over him while he slept." That's how it starts. But Maniac Magee was not born in a dump. He was an orphan who had to make decisions for his own survival. And he was good. And he brought together people who lived on opposite sides of town, people who despised each other. He was a legend. He was the kind of legend worth reading about.

Matilda Bone
FICTION

AUTHOR: Karen Cushman
HC: Clarion • PB: Yearling
THEMES: religion; survival; courage; work; education; medicine; history, medieval times

Matilda has lived a sheltered life. Raised by a priest, she has learned about right and wrong, the evils of joy and pleasure, Latin, and to pray ceaselessly. But when she is uprooted from the security of her daily rituals and delivered to Blood and Bone Alley, where she is expected to serve Red Peg the Bonesetter, Matilda finds she is alone in her belief that prayer and study are the only worthy pursuits. Here are fascinating accounts of the practice of medicine in medieval times as well as characters who will stick with you.

★ Mick Harte Was Here
FICTION

AUTHOR: Barbara Park
HC/PB: Knopf
THEMES: death; safety; bicycles; family; brothers; sisters; loss; humor

This story will make you cry. It will make you laugh. It is so real that you feel you know twelve-year-old Phoebe, who tells anecdotes about her quirky, fun-loving brother. There is a message here about the importance of wearing a bike helmet, but it never takes over the main theme of loss and its effect on all members of a family. Without sentimentality, Park deals with a difficult subject and turns it into a story to treasure.

Mississippi Bridge
FICTION

AUTHOR: Mildred D. Taylor • ILLUSTRATOR: Max Ginsburg
HC: Dial • PB: Puffin
THEMES: civil rights; African American; family; prejudice; U.S.A., the South; U.S. history, the Depression

In Mississippi in the 1930s, black people couldn't ride the bus if it meant there wouldn't be enough room for white people, even if they had purchased their tickets in advance. Taylor has melded bits of history into a moving story that illustrates the injustices of segregation.

Morning Girl
FICTION

AUTHOR: Michael Dorris
HC/PB: Hyperion
THEMES: Native American; U.S. history, pre-Columbus; siblings; Columbus; point of view; cultural diversity; prejudice; strong girls; coming-of-age; social studies

Warm, carefully chosen words take the reader into the lives of Morning Girl, a twelve-year-old Taino, and her younger brother, Star Boy, helping us to understand how and why they think and feel in the days before Columbus came to their world. The powerful ending packs a wallop and will leave the reader thinking long after the last page has been turned.

★ Nettie's Trip South
PICTURE BOOK

AUTHOR: Ann Turner • ILLUSTRATOR: Ronald Himler
PB: Aladdin
THEMES: slavery; prejudice; U.S. history, Civil War; U.S.A., the South; sadness; diaries; mail; writing; trains; comparisons; self-respect

Based on a real diary, this powerful moving story about slavery is told through a young Northern girl's letter to her friend. "Addie, I can't get this out of my thoughts: If we slipped into a black skin like a tight coat, everything would change." Don't be fooled by the picture-book format. Nettie's story will lead to difficult questions about a shameful time in our history. It's beautifully written, skillfully illustrated, and important.

Nobody Particular
PICTURE BOOK NONFICTION

AUTHOR/ILLUSTRATOR: Molly Bang
HC: Henry Holt
THEMES: women, independent; environment; community; comic-book style; determination; taking action

Strong visuals make this a compelling portrait of one woman's relentless quest to protect the environment. This is as bold a book as its subject, Diane Wilson, who waged a one-woman battle against the chemical polluters destroying the Texas Gulf ecosystem. Truly inspiring.

The Nose from Jupiter

FICTION

AUTHOR: Richard Scrimger
HC/PB: Tundra
THEMES: divorce; imagination; accidents; hospitals; memory

A novel about a kid with an alien in his nose that is fun to read and thought-provoking. You can choose to take the kid at his word or not, but Norbert the alien is a wisecracking presence that cannot be ignored.

Now Let Me Fly: The Story of a Slave Family

PICTURE BOOK

AUTHOR/ILLUSTRATOR: Dolores Johnson
PB: Aladdin
THEMES: U.S.A., the South; freedom; slavery; folklore; family; U.S. history, pre–Civil War; African American

A look at the experience of being a slave that pulls no punches in its depiction of the grueling agonies involved. Johnson's power as a writer shines through, and she does not give up her emotional intensity or devastating portrayal of the experience until it is over, and slavery is ended.

The Number Devil: A Mathematical Adventure

FICTION

AUTHOR: Hans Magnus Enzensberger
HC/PB: Henry Holt
THEMES: math; logic

A textbook in disguise, this fascinating volume embraces both math enthusiasts and the slumped-over, clock-watching math victims holding their breaths till the period is ended. It's not *Alice in Wonderland*, but it has that feel when Robert, who is no math wizard, has recurrent dreams of a number devil set on teaching him math concepts. This international bestseller adds fun and adventure to math and teaches the reader about logic in the process.

Number the Stars

FICTION

AUTHOR: Lois Lowry
HC: Houghton Mifflin • PB: Dell
THEMES: soldiers; history, World War II; prejudice; separation; escape; Jews; friendship; Denmark; hiding; courage

Ellen Rosen and Annemarie Johansen are best friends. But their friendship leads to danger when the Nazis come to Denmark. It's 1943 and Jews are being relocated. Pretending to be a member of their family, Ellen moves in with the Johansens. This gripping story of courage and friendship is difficult to put down until the last page is turned.

On My Honor FICTION
AUTHOR: Marion Dane Bauer
PB: Dell
THEMES: bicycles; drowning; friendship; death; conscience; responsibility; guilt; promises

Joel promises "On my honor" when his father asks him not to go anywhere except the park. But when Joel sets off with his friend Tony on their bicycles, he dares Tony to race him in a swim across the dangerous Vermillion River. Bauer's gripping novel about death, guilt, and peer pressure is also about love and overcoming impossible ordeals.

One World, Many Religions: The Ways We Worship NONFICTION
AUTHOR: Mary Pope Osborne • ILLUSTRATOR: Various
HC: Knopf
THEMES: religion; traditions; comparisons; rituals; faith; history, world; cultural diversity

Using more than fifty color photographs to illustrate the world's major religious faiths, Osborne describes the traditions, forms of worship, and major holidays of Judaism, Christianity, Islam, Hinduism, Buddhism, Confucianism, and Taoism. This highly accessible volume includes a glossary, map, timeline, and bibliography.

The Orphan Train Adventures FICTION
AUTHOR: Joan Lowery Nixon
HC: Bantam • PB: Dell
THEMES: individuality; orphans; family; history; foster homes; adoption; railroad; U.S. history, 19th century

Based on historical fact, this series follows the adventures of five brothers and sisters from the orphanage to foster homes in the nineteenth century. Affecting and dramatic, with characters you root for and villains you despise. Titles in the series include *A Family Apart, Caught in the Act, In the Face of Danger, A Place to Belong, Keeping Secrets, A Dangerous Promise,* and *Circle of Love.*

AUTHOR SPOTLIGHT ON
MARY POPE OSBORNE

Mary Pope Osborne can draw a crowd, including fans from six to sixteen. It's no wonder—she receives accolades for most everything she writes: picture books, early chapter books, middle-grade historical fiction, and collections of folklore.

To begin with, there is the *Magic Tree House* series: More than thirty titles (and growing), both fiction and nonfiction, which have enticed beginning readers to the pleasure of a good story while honing their reading skills. Here they travel through the times of the dinosaurs, knights, mummies, pirates, the Revolutionary War, the Titanic, the Ice Age, the Wild West, a few natural disasters—and that's just a partial list. Once they have graduated from *The Magic Tree House*, children can find plenty of insect intrigue in the *Spider Kane Mysteries*.

Magic Tree House lovers also may be hungry for longer, more compelling historical fiction, and Osborne has written several books in the *Dear America* and *My America* series (*My Secret War: The World War II Diary of Madeline Beck*; *Standing in the Light: The Captive Diary of Catharine Carey Logan*; and *My Brother's Keeper* and *After the Rain*, parts 1 and 2 of a young girl's Civil War diary), as well as a stand-alone novel, *Adaline Falling Star*, which deals with the life of the daughter of the legendary (but real) Kit Carson.

Nonfiction is also a strength of Osborne's, with several titles in *The Magic Tree House Nonfiction Companion* series going behind the scenes of earlier books to provide an in-depth look at the truth behind the stories. These are excellent books for beginning researchers. *One World, Many Religions: The Way We Worship* offers a look at the seven major religions of the world and the children who practice them.

Picture books are not neglected in her output, and *The Brave Little Seamstress*, *Rocking Horse Christmas*, *Moonhorse*, *New York's Bravest* (a retelling of the Tall Tale about Mose the Fireman, the greatest firefighter in the history of New York), and *Kate and the Beanstalk* (which turns the traditional giant tale on its ear by making the protagonist a young girl instead of the traditional boy, with surprising and satisfying results) are examples of her fine contributions to this genre. Osborne is, after all, one of the best folklorists and retellers around. Her collections *American Tall Tales*, *Favorite Greek Myths*, *Favorite Medieval Tales*, *Favorite Norse Myths*, and *Mermaid Tales from Around the World* are among our favorite places to go when we need a story from world tradition. And she has embarked on a campaign to bring the joys of Greek myths to middle grades with her chapter book series *Mary Pope Osborne's Tales from the Odyssey*.

We are grateful Mary Pope Osborne gets to enjoy the rewards of having a hit series yet has made the time to create other books in a variety of genres. Her remarkable output provides millions of children with an author they can count on.

Our Only May Amelia

FICTION

AUTHOR: Jennifer L. Holm

HC/PB: HarperCollins

THEMES: U.S.A., the Pacific Northwest; country life; brothers; strong girls; immigration; grandmothers; family; diaries

It is 1899 in Washington state and twelve-year-old May Amelia lives on the Nasel River with her parents and seven brothers. She helps out on the farm and is more interested in fishing in her overalls and chasing sheep than worrying about being a lady. Then her grandmother comes, and things begin to change. During the rough times and when times are good, May Amelia—down-to-earth, and spunky—is a character you will not soon forget.

May Amelia is not Holm's only delightful, adventurous character. In *Boston Jane*, Jane is a sixteen-year-old blossoming society lady living in Philadelphia who endures a difficult trip across the ocean to Shoalwater Bay in Washington Territory to marry her betrothed. There on the western frontier she trades her etiquette training for survival skills and discovers life isn't what she anticipated. The sequel is *Boston Jane Wilderness Days*. In all three of these engaging novels, Holm balances historical detail with riveting storytelling to create strong young women characters.

★ Out of the Dust

FICTION

AUTHOR: Karen Hesse

HC/PB: Scholastic

THEMES: Oklahoma; U.S. history, the Depression; U.S.A., the Dust Bowl; coming of age; strong girls; fathers and daughters; hardship; loss; music; courage; farms; poverty; death; poetry

The hardship and loss of a Dust Bowl family is brought to life so powerfully you can feel the caked mud on the floor and the blinding sting of dust in your eyes. But more than that, it is the aching heart of Billie Jo that fills the pages of this book as she mourns the loss of her mother and newborn brother; as she learns that she must forgive her father for his part in the accident that caused their death; as she searches for a way out of the dust and finally comes to accept the dust as part of who she is. This outstanding coming-of-age novel in verse is a flip side of *The Grapes of Wrath*, allowing us to see what happened to the families that stayed when so many were forced from their homes during one of the bleakest times in American history. Billie Jo's heart is strong, her courage inspiring, and her frailties are all too human. You will never forget her.

For another look at American history, this time in the 1920s, read *Witness*. Again writing in free verse, Hesse offers eleven distinct voices that tell the story of the Ku Klux Klan's infiltration into a small Vermont community.

Over Sea, Under Stone, Book 1 of The Dark Is Rising Sequence

FICTION-FANTASY

AUTHOR: Susan Cooper

PB: Aladdin

THEMES: fantasy; adventure; good vs. evil; England; Celtic mythology; folklore; Wales

This five-book series takes its inspiration from the great mythic history of England, weaving elements of Celtic mythology into an immensely satisfying journey into the nature of good and evil, light and dark. This is one of the great pieces of fantasy writing in the English language, and children who stay with it for the long, rewarding haul gain a basis of appreciation for Tolkien, Ursula LeGuin, and almost any adult writer of fantasy we can think of. Read them in order: follow this with *The Dark Is Rising*, then *Greenwitch*, *The Grey King* (winner of the Newbery Medal), and finally, *Silver on the Tree*.

★ The Phantom Tollbooth

FICTION-FANTASY

AUTHOR: Norton Juster • ILLUSTRATOR: Jules Feiffer

HC/PB: Random House

THEMES: humor; adventure; cleverness; diversity; cars; dogs; imagination; journeys; zany; triumph; wisdom; math; alphabet

"There was once a boy named Milo who didn't know what to do with himself—not just sometimes but always." But when a tollbooth appeared in his room, he drove through. On the other side he jumped to the island of Conclusions, met a ticking watchdog named Tock, and discovered that life wasn't boring after all. It's hard not to compare this to *Alice in Wonderland* and *The Wonderful Wizard of Oz*, where characters confront unforgettable personalities on a fantastic journey. Read it aloud and offer it as part of a permanent library.

This is a demanding book, full of clever language and allusions that can go over the heads of younger listeners. A certain amount of reading and listening experience is called for here, and I recommend it be used with children seven and up as a read-aloud. If you try this out as part of your family repertoire and it falls flat, stop. Put it away for a couple of years and bring it out again. Your children will amaze you with their ability to respond to it then. As far as reading this themselves, many adults remember it as one of their favorites from their childhood and try to give it to their own children. I don't like to be a stickler about ages, but in this case I feel strongly that there is no better way to say it: An eight-year-old can probably read this—an eleven-year-old will be more likely to love it.

★ Pink and Say

AUTHOR/ILLUSTRATOR: Patricia Polacco

HC: Philomel

THEMES: prejudice; soldiers; courage; U.S. history, the Civil War; death; friendship; storytelling; mothers and sons; fear

Don't be fooled by its picture-book format; this one is for the older child. It takes place in a time of war, deals with prejudice, and is a heartwrenching, true story. Teenager Say Curtis is wounded in a fierce battle during the Civil War. Pinkus Aylee, a young black soldier, finds him and carries him to his own home. There, Pink's mother nurtures the boys until she is killed. When they try to rejoin the troops, they are captured and sent to Andersonville Prison. Pink is hanged, but Say survives to pass the story on to his own children and grandchildren. Since he has no living descendants to remember him, Polacco's book stands as a testament to the life of Pinkus Aylee.

★ The Prydian Chronicles

AUTHOR: Lloyd Alexander

HC: Henry Holt • PB: Dell

THEMES: fantasy; adventure; journeys; courage; heroes; coming of age

As good as fantasy writing gets. In the course of five books (*The Book of Three, The Black Cauldron, The Castle of Llyr, Taran Wanderer,* and *The High King*) we hear of the adventures of Taran, the assistant Pig Keeper who wants to be a hero. Taking his cue from Welsh mythology but creating a broader canvas uniquely his own, Alexander fills his pages with enough wonderful adventure, thrills, laughter, and heartbreak for several lifetimes, but such is the nature of fantasy. We recommend that *The Prydain Chronicles* be introduced to young readers after *The Chronicles of Narnia* but before Tolkien, though whenever you begin this quintet you need to be prepared to stay with it for the long haul, as you will find yourself craving more as each book comes to an end.

Red Dirt Jessie

AUTHOR: Anna Myers

HC: Walker • PB: Puffin

THEMES: Oklahoma; U.S. history, the Depression; U.S.A., the Dust Bowl

Jessie is a young girl living in the Oklahoma Dust Bowl during the Depression. This story is so rich with the sense of time and place that the reader will forget she's not there. Myers shows her mastery of historical fiction writing for middle grades in her other books, including *Captain's Command, The Keeping Room*, and *Stolen by the Sea*.

Redwall

FICTION–FANTASY

AUTHOR: Brian Jacques • ILLUSTRATOR: Gary Chalk
HC: Philomel • PB: Berkley
THEMES: diversity; knights; fighting; magic; fantasy; weapons; adventure

While waiting for the next *Redwall* installment, fans can look for adventure in Jacques's *Castaways of the Flying Dutchman* and the sequel, *Angel's Command*, tales of mystery and seafaring adventure set among buccaneers.

This enormously popular series shows no signs of waning and can be recommended confidently for any age child who is interested in a long and involved fantasy. Imagine medieval England, with all its pageantry, chivalry, sorcery, and swordplay. Now imagine that all the characters are small, furry animals. With a cast that includes mice, ferrets, rats, and hedgehogs, this is a look at class and ethnicity, rodent-style. Great, absorbing adventure, and when kids get started on one volume, they want to keep going, so have several on hand to stay ahead of the voracious Redwall reader your child will surely become.

Regarding the Fountain: A Tale, in Letters, of Liars and Leaks

FICTION

AUTHOR: Kate Klise • ILLUSTRATOR: M. Sarah Klise
PB: Avon
THEMES: creativity; water; fountains; mystery; problem solving; letters; school; humor

Make sure to check out other books by the Klise sisters, *Trial by Journal* and *Letters from Camp*.

Something smells fishy at the town's local water company and swimming pool. When the Dry Creek Middle School principal asks artist Florence Waters to design a new drinking fountain, a villainous scheme begins to surface. Told through letters, memos, newspaper clippings, faxes, telegrams, school announcements, and lively drawings, this punny tale takes a turn when Ms. Waters solicits input from the fifth-graders and ultimately solves a muddy mystery. The fun and accessible style ensures that even reluctant readers will take on this tale.

Roll of Thunder, Hear My Cry

FICTION

AUTHOR: Mildred Taylor
HC: Dial • PB: Puffin
THEMES: courage; family; pride; U.S. history, the Depression; independence; strong girls; gifted children; prejudice; U.S.A., the South

It's an uphill battle for Cassie and her family, whose love for their land and strong family ties strengthen them against rural Southern racism during the Depression. In her author's note, Taylor describes how her history was passed from generation to generation, "a history of great-grandparents and of slavery and of the days following slavery; of those who lived still not free, yet who would not let their spirits be enslaved. From my father the storyteller I learned to respect the past, to respect my own heritage and myself." And like her father, Taylor has passed a story on to us, allowing a glimpse into the time of night riders, burnings, and public humiliation, when personal respect and family strength provided the power for survival. For further stories in the life of this remarkable family, see *Let the Circle Be Unbroken, The Land,* and *The Well.*

Sahara Special   FICTION

AUTHOR: Esme Raji Codell

HC: Hyperion

THEMES: school; teachers; fitting in; courage; humor; bad days; fear; abandonment

Fifth-grader Sahara Jones is taken out of special ed to face a regular class again. Why, she wonders, should she bother working since no one at school seems to understand her? Then enters new teacher Miss Pointy, with her wild copper-colored hair held back with sparkling dragonfly barrettes, wearing purple (eggplant) lipstick and lime eye shadow. Unforgettable characters and laugh-out-loud dialogue form this story about talented, troubled Sahara and her inspiring teacher.

 Sure, I found part of this story funny, but there were times when it was so moving, I cried out loud.

 I am certain many teachers will like this and read it to their classes, but I thought the writing was a little too enamored of the teacher and not insightful enough about the kid to be a real success with young readers.

 We'll see Walter, we'll see . . .

Sammy Keyes and the Sisters of Mercy

FICTION

AUTHOR: Wendelin Van Draanen
HC/PB: Knopf
THEMES: mystery, girls, strong; humor

The best girl sleuth since Nancy Drew and the funniest ever! Sammy is as levelheaded a seventh-grader as you will ever find; she has to be, what with the chaos that surrounds her. Living illegally in her grandmother's seniors-only community (her mother is off "finding herself" in Hollywood), Sammy has a knack for balancing the demands of her life (schoolwork, friends, not getting caught living with her grandmother). It seems only natural that she solves mysteries as well. Clever writing and oddball characters are the hallmarks of this series, and once kids read one, they will want them all.

Sarah, Plain and Tall

FICTION

AUTHOR: Patricia MacLachlan
HC/PB: HarperCollins
THEMES: family; memories; separation; mail; mothers; siblings; comparisons;
    change; fathers; love; grief; anticipation; U.S.A., the Prairie;
    stepparents; single parents; U.S. history, 19th century

Only sixty-four pages, this novel packs a wallop! Caleb was too young when his mother died to remember her, but his sister Anna helps. Now their father has sent for a mail-order bride and they wonder what life will be like when she arrives. Through letters the children first meet Sarah, and when she comes from far off by the sea they are not disappointed. This tender story shows the hardships of prairie life and the value of a strong-hearted woman. MacLachlan continues the story in *Skylark* and *Caleb's Story*.

Save Queen of Sheba

FICTION

AUTHOR: Louise Moeri
PB: Puffin
THEMES: U.S. history, Westward movement; survival; courage; Oregon;
    pioneers; Native American; brothers; sisters; adventure

"A huge greenish black fly was crawling slowly over his hand. The fly was so close to his eyes, for his hand lay tossed up on the dirt just a few inches from his face, that King David could see every leg as it moved, the iridescent wings flick, the big bulbous eyes. He wondered why he did not move his hand and brush the fly away . . ." An attack on their wagon train has killed everyone except David and his younger sister. Now they must venture ahead to find their parents on their own, and David is hurt. Here's a breath-catching story that will get the attention of adventure seekers.

 There are times when "grabbers" like this one come in handy. When I've been introduced as a storyteller in a seventh-grade English class and face a row of passive, slumped figures, legs stretched forward, arms folded, daring me to read aloud, I read the first chapter and close the book. The slumpers change position, and a few will make their way to the library to finish what I've started.

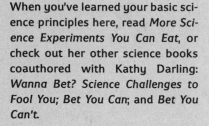 And remember, the library is free!

Science Experiments You Can Eat   NONFICTION

AUTHOR: Vicki Cobb • ILLUSTRATOR: David Cain
PB: HarperCollins
THEMES: science; science experiments; food; recipes

Cobb is a believer that learning comes from doing. These books are the proof in the pudding, er, the popsicle. Make one and learn about freezing temperatures. What has to happen for something to crystallize? Mix up some rock candy and find out.

> When you've learned your basic science principles here, read *More Science Experiments You Can Eat*, or check out her other science books coauthored with Kathy Darling: *Wanna Bet? Science Challenges to Fool You; Bet You Can; and Bet You Can't.*

Search for the Shadowman   FICTION–MYSTERY

AUTHOR: Joan Lowery Nixon
HC: Delacorte • PB: Dell
THEMES: Texas; genealogy; mystery; internet; U.S. history; secrets; family history; computers

Master of the young adult mystery, Nixon turns here to middle-grade readers and delivers a thrilling novel about family secrets and the history of Texas. Andy rights a generations-old wrong through his intrepid detective work into the history of his family. If family-tree research is fascinating your kids, they will love this book.

Searching for Candlestick Park   FICTION

AUTHOR: Peg Kehret
PB: Puffin
THEMES: divorce; fathers and sons; cats; pets; journeys; running away

 Although I found the ending contrived, this is a real page-turner about a kid's quest for his father when things in his life go wrong. My son, Anthony, devoured it in the midst of his parents' divorce and proclaimed it to be "really good, Dad. You need to read it." Read it I did, and I found the story to be strong, the characters and situations believable (except for that ending), and this portrait of a boy and his cat, Foxey, on the road in search of a missing father to be one I recommend to reluctant readers all the time.

The Secret of Sabrina Fludde

FICTION

AUTHOR: Pauline Fisk
HC: Bloomsbury
THEMES: fantasy; mystery; identity; memory

"When the day began the body was there. The night mist parted and it floated slowly on the silent river like a tree snapped at the root . . ." So begins this tale of Abren, a thin, disheveled girl looking for her identity. This first installment of a planned trilogy about the people of Pengwern, a Welsh river town with an ancient past, will keep readers glued to their chairs.

Seedfolks

FICTION

AUTHOR: Paul Fleischman
HC/PB: HarperCollins
THEMES: cultural diversity; gardening; community; city life; taking action;
    immigration; point of view; prejudice; gardens

There have been stories before about people pulled together for the purpose of good. But this one in all its simplicity has staying power. A young child starts a community garden in an empty lot behind a wasted refrigerator. Threatened by suspicion and fertilized with hope, it reminds us of the need for folks to work, to create beauty, and to be a part of a community.

 Many of Fleischman's books perform outstandingly well as reader's theater or radio plays. I have had the pleasure of directing *Seedfolks* and another book, *Seek*, for the radio with wonderful results. I'd recommend considering these titles, *Bull Run*, or *Mind's Eye*, for theater groups and schools looking for challenging, absorbing pieces to produce.

Sees Behind Trees

FICTION

AUTHOR: Michael Dorris
HC/PB: Hyperion
THEMES: Native American; blindness; coming of age

So often when we learn that someone has limited eyesight we think about what they can't do. This compelling novel concentrates instead on how a young Native American boy develops other senses, earning respect from his people.

AUTHOR SPOTLIGHT ON
PAUL FLEISCHMAN

When Paul Fleischman creates a new book, we put it aside to savor. We know that each new journey he invites readers on—whether fiction, nonfiction, picture book or poem—offers a rare insight into the ways rhythm, voice, and music connect the reader to the tale and ourselves to each other. His innovative use of form causes us to look at books in a different light.

The 1989 Newbery Medal–winning *Joyful Noise: Poems for Two Voices* was written to be spoken aloud in pairs, sometimes alternating, sometimes simultaneous. These poems offer the joy of reading aloud in harmony with another person and allow listeners to share that pleasure. While *Joyful Noise* is a poetic guide to the insect world, its companion, *I Am Phoenix: Poems for Two Voices*, celebrates the sound and the essence of birds. Once you've read aloud in twos, try *Big Talk: Poems for Four Voices*. Here Fleischman uses color to help four readers know when it's their turn to read.

We tried this in the store with teachers and staff, and were happily entertained—thought we could go on the road with a little practice.

Fleischman's approach to history gives readers something to think about. *Dateline Troy* contrasts his retelling of the Trojan War with contemporary news headlines and stories, showing readers current events that reflect the past.

The son of a great writer (Newbery winner Sid Fleischman), Paul writes novels that reflect an understanding of family and a felicity that makes them—whether happy or sad—a joy to read. In *The Borning Room* the reader is shown seventy-seven years of family life from the point of view of one room in an Ohio farmhouse. In *Graven Images* Fleischman takes three unconnected stories and subtly unites them through the common theme of unusual objects. Another historical novel, *Saturnalia*, features a story within a story about the performance of ancient Roman rites during colonial times. The possibilities for performance present themselves in much of Fleischman's later work. In *Bull Run* characters from the North and South who were affected by one of the most famous Civil War battles tell their stories in short first-person accounts that work beautifully as reader's theater. In *Seedfolks* thirteen characters of widely diverse backgrounds tell the story of the creation of a community garden that transforms a neighborhood. *Lost! A Story in String* is a picture-book story within a story. Grandmother tells her granddaughter a tale as she forms pictures out of string. Included are diagrams that allow readers to re-create the tale with string and instructions on performing. Fleischman's own string troupe includes *Lost!* as part of its regular entertainment.

Many of Fleischman's earlier picture books are out of print as of this writing, though his nature story, *Animal Hedge*, has been reissued with stunning illustrations by Bagram Ibatoulline. We'd also like to see a return of *Rondo in C* and *Shadow Play*, as well as Fleischman's first book, *The Birthday Tree*. Our favorite of his picture books remains *Weslandia*, a story of a remarkable but lonely boy who creates his own civilization.

One of our favorite things is to introduce Fleischman to someone who has not read him. It makes us look good.

Seven Spiders Spinning

FICTION

AUTHOR: Gregory Maguire • ILLUSTRATOR: Dirk Zimmer
HC: Clarion • PB: HarperCollins
THEMES: school; spiders; teachers; Halloween; humor;
    spooky stories

> Gleefully funny sequels follow: *Six Haunted Hairdos*, *Five Alien Elves*, *Four Stupid Cupids*, and *Three Rotten Eggs*.

A very funny look at the trouble seven Siberian snow spiders cause in a little town. Each has fallen in love with a different girl in Miss Earth's class, and Maguire gleefully kills off the spiders one by one as each tries to bite its beloved, all during preparation for the Halloween Pageant of Horrors. A fast pace and a classroom full of distinctly interesting children make this enjoyable even for those who don't like spiders.

Shiloh

FICTION

AUTHOR: Phyllis Reynolds Naylor
HC: Atheneum • PB: Aladdin
THEMES: dogs; pets; farms; family; abuse; humor; villains

When Marty finds Shiloh, a dog who has been badly mistreated by his owner, he can't keep him. After all, he belongs to someone else. And when Shiloh finds his way back to Marty, Marty makes a decision that could get him into a lot of trouble. *Shiloh* will have readers glued to the pages cheering, booing, laughing, crying, and wishing for a kinder, gentler world. But this is no dreary tale: We assure you there will be smiles at the turn of the last page. There are two sequels: *Shiloh Season* and *Saving Shiloh*.

Shoebag

FICTION

AUTHOR: Mary James
PB: Scholastic
THEMES: fantasy; humor; imagination; insects; school; friendship; adventure

Cockroaches are generally named for their places of birth, so Shoebag is not really unusual considering he started out as a cockroach. His mother's name is Drainboard and his father is Under The Toaster. (And speaking of names, Mary James is really writer M. E. Kerr, better known for her literary novels.) Shoebag was a happy young cockroach until one morning he woke to find he had become a human boy. What a ghastly thought. Humans could be so dirty. After all, cockroaches have to move around in human muck all the time. Original and fun, this story works read aloud or quietly alone, perhaps in the kitchen near the drainboard.

Short and Shivery

AUTHOR: Robert San Souci • ILLUSTRATOR: Katherine Coville
HC/PB: Doubleday
THEMES: horror; folklore; storytelling; diversity

FOLKLORE COLLECTION

A brilliant mix of scary stories, gathered from around the world, guaranteed to raise the hair on the back of your neck. Vivid retellings of more than thirty tales old and new make this a folklore resource as well as a great book to have at a campfire. Be sure to check out the sequels, *More Short & Shivery*, and *Even More Short & Shivery*.

The Signers: The 56 Stories Behind the Declaration of Independence

NONFICTION

AUTHOR: Dennis Brindell Fradin • ILLUSTRATOR: Michael McCurdy
HC: Walker
THEMES: United States; history; American Revolution; Declaration of Independence

Quick! Name the signers of the Declaration. Chances are you came up with Thomas Jefferson, Benjamin Franklin, and John Hancock. Good. Now how about the other fifty-three? Here are minibiographies of each of the members of the Second Continental Congress as well as snapshots of the colonies they represented. Whether telling the story of Delaware's Cesar Rodney who, despite cancer, rode eighty miles through the night to cast his vote for American independence, or John Adams who, with his brother Samuel, led the Massachusetts delegation in their fight for liberty, each signer is given his due. McCurdy's scratchboard illustrations lend just the right air of old-fashioned reverence for our founding fathers.

A Single Shard

FICTION

AUTHOR: Linda Sue Park
HC: Clarion • PB: Yearling
THEMES: Korea; orphans; homelessness; friendship; determination; pottery; jobs; artists

For a look at a different time period in Korean history, read Park's *When My Name Was Keoko*.

Tree-ear is a thirteen-year-old orphan living under a bridge in twelfth-century Korea. His village, Ch'ul'po, is known for its fine pottery, and Tree-ear wants more than anything to become a potter like the master, Min. Hunger, fear, shame, gratitude, resilience, and hard work all play a part in this Newbery Medal–winning tale of a boy who follows his heart.

I couldn't stop thinking about this story. First of all, someone putting the mastering of a skill before anything else has become a rare thing in our society. Second, I just had to get my hands on a celadon vase to see its intricate design and to touch it.

Skellig

FICTION

AUTHOR: David Almond
HC: Delacorte Press • PB: Dell
THEMES: strangers; moving; illness; angels; mystery; death; family; friendship; love; hope; new baby

Worried about his baby sister's illness (which occupies almost all of his parents' attention), and frustrated by the disorder of moving into an old house, Michael ventures into the crumbling garage and finds a mysterious stranger in the shadows beneath the spider webs. "I thought he was dead. He was sitting with his legs stretched out and his head tipped back against the wall. He was covered with dust and webs like everything else and his face was thin and pale. Dead bluebottles were scattered on his hair and shoulders. I shined the flashlight on his white face and his black suit." Is he a man, a bird, an angel? A combination of all three? He speaks in riddles, favors Chinese food and beer, and seems otherworldly. What follows is an ethereal, mystical meditation on life, death, family, and friendship. No, it isn't for everyone, but for those who prefer novels that you can chew on and that open up a reader to life's bigger questions, this will be a book to savor. Almond's writing will take your breath away. His story will haunt you long after the last page has been turned.

Stepping on the Cracks

FICTION

AUTHOR: Mary Downing Hahn
HC: Clarion • PB: Avon
THEMES: U.S. history, World War II; bullies; community; friendship; courage; secrets; conscience

A superb historical novel set during World War II. In addition to her outstanding portrayal of childhood during wartime, Hahn offers a thought-provoking tale about standing up for what you believe in, even when it isn't popular. This is our favorite of Hahn's books, and there are two sequels (*Following My Own Footsteps* and *As Ever, Gordy*), though we are also fond of her ghost stories (*A Time for Andrew, A Doll in the Garden,* and *Wait Till Helen Comes*), her historical fiction (*Promises to the Dead*), as well as her rollicking adventure novel, *The Dead Man in Indian Creek*.

AUTHOR SPOTLIGHT ON
DANIEL PINKWATER

Widely acclaimed for bringing attention to children's books through his riotous appearances on National Public Radio's *Weekend Edition*, Daniel Pinkwater is also rightly celebrated as creator of some of the best books published for children.

Possessed of an idiosyncratic sense of humor, Pinkwater writes a wide variety of books, from picture books to science fiction, and for beginning readers all the way up to high schoolers. He writes his books the way he sees 'em—you will either get his sense of humor or you won't—and his novels are read mostly by kids who are interested in fantasy or science fiction, as well as anyone who likes stories with a distinct style.

He takes his time with the narrative in his longer works, and we can imagine that many who are not tuned into his quirky eye for detail can get weary of his style. He can also get just a little too clever, often at the expense of anything happening in the story. However, we have found that the secret is to not resist—simply succumb and go along for the ride.

Many of his best novels have been collected into two volumes. The volume *4 Fantastic Novels* contains *Borgel; Yobgorgle: Mystery Monster of Lake Ontario; The Worms of Kukumlima;* and *The Snarkout Boys and the Baconburg Horror*. The volume *5 Novels* contains *Alan Mendelsohn, the Boy from Mars; Slaves of Spiegel; The Last Guru; Young Adult Novel;* and *The Snarkout Boys and the Avocado of Death*. Though we have to be in the right frame of mind for him, when we are, these compilations are treasures. It is especially wonderful to have the antics of the Snarkout Boys available once again.

Many feel that Pinkwater's masterpiece is *Lizard Music*, and it is a great book to introduce readers to his quirky style. This is the book that will either turn you into a fan or leave you cold. When Victor's parents go on vacation, leaving him in the care of his older sister, she quickly announces that she is going on a trip and leaves him home alone. Victor responds with all the glee that one would expect from an eleven-year-old—Yippee! He can stay up late and watch his favorite TV shows, order pizza (*with* anchovies for a change) and generally lead the sort of life all kids dream of. But wait! What is the weird, late-night TV program with the all-lizard band playing strange music? What is the lizards' connection to the increasing number of bizzare goings-on around town? And what does the mysterious Chicken Man have to do with it all? The answers are all here, delivered in quintessential Pinkwater style.

When he writes in shorter format, Pinkwater's deadpan style is charming and his terse dialogues deliver a lot of humor in few words. One of his funniest books is *Author's Day*, a riotous account of an author's visit to a school that goes all wrong. We suspect that Pinkwater is writing from experience here. He has collaborated with his wife, Jill, on a series of books about some lively polar bears (*Young Larry; At the Hotel Larry; Ice Cream Larry;* and *Irving and Muktuk: Two Bad Bears*). Many of his other picture books (which he often illustrates himself) are fun for all ages: *Guys From Space; The Big Orange Splot;* and *Jolly Roger*.

Pinkwater has distinguished himself as a terrific writer of chapter books for readers just moving into longer books. *The Muffin Fiend, Fat Camp Commandos, The Hoboken Chicken Emergency, Fat Men From Space*; and an early reader series, The Werewolf Club are all perfect for kids who like things a little different.

Whether on the radio or in print, Daniel Pinkwater has made a career of never talking down to kids. We are all the richer for his quirky genius, as well as his commitment to children.

The Storyteller's Beads

FICTION

AUTHOR: Jane Kurtz
HC: Gulliver
THEMES: friendship; Africa; faith; religion; hardship; journeys; Jews

Two girls from divergent cultures must come to depend on each other as they flee the political upheaval of their Ethiopian homeland. This is a transcendent novel, as beautiful a book about the meaning of faith and the healing power of friendship as one could hope for.

★ Stranded at Plimoth Plantation, 1626

NONFICTION

AUTHOR/ILLUSTRATOR: Gary Bowen
HC/PB: HarperCollins
THEMES: U.S. history, colonial America; color; Native American; survival;
pilgrims; artists; art; rituals; courage; traditions; cultural diversity;
community; orphans; new experiences; diaries

Christopher Sears is a thirteen-year-old orphan stranded at Plimoth Plantation while he waits for transportation to Jamestown. Every day he finds new things to describe in his journal: visits with Indians, eating pumpkins and lobsters for the first time, attending a birth or a funeral. He passes his time making woodcuts and printing them with natural dyes. With each turn of the page, the reader watches Christopher's artistic skill evolve from simple black-and-white woodcuts to detailed multicolored prints. We tend to stroke our hands across the cover of this book—partly because it's beautiful, and because the art and historical fiction work in perfect harmony to invite the reader in for a close-up of life in another time.

Swan Song

AUTHOR: J. Patrick Lewis • ILLUSTRATOR: Christopher Wormell
HC: Creative Editions
THEMES: animals; poetry; extinction

Remember Miss Waldron's Red Colobus, the elephant bird, the quagga, the laughing owl, or the Hawaiian O-O? In this skillfully crafted poetic tribute to these and fifteen other extinct animals you'll find an offering of hope that these and other "lost" animals will be remembered. Wormell's wood engravings are breathtaking!

Talkin' About Bessie: The Story of Aviator Elizabeth Coleman

PICTURE BOOK

AUTHOR: Nikki Grimes • ILLUSTRATOR: E. B. Lewis
HC: Orchard
THEMES: African American; strong women; pioneers; flying; airplanes;
   determination;

Bessie Coleman—the first African American woman aviator—comes to life in a series of poems written from the point of view of the people who knew her. Each poem and its accompanying painting create a rich portrait of this amazing woman. Grimes saves the best voice for last: Bessie's, which tells us, "You have never lived till you have flown!"

There's a Boy in the Girls' Bathroom

FICTION

AUTHOR: Louis Sachar
HC/PB: Knopf
THEMES: school; fitting in; bullies; self-respect; friendship; humor; lying

Bradley Chalkers doesn't fit in with the other kids in his fifth-grade class. For one thing, he's the oldest. He's also a liar and an attention-seeking bully. Fourth- through eighth-graders will recognize Bradley; kids like him have been in their classrooms. Funny and sometimes poignant, Sachar's work shows that friendship and understanding go a long way to help kids like Bradley Chalkers triumph over their own insecurities.

The Thief Lord

FICTION

AUTHOR: Cornelia Funke
HC: Scholastic
THEMES: Italy; theft; mystery; brothers and sisters; orphans; homelessness;
   escape; magic; greed; courage

This isn't just another tale about orphan siblings running away from cruel relatives to find shelter and adventure in a faraway place as cohorts to the most ingenious young thief this side of the Artful Dodger. Only a truly magical city could serve as the proper setting for Funke's tale, a city with enough mystery and intrigue of its own that the author has but to evoke it well and her work is half done. Venice is the real star, and readers of this mystery/fantasy/adventure will come to know the city well—its alleys, canals, and crumbling rooftops—by the end. They'll also discover the real identity of the Thief Lord and the story behind his Robin Hoodesque thievery. Funke is one of Germany's most popular children's authors, and this book serves as an excellent introduction to American readers.

Time Stops for No Mouse: A Hermux Tantamoq Adventure   FICTION
AUTHOR: Michael Hoeye
HC: Putnam
THEMES: mice; animals; mystery; time; friends; ladybugs; adventure

Hermux Tantamoq is a watchmaker. If you think his name is unusual, try Ms. Linka Perflinger, Tucka Mertslin, and Hiril Mennus MD. These are just a few of the characters in this story about a dashing adventurer who makes her way into the shop of an ordinary hardworking mouse to drop off a broken watch, and then disappears. Tantamoq finds himself in the midst of a mystery only he can solve. When you've finished this mouse tale, turn directly to the sequel, *The Sands of Time,* where Tantamoq teams up with artist friend Mirrin Stentrill and chipmunk historian Birch Tentintrotter to solve the mystery of an ancient cat kingdom.

 These tales are great fun to read aloud, but in case you don't have time, or are heading for a lengthy car trip, I recommend you get the unabridged audio versions narrated by Campbell Scott.

To Fly: The Story of the Wright Brothers   PICTURE BOOK BIOGRAPHY
AUTHOR: Wendie Old • ILLUSTRATOR: Robert Andrew Parker
HC: Clarion
THEMES: airplanes; flight; brothers; trailblazers; U.S. history

Well-researched and full of anecdotes and fascinating facts, this look at two intrepid Americans is a terrific balance of writing and art. Just right for readers who may not be interested a longer book.

The True Confessions of Charlotte Doyle

FICTION

AUTHOR: Avi

HC: Orchard • PB: Avon

THEMES: history, the 19th century, boats; sea; journeys; adventure; courage; strong girls; survival

Beginning with "An Important Warning," the story of Charlotte Doyle captures its reader from the start. "Not every thirteen-year-old girl is accused of murder, brought to trial, and found guilty. But I was just such a girl, and my story is worth relating even if it did happen years ago. Be warned, however . . . if strong ideas and action offend you, read no more." The terrible captain and mutinous crew were on the *Seahawk*, crossing the Atlantic Ocean in 1832. And there was one passenger, Charlotte Doyle. This is her riveting story.

★ Tuck Everlasting

FICTION

AUTHOR: Natalie Babbitt

HC/PB: Farrar, Straus & Giroux

THEMES: family; aging; change; magic; choices; taking action; kidnapping

The possibility of eternal life has been pondered since the beginning of time. Who wouldn't consider it a blessing? When ten-year-old Winnie Foster discovers the spring water that could keep her from growing old, the Tuck family, which understands the harm that one taste could bring, kidnaps her. This compelling novel, which has readers thinking about their own place in time, continues to be as popular now as it was when first published over twenty years ago.

Under the Blood Red Sun

FICTION

AUTHOR: Graham Salisbury

HC: Delacorte • PB: Dell

THEMES: friendship; prejudice; suspicion; Hawaii; U.S. history, World War II; cultural diversity; community; family; Japanese culture

Thirteen-year-old Tomizu and his best friend, Billy Davis, learn about the hardships brought on by prejudice and suspicion when the bombing of Pearl Harbor shakes up their Hawaiian homes.

★ The View from Saturday

FICTION

AUTHOR: E. L. Konigsburg

HC: Atheneum • PB: Aladdin

THEMES: teachers; students; friendship; diversity; school; tea parties; contests; handicaps; competition; gifted child; fitting in; rituals; cultural diversity; choices; community

Every once in a while we come across a novel that has so much texture woven within every sentence, we reread pages. This is one. A gifted teacher in a wheelchair, four students—bright, diverse, and best friends—all work toward the same goal, the Academic Bowl. As good a portrait of a group of misfits forming their own community as any in fiction.

The View from the Cherry Tree

FICTION-MYSTERY

AUTHOR: Willo Davis Roberts

PB: Aladdin

THEMES: mystery; murder; family; communication

> Two other orphans appear in Creech's *Ruby Holler*. Here too you'll find eccentric characters well worth knowing in an almost magical place.

From his special perch on the cherry tree, Rob sees his neighbor murdered. And when he tells what he saw, no one pays attention. That is, no one but the murderer. Suspense will keep the pages turning.

Walk Two Moons

FICTION

AUTHOR: Sharon Creech

HC/PB: HarperCollins

THEMES: comparisons; journeys; mothers and daughters; fathers and daughters; grandparents; Native American; loss; grief; death; mystery

> "Sometimes I am asked why I don't write books that reflect real-life violence in grittier settings. The answer to that is because that is not the world I want to live in, nor is it the world I want to offer children. There are beautiful places and beautiful people in this world, plenty of them, and I like to celebrate those places and those people."
> —*Newbery Medalist Sharon Creech, author of* Walk Two Moons

In chapters that shift back and forth through time, Salamanca Hiddle tells the story of the loss of her mother and how she learned the value of the Native American saying "Don't judge a man until you've walked two moons in his moccasins." Creech takes her time with the revelations, and there are a lot of them by the end, so the reader spends much of the time waiting for the answers to many of the book's mysteries, but the characters are so engaging that the contrivances of the plot hardly matter. Sal's wisdom is hard-earned and she makes an unforgettable heroine.

★ The Watsons Go to Birmingham, 1963

FICTION
AUTHOR: Christopher Paul Curtis
HC: Delacorte • PB: Dell
THEMES: prejudice; violence; family; African American; U.S. history, the 60's; Civil Rights; humor; friendship, U.S.A., the South

It made us laugh out loud and then it made us cry. Curtis's exceptional novel tells of how the struggle for civil rights affects one family, all seen through the eyes of ten-year-old Kenny, the middle child in a family known as "The Weird Watsons." Rich with character and detail of life in both the North and South during the early sixties, this is as good a first novel as we have read.

The Weighty Word Book   SHORT STORY COLLECTION

AUTHORS: Paul M. Levitt, Douglas A. Burger, and Elissa S. Guralnick • ILLUSTRATOR: Janet Stevens
HC: Court Wayne Press
THEMES: words; language; humor; puns; vocabulary; imagination; alphabet

If you mix up word meanings, this is the book for you. If you like stretching your vocabulary, making up stories, or booing at a bad pun, read this. The authors have come up with twenty-seven stories representing challenging words—from Abasement to Zealot—each ending in a word-defining pun.

Well Wished   FICTION-FANTASY

AUTHOR: Franny Billingsley
HC: Atheneum • PB: Aladdin
THEMES: magic; wishes; wisdom; adventure; friendship; love; wells; fantasy; strong girls

With wishes come responsibilities. With magic there seems always to be a catch. And there are unforeseen consequences to greedy, hasty children who wish without thinking. Nuria knows this. And yet . . . Well, surely you know what happens next. Writers have been telling us this story since the dawn of time. To the select club of Nesbit and Eager comes Franny Billingsley with her remarkable, thoughtful fantasy. Weaving elements of timeless story-telling tradition with insights fresh and bold, she has constructed an adventure that will enchant readers who will both long and fear to be in Nuria's place.

★ The Westing Game   FICTION

AUTHOR: Ellen Raskin
HC: Dutton • PB: Puffin
THEMES: mystery; detectives; contests; puzzles; wordplay

Sam Westing left a will. Now his heirs must follow clues to find his murderer. The problem is, only two people have all the clues, and you (if you choose to read this puzzle mystery) will be one of them. We don't recommend that you read this while the TV is on; Raskin's demanding game will require all your attention.

What Hearts   FICTION

AUTHOR: Bruce Brooks
HC/PB: HarperCollins
THEMES: loneliness; gifted children; stepparents; mothers and sons;
 depression; baseball; love; bullies; divorce

In four related short stories, Brooks shows us the development of young Asa from the crushed expectations and disappointment of his parents' divorce to his learning to accept the power of love. Along the way, he copes with his hard-to-like stepfather, his prone-to-depression mother, and the fact that he is often too smart for the world around him. Full of insight, this is a novel about the difference between knowledge and understanding from one of our favorite writers.

Where the Red Fern Grows   FICTION

AUTHOR: Wilson Rawls
HC: Doubleday • PB: Dell
THEMES: friendship; loss; death; pets; faith; dogs; determination; Oklahoma;
 country life; family; hunting

We defy you to read this beloved classic without crying. The story of Billy and his faithful hunting dogs, Old Dan and Little Ann, has moved legions of ten-, eleven-, and twelve-year-olds to tears, not to mention their parents and teachers. A rich sense of place and time—the Ozarks during the Depression—and the loving depiction of Bill's family make this a book to treasure.

Who Said That? Famous Americans Speak

PICTURE BOOK NONFICTION

AUTHOR: Robert Burleigh • ILLUSTRATOR: David Catrow

HC: Henry Holt

THEMES: biography; quotations; trivia; U.S. history

Young trivia seekers and Americana buffs, this is for you. Famous sayings by inventors, politicians, entertainers, and others—each accompanied by a brief biography, remind us that Americans are a diverse lot.

> Coville's adaptations of *Macbeth, The Tempest, Twelfth Night, Hamlet,* and *A Midsummer Night's Dream* are worthy companions to this book.

William Shakespeare's Romeo and Juliet

FICTION

AUTHOR: Bruce Coville • ILLUSTRATOR: Dennis Nolan

HC: Dial

THEMES: Shakespeare; romance; family; classics; Italy; love

Making Shakespeare's complex and moody plays accessible to younger readers is no small feat, and writer Coville and pulls it off beautifully in this and a number of companion books. This is a perfect introduction to the Bard's work for fourth grade and up.

> "Of all the things kids ask for in today's world, the sweetest request has got to be, 'Will you read me a story?' It says, 'Will you hold me?' 'Will you speak to me?' and 'Will you show me how the world works?'—all at the same time."
> —*Tom Bodett, author of* Williwaw!

Williwaw!

FICTION

AUTHOR: Tom Bodett

PB: Random House

THEMES: brothers and sisters; the sea; storms; fathers; adventure

September, thirteen, and her twelve-year-old brother, Ivan, are often alone. Their father is a fisherman and must leave them for long stretches of time. The two manage well in their isolated Alaska, cabin, until one day—against their father's wishes—they decide to take their boat fourteen miles to town. Here their adventure begins. You'll like these characters and will learn a thing or two about boats—and storms.

The Witches

FICTION-FANTASY

AUTHOR: Roald Dahl • ILLUSTRATOR: Quentin Blake

HC: Farrar, Straus & Giroux • PB: Puffin

THEMES: witches; grandmothers; adventure; humor; taking action; good vs. evil; disguises

When it comes to children, "Squish them and squiggle them and make them disappear" is the motto of all witches. And how does one recognize a witch? Don't count on black and dresses and broomsticks; those are from fairy tales, and this is no fairy tale. Dahl offers careful descriptions of these despicable creatures disguised as ladies. Young readers need not fear, for a boy with the help of his cigar-smoking grandmother saves the day. Laugh, imagine, marvel, and enjoy as Dahl creates another journey of characters—funny, disgusting, and perfect for a child with a soaring imagination.

Wizards: An Amazing Journey through the Last Great Age of Magic
NONFICTION

AUTHOR: Candace Savage
HC: Greystone Books
THEMES: math; science; magic; wizards; witches; Sir Isaac Newton; medicine

Readers who lose themselves in tales of fantasy will find this history of wizards fascinating. Savage begins her book with Isaac Newton who ". . . began his training as a wizard when he was twelve years old." Like Harry Potter, he lost his parents at an early age and was forced to live with relatives he detested. Chapter titles under the table of contents—*The Boy Wizard; The Philosopher's Stone; Divination; The Dark Arts*—will also have a familiar ring to Harry Potter fans.

The Wreckers
FICTION

AUTHOR: Iain Lawrence
PB: Yearling
THEMES: sea; folklore; storms; theft; England; ghosts; adventure; friendship

This story of a Cornwall community that lives off the wreckage of the ships they lure to their doom is a seafaring adventure story worthy of Robert Louis Stevenson, with characters worthy of Dickens. It is a breathtaking, rollicking good read, full of twists. There are two sequels, *The Smugglers* and *The Buccaneers*, but this first book in the trilogy is the most gripping tale.

Wringer
FICTION

AUTHOR: Jerry Spinelli
HC/PB: HarperCollins
THEMES: friendship; bullies; pigeons; birthdays; coming of age; peer
    pressure; violence; dreams; pets; courage; death

Spinelli reveals the discomfort of going along with peers who make bad choices, the thrill of being included, and the confusion that results. When boys in Palmer's city turn ten, they become wringers at the annual Family Fest. It is an honor. But Palmer is not like the others. One of the first things he knows deep inside is that he does not want to be a wringer. This is for the reader who is crossing over from the security of home to the preteen times when making the right peer choices form your future. It's heart wrenching.

A Wrinkle in Time   SCIENCE FICTION
AUTHOR: Madeleine L'Engle
HC: Farrar, Straus & Giroux • PB: Dell
THEMES: time travel; gifted children; family; science fiction; love;
    adventure

One of the most popular novels for children ever written and a smashing combination of science fiction, adventure, and a family story. Throughout the sequence of novels that begins with this book (*A Wind in the Door, A Swiftly Tilting Planet,* and *Many Water*), we are shown the fantastic adventures of the Wallace family. As a doorway to science-fiction writing, this novel is unsurpassed in its presentation of fantastic themes in a readable style, but you need not be interested in science fiction to appreciate its richness.

The Yellow House: Vincent Van Gogh & Paul Gauguin Side by Side   PICTURE BOOK
AUTHOR: Susan Goldman Rubin • ILLUSTRATOR: Jos. A. Smith
HC: Abrams
THEMES: Vincent Van Gogh; Paul Gauguin; painters; France; biography;
    diversity; artists; art; comparisons

In the fall of 1888, Vincent Van Gogh and Paul Gaugin lived together for two months in Van Gogh's Yellow House in the south of France. This is the story of their time there. A fascinating comparison of two artists, one who painted what he saw around him; the other who painted from imagination. Brief biographies of each and reproductions of actual paintings are included along with Smith's watercolor and gouache pictures and Rubin's astute observations in comparing the artists and their work. A sure way to spark the interest of young artists.

Series Fiction

Okay, so most series books aren't great literature. We can all agree on that. And some kids will read a favorite series and nothing else for a while. But most of us went through a similar phase in our own development as readers, whether it was *Nancy Drew or Sweet Valley High*. Besides, we don't all read only great literature as adults—some of us like a little "junk" once in a while ourselves. However, we hear the concerns of adults who see children reading series to the exclusion of all else. To them we say it will pass. Reading series books almost always leads to reading other books, and if a series gets them started identifying themselves as readers, it is an identity they will have for a lifetime.

Parents tell us all the time about the reading habits and tastes of their children. Here's one anecdote that perfectly illustrates the role of "junk" in the development of a lifetime reading habit:

"My son got as far as fifth grade without ever having finished a complete book. Reading intimidated him. In fifth grade, he discovered Goosebumps. He read one and finished it. Then he started reading them all, from number 1 to number 34, and he always looked forward to getting the next one in the series. But after number 34, when I offered to take him to the bookstore for number 35, he said he wasn't interested. They were getting boring and they really weren't that scary. We went to the bookstore anyway and picked out some John Bellairs books. At first, he was reluctant to try them because he didn't know what he was getting, but they were the closest thing he could find to a Goosebumps book, so he bought them. A week or two later, I asked him if he liked the books. His reply was 'Goosebumps are junk, aren't they, Mom?' So, not only did Goosebumps get my son to read, they taught him the difference between reading a book, reading a better book, and reading a good book. My son is in eighth grade now and reads voraciously. Sometimes he reads junk, sometimes he doesn't. But if it weren't for Goosebumps, I don't think he'd be reading at all."

The Young Writer's Companion

NONFICTION

AUTHOR: Sarah Ellis
HC/PB: Groundwood Books
THEMES: writing; creativity

Covering everything from journal topics to wordplay, with a healthy dose of inspiration from famous writers and their writings along the way, this is the best gift you could give to a young writer to help him become serious about the craft.

Zel

AUTHOR: Donna Jo Napoli

HC: Dutton • PB: Puffin

THEMES: history, medieval times; princes; love; family; witches; captivity; courage; mothers and daughters; folktale variations

An astonishing retelling of the Rapunzel tale from the point of view of the witch, Rapunzel, and her prince. Full of magic and heightened emotion, this is a fresh new look at a story, similar to Napoli's *The Magic Circle* in its intensity. By retelling tales in depth, the author shows us that no one is all good or evil, and in this case that the witch who locked her daughter in a tower was powerless to do otherwise. A terrific opportunity to discuss how stories get told and how what we hear depends on who is doing the telling.

Nonfiction Comes Alive!

Nonfiction is not just for book reports. Children often turn to it for their pleasure reading when a subject interests them. The books that serve children best are distinguished by the same things found in good fiction: An identifiable point of view on the part of the writer and a strong narrative drive that balances the who and what with enough texture and style to make the plot—the events chronicled in the work—come to life.

Good nonfiction for children has the pull of world-building fiction. It transcends the distribution of facts, takes the reader to a place he has never before been, and makes the trip worthwhile, whether it's written about fish, the space program, polar ice caps, woman's suffrage, or the colonization of Africa. Like good fantasy, good nonfiction begins with an introduction to the people, the land, the rules, and the traditions of this new place, equipping the reader with the lay of the land and the tools to follow her to the desired destination.

There has been much change in the world of nonfiction writing since the late 1980s. It has become more dependent upon visual elements, especially graphics, with charts, color photographs, sidebars, and graphic-design techniques that break up the text into easily digestible bites.

DK Publishing, originally from England, is largely credited with initiating this trend with its *Eyewitness Books*. Eye-popping visuals and an organizational style that flows from page to page distinguish this remarkable line of books, making them favorites with children and teachers alike. DK soon adapted this successful style across its publishing program, and while the books look much the same, there is plenty of room in the format for growth and change.

Other publishers have copied DK's highly successful style, adding their own refinements. Level Three of HarperCollins's *I Can Read Book* series adds historical fiction, nonfiction, and chapters to the early reader mix. A sampling of nonfiction titles at this level: *Egg to Chick* by Selsam, *Dolphin* by Morris, *The Josefina Story Quilt* by Coerr, *Weather Poems for All Seasons* by Hopkins, and *Hill of Fire* by Lewis.

Candlewick Press publishes a series of illustrated nonfiction books on nature topics that we feel offer outstanding information and visuals. Titles include *My Hen Is Dancing, A Piece of String Is a Wonderful Thing; I Love Guinea Pigs; All Pigs Are Beautiful, Big Blue Whale; Caterpillar, Caterpillar; Spider Watching; Think of an Eel;* and *Think of a Beaver.*

In many cases nonfiction writing has followed the visual trend by getting tighter, shorter, more to the point. Writers like Kathleen Krull (*Lives of the Writers, Lives of the Musicians,* etc.) and Diane Stanley (picture-book biographies of Charles Dickens, Cleopatra, William Shakespeare, and Queen Elizabeth I) have done much to dispel the notion that biography-writing has to be long and brimming with facts to be good. Sometimes a taste of the life of a famous person is all a young reader requires. If the taste proves intriguing, then the reader can seek out longer, more detailed biographies, of which there are many well-written examples.

The best nonfiction writers have distinctive styles of writing, distinguishing themselves by their consistently high level of excellence in their books: always informative and compulsively readable, they deliver the facts to children ages seven to fourteen on a variety of topics in a variety of ways. Each is possessed of a writer's "voice," and they use that gift to make what was once thought of as dry and boring ("Ewwww! Nonfiction!") into something children will read and reread.

The best nonfiction writers also make their subjects come vividly to life, giving a "you are there" feel to their books and a sense that they are communicating directly with the reader. Here are some of the best writers in the field, listed in order of the age of their audience, and a sampling of representative titles:

GAIL GIBBONS

When you want good, solid information for young readers on a variety of subjects, turn to Gibbons, who writes books about holidays, dinosaurs, and practically every subject an elementary schooler could be interested in:

Caves and Caverns
Wolves
The Puffins are Back
Frogs
Whales
Sea Turtles
Spiders
From Seed to Plant
Honeymakers (about bees)
The Planets
Puff . . . Flash . . . Bang!: A Book About Signals
Pirates
Recycle
Beacons of Light (about lighthouses)
Catch the Wind (about kites)
The Art Box (the best beginning art book around)

ALIKI

Communication
Corn Is Maize: The Gift of the Indians
Digging Up Dinosaurs
Milk from Cow to Carton
My Visit to the Aquarium (By the way, see if you can find the child wearing a
   "Hicklebee's" T-shirt)
How a Book Is Made

SEYMOUR SIMON

Anything by him is a safe bet, but our favorites are his books about outer space (*Our Solar System, Jupiter, Comets, Meteors and Asteroids*), and his books about the earth and its natural forces (*Earthquakes, Volcanoes, Icebergs and Glaciers*). He is so prolific and writes about so many science topics of interest that it is hard to return from a trip to the library without a Seymour Simon book!

JEAN FRITZ

Leonardo's Horse
Will You Sign Here, John Hancock?
And Then What Happened, Paul Revere?
Shh! We're Writing the Constitution!
You Want Women to Vote, Lizzie Stanton?
What's the Big Idea, Ben Franklin?

DAVID ADLER (WITH JOHN AND ALEXANDAR WALLNER)

Picture-book biography series of Crockett, Washington, Frank, Franklin, Jefferson, etc.

DIANE HOYT-GOLDSMITH AND LAWRENCE MIGDALE

This author/photographer duo has created a rich resource of books about a variety of subjects. Some of these are *Apache Rodeo; Buffalo Days; Celebrating Hanukkah; Celebrating Kwanzaa; The Day of the Dead: A Mexican-American Celebration; Las Posadas: An Hispanic Christmas Celebration;* and *Pueblo Storyteller.*

SANDRA MARKLE

Outside and Inside Snakes, . . . Birds, . . . Spiders, . . . Sharks, . . . Trees, and . . . You!

JOANNE RYDER

writes picture books that dwell on our relationship with nature. She is always thorough in her research and poetic in her language, and her books encourage young readers to become more interested in the world around them. Some of our favorites include *The Waterfall's Gift, Earthdance, My Father's Hands, Under Your Feet, Where Butterflies Grow, Without Words,* and *The Snail's Spell.*

DOROTHY HINSHAW PATENT

Gray Wolf, Red Wolf
Charles Darwin: The Life of a Revolutionary Thinker

CHERYL HARNESS

They's Off!: The Story of the Pony Express
Young John Quincy
The Amazing, Impossible Erie Canal

LAURENCE PRINGLE

Dinosaurs!: Strange and Wonderful
An Extraordinary Life: The Story of a Monarch Butterfly

RUSSELL FREEDMAN

An Indian Winter
Eleanor Roosevelt: A Life of Discovery
Give Me Liberty: The Story of the Declaration of Independence

MILTON MELTZER

Lincoln in His Own Words
There Comes a Time: The Struggle for Civil Rights
Ten Kings and the Worlds They Ruled
Ten Queens: Portraits of Women of Power

SUSAN CAMPBELL BARTOLETTI

Growing Up in Coal Country
Black Potatoes: The Story of the Great Irish Famine, 1845–1850

JERRY STANLEY

I Am an American: A True Story of Japanese Internment
Children of the Dust Bowl: The True Story of the School at Weedpatch Camp
Cowboys and Longhorns: A Portrait of the Long Drive

Listening/Interest Level: Middle Elementary to Middle School (M/M+)/ Reading Level: Middle School (M+)

These books, mostly fiction, can be read by our upper M's, but call for a level of maturity that is more often found in early teens. Just because a child can read a book does not automatically mean she must. You and your readers will have plenty to talk about here—we advocate reading with them the books that may benefit from an adult perspective.

Anne Frank: The Diary of a Young Girl

BIOGRAPHY

AUTHOR: Anne Frank

HC: Doubleday • PB: Bantam

THEMES: coming of age; diaries; autobiography; history, World War II; Anne Frank; prejudice; Holocaust; family; Jews; courage; strong girls; writing

Children who have read *The Diary of A Young Girl* often want to know more about Anne Frank; they will appreciate the photographic remembrance from the Anne Frank House museum in Amsterdam, *Anne Frank: Beyond the Diary: A Photographic Remembrance* by Ruud Van DerRol and Rian Verhoeven.

Published all over the world, Anne Frank's account of two years in hiding during World War II has come to be a symbol of the cruelties of racism and war. Entries in her diary from Sunday, June 14, 1942, to Tuesday, August 1, 1944, tell the story of thirteen-year-old Anne, who is hidden with seven other Jews in Amsterdam, fearful of being discovered by the Nazis. It's a love story. It's raw in its honesty. It's a story that will profoundly affect young adult readers.

Beyond the Western Sea

FICTION

AUTHOR: Avi

HC: Orchard • PB: Avon

THEMES: escape; adventure; England; Ireland; wealth; poverty; courage; history, nineteenth century; immigration

Book 1 in the two-part adventure *The Escape from Home* will send readers searching for Book 2, *Lord Kirkle's Money*. It's hard not to think of a Dickens novel here, in which three youths, eleven to fifteen, fight to survive in the dank alleys of England's Liverpool in the 1850s. Maura O'Connell is the oldest, and she and her brother have fled from the cruel poverty of Ireland to find a life in England. Sir Laurence Kirkle, only eleven, has left his wealthy home to seek justice in the brutal world outside. Fast paced, with no chapter lasting longer than two pages, and with enough adventure and suspense to keep the pages turning.

A Bone from a Dry Sea

FICTION

AUTHOR: Peter Dickinson

PB: Dell

THEMES: fathers and daughters; survival; archeology; strong girls; history, prehistory

Set in both ancient and contemporary times, this novel is about two girls: One lived four million years ago; the other visits the site where her father, with a team of archeologists, searches for fossil remains of ancestors. Fascinating, with strong female characters.

Corpses, Coffins and Crypts: A History of Burial

NONFICTION

AUTHOR: Penny Colman

HC: Henry Holt

THEMES: death; burial; cultural diversity; traditions; history, world; rituals

As much about the way the world deals with its dead as any all-dressed-in-black, morbid teenager could wish for, all in one handy volume. The research is extraordinary, the facts are presented in an organized and fascinating way, and the balance of quirky and serious material invites the reader to dig right in.

The Crossing

FICTION

AUTHOR: Gary Paulsen
HC: Orchard • PB: Dell
THEMES: Mexico; self-respect; friendship; mental illness; soldiers; poverty; homelessness; alcoholism; survival; orphans

Manny Bustos is an orphan, and at fourteen years old he is fighting to survive in the border town of Juarez, Mexico. Robert S. Locke is a sergeant and a Vietnam vet. He is stationed across the border at Fort Bliss, Texas. Locke drinks alcohol to hide the sound of the friends in his mind who cry for help. This is a story of their meeting and friendship with a final blend of sadness and hope. It's a story that will stick with the young adult fortunate enough to read it.

Deathwatch

FICTION

AUTHOR: Robb White
PB: Dell
THEMES: survival; resourcefulness; desert; hunting; adventure; truth

One of our favorite books to give to the boy who refuses to read anything. Ben is alone in the desert, wearing only his shorts, with no water or food, and is being pursued by a madman with a gun. How he got into that predicament is revealed in the first three chapters, with the chase taking up the better part of the book. Courageous Ben knows the desert well—he grew up here—and his survival techniques are plausible and clever. His evil pursuer, Madec, is a fast-talking, self-justifying sociopath who thinks he has the answer to everything. Will Ben escape? And if he does, how will he convince the authorities of the truth of what really happened? You just have to read it to find out . . .

My niece Patty was in the sixth grade when she asked me to read a book she complained her teacher was "making her read." She hated it. "Why would I read a book you hate?" I responded. My twelve-year-old daughter was there and offered to read it. It was <u>Deathwatch</u>. The entire time she read that book she complained, "I hate this book, Mom, you've got to read it!" When she finished it, she handed it over. I read it. I hated it and took it to work and asked the staff to read it. They too "hated" it and have been recommending it ever since. Sometimes a book is so gripping, it makes the reader breathless with frustration at not being able to step in to change the action. This is one. Read it. Maybe you too will hate it.

December Stillness
FICTION

AUTHOR: Mary Downing Hahn

PB: Avon

THEMES: homelessness; veterans; U.S. history, Vietnam War; Vietnam
 Veteran's Memorial; family; fathers and daughters; libraries

A moving novel that can help answer older children's questions about the Vietnam War. When Kelly interviews a homeless Vietnam vet for a school project, her emotional involvement produces tragic results that no one could have anticipated. It is clear to the reader, and ultimately to Kelly, that she is really trying to get answers about her own father's time in the service. Hahn's skill as a writer makes the difference between a story that could have been sappy and the emotionally involving story she delivers.

★ The Devil's Arithmetic
FICTION-FANTASY

AUTHOR: Jane Yolen

HC: Viking • PB: Puffin

THEMES: Holocaust; time travel; Germany; Jews;
 adventure; captivity; courage; good versus evil

A time-travel novel about the Holocaust that makes a gripping statement about personal response to atrocity. Hannah is tired of hearing stories about the death camps and why she should honor her Jewish heritage. When she opens the door for Elijah at the Passover Seder, she finds herself transported to 1940s Poland and learns firsthand why we must never forget the lessons of the Holocaust.

On Stories That Disturb Us

"...all stories, if continued far enough, end in death, and he is no true storyteller who would keep that from you."
—Ernest Hemingway (1899–1961)

The Dungeon
FICTION

AUTHOR: Lynne Reid Banks

HC: HarperCollins

THEMES: grief; slavery; China; anger; revenge; soldiers; Scotland; cruelty;
 castles

Anguish, anger, and an unwavering need for revenge drive this tale of Scottish laird Bruce MacLennan, who orders a deep dungeon built to hold the man who killed his wife and children. During its construction he travels to China seeking adventure, where he buys a child slave named Peony. Fans of tragedy will savor this tale of a powerful man's self-destruction, and they may cling to the hope that Peony's goodness will reawaken his lost sense of decency. But it's too late for MacLennan. His hunger for vengeance takes him back to the dungeon and the fate that awaits him—and Peony. Many readers will not guess the ending until the last turn of the page. Others will find relief in Banks's epilogue, where she reveals a promise kept and offers hope.

I agree this tale is grim, but Banks has included some lovely bits, like when the old soldier Li-wu tells Peony, "Store beauty. Furnish your memory with it. It will turn your mind into a beautiful garden that you can visit when things in the real world are hard or ugly."

The Earthsea Quartet   FICTION-FANTASY

AUTHOR: Ursula LeGuin
PB: Bantam
THEMES: responsibility; choices; dragons; gifted children; magic; wizards;
     coming of age; fantasy

A four-book meditation on the effects and uses of power, this outstanding piece of fantasy writing has been acclaimed in the adult as well as children's arena. Many bookstores keep these in the science fiction section, not with the children's books. Darker than you might expect, but it ranks at the very top of the list of world-building fantasy. Dragons, wizards, magic—it's all here, ready and waiting for the young reader done with Susan Cooper's *The Dark Is Rising* sequence and *The Hobbit* but not yet ready for *The Lord of the Rings*. The order of the books is: *The Wizard of Earthsea, The Tombs of Atuan, The Farthest Shore,* and *Tehanu.*

The Face on the Milk Carton   FICTION

AUTHOR: Caroline Cooney
PB: Dell
THEMES: separation; kidnapping; missing children; family; parents; mystery;
     secrets; truth

When Janie glanced up at the milk carton, a picture of a young girl glanced back. ". . . an ordinary little girl. Hair in tight pigtails, one against each thin cheek. A dress with a narrow white collar. The dress was white with tiny dark polka dots." The picture had been taken twelve years before. Janie recognized herself. It was impossible that her loving parents would have kidnapped her, but—there she was. There was no question. This gripping, fast-paced story will hold readers till the last page is turned. And when the reader wants to know more, the story continues in *Whatever Happened to Janie* and *The Voice on the Radio.*

Flipped

AUTHOR: Wendelin Van Draanen
HC/PB: Knopf
THEMES: friendship; neighbors; family; love; strong girls; change

A delicate balance of elements and a dual narration make for a tour de force for the author of the *Sammy Keyes Mysteries*. There is no mystery here, save for why Juliana is so obsessed with Bryce. The story starts in second grade, but the bulk of the novel takes place in seventh and eighth grades, by which time Bryce has become smitten with Juli and she has grown weary of him. A lot happens along the way, but this look at love offers the suggestion that you must truly know someone before you can love them, and that alone is reason enough to shove this book into the hands of every girl you can find.

 Who knows how we choose that first crush? This incredible story paints a perfect picture of how little sense it makes.

★ Freak the Mighty

AUTHOR: Rodman Philbrick
HC/PB: Scholastic
THEMES: bullies; gifted children; courage; friendship; handicaps;
    imagination; teamwork; computers

Two boys—misfits—combine themselves into a single entity to take on the world. This compassionate, wise, and funny book will appeal to the outcast lurking in most adolescents and deserves to be a classic, alongside *The Outsiders* and *Maniac Magee*.

★ A Girl Named Disaster

AUTHOR: Nancy Farmer
HC: Orchard • PB: Puffin
THEMES: Africa; courage; strong girls; rivers; survival;
    adventure; journeys; animals; boats; maps; ancestors;
    grandmothers; traditions

Nancy Farmer excels at fast-paced adventure fiction with a twist. Fans of *A Girl Named Disaster* will want to look for her two futuristic tales, *The Ear, the Eye and the Arm*, set in Zimbabwe two hundred years in the future, and *The House of the Scorpion*, her multiple prizewinner about Mexico, the international drug trade, and cloning.

Nhamo is eleven years old when she sets off alone on the Musengezi River to find her father. She has far to travel and the danger of starvation and drowning are ever present. Farmer has included maps of her voyage, a cast of characters, a glossary of African words, and a brief history of Zimbabwe, Mozambique, and the beliefs of the Shona. This is no textbook. It is a spellbinding adventure that offers curious readers answers with a turn of the page.

★ The Giver
SCIENCE FICTION

AUTHOR: Lois Lowry
HC: Houghton Mifflin • PB: Dell
THEMES: utopia; taking action; courage; rituals; traditions; gifted children; community; individuality; family

One of those brilliant books that come along every few years and set a benchmark of excellence that enriches the whole of children's literature. Winner of the Newbery Medal, it has shown up on school reading lists across the country, frequently for fifth or sixth grades. For many kids, this is too early to appreciate the demands this book makes upon a reader. Part of the problem lies in the fact that this is a book that begs to be discussed—it has an ending that is open to interpretation, which can frustrate readers who like their meanings clear and concise. A book that challenges readers on a variety of levels—powerful, shocking, and thought-provoking in its presentation of a world where sameness has become the standard and conformity is maintained at all costs—it will be read for generations as a warning against the deceptive virtues of utopian thinking.

> A companion book of sorts, *Gathering Blue*, offers a different possible future that connects to *The Giver* in a number of ways, the most important of which is the role of the "gifted" child in the preservation of the soul of the community.

★ The Golden Compass: Book 1 of His Dark Materials
FICTION-FANTASY

AUTHOR: Philip Pullman
HC/PB: Knopf
THEMES: fantasy; strong girls; witches; adventure; bears; religion; good versus evil

Innovative, suspense-filled and multilayered, this fantasy lifts the reader into a world where adventure is the rule and original characters cause readers to wonder, "Who is this writer Philip Pullman?" He has created personal daemons, animal familiars that accompany their humans in one form or another throughout their lives. Pantalaimon, Lyra Belacqua's daemon, has the charm, sensibilities, and loyalty that would make any of us long for a daemon of our own. And the witches? Pullman's adventure doesn't lack surprises. It challenges readers with new images and possibilities to the end, where it makes clear that the next volumes in the *His Dark Materials Trilogy* are imperative reads. Book Two: *The Subtle Knife*. The finale: *The Amber Spyglass*.

A History of US: A 10 Volume Series NONFICTION

AUTHOR: Joy Hakim

HC/PB: Oxford University Press

THEMES: U.S. history; traditions; cultural diversity; U.S. presidents; government; immigration

A ten-book set that is by far the best history of the United States available for young readers. Joy Hakim writes vibrantly, finding the balance between compulsively readable and factual. Start reading any volume, on any page, and you will find information that will fascinate—you won't be able to put it down.

Homecoming FICTION

AUTHOR: Cynthia Voigt

HC: Atheneum • PB: Simon & Schuster

THEMES: homelessness; courage; resourcefulness; taking action; change; gifted children; strong girls; family; journeys; siblings; determination; grandmother; relatives

> The Tillerman saga continues in subsequent volumes: *Dicey's Song, The Runner, A Solitary Blue, Come a Stranger, On Fortune's Wheel,* and *Sons From Afar.*

A brilliant, stand-alone read, but also remarkable as the first in a sequence of novels about the Tillerman family. Dicey is the eldest of four, and due to Mama's instability she has taken on the role of the responsible one in her family. When Mama abandons them in the book's opening scene, Dicey is faced with not only providing for the immediate survival of her family, but with getting them to the only relatives they know, miles away, on foot. Dicey and her determination are inspiring, yet she is a tough person to get to know. She is balanced by the other three siblings, each a finely crafted portrayal by author Voigt.

A Long Way from Chicago FICTION

AUTHOR: Richard Peck

HC: Dial • PB: Puffin

THEMES: farm life; grandmothers; individuality; community; taking action; U.S. history, the Depression; towns

> *A Year Down Yonder* is the second book about Grandma Dowdel (you simply must read them both.) and it is filled with the same sense of humor and even more vibrantly etched characters. Mary Alice is now fifteen and she does not look forward to spending a whole year with Grandma, who, after all, is a fox trapper, pumpkin thief, and all around troublemaker. What could they find in common? The answer brought Richard Peck a long-overdue Newbery Medal and provides a memorable reading experience, destined to become a classic of children's literature.

The year is 1929 when you first meet nine-year-old Joey, who travels with his younger sister, Mary Alice, from Chicago to spend a week with their vulgar, gun-toting, irreverent Grandma Dowdel in her small Illinois town. Each chapter represents another year and another weeklong visit, when Grandma cheats, trespasses, and tricks the authorities in an attempt to help the local underdogs. Whether read aloud or alone, these tales are downright funny.

Lord of the Deep

FICTION

AUTHOR: Graham Salisbury
HC: Delacorte • PB: Dell
THEMES: fishing; Hawaii; fathers and sons; lying; coming of age

A moving novel about a boy coming to terms with the fact that his stepfather (the only real father he has ever had) is not the perfect person he has made him out to be. Set on a deep-sea fishing boat in Salisbury's native Hawaii, this is a coming-of-age novel with a bittersweet poignancy that shows how the bonds between men can survive having their values being brought into question.

The Magic Circle

FICTION

AUTHOR: Donna Jo Napoli
HC: Dutton • PB: Puffin
THEMES: fairy tales; strong women; folktale variations; healing; witches; mothers and daughters; history, medieval times

A powerful, thought-provoking, and illuminating book to give to an intuitive reader ready for a challenge—and to adults who fit this category. Feminists, ecowarriors, mystics, shamans, and witches will find it right-on in its depiction of the price women paid for knowledge in the Middle Ages. Warning! The jacket copy gives the plot away. Hide it. Allow yourself the delicious moment of recognition when you find out that you've been reading the untold side of a familiar tale.

Make Lemonade

FICTION

AUTHOR: Virginia Euwer Wolff
HC: Henry Holt • PB: Scholastic

THEMES: poverty; teenage mothers; coming of age; determination; friendship; family

The first in a projected trilogy, aVaughn's remarkable story continues in *True Believer*, which is a ovel for teens.

Fourteen-year-old La Vaughn is determined to go to college and not end up like Jolly, the seventeen-year-old mother of the two children she baby-sits. This is a portrait of two young women who assist each other in getting their lives on track and an unblinking look at the lives of families in the grip of the cycle of urban poverty. A positive and hopeful ending that is a touch bittersweet adds just the right dose of reality.

Making up Megaboy

FICTION

AUTHOR: Virginia Walter • ILLUSTRATOR: Katrina Roeckelein
PB: Delacorte
THEMES: violence; guns; murder; point of view; heroes

This is one of the most disturbing books you will ever read, both relevant and important in our increasingly violent world. Brilliantly told in a multiview-point narrative style that interweaves comic-book and computer graphics as an essential piece of the tale. This story of a senseless murder committed by a young teen will leave lots of room for heated discussion at the book's end, because the answers aren't offered by the author—we are given the who, what, when, and where, but not the why. Is this fiction or reportage? Is it needlessly bleak or painfully real? Should all books for children offer a hopeful ending, with wrongs righted and explained and good triumphing over evil? Or can some books offer us a place to begin to discuss with our elementary school children (and they among themselves) those events in our culture over which we have no control and that leave us confused and despairing? Use this as a starting point for discussion when you and your child are ready.

★ Memoirs of a Bookbat

FICTION

AUTHOR: Kathryn Lasky
HC/PB: Harcourt Brace
THEMES: reading; coming of age; strong girls; religion; sisters; individuality; friendship; taking action; censorship; judging; self-respect

Prepare to have your love of reading be used in ways you never dreamed possible. Telling the story of a fundamentalist family that works to ban books from schools through the eyes of their book-loving oldest daughter is an inspired idea. As she grows, we know what she is reading, and our memories of childhood favorites are stroked fondly. But as her family becomes more set upon making it impossible for other people to read books they find offensive, we begin to feel our personal memories being attacked. This is a hard look from the inside at how intolerance and unquestioning fundamentalism can destroy not only communities but families. You may cheer at the ending, as we did, or you may be bothered by it. But there is no question that Lasky uses her power over words to make us think—something the book banners would like to control.

Memories of Childhood

PICTURE BOOK

AUTHOR/ILLUSTRATOR: Michael Foreman

HC: Arcade

THEMES: England; childhood; history, World War II; soldiers; family; war; coming of age; artists; school; painting; jobs

In this extraordinary book, combining his two picture-book memoirs, *War Boy* and *After the War Was Over*, Michael Foreman tells of growing up on the south coast of England during and after World War II. *War Boy* deals better with the subject of children continuing to live as children during wartime than any book we can think of. The picture-book format may mislead some into thinking this book is for young children, but the audience is decidedly older, more fifth grade and up. Some of the British vernacular may be a bit alien, but it is decidedly worth the trouble and will serve as an excellent introduction to rural English culture. The sequel, *After the War Was Over*, is notable not only for the depiction of England putting itself back together in the years after the war, but for its portrayal of a young artist in the making.

Midnight Hour Encores

FICTION

AUTHOR: Bruce Brooks

HC/PB: HarperCollins

THEMES: music; gifted child; U.S. history, the 1960s; strong girls; fathers and daughters; journeys; secrets; coming of age; single parents.

Sibilance T. Spooner (a name she made up for herself) is, at sixteen, a world-class cello player. Bright, articulate, and possessed of a mind very much her own, she has never wanted to know her mother, never wanted to understand why she was abandoned at birth and left in the care of her father, Taxi, an unreconstructed hippie. Sib and Taxi have quite a nice life together, each respecting the other and providing the right amount of love and care to give the illusion to Sib that she is complete. Then, for reasons she chooses not to share with Taxi, she decides she would like to meet her mother. Her father, never one to do anything halfway, takes this opportunity to teach his daughter about the people who made her and the times that shaped them. This brilliant novel about love, familial bonds, secrets, and self-discovery is the perfect book to give to a teenager asking, "What was the big deal about the sixties, anyway?" The writing about music and what it means to people is worth the price of the book alone.

★ Nightjohn

AUTHOR: Gary Paulsen
HC: Delacorte • PB: Dell
THEMES: slavery; reading; escape; literacy; U.S. history, pre–Civil War; African American; teachers

FICTION

Remarkable. A portrait of slave life that focuses on learning to read as a means to escape the wretchedness of life. It pulls no punches in its portrait of the cruelty, but also shines with hope and inspiration as we watch young Sarny learn to read at the hands of the runaway slave, Nightjohn. The sequel, *Sarny,* follows her life into old age.

★ Nothing But the Truth

AUTHOR: Avi
HC: Orchard • PB: Avon
THEMES: conscience; school; teachers; truth; point of view; patriotism

FICTION

A brilliantly contrived novel about the price paid when only part of the truth is revealed. Phillip Malloy is a ninth-grade student who is performing poorly in Miss Narwin's English class. His grade of a D– denies him the chance to try out for the track team, and his anger and frustration at his teacher cause him to act out during homeroom, resulting in a suspension and a major public brouhaha. The events unfold inexorably, spinning wildly out of control so quickly that reading this book is like watching a train wreck. The true genius of Avi's construction lies in the way his narrative forces the reader to choose sides in the story, while slowly coming to realize that everyone in the story is wrong because they have only part of the truth. The ending is as sad as any we have ever read, especially because if any of the main characters had stopped to consider all the sides of the situation, most of the tragedy could have been averted, which is a lot like life.

The sequel, *Broken Bridge*, tells what happens to the characters in *One More River*, twenty-five years later.

One More River

AUTHOR: Lynne Reid Banks
HC: Morrow • PB: Avon
THEMES: change; politics; Israel; kibbutz; home; Jews; peace; jobs; community; war; Mideast; Arabs

FICTION

Lesley, a wealthy fourteen-year-old cheerleader living in Canada, moves with her parents to an Israeli kibbutz where she learns about community— and about how lifetimes of discrimination affect the opportunity for peace.

Lynne Reid Banks lived on a kibbutz in Israel for eight years. Her characters are believable, and this powerful story offers a glimpse into the long-standing struggle between Jews and Palestinians.

The Outsiders
FICTION

AUTHOR: S. E. Hinton

HC: Viking • PB: Puffin

THEMES: community; friendship; prejudice; loyalty; family; gentle boys; taking action; gangs

One of the most popular books ever written for children and on more school reading lists than any other title, this first novel by then sixteen-year-old Susie Hinton (that's right—S. E. stands for Susan Elizabeth) is a classic. There are few teenagers who cannot respond to the feelings of the characters, especially when they mirror their own sense of alienation.

 I cannot prove this, but I'll bet you anything that kids who join gangs do not have books in their lives. It has always seemed to me that children who are read to and who read for themselves have a healthy ability to deal with strong, even disturbing, feelings. Could it be possible that children who have been deprived of that joy lack such inner strength and may feel that they have to search for a more concrete way to show their personal power—frequently resulting in violent expression? I'm not sure, and though it might be oversimplifying the problem, I believe a person willing to read to these children could have a strong effect on their lives. Why not books instead of guns? It sure couldn't hurt.

★ Red Scarf Girl: A Memoir of the Cultural Revolution
BIOGRAPHY

AUTHOR: Ji-Li Jiang

HC/PB: HarperCollins

THEMES: China; history; autobiography; courage; coming of age; family; jobs; school; bullies; hardship

A moving account of a Chinese family and their troubles during the upheaval of the late sixties. Young Ji-Li is bright and motivated, and has a comfortable life—her future seems assured. When Mao begins to persecute the educated and the well-to-do, her family is set upon by neighbors and friends, and Jiang's remembrances carry all the weight of similar accounts, such as *The Diary of Anne Frank*. A courageous young girl, now grown to womanhood, gives the world her childhood to stand as a testament against cruelty and inhumanity.

Singer to the Sea God

FICTION

AUTHOR: Vivian Alcock

HC: Delacorte • PB: Dell

THEMES: Greek mythology; ancient Greece; coming of age; adventure; journeys; music; singing; friendship; strong girls; gentle boys; sisters

Using the legend of Perseus and Medusa as a springboard, this is the epic tale of Phaidon and his quest to be reunited with his sister Cleo, who has been turned to stone. With the sweep and magic of great storytelling, there is enough adventure here to satisfy most readers, and enough about the Greeks and their lives to make this a useful book for supplemental reading when the time comes to learn about this period of history.

Spindle's End

FICTION-FANTASY

AUTHOR: Robin McKinley

HC: Penguin • PB: Ace

THEMES: fairy tales; folklore variations; strong girls; fairies; cleverness; fantasy

Robin McKinley has created an unforgettable character in this Sleeping Beauty tale for older fantasy enthusiasts. Readers understand at the onset that on her twenty-first birthday, princess Rosie is doomed to prick her finger on the spindle of a spinning wheel and fall into a poisoned sleep. Fortunately, a young fairy whisks Rosie away from immediate danger and disappears with her into the countryside. There, with no knowledge of her past, Rosie grows into a delightful, strong woman. As she nears her twenty-first birthday, the reader can't help but wonder whether she will be clever enough to elude the spell that has sealed her fate.

 I enjoyed every minute of this tale. I could feel the magic dust and knew in my heart that this is exactly the young woman Sleeping Beauty would become.

Stand Tall

FICTION

AUTHOR: Joan Bauer

HC: Putnam

THEMES: gentle boys; divorce; disaster; grandfathers and grandsons; family; patriotism; floods; fitting in; self-respect; confidence

Twelve-year-old Sam, known to everyone as "Tree," is six feet, three and a half inches tall and plays basketball out of a sense of obligation rather than joy. The youngest of three boys coping with their parents' divorce, he clings to his relationship with his wise grandfather, a Vietnam vet dealing with the amputation of his leg. This is an insightful, funny, moving novel by one of our favorite Newbery Honor writers.

 I am not called Walter the Giant for nothing, so I was thrilled to see how Bauer got the details of life as a tall guy so perfectly.

Stargirl FICTION
AUTHOR: Jerry Spinelli
HC/PB: Random House
THEMES: school; love; fitting in; betrayal; outcasts; desert

Reminiscent of Spinelli's Newbery-winning *Maniac Magee* in its larger-than-life tone, here is another outstanding look at the role of the nonconformist and the price children pay for being different in our society. Stargirl Carraway will probably remind you of someone you knew in high school, and you may not like her; she's just too weird. Like the narrator of the book, Leo Borlock, most kids will be enchanted by her, even as they acknowledge that she must be destroyed. Though the book is called *Stargirl*, it is about Leo and his grappling with an issue kids face every day—how to be true to yourself and still fit in.

Stones in Water FICTION
AUTHOR: Donna Jo Napoli
HC: Dutton • PB: Puffin
THEMES: history World War II, prejudice; coming of age; Italy; escape;
     friendship; hardship; hope; courage; determination

Samuel and Roberto are watching a movie in their hometown of Venice, Italy, when they are abducted by German soldiers and forced to work in a World War II labor camp. Roberto's attempts to keep secret the fact that his friend is Jewish will haunt you for weeks after you finish reading. It's a story about war and survival. It's a page turner.

Tangerine FICTION
AUTHOR: Edward Bloor
HC: Harcourt Brace • PB: Scholastic
THEMES: family; cultural diversity; soccer; disability; secrets; betrayal;
     Florida; weather; brothers; fitting in; environment

A complex and wonderfully written novel of family secrets, betrayal, coming of age, and racial inequality set in a town in Florida where nature has run amok. Paul's eyeglass lenses may be as thick as the bottom of a Coke bottle, but his emotional insight seems to make up for his legal blindness. He is wiser than his years indicate. He knows his family actively favors his mean-spirited, football star older brother. Though Paul is having trouble fitting in at his new school, where minorities are the majority and sinkholes threaten to swallow whole buildings, he is managing to get along. But the threatening lightning strikes and the burning fields of Tangerine, Florida, are a metaphor for something darker and more sinister than Paul realizes, and the revelations that come at the book's end are downright shocking. This is one heck of a read from a writer of great promise.

★ This Land Was Made for You and Me: The Life and Songs of Woody Guthrie   BIOGRAPHY

AUTHOR: Elizabeth Partridge
HC: Viking
THEMES: music; Woody Guthrie; U.S. history, the Depression; folklore; folksongs; musicians

> For a picture-book biography of this remarkable man's life, look for *Woody Guthrie: Poet of the People*, and marvel at Bonnie Christensen's woodcut illustrations.

This vibrant portrayal of a pivotal figure in twentieth-century music and politics is an example of the best kind of nonfiction writing. Partridge shows how Woody's social conscience informed every aspect of his life. Along the way she treats us to an examination of the Depression, the development of socialism in the USA, and the burgeoning folksong movement. Photos, lyrics, and memorabilia help to give the reader a rich picture of the times and a man who helped shape them.

To Be a Slave   NONFICTION

AUTHOR: Julius Lester, compiler • ILLUSTRATOR: Tom Feelings
PB: Scholastic
THEMES: slavery; African American; U.S. history, pre–Civil War; prejudice; captivity; freedom

Still as powerful as when it was originally published in 1968, Lester's oral history of slavery is all the more remarkable for being the first of such works for young readers. Slave narratives are used almost exclusively, with Lester intruding only to connect or amplify, and Feelings's art adds depth to this important piece of American history.

Touching Spirit Bear   FICTION

AUTHOR: Ben Mikaelsen
HC/PB: HarperCollins
THEMES: anger; consequences; bullies; Native American; banishment; change; bears

Fifteen-year-old Cole has been getting into trouble most of his life. But when he viciously beats and injures a classmate, he chooses "Circle Justice," an alternative sentencing program based on Native American tradition to determine his punishment. Sent to a remote Alaskan island where he must spend a year alone, Cole eats worms and rodents and is seriously injured by a bear. He survives, but in the process he learns about controlling anger, and that he can change, physically and spiritually.

Up on Cloud Nine
FICTION

AUTHOR: Anne Fine
HC: Random House
THEMES: friendship; suicide; hospitals; humor; mystery

A complex tale of two friends, one a risk taker, the other more sensible, and the mystery of how the former came to be lying in a hospital in a coma. Funnier than you'd expect for a book that features the hint of suicide and some really dreadful parenting, but the bond between the two boys drives the book, making the reader hopeful that things turn out okay at the end. They do, but not exactly how you expect.

Joan Lowery Nixon

Four-time winner of the Edgar Award, given by the Mystery Writers of America for the best children's mystery of the year, Nixon wrote dozens of books that have become favorites of thriller, horror, and mystery lovers. Some of our favorites are *The Seance*, *A Candidate for Murder*, *The Other Side of Dark*, and *The Kidnapping of Christina Lattimore*, but by all means do not be limited to our list. Any book with Joan Lowery Nixon's name on it is a fair bet to be a crackling good read.

We Were There, Too!
NONFICTION

AUTHOR: Phillip Hoose
HC: Farrar, Straus & Giroux
THEMES: U.S. history; childhood; point of view

One of the best ways we can imagine to get kids interested in history is to show them how events affected children. Here are the stories of young people at the center of most of the major American historical events. Fascinating and compellingly readable.

The Weekend Was Murder
FICTION-MYSTERY

AUTHOR: Joan Lowery Nixon
HC: Delacorte • PB: Dell
THEMES: mystery; games; contests; detectives; writing; creativity; murder; authors

A mystery weekend, complete with fictional murder, clues, and suspects, turns deadly when an actual murder occurs. Nixon's skill as a plotter serves her readers well, and this is just one in a long line of satisfying, challenging mysteries from one of the most honored writers in the genre.

Westmark

AUTHOR: Lloyd Alexander
HC: Dutton • PB: Puffin
THEMES: war; adventure; courage; heroes; peace; fighting; soldiers

Book 1 of the Westmark Trilogy, an accomplished feat of storytelling! In three books, Alexander details the course of a war raging through his imaginary land of Westmark, which looks a lot like seventeenth-century Europe. This is epic fiction at its best, and there is some awfully fine writing about the nature of war here, as well as strong, believable characters of both sexes. Book 2 is *The Kestrel*, and Book 3 is *The Beggar Queen*.

What Jamie Saw

AUTHOR: Carolyn Coman
HC: Front Street • PB: Puffin
THEMES: abuse; escape; family; stepparents

Though this is about a younger child, the intensity of the writing makes this a book for older readers. Coman's Newbery Honor book is a devastating look at the horrors of a neglected and abused childhood. Powerful and disturbing, but full of hope.

Frequently Asked Questions

We each get asked many of the same questions. We offer our responses here:

Q: I have a seven-year-old and a four-year-old. What books can I read to them both?

A: Look for books that tell a story with both words and pictures so there is plenty to see, notice, and do. Young ones enjoy challenging an older sibling to find things on the page.

For Starters, Try These:

Look Alikes (Steiner)
The Mysterious Tadpole (Kellogg)
Officer Buckle and Gloria (Rathmann)
Piggie Pie (Palatini)

Go for Action and Humor:

Possum Come A-Knockin' (Van Laan)
The Day Jimmy's Boa Ate the Wash (Noble)
The Three-Legged Cat (Mahy)

Q: My toddler gets fidgety and wants to turn the pages faster than I can read the story.

A: Let her. Don't make the reading experience a struggle for control. Figure out what's going on. Is it the story (not interesting?) or a need to move on because she's excited? If it's the latter, try having her tell *you* the story. Some toddlers have a hard time waiting. If that's the case, use books with fewer words on each page and build up to longer stories. There is nothing wrong with keeping up with her by leaving out some of the words.

Q: My ten-year-old's soccer team practices three days a week and on Saturdays. By the time he finishes his paper route, eating dinner, and doing his homework, there is no time for reading.

A: Usually, time spent reading is time taken away from something else. Is there time for TV? Is there time for computer play? If you believe reading is important, then you will find the time.

Q: My four-year-old is starting to be afraid of the dark, but he wants me to read him stories about monsters. Is this a good idea?

A: Yes, because reading and listening to scary stories help manage fears. Children usually look for things they need in their stories and it is a sign of emotional intelligence that your child seeks out a story solution to things that frighten him. Besides, often when you are concentrating on the monster in the story, you child is noticing the resilient child who has mastered his fears. Try these:

There Is a Nightmare in My Closet
   (Mayer)
There's a Monster Under My Bed
   (Howe)
Where the Wild Things Are (Sendak)

Q: My preschooler is too rough to have his own books. He still rips the pages.

A: Divide books into two stacks: HIS to do with what he likes, and OURS, which are to be treasured. You can get his books at garage sales, library sales, and used bookstores. He needs to learn to respect books, and these are the ones he learns on. Read to him from both stacks, but put OURS away for together time.

Q: What do you recommend I do to help my baby become a good reader?

A: Don't push it. Babies have no business reading, so don't try to teach them. A baby's job is to explore—frequently with its mouth, so as Valerie always says, "Give them books that are nontoxic." We could cite a host of experts on the subject of getting your child ready to read. One thing they all agree on is that a child will read when she is ready. A steady dose of stories will help her along but won't make her read any sooner than she wants to.

Here's a gift: Don't worry about teaching your child to read. Concentrate on helping her to love books. When you've done that successfully, reading will come.

Q: My son is finally reading, but he only wants to read the same series over and over. I'm concerned because he won't read better books.

A: Sameness is comforting. If your son is reading for pleasure, don't worry too much about what he is reading. A lot of great readers started off with Nancy Drew and the Hardy Boys. Make other books available to him. Give him the opportunity to go to the library and bookstore and make his own choices. He'll move on when he's ready.

I'm gonna say it one last time: Free, free, free. Libraries are free!

Q: I'm a single parent. I work full-time as well as drive the kids to their respective meetings, events, and practices. As much as I'd like to read aloud to my children, I'm exhausted by the end of the day.

A: On those days when you're worn out, have your children read to you. If they aren't yet reading, on high-energy days tape yourself reading stories and save them. There are also fine wordless books a nonreader can "read" aloud to you. Be sure you don't trade these in for read-alone times. A big value here is time, spent close.

Q: I can't get my child interested in reading.

A: You can't make a child read. If you make it into a big deal—a stand-off—you are probably going to lose. All you can really do is make sure that the opportunities for reading are there and that the books are available. If she is not interested in reading herself, at least give her the experience of being read to. Again, your job is to teach the love of books. Do what you can to help her experience the magic—fiction and nonfiction—to be found on the pages.

Q: It's time for my child to be introduced to books explaining sex. Every time I bring one out to read with him, he bolts. Any suggestions?

A: Get a copy of *It's Perfectly Normal* (Harris). Leave it where he can find it on his own.

After several self-conscious sessions attempting to read the appropriate books about sex to my daughters, I put <u>Where Did I Come From?</u> (Mayle) in their bedroom. That night I could hear them sharing a bunk pointing at pictures and laughing hysterically. I thought, at least they are hysterical over facts, which is more than I could say for my experiences at that age.

Q: My daughter wants me to read the same book to her repeatedly. I've gotten so I want to hide it. Help!

A: You are not a story-reading machine with no opinions of your own. If the story bores you, offends you, fails to engage you, or simply doesn't hold up under countless readings, don't read it. Part of the joy of reading together is shared pleasure. When you don't like a story, you're not fooling your child. Say, "I don't want to read that. You read that one on your own later. It drives me crazy." Then pick up a book you both love and read that instead.

Q: Authors put their agendas into the books they write. I'm not always comfortable with those agendas.

A: Who doesn't have an agenda? As a parent, yours may be selecting books that reinforce your values. If you have read a book and decided that your child is not ready for the issues it presents, or that it does not echo your values, don't share that book: However, when it comes time to face the challenges life presents, remember that a book will be waiting.

Q: My fifth-grader is reading at a third-grade reading level. Can you suggest titles that will interest him?

A: First of all, look for books that are not frighteningly thick, in which the chapters and the description are short and the text is a reasonable size. These should work:

Poetry collections by Shel Silverstein, Jeff Moss, Jack Prelutsky, and Kalli Dakos

Some kids need visuals:

Dogzilla (Dav Pilkey)
Eyewitness Books from DK Publishing
Amelia's Notebook (Moss)
Safari Journal (Talbott)

It may be that while there is no problem reading individual words, a sea of words without enough breaks is frustrating. Try these:

The *Dragonling* (Koller) . . . and other
   books in this series
anything by Matt Christopher

Short story collections offer the feeling of accomplishment that reading can provide, but with fewer pages per story:

Every Living Thing (Rylant)
*The Random House Book of Sports
   Stories*
The Macmillan Book of Baseball Stories

Read aloud to your older sons and daughters. Often we abandon kids who need our help, deciding that because they are old enough to read on their own, they no longer need us. Children struggling with reading at school need the comfort and reward of a good story read aloud at home.

Q: How do you share books with your kids that reinforce your values?

A: Take a look at the themes and categories at the end of this book. Choose titles that match your concerns. Don't make reading aloud into a lesson. Good stories speak for themselves. Kids can smell a moral a mile away and tend to run in the other direction.

Q: What about books with medals and gold seals on them? What do they mean?

A: There are many awards given to recognize books that have rated praise or merit, and publishers will put a gold medal on the cover of a book if they think it will generate sales. The most important awards are the Newbery Medal, given by the American Library Association for the most distinguished novel for children in a given year, the Caldecott Medal, which is awarded to the most distinguished picture book, and the Coretta Scott King Award, given to a novel and a picture book each year that is by an African American author. Each award also can have Honor books, which are similar to runners-up, and these titles, along with the award winners, receive a great deal of attention from publishers, booksellers, and librarians each year.

APPENDIX 2:

How Children's Books Are Made

If you are curious about what goes on behind the scenes of the children's book world—the writer's process, exploring different styles of illustration, the business of publishing, or learning how your favorite books came about—the following titles will be of interest:

Author Talk (Leonard S. Marcus, editor)

A Caldecott Celebration: Six Artists Share Their Paths to the Caldecott Medal (Leonard S. Marcus)

The Complete Idiot's Guide to Publishing Children's Books (Harold D. Underdown and Lynne Rominger)

Dear Genius: The Letters of Ursula Nordstrom (Leonard S. Marcus)

The Essential Guide to Children's Books and Their Creators (Anita Silvey)

From Pictures to Words: A Book About Making a Book (Janet Stevens)

How a Book Is Made (Aliki)

It's a Bunny-Eat-Bunny World: A Writer's Guide to Surviving and Thriving in Today's Competitive Children's Book Market (Olga Litowinsky)

Side by Side: Five Favorite Picture-Book Teams Go to Work (Leonard S. Marcus)

Talking With Artists (Volumes 1, 2, and 3) (Pat Cummings, editor)

Ways of Telling: Conversations on the Art of the Picture Book (Leonard S. Marcus)

Writing With Pictures: How to Write and Illustrate Children's Books (Uri Shulevitz)

Other Resources for Parents About Children's Books

If you want to know more about the world of children's books, look for these in your bookstore or library.

Books

Author Talk by Leonard S. Marcus (editor) Interviews with more than a dozen authors who give insight into their process.

A Caldecott Celebration: Six Artists Share Their Paths to the Caldecott Medal by Leonard S. Marcus The story behind the making of Maurice Sendak's *Where the Wild Things Are*; Robert McCloskey's *Make Way for Ducklings*; Chris Van Allsburg's *Jumanji*; William Steig's *Sylvester and the Magic Pebble*; Marcia Brown's *Cinderella, or The Glass Slipper*; and David Weisner's *Tuesday*.

Choosing Books for Children: A Commonsense Guide by Betsy Hearne The predecessor to every book on children's literature, now in its third edition.

From Cover to Cover: Evaluating and Reviewing Children's Books by Kathleen T. Horning Learn what reviewers need to know about what makes a book good.

The Read-Aloud Handbook by Jim Trelease The most powerful advocate for the necessity of reading aloud there is. This book has inspired more parents to read to their children than any other.

Reading Magic by Mem Fox Australian educator, bestselling author, and parent Fox speaks the plain truth about the role parents play in the development of their children's lifelong love of reading.

Side by Side: Five Favorite Picture-Book Teams Go to Work by Leonard S. Marcus Get the behind-the-scenes story of the creation of five beloved picture books: Arthur Yorinks and Richard Egielski's *Louis the Fish*, Alice and Martin Provensen's *The Glorious Flight*, Julius Lester and Jerry Pinkney's *Sam and the Tigers*, Joanna Cole and Bruce Degen's *Magic School Bus* series, and Jon Scieszka and Lane Smith's *The Stinky Cheese Man*.

Ways of Telling: Conversations on the Art of the Picture Book by Leonard S. Marcus Leonard Marcus is the historian of the children's book world. His books give insight into the creative process by allowing writers and illustrators to speak about their own work. Marcus knows which questions to ask and knows when to get out of the way and just let the answer come. In this book, he interviews William Steig, Maurice Sendak, Karla Kuskin, Rosemary Wells, Mitsumasa Anno, Jerry Pinkney, and several others about the books they create and the things that inspire them as artists.

Magazines

Most publications that cover the world of children's literature place too much emphasis on literature and not enough on children. Fine for the academics, but what about a parent who just wants to know if the latest children's books are for her child? Two magazines we consider essential are *The Horn Book* and *The Riverbank Review*. Each issue reviews new books in a manner that makes for insightful reading without requiring a master's degree in library science to understand them. Articles by authors, illustrators, and editors on themes of interest to book lovers accompany the reviews, and each issue is handsomely produced—you'll want to keep them all.

On-line Resources About Children's Books

The Internet is full of sites that can offer a lot of information, but sorting through it all wastes time. Two of our favorite sites offer a bounty of information and links to the really good stuff—they've done most of the work for you.

Kay Vandergift's Special Interest Page: The best mix of information and academic insight we have found on the Web. Kay's site thoroughly covers topics of interest to those who love children's books and will have the casual Web surface surfer fascinated for hours. http://scils. rutgers.edu/~kvander/

Cynthia Leitich Smith's Home Page: This busy-looking home page may seem at first glance to be all about Ms. Smith's books. However, a treasure trove of links and information awaits those who click on the menu on the left side of the page. This is where we go when we want to find a link or information on a children's author. If it's on the Web, Cyn Smith has linked it. http://www. cynthialeitichsmith.com/

The Out-of-Print Hall of Shame

Not that these books have anything shameful about them, quite the contrary. It is shameful that some of our favorite books (some of which received stars from us in the first edition) should be out of print as this volume goes to press. We've whined, wheedled, and wailed until we are blue in the face about some of these titles. Now we resort to what amounts to an ad in our own book begging some clever publisher to bring these books back into the hands of deserving readers. Until such time, please look for the following titles, listed from those for the youngest to the oldest, in your local public library, or from good used booksellers.

Dressing (and other titles)
BOARD BOOK
AUTHOR/ILLUSTRATOR: Helen Oxenbury

Alfie Gets in First (and other titles)
PICTURE BOOK
AUTHOR/ILLUSTRATOR: Shirley Hughes

Tom and Pippo books
PICTURE BOOKS
AUTHOR/ILLUSTRATOR: Helen Oxenbury

Cadillac
PICTURE BOOK
AUTHOR: Charles Temple
ILLUSTRATOR: Lynne Lockhart

Castle Builder
PICTURE BOOK
AUTHOR/ILLUSTRATOR: Dennis Nolan

The Cat's Purr
PICTURE BOOK
AUTHOR/ILLUSTRATOR: Ashley Bryan

Chicken Man
PICTURE BOOK

AUTHOR/ILLUSTRATOR: Michelle Edwards

The Cow Buzzed
PICTURE BOOK
AUTHORS: Andrew and David Zimmerman
ILLUSTRATOR: Clemesha Meisel

Donna O'Neeshuck Was Chased by Some Cows
PICTURE BOOK
AUTHOR: Bill Grossman
ILLUSTRATOR: Sue Truesdell

First Flight
PICTURE BOOK
AUTHOR/ILLUSTRATOR: David McPhail

My Place in Space
PICTURE BOOK
AUTHORS: Robin and Sally Hirst
ILLUSTRATORS: Roland Harvey and Joe Levine

The Ornery Morning
PICTURE BOOK

AUTHOR: Patricia B. Demuth
ILLUSTRATOR: Craig McFarland
Brown

Tommy at the Grocery Store
PICTURE BOOK
AUTHOR: Bill Grossman
ILLUSTRATOR: Victoria Chess

★ *Thirteen*
PICTURE BOOK
AUTHOR/ILLUSTRATOR: Remy
Charlip and Jerry Joyner

★ *Eeny, Meeny, Miney Mole*
PICTURE BOOK
AUTHOR: Jane Yolen
ILLUSTRATOR: Kathryn Brown

*John Patrick Norman
McHennessy: The Boy Who
Was Always Late*
PICTURE BOOK
AUTHOR/ILLUSTRATOR: John
Burningham

My Grandma Has Black Hair
PICTURE BOOK
AUTHOR: Mary Hoffman
ILLUSTRATOR: Joanna
Burroughes

*One Grain of Rice: A
Mathematical Folktale*
PICTURE BOOK
AUTHOR/ILLUSTRATOR: Demi

The Sea-Thing Child
PICTURE BOOK
AUTHOR: Russell Hoban
ILLUSTRATOR: Patrick Benson

Toad
PICTURE BOOK
AUTHOR/ILLUSTRATOR: Ruth
Brown

Turtle in July
POETRY COLLECTION

AUTHOR: Marilyn Singer
ILLUSTRATOR: Jerry Pinkney

Wombat Stew
PICTURE BOOK
AUTHOR: Marcia K. Vaughan
ILLUSTRATOR: Pamela Lofts

*Aster Aardvark's Alphabet
Adventures*
PICTURE BOOK
AUTHOR/ILLUSTRATOR: Steven
Kellogg

*Captain Snap and the Children
of Vinegar Lane*
PICTURE BOOK
AUTHOR: Roni Schotter
ILLUSTRATOR: Marcia Sewall

Charlie Drives the Stage
PICTURE BOOK
AUTHOR: Eric Kimmel
ILLUSTRATOR: Glen Rounds

Color
PICTURE BOOK NONFICTION
AUTHOR/ILLUSTRATOR: Ruth
Heller

The Day of Ahmed's Secret
PICTURE BOOK
AUTHOR: Florence Parry Heide
ILLUSTRATOR: Ted Lewin

Delphine
PICTURE BOOK
AUTHOR/ILLUSTRATOR: Molly
Bang

A Fish in His Pocket
PICTURE BOOK
AUTHOR/ILLUSTRATOR: Denys
Cazet

★ *Bo Rabbit Smart for True:
Tall Tales From the Gullah*
PICTURE BOOK
AUTHOR: Priscilla Jaquith

ILLUSTRATOR: Ed Young

★ *The Gift of Driscoll Lipscomb*
PICTURE BOOK
AUTHOR: Sara Yamaka
ILLUSTRATOR: Joung Un Kim

★ *Owl Eyes*
PICTURE BOOK
AUTHOR/ILLUSTRATOR: Frieda
Gates

Puzzle Maps U.S.A.
PICTURE BOOK NONFICTION
AUTHOR/ILLUSTRATOR: Nancy L.
Clouse

Supergrandpa
PICTURE BOOK BIOGRAPHY
AUTHOR: David M. Schwartz
ILLUSTRATOR: Bert Dodson

*Thirteen Moons on Turtle's
Back: A Native American Year
of Moons*
FOLKLORE COLLECTION
AUTHOR: Joseph Bruchac and
Jonathan London
ILLUSTRATOR: Thomas Locker

*Big Men, Big Country: A
Collection of American Tall
Tales*
FOLKLORE COLLECTION
AUTHOR: Paul Robert Walker
ILLUSTRATOR: James Bernardin

★ *Josepha: A Prairie Boy's
Story*
PICTURE BOOK
AUTHOR: Jim McGugan
ILLUSTRATOR: Murray Kimber

Tales for the Perfect Child
SHORT STORY COLLECTION
AUTHOR: Florence Parry Heide
ILLUSTRATOR: Victoria Chess

Tog the Ribber, or Granny's Tale
PICTURE BOOK
AUTHOR: Paul Coltman
ILLUSTRATOR: Gillian McClure

★ *All We Needed to Say: Poems About School by Tanya and Sophie*
POETRY COLLECTION
AUTHOR: Marilyn Singer
ILLUSTRATOR: Lorna Clark (photographs)

Chicken Soup, Boots!
PICTURE BOOK
AUTHOR/ILLUSTRATOR: Maira Kalman

City of Light, City of Dark: A Comic Book Novel
FICTION-FANTASY
AUTHOR: Avi
ILLUSTRATOR: Brian Floca

Judy Scuppernong
FICTION
AUTHOR: Brenda Seabrooke
ILLUSTRATOR: Ted Lewin

Way Home
PICTURE BOOK
AUTHOR: Libby Hawthorn
ILLUSTRATOR: Gregory Rogers

★ *Advice for a Frog*
POETRY COLLECTION
AUTHOR: Alice Schertle
ILLUSTRATOR: Norman Green

Alpha Beta Chowder
POETRY COLLECTION
AUTHOR: Jeanne Steig
ILLUSTRATOR: William Steig

★ *Boys Will Be*
COLLECTION
AUTHOR: Bruce Brooks

The Acorn People
FICTION
AUTHOR: Ron Jones

APPENDIX 5:

Lists! Lists! Lists!

It's difficult to label a book for a particular age or grade. Each child's capacity for enjoying a book depends on his reading level, his exposure to books, whether he is read aloud to, and on the book itself. Many books work on a variety of levels.

It is fine to say that your seven-year-old second-grader can read a classic like *The Secret Garden*, but "getting it" and fully appreciating the richness of the writing is another thing all together. Too often—especially in these days of standardized testing—we focus primarily on a child's ability to merely decode. For some, a popular way to see if a child is "ready" to read a book is the old five-finger rule, where you open a book at random and tell the child to place her five fingers on a page and then read to you what her fingers touch. If she is able to understand (to the adult's satisfaction) the words at the tip of her fingers, then she can read. We think it's more complicated than this. Reading is not limited to simply knowing what all the words mean. When we choose a book for a particular grade, we need to know more about the child than whether she can read the words.

A child's interests, reading history, and the culture of reading in a child's home are important factors along with comprehension in selecting a book for a child in a particular grade. However, we all like lists, shortcuts that save us time. So we've included some, neat and ready to take to the library. If you've already read all the titles, bless you, and our guess is your child is ready to choose on his own.

We feel that children need to be given access to a diverse selection so whether or not these books become their favorites is not the point—not every child will be enthusiastic over every book on this list, but every child deserves exposure to them.

Our Favorite Books for Babies

Everywhere Babies (Meyers)
Fuzzy Yellow Ducklings (Van Fleet)
Good Dog Carl (Day)
Goodnight Moon (Brown)
Hush: A Thai Lullaby (Ho)
Hush Little Baby (Long)
Mrs. Mustard's Baby Faces (Wattenberg)
My Very First Mother Goose (Opie)
Pat the Bunny (Kunhardt)
Time for Bed (Fox)
White on Black and Black on White (Hoban)

Our Favorite Books for Toddlers

Baby Says (Steptoe)
Blue Hat, Green Hat (and other Board Books by Boynton)
Brown Bear, Brown Bear, What Do You See? (Martin)
Bubba & Beau, Best Friends (Appelt)
Cars and Trucks and Things That Go (Scarry)
Chicka Chicka Boom Boom (Martin and Archambault)
Goodnight Gorilla (Rathmann)
Gossie and Gertie (Dunrea)
How Do Dinosaurs Say Goodnight? (Yolen)
It's Snowing (Dunrea)
Jessie Bear, What Will You Wear? (Carlstrom)
The Napping House (Wood)
Richard Scarry's Best Word Book Ever (Scarry)
So Much (Cooke)
Tom and Pippo books (Oxenbury)
Wake Up Big Barn (Chitwood)
Where's Spot? (Hill)

Our Favorite Books for Preschoolers

Benny's Pennies (Brisson)
Bob (Pearson)
Bread and Jam for Frances (Hoban)
Farmer Duck (Waddell)
Five Minutes' Peace (Murphy)
Flora McDonnell's ABC (McDonnell)
From Head to Toe (Carle)
How Do Dinosaurs Say Goodnight? (Yolen)
Make Way for Ducklings (McCloskey)

Max and Ruby books (Wells)
Mike Mulligan and His Steam Shovel (Burton)
Millions of Cats (Bag)
Mouse Paint (Walsh)
Mrs. Biddlebox (Smith)
Noisy Nora (Wells)
The Nutshell Library (Sendak)
One Fish Two Fish Red Fish Blue Fish (Seuss)
Shy Charles (Wells)
Tiger Tiger (Lillegard)
The Very Hungry Caterpillar (Carle)
The Wheels on the Bus (Zelinsky)
Where the Wild Things Are (Sendak)
Who Hoots? and *Who Hops?* (Davis)
The World of Christopher Robin (Milne)
Would You Rather? (Burmingham)

Taming the Halloween Willies

That first trick or treat can sometimes be a tad too scary for young children. Here is a list of books that provide a safe and comfortable introduction to the thrills and chills of Halloween.

Very Scary (Johnston)
By the Light of the Halloween Moon (Stutson)
Who Said Boo? (White Carlstrom)
When the Goblins Came Knocking (Grossnickle Hines)
Rattlebone Rock (Andrews)
Six Creepy Sheep (Enderle and Tessler)
Scary Scary Halloween (Bunting)

Our Favorite Books for Kindergarten

Abiyoyo (Seeger)
Benny's Pennies (Brisson)
Caps for Sale (Slobodkina)
Froggy Gets Dressed (London)
George and Martha (Marshall)
A House for Hermit Crab (Carle)
I Wish I Were a Butterfly (Howe)
Is Your Mama a Llama? (Guarino)
King Bidgood's in the Bathtub (Wood)
Max (Graham)
Miss Bindergarten Goes to Kindergarten (Slate)
On Market Street (Lobel)
Our Animal Friends at Maple Hill Farm (Provensen)
Stone Soup (Brown)
The Story of Ferdinand (Leaf)
To & Fro, Fast & Slow (Bernhard)
To Market, To Market (Miranda)
Wilfred Gordon McDonald Partridge (Fox)
William's Doll (Zolotow)
Would You Rather? (Burmingham)

Our Favorite Books for First Grade

17 Kings and 42 Elephants (Mahy)
Amazing Grace (Hoffman)
Anansi and the Moss-Covered Rock (Kimmel)
Bark, George (Feiffer)
Bootsie Barker Bites (Bottner)
The Dead Bird (Brown)

Don't Fidget a Feather (Silverman)

Frog and Toad Are Friends (Lobel)

Heckedy Peg (Wood)

Lily's Purple Plastic Purse (Henke)

Little Bear (Minarik)

Madeline (Bemelmans)

Miss Nelson Is Missing (Allard)

Owl Moon (Yolen)

Pete's a Pizza (Steig)

Possum Come A-Knockin' (Von Laan)

The Relatives Came (Rylant)

The Salamander Room (Mazer)

Strega Nona (De Paola)

Tacky the Penguin (Lester)

Chapter Books for First-Graders Who Are Reading Above Their Level

What do you do when you have a six- or seven-year-old that can read at a fourth- or fifth-grade level? Some kids dash through the "Easy-to-Read" level and then are ready to roll on chapter books. What are some books for older readers that will satisfy them without introducing concepts or experiences you'd prefer they wait to encounter? Try these:

Slightly Advanced (2nd/3rd-grade RL)

The A to Z Mysteries by Ron Roy

Amber Brown books by Paula Danziger

The *Annie Pitts* series by Diane DeGroat

The Bailey School Kids series by Debbie Dadey

Bunnicula books by James Howe

The Cam Jansen series by David Adler

The *Catwings* series by Ursula K. LeGuin

The *Commander Toad* series by Jane Yolen

The Dragonling series by Jackie French Koller

The *Encyclopedia Brown* series by Donald J. Sobol

Hank the Cowdog books by John R. Erickson

The Hardy Boys by Franklin W. Dixon and *Nancy Drew* by Carolyn Keane

Okay. *Nancy Drew seems a little old for this list—doesn't she drive a cool car and date and stuff?*

Yeah, but it is all quite tame. All I can tell you is, the simplistic stories and the dependable chapter length of *The Hardy Boys* were an incentive to my son when he was seven—he plowed through these for about four months and then moved on to other books. These may not work for all kids, but if they seem to want to read "big kid books," these are a safe bet.

Horrible Harry series by Suzy Kline

The Iron Giant: A Story in Five Nights by Ted Hughes

The Jake Drake series by Andrew Clements

Jigsaw Jones Mysteries by James Preller

Judy Moody series by Megan McDonald

The Kids of the Polk Street School series by Patricia Reilley Giff

The Lighthouse Family series by Cynthia Rylant

The Littles by John Peterson

Marvin Redpost series by Louis Sachar

Books by Matt Christopher (easy-to-read titles)

Mrs. Piggle-Wiggle books by Betty MacDonald

My Father's Dragon titles by Ruth Stiles Gannett

The Time Warp Trio series by Jon Scieszka

The Unicorn's Secret series by Kathleen Duey

The Zach Files by Dan Greenburg

More Advanced (4th/5th-grade RL)

I'm Sorry, Almira Ann by Jane Kurtz

Poppy and Rye and *Ereth* by Avi

The *Anastasia* books by Lois Lowry

The *Betsy* books by Carolyn Haywood

The Black Stallion books by Walter Farley

The Boxcar Children mysteries by Gertrude Chandler Warner

The *Fudge* books by Judy Blume

The *Little House* books by Laura Ingalls Wilder

The *Rowan* series by Emily Rodda

Winnie Dancing on Her Own
    by Jennifer Jacobson
And books by Beverly Cleary,
    Bill Wallace, Dick King Smith
    (especially *Upchuck and
    Rotten Willy, The Backwards
    Birddog, Lady Lollipop*, and
    the *Sophie* series), E. B.
    White, Joanne Hurwitz, and
    Marguerite Henry.

Our Favorite Books for Second Grade

Amelia Bedelia (Parish)
Bit by Bit (Saufield)
Catwings (LeGuin)
Come a Tide (Lyon)
Earl's Too Cool for Me
    (Komaiko)
Flat Stanley (Brown)
*Get Ready for Second Grade,
    Amber Brown* (Danziger)
Gus and Grandpa (Mills)
Hailstones and Halibut Bones
    (O'Neill)
Henry and Mudge (Rylant)
How Much Is a Million?
    (Schwartz)
I Love Saturdays Y Domingos
    (Ada)
The Keeping Quilt (Polacco)
*Liza Lou and the Yeller Belly
    Swamp* (Mayer)
Minnie and Moo (Cazet)
Monster Mama (Rosenberg)
My Father's Dragon (Gannett)
My Little Sister Ate One Hare
    (Grossman)
My Visit to the Aquarium
    (Aliki)
Piggie Pie (Palatini)
Sylvester and the Magic Pebble
    (Steig)
Voyage to the Bunny Planet
    (Wells)

Our Favorite Books for Third Grade

Bunnicula (Howe)
Charlotte's Web (White)
Double Trouble in Walla Walla
    (Clements)
The Gardener (Stewart)
Hawk, I'm Your Brother
    (Baylor)
*Hershel and the Hanukkah
    Goblins* (Kimmel)
John Henry (Lester)
Judy Moody (McDonald)
Little Red Riding Hood (Hyman)
Meet Danitra Brown (Grimes)
Miss Rumphius (Cooney)
Monster Mama (Rosenberg)
Mufaro's Beautiful Daughters
    (Steptoe)
New Kid on the Block
    (Prelutsky)
Rumpelstiltskin (Zelinsky)
Scary Stories to Tell in the Dark
    (Schwartz)
Some Things Are Scary (Heide)
Starry Messenger (Sis)
*The Stinky Cheese Man and
    Other Fairly Stupid Tales*
    (Scieszka)
Swamp Angel (Isaacs)
Thirteen (Charlip)
Three Pigs (Wiesner)
The *Time Warp Trio* series
    (Scieszka)

Our Favorite Books for Fourth Grade

*Amber Was Brave, Essie Was
    Smart* (Williams)
*The Araboolies of Liberty
    Street* (Swope)
Because of Winn Dixie (Di
    Camillo)
Dogzilla (Pilkey)
Frindle (Clements)
Grandfather's Journey (Say)
Hey World, Here I Am! (Little)
*If You're Not Here, Please Raise
    Your Hand* (Dukos)
James and the Giant Peach
    (Dahl)
*Jeremy Thatcher, Dragon
    Hatcher* (Coville)
Love, Rudy Lavender (Wiles)
Love That Dog (Creech)
Mick Harte Was Here (Park)
Mr. Popper's Penguins
    (Atwater)
Nettie's Trip South (Turner)
Number the Stars (Lowry)
The People Could Fly
    (Hamilton)
Riding Freedom (Ryan)
Sarah, Plain and Tall
    (MacLachlan)
A Series of Unfortunate Events
    (Snicket)
Stone Fox (Gardiner)
*Tales of a Fourth Grade
    Nothing* (Blume)
Weslandia (Fleischman)

Our Favorite Books for Fifth Grade

Belle Prater's Boy (White)
The Birchbark House (Erdrich)
The Book of Three (Alexander)
The Bridge to Terabithia
    (Paterson)
Catherine, Called Birdy
    (Cushman)
Child of the Owl (Yep)
Coraline (Gaiman)
The Egypt Game (Snyder)
A Fine White Dust (Rylant)
*From the Mixed Up Files of
    Basil E. Frankweiler*
    (Konigsburg)
Harriet the Spy (Fitzhugh)

Harris and Me (Paulsen)
The Indian in the Cupboard (Banks)
Island of the Blue Dolphins (O'Dell)
Lincoln: A Photobiography (Freedman)
Maniac Magee (Spinelli)
The Mysteries of Harris Burdick (Van Allsburg)
Pink and Say (Polacco)
Rattlesnake Dance (Dewey)
Redwall (Jacques)
Roll of Thunder Hear My Cry (Taylor)
The Sammy Keyes mysteries (Von Draanen)
Save Queen of Sheba (Moeri)
Tuck Everlasting (Babbitt)
The View From the Cherry Tree (Roberts)
The Watsons Go to Birmingham, 1963 (Curtis)
Where the Sidewalk Ends (Silverstein)
Wringer (Spinelli)
A Wrinkle in Time (L'Engle)

Our Favorite Books for Sixth Grade

Black Ships Before Troy (Sutcliff)
Chicken Soup, Boots! (Kalman)
The Dark Is Rising (Cooper)
Deathwatch (White)
The Devil's Arithmetic (Yolen)
Esperanza Rising (Ryan)
Flipped (Van Draanen)
The Folk Keeper (Billingsley)
Freak the Mighty (Philbrick)
A Girl Named Disaster (Former)
The Giver (Lowry)
The Golden Compass (Pullman)

The Great Fire (Murphy)
Hatchet (Paulsen)
Holes (Sachar)
Homecoming (Voigt)
A Long Way From Chicago (Peck)
Lord of the Deep (Salisbury)
Nightjohn (Paulsen)
Shipwreck at the Bottom of the World (Armstrong)
Starry Messenger: Galileo Galilei (Sis)
Tangerine (Bloor)
The True Confessions of Charlotte Doyle (Avi)
The Westing Game (Raskin)
Where the Red Fern Grows (Rawls)
Zoom (Banyai)

Classics to Read Aloud

Ask ten different people what they think the definition of a classic is and you'll get ten different answers. Bookstores often have a section called classics; libraries do not. One definition of classics is any piece of literature that has stood the test of time, but how much time are we talking about? Another interpretation is a book that has stuck around long enough to be taught as part of a school curriculum. Webster defines it as "a work of enduring excellence." For us, a classic is a book over fifty years old that continues to be read by children and their families. The following list will make for several years' worth of reading aloud:

20,000 Leagues Under the Sea (Verne)

The Adventures of Huckleberry Finn (Twain)
The Adventures of Pinnochio (Collodi)
The Adventures of Tom Sawyer (Twain)
Alice's Adventures in Wonderland (Carroll)
Anne of Green Gables (Montgomery)
Around the World in Eighty Days (Verne)
Black Beauty (Sewell)
The Black Stallion (Farley)
The Borrowers (Norton)
Call it Courage (Sperry)
The Call of the Wild (London)
Charlotte's Web (White)
The Chronicles of Narnia (Lewis)
Doctor Doolittle (Lufting)
Five Children and It (Nesbit)
Five Little Peppers and How They Grew (Sidney)
A Girl of the Limberlost (Stratton-Porter)
Heidi (Spyri)
The Hobbit (Tolkein)
The Hound of the Baskervilles (Doyle)
The Incredible Journey (Burnford)
The Jungle Book (Kipling)
Just So Stories (Kipling)
Kidnapped (Stevenson)
Little House on the Prairie (Wilder)
The Little Princess (Burnett)
Little Women (Alcott)
Mary Poppins (Travers)
The Merry Adventures of Robin Hood (Pyle)
Old Yeller (Gipson)
Peter Pan (Barrie)
The Pickwick Papers Dickens)

The Prince and the Pauper (Twain)
The Railway Children (Nesbit)
The Secret Garden (Burnett)
Swallows and Amazons (Ransome)
The Swiss Family Robinson (Wyss)
The Three Musketeers (Dumas)
Treasure Island (Stevenson)
Understood Betsy (Fisher)
The Wind in the Willows (Grahame)
The Wizard of Oz (Baum)

And don't forget Edgar Allen Poe! A collection of Poe is essential to have on hand for a night when the power goes out. Better than any of the horror writers your kids are accustomed to, this guy will provide an evening of suspense and terror that will turn schlocky horror fans into Poe-heads. Read *The Tell-Tale Heart* aloud and watch them grow quiet and still as your voice gets more intense. Be sure to shriek the last line for maximum effect!

Walter, be sure I'm nowhere near when you start shrieking. When the lights go out, hopefully I'll be curled up on a soft chair with my grandson, telling made-up gentle stories or making flashlight characters on the walls. It's scary enough to be suddenly immersed in darkness without creating Poe-heads!

You may wish for Mr. Poe when your grandson gets older and wants to make scarier images with that flashlight. My grandmother used to read *The Fall of the House of Usher* to me with a single candle illuminating her face. I loved it!

Long Picture Books

Don't be afraid of picture books with long texts. Some readers, through their early teen years, need the visuals to drive them forward.

Not to mention the young artist who anticipates a powerful image at the turn of a page.

Try books like:

Black Ships Before Troy (Sutcliff)
The Weaving of a Dream (Heyer)
Good Griselle (Yolen)
Excalibur (Talbott)
Charlie Drives the Stage (Kimmel)
Dippers (Nichol)
Pink and Say (Polacco)
Reading to Matthew (Vivelo)

Great Openings: Books That Will Grab Them in Seconds

Try one of these when you need a story in which the first line or paragraph is so compelling they'll want to know what is next.

"The night Max wore his wolf suit and made mischief of one kind and another his mother called him wild thing . . ."

Where the Wild Things Are

"Seventeen kings on 42 elephants going on a journey through a wild wet night . . ."

Seventeen Kings and 42 Elephants

"Henry had no brothers and sisters. 'I want a brother,' he told his parents. 'Sorry,' they said. Henry had no friends on the street. 'I want to live on a different street,' he told his parents. 'Sorry,' they said. Henry had no pets at home. 'I want to have a dog,' he told his parents. 'Sorry,' they almost said."

Henry and Mudge: The First Book

"Patrick Edward was a wonderful boy, but his mother was a monster."

Monster Mama

"Go away, you bad old dog. Go away from me."

Go Away Dog

"My name is Ora Mae Cotton of Crabapple Orchard and last night somebody stole my tooth."

Airmail to the Moon

"City lights flicker in the dusk like winking fireflies. I hold my Auntie Maita's papery hand. Together we stare at the shiny photo in her lap, touched so often with hope, the edges curl. My heartbeat rushes in an impatient waltz as we watch for the stranger to arrive."

The Sea Chest

"Down the dusty roads and far away, a poor mother once lived with her seven children named Monday, Tuesday, Wednesday, Thursday, Friday, Saturday and Sunday."

Heckedy Peg

"Old black fly's been buzzin' around, buzzin' around, buzzin' around. Old black fly's been buzzin' around, and he's had a very busy bad day."

Old Black Fly

"My little sister ate one hare. We thought she'd throw up then and there."

My Little Sister Ate One Hare

"Before Julius was born, Lilly was the best big sister in the world."

Julius, the Baby of the World

"Swallow a slug by its tale or its snout. Feel it slide down. Feel it climb out."

Slugs

"Before George Hogglesberry went into his new class, he put a nose on his face."

George Hogglesberry, Grade School Alien

"My dad and I live in an airport."

Fly Away Home

"On August 1, 1815, when Angelica Longrider took her first gulp of air on this earth, there was nothing about the baby to suggest that she would become the greatest woodswoman in Tennessee. The newborn was scarcely taller than her mother and couldn't climb a tree without help."

Swamp Angel

"On Monday in math class, Mrs. Fibonacci says, 'You know, you can think of almost everything as a math problem.' On Tuesday I start having problems."

Math Curse

"Everybody in my class knows my name. It's Fran Ellen Smith. I'm nearly ten. I suck my thumb, and everybody says I smell bad."

The Bears' House

"Take this guy. See how grumpy he is? He's been grumpy since he got out of bed, stepped on his little boy's beach ball, slid halfway across the house, and flew out the window into the rosebush."

A Barrel of Laughs, a Vale of Tears

"Dawn was indeed well up the sky, but over the Greek camp there was little light, for Zeus had spread a churning mass of black cloud across the sky above them: though where the Trojans gathered on the higher ground the sky was clear and the light strong. And soon, from the menacing cloud roof rain began to fall: rain that was as red as blood."

Black Ships Before Troy

"They say Maniac Magee was born in a dump. They say his stomach was a cereal box and his heart a sofa spring. They say he kept an eight-inch cockroach on a leash and that rats stood guard over him while he slept."

Maniac Magee

"Manny Bustos awakened when the sun cooked the cardboard over his head and heated the box he was sleeping in until even a lizard could not have taken it, and he knew, suddenly, that it was time. This was the day."

The Crossing

"Eleven-year-old Muhammad Bilal flinched. The sore on his ankle rubbed against the iron shackle that held him, sending shivers of pain up his thin leg. He pushed his foot closer to the wooden board to which he was fastened and tried to shift his body."

The Glory Field

"12th Day of September—
I am commanded to write an account of my days: I am bit by fleas and plagued by family. That is all there is to say."

Catherine, Called Birdy

"Coraline discovered the door a little while after they moved into the house."

Coraline

"If you're interested in stories with happy endings, you would be better off reading some other book. In this book, not only is there no happy ending, there is no happy beginning and very few happy things in the middle."

A Series of Unfortunate Events:
The Bad Beginning

"It was hard to understand Barney with the air tubes up his nose. It made his voice sound funny and he couldn't talk very loud."

Child of the Owl

"Ba-room, ba-room, ba-room, baripity, baripity, baripity, baripity—Good."

Bridge to Terabithia

"Here we go again. We were all standing in line waiting for breakfast when one of the case-workers came in and tap-tap-tapped down the line. Uh-oh, this meant bad news, either they'd found a foster home for somebody or somebody was about to get paddled. All the kids watched the woman as she moved along the line, her high-heeled shoes sounding like little firecrackers going off on the wooden floor. Shoot! She stopped at me and said, 'Are you Buddy Caldwell?'"

Bud, Not Buddy

"When the day began the body was there. The night mist parted and it floated slowly on the silent river like a tree snapped at the root. Its hair spread across the water like a halo of little branches. Its face was deathly white. Its eyes stared like knots of wood, shiny and unseeing as a town approached."

The Secret of Sabrina Fludde

"As summer wheat came ripe, so did I, born at home, on the kitchen floor."

Out of the Dust

"If you asked the kids and teachers at Lincoln Elementary School to make three lists—all the really bad kids, all the really smart kids, and all the really good kids—Nick Allen would not be one of them. Nick deserved a list all his own, and everyone knew it."

Frindle

THEMATIC INDEX

Want to know if there's a good book about dogs? Is your child having trouble adjusting to a move, a new school, or other problems? Looking for a story that will give comfort, teach a lesson, or make a point? Look here. This index of nearly 1,000 themes is designed to help you make a connection between your child and books using interests, situations, and issues as a guide.

We chose books because we liked them and not because they fit a particular theme, so some themes have only a few titles, while others have many. Most are self-explanatory, but when we felt there was a need for a description we added one. We encourage using these themes as a starting place for those who need them or as an indepth reference for others. We're sure there are ways to use them we haven't considered, and we look forward to hearing from readers about how you use them.

In order by theme, with an alphabetical listing of the books for each:

John Patrick Norman McHennessy, the
  Boy Who Was Always Late, 430
Masai and I, 212
Meanwhile . . . , 244
Monster Motel, 330
Mr. Rabbit and the Lovely Present, 135
My Mama Says There Aren't Any
  Zombies . . . , 181
My Pony, 136
Mysteries of Harris Burdick, 246
Nose from Jupiter, 372
On Market Street, 142
Pete's a Pizza, 144
Phantom Tollbooth, 376
Rootabaga Stories, 76
Roxaboxen, 252
Runaway Bunny, 148
Secret Garden, 313
She'll Be Comin' Round the Mountain,
  39
Shoebag, 384
Sing, Sophie!, 58
Snail's Spell, 401
Someone Says, 90
Tar Beach, 59
Tell Me a Picture, 80
Tiger, Tiger, 186
Tog the Ribber, or Granny's Tale
Tuesday, 30
Until I Met Dudley, 321
Voyage to the Bunny Planet, 30
Weighty Word Book, 393
When I'm Sleepy, 159
Winnie the Pooh, 188
Wolves in the Walls, 326
World of Pooh, 188
Would You Rather . . . ?, 160

IMMIGRATION (includes emigration)
All the Lights in the Night, 266
Always Prayer Shawl, 219
Beyond the Western Sea, 404
Grandfather's Journey, 235
History of US, 410
I Am an American, 402
I Hate English, 171
If Your Name Was Changed at Ellis
  Island, 294
Josepha, 430
Keeping Quilt, 47
Lotus Seed, 204
Make a Wish, Molly, 302
Molly's Pilgrim, 304
Night Journey, 299
Our Only May Amelia, 375
Peacebound Trains, 307
Peppe the Lamplighter, 247
Seedfolks, 382
Who Belongs Here?, 325

INDEPENDENCE
Catherine, Called Birdy, 344
Eeny, Meeny, Miney Mole, 430
I Can, 87
Miss Rumphius, 245
Olivia, 182

Roll of Thunder, Hear My Cry, 378
Story About Ping, 152
Tiger, Tiger, 186

INDIA
Buddha, 223
One Grain of Rice, 430
People Who Hugged Trees, 75
Rikki-Tikki-Tavi, 250
Seven Blind Mice, 149
Talking Walls, 319

INDIVIDUALITY
All the Places to Love, 163
All We Needed to Say, 431
Brown Honey in Broomwheat Tea, 222
Carrot Seed, 102
Chicken Soup, Boots!, 431
Cinder Edna, 278
Cow That Went Oink, 104
Daydreamer, 349
Dot, 208
Eeny, Meeny, Miney Mole, 430
Emily, 283
Everybody Needs a Rock, 183
Girl Who Loved Caterpillars, 111
Giver, 409
Gooney Bird Greene, 201
Harvey Potter's Balloon Farm, 70
Hip Cat, 291
Jeremy's Decision, 25
Lily's Crossing, 368
Long Way from Chicago, 410
Maniac Magee, 369
Memoirs of a Bookbat, 412
Miss Rumphius, 245
My Grandma Has Black Hair, 430
Oh, the Places You'll Go!, 53
Oliver Button Is a Sissy, 138
Orphan Train Adventures, 373
Sisters, 28
Story of Ferdinand, 152
Tacky the Penguin, 153
Three Hat Day, 257
Town Mouse, Country Mouse, 187

INDONESIA
Komodo, 211

INFINITY
Re-Zoom, 32
Zoom, 32

INSECTS
Bugs (Wright), 165
Bugs! Bugs! Bugs!, 101
Fire Race, 169
Girl Who Loved Wild Horses, 286
I Wish I Were a Butterfly, 121
Insectlopedia, 330
Jack's Garden, 173
Joyful Noise, 366
My Visit to the Zoo, 181
Old Black Fly, 181
Shoebag, 384
Spider and the Fly, 315
Turtle in July, 430
Very Quiet Cricket, 157
What About Ladybugs?, 80

Why Mosquitoes Buzz in People's Ears,
  188

INTERNET
Search for the Shadowman, 381

INTERNMENT, JAPANESE (see captivity)

INUIT
Eagle's Gift, 191
Julie of the Wolves, 366
On Mother's Lap, 143
Small Tall Tale from the Far, Far North,
  315

INVASION
City of Gold and Lead, 348
Wolves in the Walls, 326

INVENTIONS AND INVENTORS
101 Ways to Bug Your Parents, 264
Ben and Me, 338
How Ben Franklin Stole the Lightning,
  292
Made in China, 369
Mistakes That Worked, 303
New Way Things Work, 74
Piece of String Is a Wonderful Thing,
  400
Real McCoy, 310
So You Want to Be an Inventor?, 315
Ug, 259

IRELAND
Beyond the Western Sea, 404
Black Potatoes, 402
Fin M'Coul, the Giant of Knockmany
  Hill, 138

IRISH AMERICANS
Ten Mile Day and the Building of the
  Transcontinental Railroad, 319

ISLAM
Celebrating Ramadan, 58
Magid Fasts for Ramadan, 58
Ramadan (Ghazi), 57

ISLANDS
Abel's Island, 333
Island of the Blue Dolphins, 364
Last Princess, 297
William Shakespeare's The Tempest, 395

ISRAEL
All the Lights in the Night, 266
Chicken Man, 429
One More River, 414
Talking Walls, 319

ITALY
Angelo, 220
Clown of God, 226
Days of the Blackbird, 138
King of Capri, 174
Leonardo's Horse, 367
Rome Antics, 311
Saint Francis, 312
Starry Messenger, 316
Stones in Water, 417
Strega Nona, 138
Thief Lord, 389
Tony's Bread, 138
William Shakespeare's Romeo and
  Juliet, 395

INDEX

Ghazi, Suhaib Hamid, *Ramadan*, 57–58
The Ghost Dance (McLerran and Morin), 286
The Ghost-Eye Tree (Martin, Archambault, and Rand), 110–11
The Ghost in the Mirror (Bellairs), 362
Ghost Wings (Joosse and Potter), 201
Gibbons, Gail:
  The Art Box, 400
  Beacons of Light, 400
  Catch the Wind, 400
  Caves and Caverns, 400
  Frogs, 400
  From Seed to Plant, 400
  Honeymakers, 400
  Pirates, 400
  The Planets, 400
  Puff . . . Flash . . . Bang!: A Book About Signals, 400
  The Puffins Are Back, 400
  Recycle, 400
  Sea Turtles, 400
  Spiders, 400
  Whales, 400
  Wolves, 400
Giff, Patricia Reilly:
  The Kids of the Polk Street School, 126
  Lily's Crossing, 368
The Gift of Sarah Barker (Yolen), 78
The Gift of the Magi (Henry), 57
Gila Monsters Meet You at the Airport (Sharmat and Barton), 41–42
Gilchrist, Jan Spivey, *Nathaniel Talking*, 246–47
Gilman, Phoebe, *Something from Nothing*, 98
Ginger (Voake), 111
Gingerbread Baby (Brett), 169
The Gingerbread Boy (Egielski), 111
The Gingerbread Boy (Galdone), 116
Gingerbread Days (Thomas and Cooper), 222
Ginsburg, Max, *Mississippi Bridge*, 370–71
A Girl from Yamhill (Cleary), 354
A Girl Named Disaster (Farmer), 361, 408–09
Girls of Many Lands series (various), 354–55
Girls to the Rescue (Lansky), 286–87
The Girl Who Cried Flowers and Other Tales (Yolen), 78
The Girl Who Loved Caterpillars: A Twelfth Century Tale, from Japan (Merril and Cooper), 111
The Girl Who Loved Wild Horses (Goble), 286
The Girl Who Spun Gold (Hamilton), 308
Give a Dog a Bone: Stories, Poems, Jokes, and Riddles About Dogs (Cole and Calmenson), 51
Give Me Liberty: The Story of the Declaration of Independence (Freedman), 402

The Giver (Lowry), 409
Gladiator (Watkins), 355
The Glory Field (Myers), 358
Go, Dog, Go! (Eastman), 112
Go Away, Green Monster! (Emberley), 112
Goble, Paul:
  Adopted by the Eagles: A Plains Story of Friendship and Treachery, 265
  Buffalo Woman, 286
  The Girl Who Loved Wild Horses, 286
  Star Boy, 286
God Bless the Gargoyles (Pilkey), 42
Godkin, Celia, *What About Ladybugs?*, 80
Godwin, Laura:
  The Doll People, 281–82
  The Meanest Doll in the World, 281
Go Hang a Salami! I'm a Lasagna Hog! (Agee), 214
The Going to Bed Book (Boynton), 85
Going to Daycare (Rogers), 88
Going to the Dentist (Rogers), 88
Going to the Hospital (Rogers), 88
Going to the Potty (Rogers), 88
Goldberg, Barry, *The Rugrats' Book of Chanukah*, 231
The Golden Books Treasury of Christmas Joy: Favorite Stories, Poems, Carols, and More (Skwarek, ed.), 57
The Golden Compass: Book 1 of His Dark Materials (Pullman), 409
The Golden Mountain Chronicles (Yep), 346
Goldilocks and the Three Bears (Brett), 112
Goldilocks and the Three Bears (Marshall), 191
Goldilocks Returns (Ernst), 226
Goldin, Barbara Diamond, *A Mountain of Blintzes*, 237
Gold Rush Fever: A Story of the Klondike (Greenwood), 248
Golem (Wisniewski), 235
Golenbock, Peter, *Teammates*, 256–57
Gonsalves, Rob, *Imagine a Night*, 24
Gonzalez, Ralfka and Ana, *My First Book of Proverbs/Mi Primer Libro De Dichos*, 245–46
Good-Bye Curtis (Henkes and Russo), 177
Goodbye Mousie (Harris and Ormerod), 20, 112–13
Good Dog, Carl (Day), 24
Good Griselle (Yolen), 77
Good Luck Gold and Other Poems (Wong), 330
Good Night, Gorilla (Rathmann), 113
Goodnight Moon (Brown and Hurd), 87, 113, 151
The Good, the Bad, and the Goofy (Scieszka and Smith), 320
Gooney Bird Greene (Lowry and Thomas), 201

Gopher Up Your Sleeve (Johnston and Park), 42
Gorey, Edward:
  The Shrinking of Treehorn, 314
  Treehorn's Treasure, 314
  Treehorn's Wish, 314
Gossie (Dunrea), 86–87
Gottfried, Maya, *Last Night I Dreamed a Circus*, 127
Grace, Catherine O'Neil, *I Want to Be a Veterinarian*, 293
The Graduation of Jake Moon (Park), 355
Graham, Bob:
  Jethro Byrd Fairy Child, 173
  Max, 179
Graham, Ruth Bell, *One Wintry Night*, 56, 74
Gramatky, Hardie, *Little Toot*, 129–30
Grand Central Station (Kalman), 233
Grandfather's Journey (Say), 235–36
Grandfather Tang's Story (Tompert and Parker), 209–10
Grandmother Bryant's Pocket (Martin and Mathers), 287
Grandmother's Nursery Rhymes/Las Nanas De Abuelita (Jaramillo and Savadier), 170
Grandpre, Mary, *The Sea Chest*, 253
The Grapes of Math (Tang and Briggs), 355–56
The Graphic Alphabet (Pelletier), 287, 393
Grass Sandals: The Travels of Basho (Spivak and Demi), 236
Graven Images (Fleischman), 383
Gray, Libba Moore, *Dear Willie Rudd*, 228–29
Gray Wolf, Red Wolf (Patent), 402
The Great Ball Game: A Muskogee Story (Bruchac and Roth), 70, 190
The Greatest: Muhammad Ali (Myers), 358
The Great Fire (Murphy), 356
The Great Gilly Hopkins (Paterson), 342
The Great Kapok Tree (Cherry), 287
The Great Piratical Rumbustification (Mahy and Blake), 287–88
The Great White Man-Eating Shark: A Cautionary Tale (Mahy and Allen), 236
The Greek News (Powell and Steele), 356
Greenberg, David, *Slugs*, 254
Greenberg, Jan, *Action Jackson*, 333–34
Greenberg, Martin, *The Haunted House: A Collection of Original Stories*, 78
Greene, Stephanie, *The Rugrats' First Kwanzaa*, 58
Green Eggs and Ham (Seuss), 95
Greenfield, Eloise:
  Honey, I Love and Other Love Poems, 329
  Nathaniel Talking, 246–47

VALERIE V. LEWIS is a leading children's book consultant and co-founder of Hicklebee's, a thriving, community-based children's bookstore in San Jose, California. She reviews books on CBS's *The Early Show* and was a regular guest on NPR's *Looseleaf Book Company*. She served on the Board of Directors of the American Bookseller's Association as chair of the national ABA's Children's Issues committee. A highly popular speaker, Valerie takes her expertise to teachers, librarians, parents, and booksellers across the United States and in Europe. She lives in San Jose, less than an hour's drive from her daughters, Laura and Kaela, and granchildren Joey and Alissa.

WALTER M. MAYES . . . aka WALTER THE GIANT STORYTELLER is really six feet, seven-and-a-half inches tall! WALTER has spent most of his adult life entertaining and enlightening both children and adults with stories, as well as with his message of the importance of books and the power of stories in all our lives. He is the library media specialist at The Girls' Middle School in Mountain View, California, where he spends as much time as he can putting books into the hands of 120 girls, most of whom are voracious readers. His understanding of the needs of teens concerning reading and other aspects of adolescent life gets refined every day he works there. Walter makes his home in San Francisco, California, and is the proud father of a teenage son.

To contact Walter, to offer feedback on this book, or to arrange an appearance by Walter the Giant Storyteller, call (760) 752-9973 or e-mail him at *WMMayes@aol.com*.